Crucial Dimensions
in World
Evangelization

CRUCIAL DIMENSIONS

IN WORLD

EVANGELIZATION

Arthur F. Glasser
Paul G. Hiebert
C. Peter Wagner
Ralph D. Winter

William Carey Library

533 HERMOSA STREET • SOUTH PASADENA, CALIF. 91030

Published by the William Carey Library
533 Hermosa Street
South Pasadena, Calif. 91030
Telephone 213-799-4559

International Standard Book Number 0-87808-732-X
Library of Congress Catalog Number 76-42l65

PRINTED IN THE UNITED STATES OF AMERICA

Contents

PART V: CHURCH/MISSION TENSIONS TODAY

PART VI: THIRD WORLD MISSIONS

PART VII: INTRODUCING THEOLOGICAL EDUCATION BY EXTENSION

Foreword

All around the world there is new and rising interest in finishing the task of world evangelization. From country after country we hear of new efforts, new kinds of meetings, new organizations, new levels of concern about the need for humble, energetic devotion to a task that has long been the primary obligation of the Church of Jesus Christ.

Missiologists--the people for whom the study of Christian outreach is a scholarly and professional concern--report their estimate that the doors of at least 1,000 new churches are flung open for the first time each Sunday, and that in no country of the world is the percentage of committed Christians getting smaller. Does this mean there are no longer nearly three billion people without Christ? No, but it does enable us to lift up our heads and accept the Great Commission as a realistic goal. It enables us to know that books like this cut away at a *vital* edge and deal with a challenge which God through his Holy Spirit has put *within our grasp*.

It is a significant thing when a group of four outstanding missiologists put their hand to a project like this, drawing from still others--all scholars with field experience. I pray that thousands will find both delight and deep challenge in these pages.

Leighton Ford

Preface

Four of us, with experience ranging from Guatemala and Bolivia to India and China, have worked together to produce in a single book key chapters on the crucial dimensions of world evangelization. In order to do so, we have called upon six other men, with additional experience in Japan, Mexico, Argentina, Colombia, Taiwan, Pakistan, Singapore and the Fiji Islands. Short biographical sketches are scattered through the book to introduce each of the ten people who are contributors. (Usually these occur at the beginning of a section, but sometimes at the beginning of a chapter so as not to destroy the format of the original material.)

However, the chief spectrum in this handbook is not geographical but strategic. As you glance through this book you will encounter not a continental breakdown but the significant categories of the task of world evangelization. The contents page spells this out in exciting detail.

We do not apologize for this joint authorship because no one person could possibly write as knowledgeably as a group of ten about this dramatic rainbow of themes that illuminate every major mission field in the world today.

In some ways this book is like an advanced reader that builds upon three other books in relation to which its selections have been made consciously supplementary. We refer to two books by C. Peter Wagner, *Stop the World, I Want to Get On* (Regal Books) and *Frontiers of Missionary Strategy* (Moody Press). The third is *The Twenty-Five Unbelievable Years, 1945-1969* (William Carey Library) by Ralph D. Winter. Moreover, there is still another book, *Understanding World Evangelization* (also William Carey Library), which functions as a study guide not only to this reader but to the other three books mentioned above.

This book and the three first mentioned are all perfectly able to stand on their own, however. *Stop the World* is a highly readable, ideal introduction to the subject of world evangelization. *Frontiers* tackles the whole range of problems and issues missionaries and mission agencies face. *The Twenty-Five Unbelievable Years* tells how following World War II, the Western colonial empire collapsed but both national churches and even the mission agencies not only survived but made unbelievably giant strides forward. As you can see, none of these books is as comprehensive as this one.

It would be unfair if we did not warn everyone who takes this book in hand, or who in any way senses the import of this subject, that these are *crucial* dimensions of a highly crucial task. This is not a book about a species of penguins that is in danger of becoming extinct. Rather, with arresting strategy, it wrestles with the open sores and fearful spiritual darkness which ravage and wreck the lives of hundreds of millions of real people, creatures that are the highest of all creation, creatures for whom God's own Son endured the cross, despising the shame, and is set down on the right hand of God...the Son who said 'as my Father sent me, so send I you.'

No, you can no longer hide your eyes if you probe these pages. They will show the permanence, the complexity, the scope, and yet *the obligation* deriving from the *feasibility* of the emergency task to which all who acknowledge Jesus Christ as Lord are called.

Ralph D. Winter

Part I

An Introduction
to Mission Theology

Arthur F. Glasser

Arthur Glasser is the dean of the faculty and Associate Professor of the Theology of Mission at the School of World Mission of Fuller Theological Seminary. Prior to this position he served for twelve years as the home secretary for the Overseas Missionary Fellowship (formerly the China Inland Mission) under whose auspices he began his career as a missionary in Western China at the end of World War II. He has taught on the faculty at Columbia Bible College and is co-author with Eric Fife of *Missions in Crisis*. His articles appear frequently in *Missiology: An International Review, His, Eternity, Sunday School Times, Christianity Today,* and *Evangelical Missions Quarterly.* Concurrently with his position at the School of World Mission he is the editor of *Missiology: An International Review,* the official organ of the American Society of Missiology.

The material in these four chapters is all original to this text.

1

The Missionary Task
-
An Introduction

> "As the Father has sent me, even so I send you"
> (Jn. 20:21). "Go into all the world and preach
> the gospel to the whole creation" (Mk. 16:15).
> "Repentance and forgiveness of sins should be
> preached in his name to all nations" (Lu. 24:47).

With these words the Lord Jesus Christ, on the evening of the
day of his resurrection, commenced the revelation of his will
for his Church in the world. Into all the world! To every
creature! What Commander ever conceived so vast a campaign!
What Leader ever confronted so small a band of followers with
so formidable, so impossible a task! Truly, this is the command
of Deity: this is the program of God! Such a gracious purpose--
that the whole world of sinning men have the opportunity to hear
the liberating good news of the grace of God and of the Kingdom
(Acts 20:24,25).

Our Lord had previously intimated that the future work of his
disciples would be to evangelize the world (Mk. 14:9; Jn. 4:42;
10:16; Mt. 4:12-16; Lk. 4:18, 19). A most striking and significant statement was made on Tuesday evening of Passion Week,
shortly after his last public appearance in the temple and final
appeal to the leaders of Israel (Mt. 23:13-39; Jn. 12:44-50).
In great grief he slowly left the temple, never to return
(Mt. 24:1). While departing, in response to a casual remark
from his disciples calling attention to its beauty and adornment,
he solemnly predicted its coming destruction. Not one stone
would be left upon another (Mt. 24:2, 3). The disciples were
amazed and followed him in silence out of Jerusalem and on to
the slopes of the nearby Mount of Olives. They sat down and

looked across the valley over to the mighty city whose coming
doom they had just heard announced. Finally, they could contain
themselves no longer. In considerable confusion they blurted
out several questions relating to the future. Christ's reply,
known as the Olivet Discourse, constitutes his major prophetic
utterance and consists of a panoramic sketch of future human
history, from the Roman conquest of Jerusalem to the final consummation of the age. It is in this discourse that one finds
our Lord saying: "The gospel must first be published among all
nations." Then, and only then, would "the End" come.

This reference to the centrality of the work of evangelizing
the world should never be forgotten, much less its context:
the prophecies of Christ relating to the future. One of the
great strengths of the Christian message is its Eschatology or
doctrine of the "last things." The Revelation of God contains
not only the solution to all individual needs, both now and for
eternity, through the establishment of a right, personal relationship with Christ. It also describes his majestic solution
to the vast problem of history, resolving its enigmatic past and
describing its future consummation through his glorious Return
and subsequent righteous reign "on the earth" (Rev. 5:10). How
immeasurably comforting to realize that even in this day of
crisis and conflict, the discerning Christian can see in the
present world scene significant happenings that indicate not
only God's sovereign power, but that his program for this age
is rapidly being realized. Ancient Israel's return (after 1900
years) to the land of Palestine, despite the violent persecutions
of the Nazis in which over 6,000,000 Jews were liquidated--Did
not Scripture prophesy their ultimate survival? The seemingly
irresistible onward march of Communism, with its insatiable
hunger for world conquest, its drastic transformation of even
the essential cultures of the peoples it conquers, and its naked,
brutal opposition to God and his people--Did not Christ say that
this age would end in violence and oppression, in tribulation
and with Antichrist? The mysterious, paradoxical picture of the
established Church, and worldly-minded in the larger sense, but
because of the labors of a devoted minority, engaging in world-
wide missionary activity on an unprecedented scale--Did not
Christ say the gospel must "first" be published among all
nations? These are significant days in the vast movement of
history, and the progress being made in world evangelization is
anything but incidental to it. For the Christian, it is a fact
of greatest significance.

Scripture distinctly states that God greatly desires that his
people keep the prospect of Christ's triumphant Return ever
before them. The Apostle Paul is a striking example of his
ideal in this regard. Just prior to his martyrdom he revealed
that in his intense missionary labors: in his fighting the

good fight of faith and seeking to preach the gospel "not where Christ was named," his inner heart continually dwelt with love on the prospect of Christ's appearing. The fact that Christ was coming back, and that at that Day all Christians would have to stand in his holy Presence, and give personal account of their stewardship--this truth well-nigh overwhelmed Paul. It kept him from all the trivia of life, and made him single-minded in his devotion to this central task (Rom. 15:16-21: II Tim. 4:5-8).

MAKING DISCIPLES

Several weeks after Jesus' Jerusalem instruction, referred to above, he amplified this mandate in the following fashion:

> Make disciples of all nations, baptizing them in
> the name of the Father and of the Son and of the
> Holy Spirit, teaching them to observe all that I
> have commanded you (Mt. 28:19, 20).

You will note that like a good teacher he first reviewed his initial instructions, before moving on to describe the new material. In restating the call to world evangelization, he deliberately replaced the basic verb "preach" ("to proclaim after the manner of a herald") with the imperative "make disciples" and adds that this is accomplished by "baptizing" and "teaching." At this point the scholars are needed to tell us how to fit all this together. Some argue that this merely means that we first enlist a man through our evangelistic witness. Later, we baptize him into the life and witness of a local congregation, and in the days ahead he becomes involved in the ongoing teaching that normally follows conversion. Others argue that one is not a disciple of Jesus until he has been baptized; and they reserve the teaching mandate for post-conversion education. In more recent days a third group of scholars feels that the grammar of the text forces them to conclude that both baptizing and teaching are directly related to making disciples. Baptism marks that the disciple has indeed placed himself under divine authority and become God's possession without qualification. And the teaching must refer to the initial communication of the gospel, especially in the area of making known what following the Lord truly means. We would agree to this, but feel that as a man receives Christ Jesus the Lord, so he is to live in him (Col. 2:6). The teaching that brings a man to his first commitment to Christ is to be given to him all the rest of his days.

Down through the ages the Church has found in this training aspect of the Great Commission, ample authority for its program of education, ranging from primary church schools on through to

theological seminaries. And God has used many a Christ-centered
school to prepare young people for a life of usefulness in his
service. Unfortunately, however, the training that is specifically designed to transform conduct is minimized, or altogether
overlooked. The training of the mind is conceived as the central
task. But the Great Commission is a call to evangelize the world
and produce men and women who would be more than well-informed
"believers" (not a common New Testament word). Jesus Christ
wants disciplined disciples.

PLANTING CHURCHES

  But the Christian movement needs even more than strong, committed individuals. Christians need to be gathered together in
communities. The missionary task is incomplete if it stops
short of planting churches.

  Our Lord did not reveal this added ministry until after
Pentecost. Even then, it was unfolded only gradually by his
Spirit. By his reference to "baptizing" in the Name of the
Father, and of the Son, and of the Holy Spirit in the Great
Commission, he had intimated this, but gave no further details.
The disciples first needed to have individual, experiential
knowledge of the great transformation wrought on the Day of
Pentecost by the Holy Spirit. Until he descended, baptizing
them "into one Body," bringing them into vital, mystical union
with Christ, and making them members of his Church ("which is
his Body"), the water baptism he had enjoined was devoid of full
significance. The spiritual verities it represented had not as
yet been accomplished. This Holy Spirit baptism had been
promised frequently prior to Pentecost (by John the Baptist in
Matt. 3:11 and by Jesus in Acts 1:5, etc.), was consummated on
that Day (Acts 2:1-4) and described thereafter in the New
Testament as a past, historical event (I Cor. 12:13).

  When the Holy Spirit came on the Day of Pentecost, he endued
the first disciples with power, and they began immediately under
his direction to preach and witness. They won men and women to
Christ and commenced meeting with them, leading them into a
pattern of ongoing discipleship (Acts 2:5-47). It was then that
they began to discover that God had given to them a corporate
life quite distinct from their individual relationship to Christ.
They started meeting together for worship, celebrating the Lord's
Supper, and receiving instruction in the Word of God from the
Apostles. The refreshing fellowship thus experienced was used
by God's Spirit to draw them together, and they continued to
sense, under his leadership, an obligation to continue their
evangelistic outreach, an obligation that quickened their
burden to pray together for the victory of God in the hearts
of men.

Being all of Jewish background, this activity of public worship, reading the Scriptures, preaching and praying reminded them of the pattern they formerly had followed at their old synagogue services. It was natural for them to consider the probability that God wanted them to continue this pattern. It had a four-fold function. It was to be an assembly for worship, a family for fellowship, an organism for vigorous evangelistic outreach, and a school for training disciples. When the need arose for a pattern of organization, it was found that God's will embraced the use of deacons and elders, each with a distinct sphere of responsibility, whether material or spiritual. As to ministries, the Lord provided apostles, prophets, evangelists, pastors, and teachers.

Taking the Church at Corinth as an example, one notes that local churches developed at least three distinct types of meetings--one, for the purpose of instruction, coupled with prayer and exhortation, another for the purpose of thanksgiving and worship, beginning with a common fellowship meal and ending with the celebration of the Lord's Supper, and the third, a sort of congregational meeting to conduct the business of the local church.

God's program for the evangelization of the world involves the local church. Unless local congregations are firmly established in each population center that has been evangelized, there is no satisfactory way of conserving the results of evangelistic efforts. Without local churches new converts cannot be readily trained, for that training involves working in a group and participating in group worship as well as walking alone with God. Without the varied, extensive outreach of a spiritually-minded church, it is difficult to train young converts to discharge their responsibility under God to participate in gospel outreach. In fact, it is almost impossible to evangelize souls and train converts adequately without the healthy functioning of a local church.

Planting these churches, then, is ever the ultimate objective of all missionary work. Missionary labor, no matter how brilliant, will have little permanence unless this is accomplished. In the final analysis, it is the local congregations, rather than individual believers, that bring lasting changes to the spiritual life of a region. Only through the establishment and functioning of local churches scattered throughout the population centers, integrated in part to the culture of the area, and independent of all outside control and support can an area originally designated as a "mission field" lose that title. "Mission fields" are areas where there are no churches. And the tragedy is that after more than 1900 years of Christianity there are still many dark places in the earth in which there are no indigenous churches witnessing to the true faith.

If one were asked to describe the relative importance of the
different components of the missionary task, he would be obliged
to confess that evangelism is 100% important: men are lost, and
"the Coming of the Lord draws near." Training is 100% important:
converts are babes, and God needs mature men, if his work is to
go forward. Church-planting is 100% important: to ignore the
Church and its corporate ministry is to remove all possibility
of permanence from evangelistic or training efforts, and to
violate a fundamental principle of the Word of God. No ministry
is primary; no ministry is secondary. All are of fundamental
importance. The program of God embraces all three.

MOTIVATION FOR MISSION

One factor remains. When our Lord issued the Great Commission,
he twice used the word "go." In most English versions its gram-
matical force is the imperative mood, the mood of command. "Go
ye!" But when one examines these statements in the original
language, the force is strikingly different. In the Greek the
imperative mood of command is limited to the words, "preach" and
"make disciples." The words which convey the concept of "going"
are participles. It is true that under certain conditions they
may be given an imperative force, but they do not have to be so
translated in this context. Rendering these passages literally,
one might translate Mark 16:15, "Having gone (or, when you go)
into all the world *proclaim* the glad tidings to all the creation,"
and Mt. 28:19, "In your going (or, going), therefore *make disciples* of all the peoples."

This striking fact arouses a natural query. Why do these
solemn elements of the Great Commission convey such an unexpected
impression? It is as though our Lord said to his disciples, "Of
course you will go...but when you do go, don't forget that my
command to you is to evangelize and to make disciples."

The only satisfactory solution to this problem is found in
Acts 1:8 with its majestic statement regarding the central
function of the Holy Spirit in the program of world evangelism.
Our Lord speaks prophetically in this passage, "But ye shall
receive power when the Holy Spirit has come upon you; and you
shall be my witnesses in Jerusalem and in all Judea and Samaria
and to the end of the earth."

The meaning is clear. When the Holy Spirit comes upon the
disciples and begins to administer the Lordship of Christ, a
new dynamic will enter their lives, and under his leadership
they will be borne along ever onward in the program of God.
However, should his sovereign authority be resisted and refused,
being replaced with self-will and self-direction, the momentum
of moving forward and outward will diminish, and inevitably the

the program of God will come to a standstill. Sadly, the
history of the Church records periods when there was little
missionary outreach: tragic evidence of the essential disobedience of the Lord's people to the inner authority of the Holy
Spirit. By their fruits they are known. Even today, the
Christian or church not concerned about missions is a Christian
or church that is either ignorant of God's Word or grieving his
Holy Spirit. Christians need no missionary appeals when they
are led by the Spirit.

This is a searching word. It has its primary application to
the task of training converts. Are they being discipled from
the very outset to be filled with the Holy Spirit? If not
filled with his holy Presence, they will not respond to his
leadership. They will remain out of the directive will of God.
Hence, they will hinder, not help, the cause of Christ.

CONCLUSION

This is a day in which evangelistic movements are enjoying
unprecedented success. The anguish of the world and the ominous
aspect of the future are causing many to hunger after spiritual
reality. But, there is a growing realization that the churches
of the day need greater spiritual vigor if they are to cope with
the vast opportunities of the present hour. Many churches are
beginning to feel they need better men: men who love Christ
supremely, who hate sin intensely, and who desire with great
compassion to see the unsaved won to the Savior.

Then too, the recent successes of the Communists are causing
many Christians to realize that there is another program of
world conquest abroad in the earth today. These Communists
are after the same peoples, tribes, tongues, and nations that
are Christ's concern. Their movement likewise embraces evangelism, training, and the planting of permanent centers of indoc-
trination and outreach. And they know how to train men. One
of the most critical books describing their activities is
obliged to confess: "The disciples of Marx are the most energetic, the most self-sacrificing, the most self-confident, and
the most disciplined group in modern society" (Parkes 1939:5).
In the present critical hour, then, the crux of the program of
God is in the training of its converts. For, if it is a matter
of Christianity versus Communism, it is a matter of Christian
versus Communist, a matter of disciple versus disciple.

Never has there been such a need to master and apply the
principles of mission outlined in the New Testament. They are
as true and workable now as when first applied: when a Roman
world was won to Christ. They need to be used today if the
cause of Christ is to advance in the teeth of the gathering
storm.

BIBLIOGRAPHY

PARKES, Henry B.
  1939   *Marxism: An Autopsy*. Boston, Houghton Mifflin Co.

2

Jesus Christ Making Disciples - A Study in Method

"Do the work of an evangelist" (II Ti. 4:5)

When our Lord began his final journey to Jerusalem--the one that
would climax with his death, burial and resurrection--his
disciples "supposed that the Kingdom of God was to appear
immediately" (Lu. 19:11). They did not realize that he would
be rejected by the nation and crucified, and that a long historic period would elapse before his final consummation of
human history with his glorious Return. In order to prepare
his disciples for what we call the "Church Age"--the long period
between his first and second Advent--the Lord gave the parable
of the pounds (Lu. 19:11-27). Its details are familiar. Prior
to a nobleman's departure he gives each of his servants the same
deposit--a pound--and tells them to trade with it until he
returns. Our Lord sought thereby to underscore the fact that
all God's servants have the same opportunity: each pound is
capable of multiplication if permitted to do its own work.
However, on the day of reckoning not all report the same
results: "Lord, your pound has made ten pounds" (v. 16).
"Lord, here is your pound" (v. 20). Apparently a capacity for
risking everything is an essential ingredient if the pound is
to multiply.

We naturally are curious as to what this pound represents.
Campbell Morgan confirms the obvious: "The pound...is the
gospel of the grace of God" (1943:247). There is life in the
gospel; it can transform the lives of men. But it must be let
loose.

Not many Christians think that they have what might be called
the "gift of evangelist." But to every one God has committed
the priceless treasure of the gospel. This would imply that all
possess grace for confessing Christ before men. Indeed, those
who follow him are automatically enrolled in his school of
evangelism: "Follow me, and I will make you fishers of men"
(Mt. 4:19). Those who respond truly begin to fish. Those who
do not fish betray possible flaws in their discipleship.

But what does it mean to be enrolled in his school? If it
means imitating his evangelistic method, as described in the
Gospels, we can only throw up our hands. His insight into man
was total; he employed a different approach with each person,
and dealt with no two seekers alike. Of course, he was eminently
successful! But how can mere humans ever be expected to follow
his example?

I used to be utterly bewildered over the very complexity of
this task of "making disciples" until I came upon some counsel
the Lord gave a new convert, Saul the Pharisee, when commissioning him to his service. When I examined this closely, I was
amazed; here was a basic formula that he apparently used himself
and which could be superimposed on the record of his dealings
with men and women of differing temperaments and different
situations. Because of his universal presuppositions--all
humans are "spiritual in essence, sinning in experience, and
savable by grace"--he followed the same deliberate sequence
with them all (Morgan 1937:5).

What then is the formula? Our Lord told the Saul who became
Paul that his task "under God" among the Gentiles was "to open
their eyes, that they may turn from darkness to light and from
the power of Satan to God, that they may receive forgiveness of
sins and a place among those who are sanctified by faith in me"
(Acts 26:18).

The use of this statement with its detailed pattern for
dealing with a man may be objected to. Some might ask in all
sincerity, "Why complicate anything as simple as the task of
winning men to Christ? The facts are clear: 'All have sinned
and fall short of the glory of God,' 'The wages of sin is death'
and 'Christ died for our sins.' Ask if the man believes these
truths. If he does, get him to assent to the Scriptural proposition: 'Believe in the Lord Jesus, and you will be saved.' If
he believes, he is automatically saved, right then and there.
It is as simple as that. Why complicate it?"

While it is a sad fact that in American Evangelical circles
today, the gospel tends to be simplified to the irreducible
minimum of believing three facts and agreeing to a simple

proposition that appears to make automatic the whole matter of
becoming a Christian, this is in sharp contrast with the method
employed by our Lord. In fact, a careful study of his method
will reveal how inadequate is the popular concept of getting a
man to "take Jesus as his own personal Savior." It is not without reason that whereas many go through this "formula" and
profess to receive Christ, not a few subsequently fall by the
wayside and manifest by their lives that they never really
experienced the new birth. We stand against this "easy
believism" and "cheap grace" and turn to the sequence of our
Lord's method for "making disciples." The steps follow:

"OPEN THEIR EYES"
--Make Men Conscious of Spiritual Need

What is man? Only God himself in his infinite omniscience
knows the full answer to this ancient question. When he regards
man from the viewpoint of his compassion and love, his heart is
strangely moved. He sees man as poor, weak, without strength,
broken-hearted, enslaved, blind, bruised. And he desires to
help man, to save man. But when he regards man from the viewpoint of his holiness and justice, his indignation is deeply
aroused. He sees the human race as rebellious, sinful, ungodly,
enemies by wicked works, children of wrath, children of the
devil, unrighteous. His sense of justice demands that he judge
man.

But how can God both save and judge? This is the dilemma
that only the substitutionary death of Christ could resolve,
when "God was in Christ, reconciling the world to himself"
(II Cor. 5:19). At the Cross, God punished the innocent
Substitute that he might forgive the penitent guilty. But can
man be reached by God when he has his back so stubbornly turned
toward him? How can he be so broken in repentence and submission
that he will reach out and take from God's pardoning hand full
provision for his individual need? Surely the power of God is
needed to work so mighty a miracle. Thank God, the initial
impulse comes from God himself. Were he not a gracious, seeking
God, man would never go to him of his own free will.

There are three forces that must work together to bring this
about: the Christian, the Word of God (which is "living and
powerful" (Heb. 4:12)), and the Holy Spirit. Just to list these
three is to make very evident the fact that the Christian's
chief responsibility is to cooperate with God as he brings the
message of his Word to the needy soul. For, in the final analysis, it is God alone who draws people to himself (John 6:44;
12:32; Eph. 2:8-10; Phil. 1:29; 2:12, 13; etc.).

Consider man. An additional aspect of his condition must now
be mentioned. Not only is man blind to the things of God,

unable of himself to enter his Kingdom, and a rebel against his
will. He is also living in an almost hermetically-sealed
compartment of self-centeredness. The familiar illustration
is of his dwelling in a windowless, doorless room whose floor,
walls, and ceiling are surfaced with innumerable mirrors.
Everywhere he looks, the primary image he sees is himself.

A widely heralded text in human relations frankly admits:

> When dealing with people, let us remember we are
> not dealing with creatures of logic; we are dealing
> with creatures of emotion, creatures bristling with
> prejudices and motivated by pride and vanity...
> when not engaged in thinking about some definite
> problem, people usually spend about 95% of their
> time thinking about themselves (Carnegie 1937:41,
> 55).

Indeed, the more a Christian worker ponders the mystery of the
human heart, the more he casts himself upon his God for some
solution to the almost insurmountable problem of reaching his
fellow-men. He gives himself to prayer. He earnestly beseeches
his God to reveal some hidden door, some secret passageway that
will open to the inner citadel of Mansoul. And he is confident
that his God will hear his cry and undertake on his behalf. The
One who commands his people to preach the gospel to every creature delights to work with them as they go forth in his Name.

John 4:7-42 records the story of Christ bringing the blessing
of God to a Samaritan city called Sychar. It all began when he
established contact at a well with a jaded, middle-aged woman
who had come to draw water. When first they met she was completely wrapped up in herself. She was neither interested in
him nor in his message. But very soon she began to change.
The manner in which he dealt with her is very revealing and
most instructive. It cannot be improved upon. Its essential
elements should be mastered. They are capable of wide application.

How did our Lord "open the eyes" of this woman so that she
became aware of her spiritual condition? His method was simple;
all of us can use it. He had to build a bridge of love and
understanding to her heart. She had to have confidence in him
before she could have confidence in his message. He, therefore,
had to deny himself and deliberately project himself into her
situation, using what modern parlance would term the "you-
centered" approach. He deliberately sought to express the
love of God to her. He was friendly. He was respectful. He
was determined to be a good listener. He knew that if he was

not interested in what she might want to tell him, he could not reasonably expect her to be interested in what he had to say.

His opening word was, "Give me drink" (4:7). So simple, and yet what a wealth of wisdom behind this request. So tactful, and gracious, but how wonderfully it put him under her obligation. And the results were far-reaching. Although she gave a curt reply voicing her surprise that he should overlook the old racial prejudice that had separated Jews from Samaritans for centuries, she somehow sensed a drawing to him. When in his quiet way he replied, ignoring completely the vexing question she had raised, and started to speak of giving her something, she unconsciously sensed that she was "accepted" by this winsome, gentle Stranger. The request for a drink had worked wonders. His bridge to her heart had been speedily and solidly built. He accepted her, and she accepted him.

The Lord then sought to arouse her interest and create a hunger for his solution to the vast problem of her social and spiritual need. He knew of her self-centeredness. He also knew of her shameful past. But he did not use a negative, critical approach. To do so would have defeated his purpose and put her on the defensive. He had to be positive. He had to arouse her curiosity. Although it soon developed that she had a religious background of a sort, he did not even begin with a reference to religion. Note his words: "If you knew the gift of God and who it is that is saying to you, 'Give me a drink,' you would have asked him, and he would have given you living water" (4:10).

What was the result? The racial question was forgotten. When he uttered these simple words her curiosity began to mount by leaps and bounds. Was there a "gift of God" she had not as yet received? What was this "living water"? And it was to be had for the asking? Who is this Jewish Stranger that is so ready to give her this water, if she will but ask?

At this point the woman began to sense, however vaguely, her need. Apparently she had a religious background but no vital experience of God. She had not as yet sought God's solution to the problems of her life. Her feverish seeking had all been on the human level. Her heart was still empty and hungry, though "the fires of passion had long since burnt themselves out, leaving nothing but ashes" (Morgan 1937:76). But now she was beginning to hope. A few friendly words from One who was apparently interested in her made all the difference.

This is the Scriptural method of contacting people: erecting the bridge of love; experience of another; awakening a sense of need so that you can speak further to their heart. It should be

noted, however, that in the great majority of our Lord's
dealings with the unsaved he did not have to awaken interest
as he did with this Samaritan woman. Recall Nicodemus (John
3:1-21) and the rich young ruler (Matthew 19:16-22). With
Zacchaeus, that "notorious rogue," there already was curiosity
about the Lord, but little else. By a personal word, our Lord
sought his hospitality, despite the adverse publicity it would
create. He thereby won his confidence, and Zacchaeus opened
his heart to him (Luke 19:1-10).

"TURN THEM FROM DARKNESS TO LIGHT"
--Revealing the Sufficiency of Christ

In arousing desire our Lord but commenced his dealings with
the Samaritan woman. Her mind was still darkened and confused.
But there was now a difference. She wanted to hear more. So
our Lord went further. He now expanded what he meant by "living
water" and brought himself more clearly into her conscious
thought as the solution to all her need. The entrance of his
words brought light, giving her understanding. This was his
work of enlightenment. In no time at all, after patiently
hearing her reactions, he spoke that word which caused her sin-
darkened mind to fill with light. Pointing to the water deep
within the well, he said: "Every one who drinks of this water
will thirst again, but whoever drinks of the water that I shall
give him will never thirst; the water that I shall give him will
become in him a spring of water welling up to eternal life"
(4:13-14).

With this word all the Samaritan woman's latent hungerings
were fully aroused. It was as though he had said, "Come to me,
all who labor and are heavy laden, and I will give you rest."
What she truly needed, she now realized, was rest of heart,
happiness, joy, contentment, peace, security, everlasting life.
And he was willing to give them to her! A "spring of water"
within her! Such happiness! Such joy! This wonderful One was
promising so much! Almost impatiently she grasped his offer
with wonder and amazement. "Sir, give me this water, that I
may not thirst, nor come here to draw." So much more than mere
desire had been aroused. A new conviction had seized her. She
now clearly discerned that he was the One able to meet her need.

This is the Scriptural method of turning men "from darkness
to light." As one continues to witness to the one whose interest
has been awakened, he moves from the general to the specific.
The written Word of God, revealing the living Word of God, is
now opened and examined. Its authoritative, loving voice is
made central. What is the need? Christ is greater than that
need! Christ, moreover, wills to meet that need!

Is there weakness before some debasing personal habit?
Christ is Power against all temptation. Is there anxiety and
fear in the heart? Christ is Peace. Is life a monotonous
existence without meaning? Christ is Purpose. He has his
perfect will for each one of his Own. Is there loneliness and
heart-hunger? Christ is Presence. He is the "Friend that
sticketh closer than a brother." By his holy Presence within
the believing heart, he makes loneliness impossible forevermore.
Is life too great a mystery to be resolved? Christ is Light.
Those abiding in his Word find all life's mysteries wonderfully
resolved. His truth dispels all shadows. Is there material
insecurity with fears of the unknown future gnawing at the
heart? Christ is Provision. He promises to supply all the
material and spiritual needs of his people and will walk with
them into the unknown future still providing each and every
need. Is there the fear of sickness and death? He is the
Resurrection and the Life, the Comforter who comforts the
afflicted and alone is able to make death, that fearsome enemy,
but a portal through which one passes into the eternal Presence
of God.

"TURN THEM FROM THE POWER OF SATAN UNTO GOD"
--Presenting the Necessity for Repentance and Submission

One would think that if a person is conscious of his need and
aware that Christ is able to meet that need, he has but to call
upon the Lord and request his salvation. Surely Christ would
not deny such a request! But to do this would be quite foreign
to the spirit of the New Testament. When the Samaritan woman
asked him for the "living water" he countered with a strange
word. To the casual reader it almost appears as though he
ignored her plea and issued an utterly irrelevant command.
John tells us that he abruptly said, "Go, call your husband,
and some here" (4:16).

Christ had to introduce the moral aspect. Moreover, he had
to get beyond the mere surface needs of the woman and on to her
real need which was spiritual. He was not solely interested in
enabling her to become a well-integrated, contented person. He
was desirous of bringing her to God. So he said in effect, "I
must ask you about your hidden life, your shameful past. You
must realize that in calling upon me for help you are calling
upon God. And God is holy and just. I cannot overlook your
sin. If I am to help you--and I truly desire to help you--I
must help you on my terms, not on your terms. And my terms
involve the confession of sin and the repudiation of the self
that did the sinning. Your sin must be confessed. Your self
must be dethroned from your heart. And since I do not desire
to separate myself from my gifts, I must deal with you with the
object of getting you of your own free will to enthrone me as

your Lord, to give me the solitary place in your heart.
Hitherto another power has had dominion over you. His spirit
of disobedience has been actively at work within your heart
these many years. Now it must leave. By my spirit I must
reign supreme. So let me talk with you. Go, call your husband,
and come!"

When the woman was commanded to go call her husband and
return, conflict for the first time entered their conversation.
This was to be expected. When one seeks, under God, to turn a
soul from the power of Satan unto God, all of the unregenerate,
Adamic nature of man bursts forth with its age-long defiance,
"We will not have this man to reign over us!" Furthermore, the
"power behind" man, even Satan himself, now entered the conflict
as well. But our Lord would not "give place to the devil. He
resisted him, and although the conversation for the time seemed
to range far from the main issue, in the end full victory was
achieved.

The woman sought to prevaricate. She said, "I have no
husband." She did not realize how completely Christ knew her
hidden past. But when he replied, revealing his knowledge of
her five past husbands and of the man with whom she was living
at that moment, the conflict suddenly sharpened. She attempted
to escape through introducing a side issue, a religious dispute,
of all things! But he quickly directed even this religious
question back to the main issue at hand. He went on to show her
that if she is to approach God and have him meet her need, she
must go in spirit and in truth. She must hide nothing. She
must be honest with herself, and with God. There was no alternative. Her past had to be confessed and utterly repudiated.

At this point, deep down in the woman's heart resistance
began to crumble. Wistfully she expressed the hope that when
Messiah came he would reveal all things. Our Lord promptly
countered by showing her that he was the Messiah. He claimed
to be the fulfilment of her most lofty religious conception.
With that she yielded.

The water-pot was forgotten. She had a new center to her
being, a new purpose in life. She had Jesus Christ. She was
now rightly related to her Creator by the dual bond of repentance and submission.

Although the climax to this encounter seems so sudden, so
simple, we cannot lightly pass it by. In a very real sense it
represents the most important part of our Lord's evangelistic
technique. For, the great theme of Christ's public ministry
was "The Kingdom of God." This message was the embodiment of
the very substance of the Old Testament wherein God, in calling

Israel, began to prepare for the rule of heaven and the kingship
of its Lord. He did this by precept, by example, and by prophetic utterance. When our Lord preached "repentance" and the
"kingdom of God," he was calling individuals to respond to the
rule of God over their hearts.

At this point, lest one misconstrue the force of this highly
simplifed description of the message of Christ, one might add
that an analysis of all the passages (116 approximately) referring to the Kingdom in the New Testament would show that it
means the essential rule of God; manifested in and through
Christ during his earthly ministry, apparent in the Church to
a greater or lesser degree as she seeks to "know him and make
him known" in the vast program of world-wide testimony; triumphant at the Second Coming of Christ; fully realized in his
millennial reign, and finally perfected in the world to come in
the new heavens and new earth.

If one overlooks the fact that Christ's evangelistic work
was primarily to bring the rule of God to individual hearts,
much of what he said to individuals appears irrelevant and
beside the point. In fact, some have wondered why he spent so
much time pressing the necessity for repentance. Why so much
stress on the cost of discipleship when Divine Grace was offered
so freely in the Gospel?

Apparently, if a man is to receive Christ in all the fullness
of meaning contained in the biblical word "receive," more is
required than mere intellectual assent to the truth of certain
statements in the Bible. Even the attempt to project something
"simple" into the meaning of the word "believe" runs head-on
into the stone wall of biblical reality when confronted by such
a statement as "How can you believe, who receive glory from one
another and do not seek the glory that comes from the only God?"
(John 5:44) To believe in God without submitting to the authority of God is unthinkable. To call Christ "Lord" is easy, but
the belief which saves is a belief that involves complete
repudiation of self as the cause for all past failure and the
source of all rebellious sinning against God. Unless the Cross
with its sharp mark of death is accepted as the new, abiding
principle of life, how can one be certain that there was a true
repentance to God in the first place? How can Christ be Lord
if there is no continuous, glad song within the heart saying
"None for self; all for Christ"? Unless the impelling drive in
life is to "follow Christ," self is still in control. And when
has the Crucified ever tolerated self-centeredness in the heart
of any of his disciples?

But return to Christ's evangelistic technique. How did he
bring men to this place of brokenness? Although he dealt with

men and women of different temperaments and in different circumstances, he always regarded them as sinful. To bring them to an
awareness of their own sin that they might sense their spiritual
need, he used two mighty weapons. "Through the law comes knowledge of sin" (Rom. 3:20). How frequently he applied the law to
a man's heart until the Spirit brought real conviction of sin
(e.g. Lu. 18:18-24). "God's kindness is meant to lead you to
repentance" (Rom. 2:4). How frequently he spoke of the grace of
God that lets the prodigal know he is welcome in the Father's
House (e.g. Lu. 15:11-24; Jn. 3:14-21).

This then is the Spriptural method of turning men "from the
power of Satan unto God": resolute prayer and faith in the name
of Jesus on the ground of his shed blood to dislodge Satan's
hold on a man and beat off his counter-attacks as the claims
of Christ are pressed; presenting the moral demands of God and
the true nature of discipleship; stressing the dethronement of
self and the enthronement of Christ; then, presenting the heart
of the gospel, the sinfulness of sin as revealed through the law
and the goodness of God as revealed through the Cross. These
mighty levers are able to move the heart to deny itself, take
up the Cross, and begin to follow Christ. True repentance and
submission are as the oath of allegiance the soldier takes when
he forsakes civilian life to enter the armed forces of his
country. They are not unlike the total surrender the bride
makes when she forsakes her independence and accepts the
authority of one who loves her and desires her to be his until
death breaks their union. Repentance and submission are the
two aspects of the response of the human heart to the conquering
love of Christ, who came to seek and to save that which was lost.

"THAT THEY MAY RECEIVE FORGIVENESS OF SINS...BY FAITH IN ME"
--Leading the Awakened to Exercise Faith
in God's Pardoning Grace

Once the Holy Spirit has produced in the heart an attitude of
submission to the Lordship of Christ, the work of evangelism is
almost concluded. But not quite. The awakened sinner must
receive by faith the forgiveness of his sins. He must receive
the moral cleansing that Christ provides. And he must come to
that subjective conviction, based upon the Word and inwrought
by the Holy Spirit, that he has peace with God.

Without this exercise of faith a soul cannot please and serve
God. Without the subjective experience of release that comes
when the conscience is purified, he will not be able to offer
Christ freely to his fellow-men. He will not be able to testify
with conviction that God is merciful and gracious and ready to
pardon, unless he has himself entered into this blessing.

Christ promises to meet every need, especially the fundamental spiritual need for forgiveness. When people accept his pardoning grace, taking him at his word, he rejoices. They have not believed "in vain." They have believed that to ask for forgiveness is to receive forgiveness. They have acted on Christ's faithfulness. Did he not say, "Shall not your Father who is in heaven give good things to those who ask him?" (Mt. 7:10) What greater "good thing" is there than the forgiveness of sins? On another occasion Christ said,"If any one thirst, let him come unto me and drink" (Jn. 7:37). It is by accepting by faith the full forgiveness of sins, on the grounds of Christ's redemptive work on the Cross, that a thirsty, repentant soul drinks of the grace of God.

This then is the Scriptural method of leading a repentant sinner to receive the forgiveness of his sins. It is the simple technique of leading him to exercise appropriating faith, based on some clear promise made in the Bible concerning God's willingness to forgive sin. It is concluded with a prayer of thanksgiving.

"THAT THEY MAY RECEIVE...INHERITANCE AMONG THEM THAT ARE SANCTIFIED BY FAITH IN ME" --Leading the Awakened to Enter by Faith Into the Family of God

In the Divine economy forgiveness and relationship are intimately related. It is impossible for a sinner to receive the forgiveness of his sins and at the same time leave unchanged his essential relationship to God and his people. The very essence of forgiveness is that a new relationship has been established between sinning man and a grieved and righteously angry God. Alienation gives way to acceptance. The penitent becomes the object of Divine affection and favorable regard. More, he senses a drawing to the people of God. The apostle John made this a test of the reality of the new birth: "We know that we have passed out of death into life, because we love the brethren. He who does not love remains in death" (I Jn. 3:14).

But these feelings of acceptance and belonging need to be translated into speech and action. Although the man who believes with his heart is justified, it is when he confesses with his lips that Jesus is Lord that he is saved (Rom. 10:9, 10). It is only by the indwelling Spirit that such a confession can be made, and that one is enabled to address the God who forgives as his Father in heaven (I Cor. 12:4; Rom. 8:15-17; Gal. 4:6).

The action required is the submission to baptism and entrance into the life and witness of the local congregation. Was it not Ananias who told the newly converted Saul of Tarsus: "Why do

you wait? Rise and be baptized, and wash away your sins,
calling on his name" (Acts 22:16)? Baptism marks the end of
the former life with its aloneness and alienation; it is the
initiatory rite into the church. By it one breaks with his
past and accepts the privilege and the responsibility of sharing
with brothers and sisters the life and liberty of the Lord Jesus.

This then is the Scriptural method of evangelism. It ends
with the incoporation of the new convert into the church. How
important this last step is. For, it is in the church and
through the church that the fruit of evangelism can be best
conserved.

BIBLIOGRAPHY

CARNEGIE, Dale S.
    1937   *How to Win Friends and Influence People.* New York,
            Simon and Schuster.

MORGAN, G. Campbell
    1937   *The Great Physician; the Method of Jesus with
            Individuals.* New York, Fleming H. Revell Company.

    1943   *The Parables and Metaphors of our Lord.* New York,
            Fleming H. Revell Company.

3

The Apostle Paul
and the Missionary Task
-
A Study in Perspective

By the power of the Holy Spirit...I have fully
preached the gospel of Christ...not where Christ
has already been named, lest I build on another
man's foundation, but as it is written, "They
shall see who have never been told of him, and
they shall understand who have never heard of
him" (Rom. 15:19-21).

It is our task in this chapter to trace the Apostle Paul's
approach to the task of evangelizing the nations. Obviously,
we cannot examine in detail all the references in the New
Testament record to his mission perspectives and labors.
Before we review the calling of God that made him an apostle
and set him apart for the gospel of God...(to bring about the
obedience of faith for the sake of his name among all the
nations (Rom. 1:1, 5-6)), we must review those earlier events
which gave birth to the New Testament church and launched the
missionary movement.

When John the Baptist announced that the coming One would
baptize his people with the Holy Spirit and fire (Matt. 3:11),
he was announcing the event that would preeminently mark the
distinction between the Old and New Testaments. The Spirit
would come upon the apostolic community Jesus had gathered and
empower it to become a missionary movement. This climactic
event took place early on the morning of the Day of Pentecost.
It was then that the Holy Spirit came upon a small company in
an upper room (only 120) and "they began to speak" under his
unction. Spirit and speech: by these the Church emerged as a

witnessing community. From this time forward it was of her
very essence to witness to the resurrected and glorified Christ.
Out of this witness all her other activities would arise.

The story of Pentecost is well known. A living organism was
created (I Cor. 12:12, 13) and it soon demonstrated its capacity
as a life-communicating presence among men. On that first day
its numbers increased by 3,000. The flame went from heart to
heart. In the weeks and months that followed, this living
Church demonstrated its capacity to reach outward in a spontaneous fashion with the good news of Jesus Christ. In the early
chapters of the Acts (2-12) we see evidence of the existing
possibilities of what has been termed "near neighbor evangelism."
Jerusalem, Judea, Samaria, Galilee--among the people of Palestine
the devoted believers reaped the harvest where Jesus and his
disciples had earlier sowed the good seed of the gospel of the
Kingdom.

During this period, and scholars believe it lasted for some
years, many things happened. The churches grew in size and
number, the new "messianic Jews" faced courageously the persecution of their countrymen, many priests were converted, Stephen
was stoned to death, revival broke out in Samaria and Peter took
the gospel to Cornelius and his household, the first Gentile
converts. But of central significance was the fact that God
singled out a rabid persecutor of this new faith to be transformed into its greatest missionary.

CALLED TO BE AN APOSTLE

It is generally agreed that the first century of the
Christian era was marked by intense missionary activity on the
part of the Jews. We can well believe that Saul the Pharisee
who later became Paul the Apostle was among those ardent Jews
whose life was dedicated to bringing the blessings of the Jewish
law to his contemporaries. Perhaps he was referring to this
when he later wrote: "I advanced in Judaism beyond many of my
own age among my people, so extremely zealous was I for the
traditions of my fathers" (Gal. 1:14). Incidentally, we should
remember that although he had been born in Tarsus, a largely
Gentile city in Cilicia, Asia Minor, Saul had been "brought up
in Jerusalem at the feet of Gamaliel, educated according to the
strict manner of the law" (Acts 22:3). This means he was no
typical Jew of the Diaspora (the Jews scattered throughout the
Mediterranean world). As a youth his direct contact with
Gentiles had been minimal; some scholars feel he moved to
Jerusalem with his parents shortly after his sixth birthday.

At any event, at his first appearance in the New Testament
Saul is a young man, approving the stoning of Stephen (Acts 8:1)

and persecuting the Church violently, even trying to destroy it
(Gal. 1:13). But then, on the road to Damascus, he is chosen
by Jesus Christ (Phil. 3:12). In those moments of initial
encounter between Saul and Jesus, the divine call was given and
received. As Paul later wrote: "It pleased God...to reveal
his Son to me, in order that I might preach him among the
Gentiles" (Gal. 1:16). Where previously he gave the law to men,
now he had a person to share with them, Jesus Christ. From that
time on Paul was possessed by one determination: to know Christ
and to make him known.

PREPARED FOR MISSIONARY SERVICE

The seven, or perhaps nine years (?) following his conversion
and calling were Paul's hidden years. During this time he
apparently received relatively little help from mature believers.
In Damascus, Arabia, Jerusalem, Tarsus, the rural parts of
Cilicia and finally Antioch, Paul went through a succession of
experiences that have come to characterize the training period
of many men of God. Note the succession: quiet fellowship,
active witness, persecution, rejection by fellow-believers,
enforced retirement, years of study then active service under
experienced leaders. Apparently this strange sequence was
necessary. At first he fellowshiped with Christians in worship
and ministry to the Lord (Damascus), then witnessed with them
in the Jewish synagogues. A period of persecution followed,
forcing Paul to turn to God for retirement, communion and
divine instruction (Arabia). This meant separation from all
his usual sources of strength and counsel and was apparently
necessary so that Paul could find in God himself the sole
source of all life and blessing. It is interesting to note
that Paul was then sent back to his home environment (Tarsus,
Syria and Cilicia) to serve, before being thrust out into
ministry further afield. Finally, God deliberately called this
man, destined for future leadership in his Church, to work
under human authority for a time before giving him an independent ministry (Antioch). What seems amazing is that God spent
such a long period training one who already knew the Jewish
Scriptures so well. This suggests that it is unwise to push
young believers too soon into active service, or even into
places of responsibility and leadership in a local church or
mission. Paul later wrote: "Do not be hasty in the laying
on of hands" (ie setting people apart to bear responsibilities
in the local congregation--I Tim. 5:22). Perhaps he was putting
into words his recognition that God was deliverately slow in
sending him forth as a missionary to the Gentiles.

THE SIGNIFICANCE OF THE APOSTOLIC BAND

We have mentioned that Acts 2-13 describes the evangelistic possibilities for "near neighbor outreach" latent within the local congregation. We have referred to the manner in which the Christian movement expanded from Jerusalem to Judea to Samaria and from there to the edges of Jewish Palestine. Chapter 11 brings this story to a climax by showing how a largely Gentile church was planted in Antioch, the fourth largest city in the Mediterranean world. Its cluster of small congregations ("house churches") was so dynamic that Barnabas, who was sent from Jerusalem to supervise and aid in its ministry, became convinced that a more vigorous and able man was needed to prepare the new converts for incorporation into the life of the emerging congregations. He thought of Paul and set forth to Cilicia to seek him. Eventually he found him and the two men combined their strength to lead the church "for an entire year." It is impossible to speak of this church without using superlatives. It was noteworthy as a truly cosmopolitan, most evangelistic, well-taught and outstandingly generous company of the Lord's people. And yet, in Acts 13:1-5 the church is described as burdened, and on its knees "worshipping the Lord and fasting."

Why so? What was the problem? The fact that the church was fasting conveys the impression that it was seeking guidance as it sensed its responsibility to take the gospel beyond Antioch to the diverse peoples of the Mediterranean world. Antioch's Christians had no doubt as to the suitability of the gospel for all men; what they lacked was a new method for sharing the gospel with them. The earlier method of near-neighbor, spontaneous outreach would only work within a homogeneous culture. What was now needed was a structured way of extending the knowledge of Christ, one that would surmount all the barriers, whether geographic, linguistic, cultural, ethnic, sociological or economic. So they prayed and fasted.

In response, the Holy Spirit led them to take a decisive step for which there was no precedent. The account twice refers to this, perhaps to underscore that the decision was in response to the Holy Spirit's presence and direction. They "organized what in later times would have been called a foreign mission" (Neill 1968:80). When Barnabas and Saul were designated as its charter members, the church merely "let them go" (vs. 3) because it was essentially the Holy Spirit whose authority and designation were behind his "sending them forth" (vs. 4).

From this, we cannot but conclude that both the congregational parish structure and the mobile missionary band structure are equally valid in God's sight. Neither has more right to the

name "church" since both are expressions of the life of the
people of God. Indeed, this record clearly challenges the
widely held notion that "the local assembly is the mediating
and authoritative sending body of the New Testament missionary"
(Peters 1972:219). And, there is no warrant for the view that
Paul, "for all his apostolic authority, was sent forth by the
church (God's people in local, visible congregational life and
in associational relationship with other congregations) and,
equally important, felt himself answerable to the church" (Cook
1975:234 quoting Rees). This mobile team was very much on its
own. It was economically self-sufficient, although not unwilling to receive funds from local congregations. It recruited,
trained and on occasion disciplined its members. The Holy
Spirit provided direction: like Israel in the wilderness, it
had both leaders and followers.

The band was apostolic in the sense that its members regarded
themselves as the envoys of God to the unbelieving world. They
lived "under the continual constraint of crossing the border
between belief and unbelief in order to claim the realms of
unbelief for Christ" (Bocking 1961:24). Only when there are no
more frontiers to be crossed--only when Jesus Christ has returned
and subdued all peoples under his authority will it be possible
to say that the need for such missionary bands has finally come
to an end.

From this time on the Apostle Paul's missionary methodology
was an expression of the activities of the apostolic band (what
Catholics call the "sodality" structure). It should be noted
that the sodality is not biologically self-perpetuating, as the
local congregation would be. One joins the band (or mission) by
commitment to the Lord for full-time involvement with the extension of the Christian movement. Acts 14:21-23 describes the
sequence of activities: preaching the gospel; making disciples;
bringing converts to a sense of their corporateness as members
of Christ and of one another, and custodians of the gospel of
the kingdom; and finally, organizing them into local congregations in which individual members commit themselves to one
another and to the order and discipline of the Spirit of God.
After a missionary journey was completed, the band returned to
its base (Antioch) and rehearsed before the church all that God
had accomplished through them (Acts 14:23, 28).

But what plan did the band follow in its missionary outreach?
It seems to have had two general objectives. One, the band
sought to visit all the Jewish synogogues scattered throughout
the Roman Empire, beginning in Asia Minor. Since the gospel was
"to the Jew first" (Rom. 1:16) this was natural. Indeed, Paul
was very explicit on the subject. Only after the Jews in any

one place rejected his message did he go out to the Gentiles.
We recall his words in Pisidian Antioch:

> It was necessary that the word of God should be
> spoken first to you (Jews). Since you thrust
> it from you, and judge yourselves unworthy of
> eternal life, behold we turn to the Gentiles.
> For so the Lord has commanded us, saying, "I
> have set you to be a light for the Gentiles,
> that you may bring salvation to the uttermost
> parts of the earth" (Acts 13:46, 47).

It should be noted that this initial outreach to the Jews was
not "mission" in the modern sense of the term. Nor should it
be. Mission implies reaching those without faith in God. In
contrast, the Jews already possessed "the sonship, the glory,
the covenants, the giving of the law, the worship, and the
promises; to them belong the patriarchs, and of their race,
according to the flesh, is the Christ" (Rom. 9:4, 5). The Jews
of the synagogue, because they have rejected in principle the
gospel, are to be "made jealous." By this strategy Paul sought
to "save some of them" (Rom. 11:11, 14). What does this mean?
Probably, he felt that the Christian movement in the totality
of its existence must convincingly demonstrate to the Jews that
Jesus of Nazareth is attractive, desirable and illuminating as
the Messiah who has already come. The Apostle Paul wanted to
live with true Jewry. They were not people of another religion
but remained the holy root to which the Gentile Church had been
grafted. As a result he went wherever there were Jewish synagogues. It was only because they were largely to be found in
the cities of the Empire that he went to the cities. God had
unfinished business to complete with his ancient people. And
this particular responsibility is still a priority task for the
Church in our day. The gospel is "to the Jew first."

The second general objective that underlay Paul's missionary
strategy was to plant Messianic synagogues or local congregations
wherever he found people responsive to the gospel. Keep in mind
that that first century of the Christian Era was *par excellence*
the great century of Jewish missionary activity. Jesus referred
to this when he reminded the Jewish leadership of his day that
their scribes and Pharisees "traversed sea and land to make a
single proselyte" (Matt. 23:15). This meant that circling
virtually every synagogue was a ring of Gentiles, mostly Greek
"God-fearers," who had been drawn by the witness of the Jews to
the worship of one God and to a quality of life far surpassing
anything practiced in the Roman world. Although compelled by
Jewish moral strength, intellectual vigor, disciplined living
and wholesome family life, these Gentiles stopped short of
receiving circumcision and becoming Jews. Inevitably Paul was

determined to win these spiritually hungry Gentiles to faith in
Jesus and make them the nuclei of Messianic (generally Greek-
speaking) synagogues (local congregations) of the emerging
Christian movement. So then diaspora Judaism "ploughed the
furrows for the gospel seed in the Western world" (Deissmann)
and the Jews "were robbed of their due reward...and prevented
from gathering in the harvest which they prepared"--all this by
Paul and his team, "a generation of fanatics" (to borrow from
the atheist Renan). When Luke wrote that "All the residents of
Asia heard the word of the Lord, both Jews and Greeks" (Acts
19:10), he probably meant that the band's outreach from the
Jewish presence in Ephesus extended throughout Asia, the south-
western portion of present day Turkey, and that the new congregations of converted Jews and non-Jewish Greeks were uniformly
involved in preaching the new faith. Inevitably, those Jews
who remained deep within rabbinic Judaism were "made jealous."
So it is today: the missionary obedience of the churches cannot
but stir Jewish people to reflect on why they are unwilling to
share their knowledge of the one God, the Creator of all men.

SPIRITUAL GIFTS AND THE MINISTRY

In his letters to the newly founded congregations Paul frequently stressed the wonderful fact that God at Pentecost "gave
gifts" to his people and thereby fully provided for their growth
in grace and their participation in evangelistic witness. When
he said that there were "varieties of service (ministry)"
(I Cor. 12:5), he was underscoring the diversity which characterizes the service of Christians within the fellowship of local
congregations and among the peoples of the world. To Paul the
word "ministry" embraced the total range of Christian duties
(Eph. 4:8, 12). All disciples of Christ are called to this
Diakonate. When every part of the Body is "working properly"
it grows in size, in spiritual depth and in extent (vs. 16).

Internal "service" embraces the local congregation's ministry
to the Lord in worship (by prayer, praise, sacrament and the
hearing of the word of God), the ministry of its members to one
another "For their common good" (I Cor. 12:7; II Cor. 8:4),
and the ministry of teaching by which the believing congregation
is inculcated with the norms of the apostolic tradition (Acts
6:4; Rom. 12:7). These three: worship, sharing, and instruction are essential to the vitality of any local congregation's
inner life--the "koinonia" of the people of God.

External "service" likewise has three components. They are
frequently described as the "mission" of the Church since they
embrace all that Christians have been sent into the world to
accomplish. There is the specific calling to minister to those
in special need: the poor, the sick, the widow, the orphan, the

prisoner, the homeless and "the stranger within the gate." Paul
clearly taught that God has equipped certain men and women for
such works of mercy and relief (Rom. 12:7; Gal. 6:10a).   In
addition, there is the ministry of reconciliation whereby
Christians work for concord between men and for social justice
within society. Since Paul preached a gospel which proclaimed
that sinners could be reconciled to God through Christ's redemptive cross, he was also not indifferent to the obligation to
work for the reconciliation of hostile groups within society
(II Cor. 5:18-21). Finally, there is the ministry of evangelism
whereby Christians confront men and women with the good news of
redemptive salvation through Christ's death, burial and resurrection. Christians are to serve their unsaved contemporaries
because they are the followers of the Great Servant. And their
supreme service is to bring non-Christians to the Servant himself.

So then, we can conclude that through Paul's pointed instruction that all "born again" Christians have been given "the
manifestation of the Spirit for the common good" (I Cor. 12:7),
he was relaying the mandate of Christ's Great Commission to the
churches. In this connection none of Paul's exhortations was
more pointed than the challenge he pressed on Corinthian
believers at the end of a lengthy discussion of spiritual gifts.
He urged them to "covet earnestly the higher gifts" (12:31).
His concern was that they should seek those gifts which concerned
the oral ministry of the word of God. Covet the apostolic gift
and become God's envoy, his evangelist, his church-planter in the
unbelieving world. Covet the prophetic gift and become his
spokesman, his revivalist to the professing Church. Covet the
pastoral gift and become his teacher, his shepherd to the local
congregation. As D. L. Moody used to say: "Covet usefulness!
Make your plans big, because God is your Partner."

CHURCH AND MISSION

"I was appointed a preacher and apostle (I am telling the
truth, I am not lying), a teacher of the Gentiles in faith and
truth" (I Tim. 2:8). Paul was determined to see the Church
grow. Indeed, he regarded it her chief and irreplaceable task:
to preach the gospel to all mankind and incorporate all those
who believed into her communal life. He felt that only through
the deliberate multiplication of vast numbers of new congregations would it be possible to evangelize his generation. As an
apostle, a member of an apostolic band, he saw himself laboring
on the fringes of gospel advance, doing this priority work.

This inevitably meant that Paul made crucial the relation
between his band and the new congregations. Indeed, we cannot
understand his preoccupation with gathering funds from the

Gentile churches to bring relief to the Jewish churches, unless it was somehow related to his desire that the churches be one "that the world may believe" (John 17:21).

Furthermore, Paul also struggled to achieve and maintain a symbiotic relationship between his apostolic band and the churches it had planted. True, some of the churches promptly forgot him and displayed little interest in his evangelistic and missionary endeavors. Other churches opposed Paul and showed a surprising vulnerability to syncretistic thinking, false teaching and gross carnality. Still other churches remained so weak that he had to care for them as a nurse cares for little children. But there were churches, such as the one in Philippi which loved him and expressed that love with sacrificial gifts. In turn, by his example, his teaching and his prayers, Paul constantly reminded the churches of their apostolic calling. They had been sent by God into the world to reach beyond their borders with the gospel. Their task was to bring into God's kingdom the nations for which Christ died and which had yet to acknowledge him as their king.

The most striking illustration of Paul's desire to establish this symbiotic relationship between local church and mobile mission is found in his epistle to the church in Rome. When he wrote this letter he was midway through his great missionary career: his work in the Eastern Mediterranean just completed. Indeed, he could state that "from Jerusalem and as far around as Illyricum" (present day Yugoslavia) he had "fully preached the gospel of Christ" (Rom. 15:9). However, the Western Mediterranean represented unrelieved darkness, with but one point of light: the church in Rome. Apparently, this solitary fact had been on Paul's mind for some years as he agonized in prayer and deliberated about his future ministry (15:22).

So, he took pen in hand and wrote this tremendous epistle. As a "task theologian" he carefully selected certain themes, and developed them to prepare the Roman Christians for his missionary strategy. They had to realize anew 1) the abounding sin of man, with all the world guilty before God (1:18-3:20); 2) the abounding grace of God to sinners, with justification offered to the believing because of Christ's redemptive work (3:21-5:21); 3) the abounding grace of God to Christians, with sanctification made possible through the Holy Spirit's indwelling presence and power (6:1-8:39); 4) the abounding grace of God to the nations for although Israel had failed through unbelief, God was nonetheless determined to reach them with the gospel through the Church and restore Israel at his return (9:1-11:36); and 5) various practical matters such as the exercise of spiritual gifts (12:1-21), the relation of Church and State (13:1-7), and the importance of love to enable the diversity within the Church

effectively to put united heart and conscience to reaching the
nations (13:8-15:6). Only after this extensive review (15:15)
does Paul reveal his strategy for the church at Rome: that it
was to become a second Antioch, the new base of operations for
his mission to Spain and the Western Mediterranean (15:22-24).
It would have a significant role, providing Paul with experienced
men and undertaking for their financial and prayer support. In
other words, this epistle was written to give a strong cluster
of house-churches in a great pagan city a sense of their missionary responsibility for peoples beyond their borders.
Through its participating in the missionary obedience of Paul's
apostolic band, the church at Rome would attain a new sense of
its role as the "sent people" of God (1:11-15). We conclude:
the local congregation needs the mobile team. Church needs
mission that the "gospel of the kingdom will be preached throughout the whole world, as a testimony to all nations; and then the
end will come" (Matt. 24:14).

THE STRATEGY OF SUFFERING

    One final element remains. We cannot trace the Apostle Paul's
missionary career without being impressed again and again with
the fact that his whole life was marked by suffering. When the
Lord Jesus called him to the apostolate he said: "I will show
him how much he must suffer for the sake of my name" (Acts 9:16).
Although set free by Christ, he knew that this freedom was only
granted that he might take God's love to all, which meant that
he would have to become the slave of all (I Cor. 9:19-23).

    All this brings us to the deepest levels of Christian exper-
ience where life is lived in the tension of one's times and in
spiritual encounter with the forces of darkness. It is these
forces that seek to hinder the efforts of the people of God to
liberate people with the gospel. Indeed, one cannot enter into
the fabric of Paul's thought and experience without becoming
aware that all his letters (with the possible exception of
Philemon) make reference to Satan who constantly sought to
thwart this plans (e.g. I Thess. 2:18). Paul writes of "the
mystery of lawlessness," "the elemental spirits of the world,"
the "god of this age," "principalities and authorities"--
indeed, these "world powers" penetrated every component of his
thought, and although he knew they were vanquished by Christ at
the cross, they still posed tremendous obstacles to his missionary obedience. And Paul knew these powers could only be overcome by faith, love, prayer and suffering. He wrote: "We are
appointed unto afflictions" (I Thess. 3:3). This points up a
cardinal principle: the gospel cannot be preached and the
people of God cannot be gathered into one from the nations
(John 11:52) without individuals here and there "completing
what is lacking in Christ's afflictions" in order to accomplish

this task (Col. 1:24). Apparently, one cannot become involved in proclaiming the gospel of the kingdom without paying a price for the privilege. And that privilege is extended to us as well.

The spirit world is always present and the demons are never friendly. This was Paul's experience. And he suffered in order to overcome them, using the weapons provided by his victorious Lord. Were he among us today he would call for our active resistance to all that hinders the ongoing purpose of God--the powers in religious structures, in intellectual structures ('ologies and 'isms), in moral structures (codes and customs) and in political structures (the tyrant, the market, the school, the courts, race and nation) (Yoder 1972:465). The good news our generation needs to hear today includes the breaking in of the kingdom of God by the One who rendered inoperative all opposing forces. But those who serve in his name will suffer. The cross is still the cross.

BIBLIOGRAPHY

BOCKING, Ronald
   1961   *Has the Day of the Missionary Passed?* Essays on
          Mission, No. 5. London, London Missionary Society.

COOK, Harold R.
   1975   "Who Really Sent the First Missionaries?" *Evangelical
          Missions Quarterly*, October 1975:233-239.

NEILL, Stephen
   1968   *The Church and Christian Union.* London, Oxford
          University Press.

YODER, John Howard
   1972   *The Politics of Jesus.* Grand Rapids, William B.
          Eerdmans Publishing Co.

4

Mission in the Early Church
-
From the Apostle John
to Constantine
A.D. 90-313

"Probably no period in the history of the world
was better suited to receive the infant Church
than the first century A.D." (Green 1970:13).

The New Testament ends with the Church moving on into its
second generation, a time when many congregations were beginning to experience a wide range of unexpected problems, internal
as well as external. Some were "losing their first love"
(Rev. 2:4). Harrassed by Jewish and pagan persecutors, others
were being exhorted to be "faithful unto death" (Rev. 2:10), as
though facing total catastrophe--which they were. Still others
were troubled by power struggles and doctrinal disputes that
threatened their unity (II John 7-11 and III John 9, 10). The
thoughtful student cannot but be curious about the outcome of
all this: what happened to those apostolic churches in the
years that followed?

   Strange as it may seem, this question is not easy to answer.
Although historians largely agree that by the beginning of the
second century there were churches in most of the cities of the
Roman Empire, minor as well as major, exactly how they came into
existence lies buried in legend. The fact remains that written
records do not exist. All we know is that the principle: "to
the Jew first" was rigorously maintained. There were colonies
of Jews in most of the Roman provinces surrounding the Mediterranean and Black Sea areas, as well as throughout the Middle
East. These Jews had their synagogues, and every synagogue had
its ring of Gentile onlookers, of whom not a few had begun to
profess a measure of allegiance to the God of Abraham, Isaac
and Jacob. They were apparently willing to put up with their

second-class religious status (in Jewish eyes!) in order to study the Scriptures and "seek God, in the hope that they might feel after him and find him" (Acts 17:27). When they heard of Jesus--and what synagogue was not eventually confronted by the gospel? (Acts 28:22)--it was these Gentile "God fearers" who were drawn by the message of a classless society: the kingdom of God with Jesus as the King. And so, in a relatively short time this outer ring of "second-class" followers of Judaism turned to him and became first-class citizens in his kingdom (Phil. 3:20, 21).

Actually, throughout the Roman Empire the second century was a time of spiritual hunger and religious inquiry. Only the synagogue witness was positive and uncompromising. All the old ethnic faiths were on the defensive: some were breaking up rapidly because the ethnic groups themselves were disappearing. Indeed, had this vacuum not been developing there would hardly have been the apparently irresistible movement forward of those proclaiming new life in Christ. The ancient world with all of its divisions was fading and the "idea of universal humanity" was gaining credence. Slaves, women and children were being treated with growing deference and a desire for change was in the air. As the new Gentile converts turned from the synagogues to share their new faith with Greek, Latin and "barbarian" neighbors, they encountered a widespread disposition to listen to their message of forgiveness, resurrection and hope.

THE RETREAT OF JUDAISM

Christianity represented a universal faith. Jesus had seen to that! Men, not Jews, were the objects of his love and redemptive concern. His task was "to gather into one the children of God who were scattered abroad...to draw all men to himself" (John 11:52 and 12:32). As a result, in the apostolic age, and until the Jewish war of A.D. 68-70, both Jewish and Gentile believers were in dynamic interaction with one another. They constituted two components of the larger unity of the people of God. But when Jerusalem was destroyed and the temple burnt, Jewish believers in Jesus began to dwindle in numbers and significance. Within the next hundred years, helped along by a growing Gentile church bigotry, the situation had so altered that by 180 A.D. Jewish believers were officially regarded as heretics. Their total demise was imminent. From the second century until the present, the division between Jews and Christians has persisted, aided and abetted by a "Christian anti-Semitism" that is the worst stain on the record of Gentile Christendom. Only in our day are we witnessing a resurgence of Messianic Judaism. Many Jewish believers in Jesus are seeking to retain their identity with the totality of Jewish life and culture. Some might object to this and affirm that when anyone,

Jew or Gentile, believes in Jesus, he theologically loses his
cultural identity, for in Christ there is neither Jew nor Greek
(Gal. 3:28). And did not Paul himself deliberately become a
Jew in order to win Jews (I Cor. 9:20)? But it is equally true
that he was proud of his Jewish antecedents (Acts 21:39; 22:3)
and warned other Messianic Jews against attempting to disavow
or repudiate their cultural origins (I Cor. 7:17-24). The Jew
was not to be converted from Judaism so much as to be converted
to Christ. We would feel it a veiled form of anti-Semitism to
press the Jewish believer today to divest himself of his Jewish
culture and assimilate into the life of the Gentile church.

Almost all of the sub-apostolic writers speak approvingly of
the way in which the Gentile church took over Judaism's trea-
sures (her Scriptures, salvation history, heroes and some of her
festivals) and then condemned her. The consensus was that

> by their rejection of Jesus, the Jewish people
> disowned their calling and dealt a deathblow to
> their own existence; their place was taken by
> Christians as the new People, who appropriated
> the whole tradition of Judaism, giving a fresh
> interpretation to any unserviceable materials
> in it, or else allowing them to drop (Harnack
> 1972:69, 70).

The Christians merely

> established themselves in the strongholds
> hitherto held by Jewish propaganda and
> Jewish proselytes. Japeth occupied the tents
> of Shem and Shem had to retire (70).

WHAT WAS THE GOSPEL?

Even in the New Testament we can detect the steady enlarge-
ment of the message that was proclaimed during those early
decades. At first the thrust was that men should repent because
the kingdom of God was at hand (Matt. 10:7). Then, following
the crucifixion and the resurrection, the message was confined
to Jesus as the risen Messiah who will return to establish his
kingdom (Acts 2:29-37; 3:19-26). In no time at all a buttres-
sing of the Old Testament came to the fore and a soteriological
exposition was given to show that Christ died as the sin-
offering on behalf of mankind (Acts 13:38; I Cor. 15:4). Ampli-
fication called for the turning away from idols and the confession that "Jesus is Lord" (I Thess. 1:9, 10 and I Cor. 12:1-3).
To the Greek philosophers in Athens Paul preached God as Creator
and as the Providence superintending human history and climaxed
it with the theme: "Jesus and the Resurrection" (Acts 17:22-30).

Over the years details were added, such as the necessity for
adopting a life-style characterized by self-abnegation and
simplicity. Heretics appeared from time to time with their
additions to or subtractions from this deposit of truth (Rev.
22:19). Throughout the first three centuries the majority of
Christians held to the basic facts of the gospel (although they
did not always agree about their interpretation!). They sought
to transmit this message faithfully to all with whom they came
in contact. The witness was borne by "the little man, the
unknown ordinary man, the man who left no literary remains."
He was "the prime agent in mission" (Green 1970:172). The
Roman world was not conquered by a sophisticated philosophical
message: the gospel was readily grasped by ordinary people and
they passed it on in ordinary ways.

CONFRONTING THE POWERS

The early Christians believed the world was filled with
intelligent, unseen beings who opposed God and afflicted the
human race. Apparently, during the second century this belief
also became widespread among pagans. People lived in fear of
evil spirits, and sought relief from their malevolence. What
turned the tide was the Christian confession that Jesus is Lord,
that by his cross he "disarmed the principalities and powers and
made a public example of them, triumphing over them" (Col. 2:15).
It was inevitable that Christians sought to exorcise the tor-
mented.

Since it was widely believed that sickness was also due to
the activity of demonic forces, all bodily ailments came under
the challenge of Jesus' name.

Indeed, as Harnack states: "Exorcism formed one very powerful
method of the Christian mission and propaganda. It was a question not simply of exorcising and vanquishing the demons that
dwelt in individuals, but also of purifying all public life from
them" (1972:131). When it became apparent that the demons could
not stand up to the Christians, it was inevitable that unworthy
people became involved. The church was soon excoriated for
tolerating in its midst those who were no more than magicians
and necromancers, charlatans and exploiters of the credulous.
Serious people were often repelled, especially by those frivolous
Christians who too readily blamed their own sins on the work of
demons. Nonetheless, it was this vigorous confrontation of the
spirit world by ordinary Christians desirous of liberating their
fellow men that greatly increased people's willingness to listen
carefully to the gospel and face seriously the claims of Christ.

CHRISTIAN LOVE IN ACTION

Jesus had underscored the importance of displaying the love of God through works of mercy and charity (Matt. 25:31-46). And the early Christians, although themselves a despised minority--a lower class movement in Roman society--were most careful to obey his precepts and follow his example of self-giving love. They were extremely conscientious about giving alms, supporting widows and orphans, and caring for the sick, the infirm and the indigent. They extended this ministry to non-Christians. As Julian reluctantly admitted: "These godless Galileans feed not only their own poor but ours; our poor lack our care" (quoted in Harnack 1972:162). They visited prisoners, especially those in the mines, and they made sure the dead were given a decent burial. Most important, Christians continually sought to ameliorate the conditions of the slaves, although the thought of striking at the roots of the slave system does not seem to have occurred to them.

We can do no better than to quote a familiar statement written by an unknown Christian to Diognetus in the second century. Is he describing the actual conduct of Christians in the midst of most difficult pagan surroundings, or is he defining an ideal to which they should strive? We do not know for sure, but there is something in his words that evokes a positive response from the best that is within us:

> Christians are distinguished from other men
> neither by country nor language nor the customs
> which they observe. For they neither inhabit
> cities of their own, nor employ a peculiar form
> of speech, nor lead a life which is marked out
> by any singularity...But inhabiting Greek as
> well as barbarian cities...and following the
> customs of the natives in respect of clothing,
> food and the rest of their ordinary conduct,
> they display to us their wonderful and confes-
> sedly paradoxical manner of life. They dwell
> in fatherlands of their own country, but only
> as aliens. As citizens they share in all things
> with others, and yet endure all things as
> foreigners. Every foreign land is their father-
> land and every fatherland a foreign land. They
> marry as do all; they beget children, but they
> do not destroy their offspring. They have a
> common table, but not a common bed. They are in
> the flesh but they do not live after the flesh.
> They pass their days on earth, but they are
> citizens of heaven. They obey the prescribed
> laws, and at the same time surpass the laws by

> their lives. They love all men, and are
> persecuted by all... (Green 1970:135, 6)

This display of love was not without power. Behind all the
grace and kindness shown by those early disciples to their non-
Christian neighbors, there was strength--the confirming witness
of God. This reality was unmistakable: "God bore witness by
signs and wonders and various miracles and by gifts of the Holy
Spirit distributed according to his own will" (Heb. 2:4).
Whereas the ethnic religions and cults had their moments of
ecstasy and vision along with their demonic and anti-demonic
manifestations, the sheer wealth of the Spirit's activity coupled
with the moral force of ordinary Christians was a tremendous
demonstration of the superiority of the way of Jesus. True, in
time, the life of congregations centered more directly on their
leaders--priests and teachers--along with altars, sacraments,
the *regula* of faith and the Scriptures. But, this vitality of
the Spirit did not really diminish until the third century. The
Christian movement was a moral enterprise of transforming power
led by those who out-loved, out-thought and out-did their contemporaries. They were the "third race," different from the
Jews and morally superior to the Gentiles. They waged warfare
against idolatry, against its vices that defile men, against its
luxury and against its astrology. As Harnack pointedly stated:
"It was significant, highly significant indeed, that gross and
actual idolatry was combatted to the bitter end. With it Christianity never came to terms" (1972:311).

MISSIONARY METHODOLOGY

In the New Testament we trace the emergence of the apostolic
band. In the second and third centuries sodalities continued to
function. It is striking that in an early catechetical manual,
the Didache (c. 120 A.D.), the unknown writer speaks of only one
class of people who were to be honored in the church: those who
preached the word of God as *ministri evangelii*. One is reminded
of a similar exhortation in Hebrews 13:7, 17. Nameless, these
itinerant apostles (missionaries), teachers and prophets tended
to be received by the local congregations with much respect,
although, as would be expected, charlatans occasionally joined
their ranks. With the passage of time, however, and the mounting
persecution of Imperial Rome, these bands dissolved and the task
of extending the knowledge of Christ and the gospel was largely
undertaken by lay witnesses. Gager summarizes:

> In general we must imagine Christian missions
> as rather quiet and unobtrusive, depending heavily
> on personal contact within closely defined social
> circles. ...Interest seems to have been aroused
> by word of mouth rather than by public announce-
> ments. ...families, friends and fellow workers

> provided a ready social basis for converts
> (pre-existing friendship nets). ...such
> restricted social units supplied a convenient
> means of communication as well as the rudi-
> ments of social relations (affective bonds)
> that could be carried over into the new group
> (1975:130).

   In those early years the living faith we know as Christianity
seemed to grow and reach but without special "methods" for its
propagation. It was a lay movement through and through. Its
members loved and rejoiced and served and witnessed. And the
pagans round about "saw...a quality of living, and supremely of
dying, which could not be found elsewhere. ...Men will not
believe that Christians have good news to share until they find
that bishops and bakers, university professors and housewives,
bus drivers and street corner preachers are all alike keen to
pass it on, however different their methods may be" (Green 1970:
275). In the end, the royal house was penetrated. Even the
Emperor Constantine capitulated, and during his reign Christianity not only gained the official recognition of the State, but
became the State religion.

BIBLIOGRAPHY

GAGER, John G.
   1975   *Kingdom and Community The Social World of Early
           Christianity*. Englewood Cliffs, New Jersey,
           Prentice-Hall, Inc.

GREEN, Michael
   1970   *Evangelism in the Early Church*. Grand Rapids,
           William B. Eerdmans Publishing Co.

VON HARNACK, Adolf
   1972   *The Mission and Expansion of Christianity in the First
           Three Centuries*. (Harper Torchbook) New York, Harper
           and Row, Publishers.

Part II

An Introduction to

Mission Anthropology

Paul G. Hiebert

Paul Hiebert, the author of Part II, "An Introduction to Mission Anthropology," is Associate Professor of Anthropology and South Asia Studies at the University of Washington in Seattle. He began his career as a missionary in India for the Mennonite Brethren Board of Missions and Services, of which he is now a director of research. He obtained a doctorate in the field of cultural anthropology from the University of Minnesota. He has served on the faculties of Kansas State University, University of Wisconsin, Fresno State University and Osmania University in Hyderabad, India, and has received high marks for his teaching abilities from the students at the Summer Institute of International Studies (held at Wheaton College each summer). He is the author of the recently published *Cultural Anthropology* (Lippincott, 1976) and has published articles in *The American Anthropologist, Folklore, Church and Mission* and *Missiology: An International Review.*

The diagrams occurring in these pages are all reprinted by permission of Lippincott publisher, but all other material is original to this text.

Introduction

This section is a brief introduction to mission anthropology. Anthropology itself is the study of human beings in an attempt to understand how they think and live. Why do they build houses, wear clothes, speak languages and organize families? How do they create societies and cultures, and how do these, in turn, mold them? And how do people and cultures change? These and many more are the questions anthropologists ask.

They seek the answers by studying people and their environments--by living with them, observing their behavior, listening to what they say, and sharing in their activities. The results have given us a great many insights into what it means to be human.

Mission anthropology seeks to apply the insights gained by anthropology to the mission task of the Church. In doing so it does not deny that people are spiritual beings. To the contrary, it recognizes that the Bible has a great deal to say about human beings: that they have sinned and need the salvation provided by Jesus Christ, that they should grow in fellowship with God and in harmony with His creation, and that they have an eternal destiny.

But mission anthropology does take the doctrine of the incarnation seriously. For some reason God chose to create people not only divine but also human. Their bodies are subject to natural and biological laws, their minds and spirits operate in accord with psychological and sociocultural principles. In order to understand people, we must recognize both their natural and their spiritual dimensions, and the relationships between these.

Since the spiritual issues in missions are dealt with elsewhere in this book, we will confine ourselves here to some of
the insights anthropology can bring to our task.

5

Culture and
Cross-Cultural Differences

One of the first shocks a person experiences when he or she leaves his home country is the foreignness of the people and their culture. Not only do they speak an incomprehensible language, but also dress in strange clothes, eat unpalatable foods, organize different kinds of families and have unintelligible beliefs and values. How do these differences affect the communication of the Gospel and the planting of churches in other societies?

THE CONCEPT OF CULTURE

In ordinary speech we use the term "culture" to refer to the behavior of the rich and elite. It is listening to Bach, Beethoven and Brahms, having the proper taste for good clothes, and knowing which fork to use when at a banquet.

But anthropologists in their study of all humankind, in all parts of the world and at all levels of society, have broadened the concept and freed it from value judgements, such as good or bad. There has been a great deal of discussion on how to define the term. For our purposes we will define culture as *the integrated system of learned patterns of behavior, ideas and products characteristic of a society*.

1. Patterns of Learned Behavior

The first part of this definition is "learned patterns of behavior." We begin learning about a culture by observing the behavior of the people and looking for patterns in the behavior. For example, we have all seen two American men on

meeting grasp each other's hand and shake it. In Mexico we
would see them embrace. In India each puts his hands
together and raises them towards his forehead with a slight
bow of the head--a gesture of greeting that is efficient,
for it permits a person to greet a great many others in a
single motion, and clean, for people need not touch each
other. The latter is particularly important in a society
where the touch of an untouchable used to defile a high
caste person and force him to take a purification bath.
Among the Siriano of South America, men spit on each other's
chests in greeting.

Probably the strangest form of greeting was observed by
Dr. Jacob Loewen in Panama. On leaving the jungle on a
small plane with the local native chief, he noticed the
chief go to all his fellow tribesmen and suck their mouths.
When Dr. Loewen inquired about this custom, the chief
explained that they had learned this custom from the white
man. They had seen that every time he went up in his plane,
he sucked the mouths of his people as magic to insure a safe
journey. If we stop and think about it a minute, Americans,
in fact, have two types of greeting, shaking hands and suck-
ing mouths, and we must be careful not to use the wrong form
with the wrong people.

Like most cultural patterns, kissing is not a universal
human custom. It was absent among most primitive tribesmen,
and considered vulgar and revolting to the Chinese who
thought it too suggestive of cannibalism.

Not all behavior patterns are learned. A child touching
a hot stove jerks his hand away and yells "Ouch!" His
physical reaction is instinctive, but the expletive is
culturally learned.

2. Ideas

Culture is also the ideas people have of their world.
Through their experience of it, people form mental pictures
or maps of this world. For instance, a person living in
Chicago has a mental image of the streets around his home,
those he uses to go to church and work, and the major arter-
ials he uses to get around town. Obviously, there are a
great many streets not on his mental map, and as long as he
does not go to these areas, he has no need for knowing them.
So also people develop conceptual schemes of their worlds.

Not all our ideas reflect the realities of the external
world. Many are the creations of our minds, used to bring
order and meaning in our experiences. For example, we see
a great many trees in our lifetime, and each is different

from all others. But it would be impossible for us to give
a separate name to each of them, and to each bush, each
house, each car--in short, to each experience we have. In
order to think and speak we must reduce this infinite variety of experiences into a manageable number of concepts by
generalization. We call these shades of color red, those
orange, and that third set yellow. These categories are the
creations of our mind. Other people in other languages lump
them into a single color, or divide them into two, or even
four colors. Do these people see as many colors as we?
Certainly. The fact is we can create as many categories in
our minds as we want, and we can organize them into larger
systems for describing and explaining human experiences.

In one sense, then a culture is a people's mental map of
their world. This is not only a map *of* their world, but
also a map *for* determining action (Geertz 1972:169). It
provides them with a guide for their decisions and behavior.

3. Products

A third part of our definition is "products." Human thought
and actions often lead to the production of material arti-
facts and tools. We build houses, roads, cars and furniture.
We create pictures, clothes, jewelry, coins and a great many
other objects.

Our material cuture has a great effect on our lives.
Imagine, for a moment, what life in America was like a
hundred years ago when there were no cars or jets. The
invention of writing, and more recently of computers has
and will have an even more profound effect upon our lives
for these permit us to store up the cultural knowledge of
past generations and to build upon it.

4. Form and Meaning

Behavior patterns and cultural products are generally linked
to ideas or meanings. Shaking hands means "hello." So does
kissing in certain situations. We also assign meaning to
shaking our fists, to frowning, to crying, to letters of the
alphabet, to crosses and to a great many other things. In
fact, human beings assign meaning to almost everything they
do and make.

It is this linkage between an experienceable *form* and a
mental *meaning* that constitutes a symbol. We see a flag,
and it carries the idea of a country, so much so that men in
battle will even die to preserve their flags. A culture
can be viewed as the symbol systems, such as languages,
rituals, gestures and objects, that people create in order
to think and communicate.

5. Integration

Cultures are made up of a great many patterns of behavior,
ideas and products. But it is more than the sum of them.
These patterns are integrated into larger cultural complexes,
and into total cultural systems.

To see this integration of cultural patterns we need only
observe the average American. On entering an auditorium to
listen to a musical performance, he looks until he finds a
chair on which to perch himself. If all these platforms are

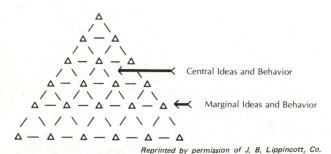

Reprinted by permission of J. B. Lippincott, Co.

Figure 1. Culture is an integrated set of ideas
and their associated behavior patterns and products.

occupied, he leaves because the auditorium is "full."
Obviously, there are a great many places where he can sit
on the floor but this is not culturally acceptable, at
least not at the performance of a symphony orchestra.

At home the American has different kinds of platforms for
sitting in the living room, at the dining table and at his
desk. He also has a large platform on which he sleeps at
night. When he travels abroad his greatest fear is being
caught at night without a platform in a private room, so
he makes hotel reservations well ahead of time. People
from many parts of the world know that all you need is a
blanket and a flat space in order to spend the night, and
the world is full of flat places. In the airport, at three
in the morning, the American traveler is draped uncomfortably
over a chair rather than stretched out on the rug. He would
rather be dignified than comfortable.

Not only do Americans sit and sleep on platforms, they build their houses on them, hang them on their walls, and put fences around them to hold their children. Why this obsession with platforms? Behind all these behavior patterns is a basic assumption that the ground and floor are dirty. This explains their obsession for getting off the floor. It also explains why they keep their shoes on when they enter the house, and why the mother scolds the child when it picks a potato chip off the floor and eats it. The floor is "dirty" even though it has just been washed, and the instant a piece of food touches it, the food becomes dirty.

On the other hand, in Japan the people believe the floor is clean. Therefore they take their shoes off at the door, and sleep and sit on mats on the floor. When we walk into their home with our shoes on, they feel much like we do when someone walks on our couch with their shoes on.

At the center, then, of a culture are the basic assumptions the people have about the nature of reality and of right and wrong. Taken together, they are referred to as the people's *world view*.

This linkage between cultural traits, and their integration into a larger system have important implications for those who seek to introduce change. When changes are made in one area of culture, changes will also occur in other areas of the culture, often in unpredictable ways. While the initial change may be good, the side effects can be devastating if care is not taken.

CROSS-CULTURAL DIFFERENCES

In their study of various cultures, anthropologists have become aware of the profound differences between them. Not only are there differences in the ways people eat, dress, speak and act, and in their values and beliefs, but also in the fundamental assumptions they make about their world. Edward Sapir pointed out that people in different cultures do not simply live in the same world with different labels attached, but in different conceptual worlds.

Edward Hall points out just how different cultures can be in his study of time (1959). When, for example, two Americans agree to meet at ten o'clock, they are "on time" if they show up from five minutes before to five minutes after ten. If one shows up at fifteen after, he is "late" and mumbles an unfinished apology. He must simply acknowledge that he is late. If he shows up at half past, he should have a good apology, and by eleven he may as well not show up. His offense is unpardonable.

In parts of Arabia, the people have a different concept or
map of time. If the meeting time is ten o'clock, only a servant
shows up at ten--in obedience to this master. The proper time
for others is from ten forty-five to eleven fifteen, just long
enough after the set time to show their independence and equality. This arrangement works well for when two equals agree to
meet at ten, each shows up, and expects the other to show up, at
about ten forty-five.

The problem arises when an American meets an Arab and
arranges a meeting for ten o'clock. The American shows up at
ten, the "right time" according to him. The Arab shows up at
ten forty-five, the "right time" according to him. The American
feels the Arab has no sense of time at all (which is false), and
the Arab is tempted to think Americans act like servants (which
is also false).

1. Culture Shock

   Our first reaction to the prospect of going overseas is one
   of excitement and anticipation. The flight, the new sights
   and strange customs--is this really happening to me? The
   market place is colorful with its bargains, if only the
   vendors could speak English. The village is fascinating.
   Is there a drugstore where I can get some medicine for my
   stomach pains? Not until next week when I return to the
   city?! The food is interesting, to say the least. I like
   to try new dishes, but I suppose I couldn't stand this as a
   steady diet. You mean to say the people here eat it twice
   a day, every day? And so will I when I move to the village?
   For three years? In this house with no running water? No
   doctor? No one who can talk a decent English? How did I
   get into this anyway?

   Our first confrontation with cultural differences is
   culture shock, the sense of confusion and disorientation we
   face when we move into another culture. This is not a
   reaction to poverty or the lack of sanitation, for foreigners coming to the U.S. experience the same shock. It is
   the fact that all the cultural patterns we have learned are
   now meaningless. We know less about living here than even
   the children, and we must begin again to learn the elementary things of life--how to speak, to greet one another, to
   eat, to market, to travel, and a thousand other things.

   We never really enter culture shock as tourists, for then
   we launch out daily from our little American style hotels to
   see the people, but not to settle down among them and build
   stable relationships. It is when we realize that this now
   is going to be our life, and for a long time to come, that

the shock comes. Disorientation, disillusionment and depression strike, and we would go home if only we did not have to face the folks there.

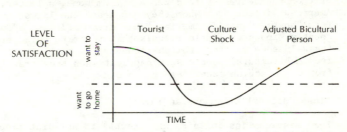

Figure 2. Culture shock is a sense of cultural disorientation that comes when one enters a new culture.

But this reaction is perfectly normal. As we learn to speak the new language, make a few friends, find out that we can travel by bus, learn to count the now not so strange coins, and realize that we can keep our health, we begin to fit into the new cultural setting. We need to avoid the temptation to withdraw into ourselves and our houses, or to try to return in part to our old culture by creating a little America in which we live. We can get out and learn to live in the new culture, and, in time, we will feel as at home in it as our own, possibly even more so.

Something happens to us when we adapt to a new culture, we become bicultural people. Our parochialism, based on our unquestioned feeling that there is really only one way to live, and our way is it, is shattered. We must deal with cultural variety, with the fact that people build cultures in different ways, and that they believe their cultures are better than ours. Aside from some curiosity at our foreignness, they are not interested in learning our ways.

But to the extent we identify with the people and become bicultural, to that extent we find ourselves alienated from our kinsmen and friends in our homeland. This is not reverse culture shock, although we will experience that when we return home after a long stay abroad. It is a basic difference in how we now look at things. We have moved from a philosophy that assumes uniformity to one that has had to cope with variety, and our old friends often don't understand us. In time we may find our closest associates among other bicultural people.

In one sense, bicultural people never fully adjust to one culture, their own or their adopted one. Within themselves they are part of both. When Americans are abroad, they dream of America, and need little rituals that reaffirm this part of themselves—a food package from home, a letter, an American visitor from whom they can learn the latest news from "home." When in America, they dream of their adopted country, and need little rituals that reaffirm this part of themselves—a visitor from that country, a meal with its food. Bicultural people seem happiest when they are flying from one of these countries to the other.

2. Cross-Cultural Misunderstandings

Some missionaries in Zaire had trouble in building rapport with the people. Finally, one old man explained the people's hesitancy to befriend the missionaries. "When you came, you brought your strange ways," he said. "You brought tins of food. On the outside of one was a picture of corn. When you opened it inside was corn and you ate it. Outside another was a picture of meat, and inside was meat, and you ate it. And then when you had your baby, you brought small tins. On the outside was a picture of babies, and you opened it and fed the inside to your child."

To us the people's confusion sounds foolish, but it is all too logical. In the absence of other information, they must draw their own conclusions about our actions. But we do the same about theirs. We think they have no sense of time when, by our culture, they show up late. We accuse them of lying when they tell us things to please us rather than as they really are (although we have no trouble saying "Just fine!" when someone asks "How are you?"). The result is cultural misunderstanding, and this leads to poor communication and poor relationships.

Cultural misunderstandings often arise out of our subconscious actions. Hall illustrates this (1959) is the way people use physical space when they stand around talking. North Americans generally stand about four or five feet apart when they discuss general matters. They do not like to converse by shouting to people twenty feet away. On the other hand, when they want to discuss personal matters, they move in to about two or three feet and drop their voices. Latin Americans tend to stand about two or three feet apart in ordinary conversations and even closer for personal discussions.

Misunderstandings arise only when a North American meets a Latin American. The latter subconsciously moves in to

about three feet. The former is vaguely uneasy about this
and steps back. Now the Latin American feels like he is
talking to someone across the room, and so he steps closer.
How the North American is again confused. According to his
spacial distance, the Latin American should be discussing
personal matters like sharing some gossip or arranging a
bank robbery. But, in fact, he is talking about public
matters, about the weather and politics. The result is the
North American thinks Latin Americans are pushy and always
under his nose; the Latin American concludes that North
Americans are always distant and cold.

Misunderstandings are based on ignorance about another
culture. This is a problem of knowledge. The solution is
to learn to know how the other culture works. Our first
task in entering a new culture is to be a student of its
ways. Even later, whenever something seems to be going
wrong, we must assume that the people's behavior makes sense
to them, and reanalyse our own understandings of their
culture.

3.   Ethnocentrism

Most Americans shudder when they enter an Indian restaurant
and see the people eating curry and rise with their fingers.
Imagine going to a Thanksgiving dinner and diving into the
mashed potatoes and gravy with your hand. Our response is
a natural one, to us. Early in life each of us grows up in
the center of our own world. In other words, we are egocen-
tric. Only with a great deal of difficulty do we learn to
break down the circle we draw between I and You, and learn
to look at things from the viewpoint of others. We also
grow up in a culture and learn that its ways are the right
ways to do things. Anyone who does differently is not quite
"civilized." This ethnocentrism is based on our natural
tendency to judge the behavior of people in other cultures
by the values and assumptions of our own.

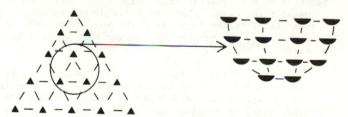

Reprinted by permission of J. B. Lippincott, Co.

Figure 3.   Ethnocentrism is judging other people's behavior
by one's own values and assumptions.

But others judge our culture by their values and assumptions. A number of Americans went to a restaurant with an Indian guest, and someone asked the inevitable question, "Do people in India really eat with their fingers?" "Yes, we do," the Indian replied, "but we look at it differently. You see, we wash our hands carefully, and besides, they have never been in anyone elses mouth. But look at these spoons and forks, and think about how many other people have already had them inside their mouths!"

If cross-cultural misunderstandings are based on our knowledge of another culture, ethnocentrism is based on our feelings and values. In relating to another people we need not only to understand them, but also to deal with our feelings that distinguish between "us" and "our kind of people," and "them" and "their kind of people." Identification takes place only when "they" become part of the circle of people we think of as "our kind of people."

4. Translation

How do you translate ". . .lamb of God . . ."(John 1:29) into Eskimo in which there is no word for, or any experience of animals we call sheep? Do you make up a new word and add a footnote to describe the creature that has no meaning in their thinking? Or do you use a word such as "seal" that has much the same meaning in their culture as "lamb" does in Palestine? Obviously cultural differences raise problems when we translate a message from one language and culture to another.

Here it is well to recall that cultural symbols have both form and meaning. Many early translators failed to note this difference and assumed that when they translated the form, the people would understand the meaning correctly. In other words, if in one language we find the world "lamb," we need only find the word in another language for the same kind of animal and the people will understand what we "mean." But this does not necessarily follow. In fact, the contrary is usually the case. The same forms do not carry the same meaning in different language. The more accurately we translate the form, the greater the danger that we will lose the meaning.

An example of this variance of meanings assigned to the same form is found in the Christmas story. In Palestine shepherds were respected and devout men. In India shepherds are the village drunkards, and in Christmas pageants in more than one instance they have come onto the stage reeling drunk. In this case the form has been kept, but some of the meaning lost. The same loss can occur whenever we translate

cultural forms such as campfire services, Christmas trees
and alter calls.

More recently translators have been concerned with
"dynamic equivalent" translations, in which the meaning is
preserved, even if a different form is used. The result is
translations that are better understood by the people. But
the task is not as simple as it seems. We cannot simply
translate word for word, using words with equivalent meanings,
for words, themselves, are products of a culture and
reflect the basic values and assumptions of that culture.
The fact is, there are no words in one culture that carry
exactly the same meanings as the words in another culture.

This fundamental variance, even at the level of simple
language, is best seen by way of illustration. Most Americans
divide their concepts of living beings into a number of
discrete categories. At the top is God who, in the Judeo-
Christian tradition, is categorically different from all
other beings. He is creator, they creation. He is infinite
and eternal. They are finite and temporal.

Below God are other spirit beings, angels and demons.
These belong to the realm of the supernatural which is
sharply distinguished in the West from the natural.

At the top of the natural realm are people. Because they
belong to a single category, they are thought, at least
ideally, to be equal. Below humans are animals. For all
practical purposes they are treated as different from humans,
for one can kill and eat, or enslave animals, but not people.
Finally, at the bottom, are plants. Beneath this hierarchy
of *different kinds* of life there is inanimate matter that is
thought to have no life at all.

In India people look at life differently. They see all
life as one, and all living beings have different quantities
of this *one kind* of life. At the top are the gods and demi-
gods who are pure life or spirit. Below them are various
kinds of demons, then saints, high caste people, low caste
people, cows, horses, sheep, snakes, fish, insects, plants
and all other forms of this life. The differences between
them is one of degree, not of kind. And through the process
of reincarnation, the same being may be reborn in one life
as a human, and in the next as an animal or god.

Because they feel all life is one, Indians make no sharp
distinction between gods and people. Saints may be worshipped just as deities. It is not uncommon, therefore, for
the people to reverence Krishna, Mahatma Gandhi and J. F.
Kennedy at the same time. On the other hand, there is no

AMERICAN CONCEPT OF LIFE   INDIAN CONCEPT OF LIFE

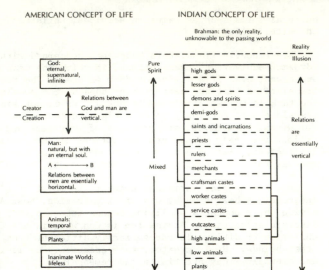

Figure 4. A comparison of American and Indian views of life.

sharp distinction between people and animals. To kill
either is wrong. When a United States development agent
suggested Indians kill many of their cows and eat them, the
people reacted much as we might if an Indian suggested we
solve our poverty problem by shooting the poor. We keep our
poor in ghettos, but we cannot kill them. So, too, an
Indian may work his cow in the field, but he should not kill
it.

Now back to the discussion of translation. Beginning in
Genesis we read, "In the beginning God. . ." The question
is, how shall we translate the word "God"? In Telugu, a
south Indian language, we can use the words "Isvarudu,"
"Devudu," "Bhagavanthudu," or a number of others. The
problem is that each of these carries the Hindu connotation
that gods have exactly the same kind of life as human beings,
only more of it. They are not categorically different from
people. There is no word that carries the same connotations
as the Biblical concept of God.

This also raises the problem of translating the Biblical
concept of "incarnation." In the Biblical setting incarnation is seen as an infinite God crossing the great gulf
between Himself and human beings, and becoming a person. In

other words, He crossed from one category to another. In
the Indian setting gods constantly become incarnate by moving down within the same category to the level of people.
Obviously this concept of incarnation is fundamentally different from the Christian one. To use it is to lose much
of the meaning of the Christian message. But how then can
we translate the Biblical concepts of God and incarnation in
Telugu or other Indian languages?

We might coin a new word for "God" or "incarnation," but
then the people will not understand it. Or we can use one
of the Telugu words, but then we face the danger that the
Biblical message will be seriously distorted. Often the
best we can do is use a word with which the people are
familiar, but then to teach them the meaning we are giving
to it. It may take years and even generations before the
people understand the new meanings and the total Biblical
world view within which these meanings make sense.

This process may seem to take too long. What about the
illiterate peasant who accepts Christ at an evening service?
Do not his concepts and world view change immediately?
Obviously not. But his salvation is not dependent on
whether he has a Christian world view or not, but on whether
he accepts Christ's salvation however he understands it, and
becomes His follower. However, for the long range building
of the church, the people and their leaders must have an
understanding of the Biblical concepts and world view if the
message is to be preserved over the generations.

IMPLICATIONS OF CULTURAL DIFFERENCES FOR MISSIONS

It is clear that cultural differences are important to a
missionary who must go through culture shock, learn to overcome
misunderstandings and ethnocentric feelings, and translate his
message so that it is understood in the local language and culture. But there are a number of other important implications
that need to be touched briefly.

1. The Gospel and Culture

We must distinguish between the Gospel and culture. If we
do not, we will be in danger of making our culture the
message. The Gospel then becomes democracy, capitalism,
pews and pulpits, Robert's Rules of Order, clothes, and
suits and ties on Sunday. One of the primary hinderances
to communication is the foreignness of the message, and to
a great extent the foreigness of Christianity has been the
cultural load we have placed upon it. As Mr. Murthi, an
Indian evangelist, put it, "Do not bring us the Gospel as
a potted plant. Bring us the seed of the Gospel and plant
it in our soil."

The distinction is not easy to make, for the Gospel, like any message, must be put into cultural forms in order to be understood and communicated by people. We cannot think without conceptual categories and symbols to express them. But we can be careful not to add to the Biblical message our own.

A failure to differentiate between the Biblical message and other messages leads to a confusion between cultural relativism and Biblical absolutes. For example, in many churches where it was once considered sinful for women to cut their hair or wear lipstick, or for people to attend movies, these are now acceptable. Some, therefore, argue that today premarital sex and adultery are thought to be sinful, but that in time they too will be accepted.

It is true that many things we once considered sin are now accepted. Are there then no moral absolutes? We must recognize that each culture defines certain behavior as "sinful," and that as the culture changes, its definitions of what is sin also change. There are, on the other hand, certain moral principles in the Scriptures that we hold to be absolute. However, even here we must be careful. Some Biblical norms, such as leaving the land fallow every seventh year and not reaping the harvest (Lev. 25) or greeting one another with a holy kiss (I Thess. 5:26) seem to apply to specific cultural situations.

2. Syncretism versus Indigenization

Not only must we separate the Gospel from our own culture, we must seek to express it in terms of the culture to which we go. The people may sit on the floor, sing songs to native rhythms and melodies, and look at pictures of Christ who is Black or Chinese. The Church may reject democracy in favor of wise elders, or turn to drama to communicate its message.

But, as we have seen, translation involves more than putting ideas into native forms, for these forms may not carry meanings suitable for expressing the Christian message. If we, then, translate it into native forms without thought to preserving the meaning, we will end up with *syncretism*—the mixture of old meanings with the new so that the essential nature of each is lost.

If we are careful to preserve the meaning of the Gospel even as we express it in native forms we have *indigenization*. This may involve introducing a new symbolic form, or it may involve reinterpreting a native symbol. For example, bridesmaids, now associated with Christian weddings, were originally used by our non-Christian ancestors to confuse the demons who, they thought had come to carry off the bride.

3. Conversion and Unforeseen Side Effects

Since cultural traits are linked together into larger wholes,
changes in one or more of them leads often to unforeseen
changes in other areas of the culture. For example, in one
part of Africa, when the people became Christians, their
villages also became dirty. The reason for this was that
they were now not afraid of evil spirits which they believed
hid in the refuse. So they no longer had to clean it up.

Many cultural traits serve important functions in the
lives of the people. If we remove these without providing
a substitute, the consequences can be tragic. In some
places husbands with more than one wife had to give up all
but one when they became Christians. But no arrangements
were made for the wives who were put away. Many of them
ended up in prostitution or slavery.

4. Theological Autonomy and World Christianity

As Christianity becomes indigenous in cultures around the
world, the question of the unity of the church arises.
There is an increasing stress that the church in each
cultural setting become autonomous; self supporting, self
administering and self propagating. But how do we cope with
theological variety? How do we react when the churches we
help plant want theological autonomy and call for a socialist
or even Marxist evangelical Christianity?

It is clear that cultures vary a great deal. As the
Gospel becomes indigenous to them, their theologies--their
understandings and applications of this Gospel--will also
vary. What, then, does it mean to be a Christian? And how
can Christians who disagree in some points of theology have
true fellowship with one another?

Here we must remember two things. In the first place, we
need to understand the nature of human knowledge and recognize its limitations. People experience an infinitely varied
world around them and try to find order and meaning in their
experiences. In part they discover the order that exists
in the world itself, and in part they impose a mental order
on it. They create concepts that allow them to generalize,
to lump a great many experiences into one. They also act
like a movie editor, linking certain experiences with certain
other ones in order to make sense of them. For example,
experiences in the same classroom on a number of different
days are put together and called Introduction to Anthropology.

A different set is thought of as "church activities."

When we read the Scriptures, we must remember that we interpret them in terms of our own culture and personal experiences. Others will not interpret them in exactly the same way. We must, therefore, distinguish between the Scriptures themselves, and our theology or understanding of them. The former is the record of God's revelation of Himself to humankind. The latter is our partial, and hopefully growing, understanding of that revelation. If we make this distinction, we can accept variations in interpretation, and yet find fellowship with those who are truly committed followers of Christ.

In the second place, we must never forget that the same Holy Spirit who helps us to understand the Scriptures, is also interpreting it to believers in other cultures. Ultimately it is He and not we who is responsible for preserving divine truth and revealing it to us. We must make certain that we are committed followers of Jesus Christ and open to the instruction of His Spirit.

6

Social Structure
and Church Growth

The second anthropological concept we will use to analyze
mission processes is *social structure*. People are social
beings, born, raised, married, and usually buried in the
company of their fellow humans. They form groups, institutions
and societies. Social structure is the ways in which they
organize their relationships with one another and build societies.

Societies can be studied on three levels: that of interpersonal relation, of groups, and of the society as a whole.
A study of missions at each of these levels can help us a great
deal to understand how churches grow.

INTERPERSONAL RELATIONSHIPS: THE BICULTURAL BRIDGE

When a missionary goes overseas and settles down, what does
he do? Whatever his specific task, he is involved in interpersonal relationships with a great many people. Many of these
are not Christians, but, most likely, he will spend much of his
time with Christian converts. He will go to the market, or
preach in the village square, but his closest relationships will
be with national pastors, evangelists, teachers and other
Christians. What are the characteristics of these carious
relationships?

It is clear that in most cases communication across cultures
is multistepped. The missionary received the message in his
family, church and school. He communicates it to national
Christian leaders who in turn pass it on to local Christians
and nonchristians in the cities and villages. With few

exceptions, the greatest share of the mission work in a country
is done by these unheralded nationals.

Here, in order to see how a structural analysis is used, we
will look at one link in this chain of communication--the relationships between the missionary and his national counterpart.
This has sometimes been called the bicultural bridge, and is the
critical step in which much of the translation of the message
into a new culture occurs.

The bicultural bridge is a set of relationships between
people from two cultures. But it is more. It is itself a new
culture. The missionary rarely can "go native." He will set
up housing, institutions and customary ways of doing things
that reflect his home culture, in part, and, in part, are adapted
from the culture in which he finds himself. His national counterparts do the same. It is true that they have not moved out
of their own culture, but their interaction with the missionary
exposes them to a great many foreign missionary will be increasingly alienated from their home culture.

A great deal of energy in the bicultural setting is spent on
defining just how this new culture should operate. Should the
missionary have a car in a society where most of the people do
not? If so, should his national counterparts have them too?
Where should the missionary send his children to school--to the
local schools, to a school for missionary children, or to those
in North America? What food should the missionary eat, what
dress should he wear and what kind of house should he and the
national workers have? These and a thousand more questions
arise in the bicultural setting.

1. Status and Role

The term "status" has a number of common meanings, but
anthropologists use it in a specific sense, defining it as
the "positions in a social system occupied by individuals."
At the level of interpersonal relationships a social organization is made up of a great many such positions: teachers,
priests, doctors, fathers, mothers, friends and so on.

Each status is associated with certain behavioral expectations. For example, we expect a teacher to act in certain
ways towards his students. He should show up for class and
lead it. He should not sleep in class, or come in a dressing
gown. A teacher should also act in certain ways vis-a-vis
his administrators, the parents of the students, and the
public.

All interpersonal relationships can be broken down into
complimentary role pairs: teacher-student, pastor-

parishioner, husband-wife, etcetera. The nature of the
relationship between two individuals is based very much on
the statuses they choose.

The Missionary and the Nationals. "What are you?" This
question repeatedly asked of a person who goes abroad to
settle. The people ask because they want to know how to
relate to the newcomer.

Missionaries generally answer, "We are missionaries." In
stating this they are naming a status with its associated
roles, all of which are perfectly clear to themselves. They
know who "missionaries" are, and how they should act. But
what about the nationals, particularly the nonchristians
who have never met a missionary before. What do they think
of these foreigners?

Here we must come back to cultural differences, again.
Just as languages differ, so also the roles found in one
culture differ from those found in another culture.
"Missionary" is an English word, representing a status and
role found in the West. In most other cultures it does not
exist. When a missionary shows up in these cultures, the
people must observe him and try to deduce from his behavior
which of their roles he fits. They then conclude that he
is this type of person and expect him to behave accordingly.
We, in fact, do the same thing when a foreigner arrives and
announces that he is a "sannyasin." From his looks we might
conclude he is a hippie, when, in fact, he is a Hindu saint.

How have the people perceived the missionaries (for an
excellent discussion of missionary roles see Loewen 1975:
and Smalley 1967:276-285   )? In India the missionaries
were called "dora." The word is used for rich farmers and
small-time kings. These petty rulers bought large pieces
of land, put up compound walls, built bungalows, and had
servants. They also erected separate bungalows for their
second and third wives. When the missionaries came they
bought large pieces of land, put up compound walls, built
bungalows, and had servants. They, too, erected separate
bungalows, but for the missionary ladies stationed on the
same compound.

Missionary wives were called "dorasani." The term is
used not for the wife of a dora for she should be kept in
isolation away from the public eye, but his mistress whom he
often took with him in his cart or car.

The problem here is one of cross-cultural misunderstanding. The missionary thought of himself as a "missionary,"

not realizing that there is no such thing in the traditional
Indian society. In order to relate to him, the people had
to find him a role within their own set of roles, and they
did so. Unfortunately, the missionaries were not aware of
how the people perceived them.

A second role into which the people often put the missionary in the past was "colonial ruler." He was usually white,
like the colonial rulers, and he sometimes took advantage of
this to get the privileges given the rulers. He could get
railroad tickets without waiting in line with the local
people, and he could influence the officials. To be sure,
he often used these privileges to help the poor or oppressed,
but by exercising them, he became identified with the colonial rulers.

The problem is neither of the roles, rich landlord or
colonial ruler, permitted the close personal communication
or friendship that would have been most effective in sharing
the Gospel. Their roles often kept the missionaries distant
from the people.

But what roles could the missionaries have taken? There
is no simple answer to this, for the roles must be chosen
in each case from the roles in the culture to which he goes.
At the outset he can go as a "student," and request that the
people teach him their ways. As he learns the roles of
their society, he can choose one that allows him to communicate the Gospel to them effectively. But when he chooses a
role, he must remember that the people will judge him according to how well he fulfills their expectations of that role.

The Missionary and National Christians. The relationship
between a missionary and national Christians is different
from that between him and nonchristians. The former, after
all, are his "spiritual children" and he their "spiritual
father."

This parent-child relationship is vertical and authoritarian. The missionary is automatically in charge. He is
the example that the people must imitate, and their source
of knowledge. But people soon become tired of being children,
particularly when they are older and in many ways wiser than
their parents. If not permitted to be responsible for themselves, they will never mature, or they will rebel and leave
home.

The missionary is also imprisoned by this parental role.
Not only is it difficult for him to form close relations
with the people, with them as his equals, but also he feels

he can admit to no wrong. If he were to confess personal
sins and weaknesses to the people, he fears that they will
lose their faith in Christ. But he is also their model for
leadership roles, and they soon come to believe that no
leader should admit to sin or failure. Obviously the missionary and the national leaders do sin, and because of
their roles, they have few ways of confessing sin and
experiencing the forgiveness of the Christian community
without destroying their ministry.

Another role into which missionaries can slip, often
unawares, is that of "empire builders." Each of us needs
to feel that we are part of an important task. From this it
is only a small step to seeing ourselves as the center of
this task and indispensible. We gain personal followers and
build large churches, schools, hospitals and other institutions that prove our worth.

However, this role, like the first, is not the best for
effective communication. From a structural perspective, it
is a vertical role in which communication proceeds from the
top down. There is little feedback from the bottom up.
People below comply with the orders from above, but often
do not internalize the message and make it their own. From
a Christian perspective, this role does not fit the example
of Christ. On the contrary, it can lead to an exploitation
of others for our own personal gain.

What roles can the missionary take (see Laewen 1975)?
Here, because the missionary and the nationals are Christians,
we can turn to a Biblical model--that of brotherhood and
servanthood. As members of one body we must stress our
equality with our national brothers and sisters. There is
no separation into two kinds of people, "we" and "they."
We trust the nationals just as we trust our fellow missionaries, and we are willing to accept them as colleagues and
as administrators over us. Assignments of leadership within
the church are not based on culture, race or even financial
power. They are made according to God given gifts and
abilities.

There is leadership in the Church, just as there must be
in any human institution if it is to function. But the
Biblical concept of leadership is servanthood. The leader
is one who seeks the welfare of the others and not himself
(Matt. 20:27). He is dispensable, and in this sense the
missionary is most dispensable of all, for his task is to
plant the church and to move on when his presence begins to
hinder its growth.

2. Identification

Good relationships involve more than choosing suitable roles.
Within a role the individual expresses different attitudes
that show his deep feelings towards the other person.

If we feel that somehow we are a different kind of people
from those with whom we work, this will be communicated to
them in a number of subtle ways. We may live apart from
them, allow them only into our living rooms which are public
space, and not permit our children to play with theirs. Or
we may allow no nationals on mission committees.

When we identify with the people, we will do so in formal
ways--at an annual feast given to the staff of the school or
Hospital, in their homes, but only on formal invitation, and
on the committees by allowing a few to participate. We may
even wear the native dress on certain occasions. But formal
identification is identification at an arms length. It
stresses the basic difference between people, even as it
demonstrates their superficial oneness.

The real test of identification is not what we do in
formal, structured situations. It is how we handle our
informal time, and our most precious belongings. When the
committee meeting is over, do we go aside with fellow Americans to discuss cameras, and thereby exclude our national
colleagues by our use of space and the topic of discussion?
Do we frown on our children playing with the local children?

But is it possible for a missionary ever to "go native?"
Obviously not. It takes immigrants from Northern Europe
three or four generations to assimilate into American culture, and where the cultural differences are greater, it
takes even longer.

The basic issue in identification is not formal equiva-
lence--living in the same houses, eating the same food and
wearing the same dress. We can do so and still communicate
to people the mental distinction we make between them and
us. The issue is one of mental maps and basic feelings.
If we, indeed, see and feel ourselves to be one of them,
this message will come through, even if we have different
life styles. A national gives us his best food, lets us
sleep in his guest room and use his oxcart, and we share
with him our best food, guest room and car. The principle
is not formal equality but true love and mutual reciprocity
(see Nida 1960:158-170).

A sense of oneness with the people creates in us an interest in learning more about them, and in sharing in their culture. Our example is Christ who, because of His love, became incarnate among us in order to bring us God's good news.

GROUP STRUCTURES: MISSION MODELS

Missionaries are involved in a great many groups: in churches, schools, hospitals, committees, families, neighborhoods and so on. One example will illustrate how a social structural analysis can give us a great many insights into the ways these operate.

What is the relationship between the mission and the church? This is a theological question, but it is also a structural question. Unfortunately, if there is any discrepancy between theology and structure, the latter will speak louder than what we say. What are some of the structural answers that have been given to the question?

1. Missions as Part of the Church

In some churches, missions is seen as one of the tasks carried out by the corporate church or denomination. These bodies organize mission boards, and send and support missionaries abroad. Abroad the missionaries become members of the churches they plant, and take offices within it such as pastor and treasurer. The missionaries are never part of a distinct group, the Mission, that is set apart from the national church (see Figure 5)

This model of mission organization has certain strengths and certain weaknesses. It tends to have a strong concept of "the church," because it is deeply rooted in the church and committed to planting churches. It also tends to minister to the whole person, for it sees mission as part of the larger task of the church. This model for mission work has little problem with indigenizing the work and transferring responsibility to nationals. The missionaries are part of the church structure and this structure remains. Transfer of authority takes place as national leaders replace missionaries in the church offices. There is no mission structure that must be broken down.

The danger of this approach is that the parent churches may lose their vision for missions. There are so many activities and needs at home, that they cease to be missionary in nature.

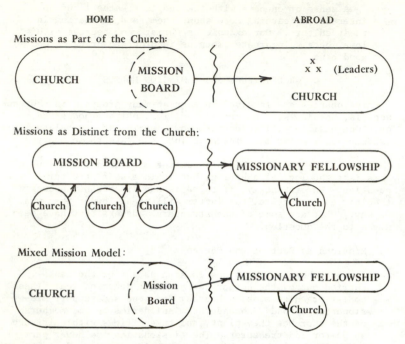

Figure 5. Three common social structures used in mission work.

2. Missions as Distinct from the Church

Because many churches had no vision for missions, another model for missions was developed. In this missions was seen as distinct from the church. Independent faith mission boards arose that recruited missionaries from the churches, but the boards themselves were never subject to any corporate church.

Abroad, this led to a pattern in which the missionaries formed a "Missionary Fellowship" distinction from the "Church." Their task was to start the church, and to turn the work over to this church when it was ready. The missionaries generally did not become members of the national church or hold offices in it. Their primary ties and memberships were with the sending churches (see Figure 5).

The strength of this approach was a strong zeal for missions. Because there was only one focus--the

evangelization of the world--there was less likelihood of
distraction. Moreover, this model was particularly suited
for specialized ministries such as translating and printing
the Scriptures, radio and television broadcasting, Christian
literature and medical services. These ministries are used
by churches from a wide range of denominations, and, therefore, have an appeal in a great many churches of different
kinds. Moreover, these ministries are not directly involved
with planting churches, which raises the delicate question
of their denominational affiliations, and the difficult
problems of indigenizing the work.

This model tends to have a weak concept of the church for
structurally the mission is distinct and independent from
the church. Its strength is evangelization. It is often
weaker in the long range task of planting churches.

This model also has a problem with indigenizing the work.
There are two distinct structures, mission and church, and
the question is when and how to transfer responsibility from
one to another. Can the church maintain the institutions
once funded by the mission? And how does the mission relate
to the national church once the transfer has taken place--
is there still a place for it, is it subordinate to the
church, and what is its responsibility if the national
church asks it to leave even though the church has no evangelistic outreach of its own?

Finally, the dichotomy between mission and church tends
to lead to a dichotomous view of human beings, and a view
of missions that ministers only to the spiritual needs of
man and not to the total person.

3. A Mixed Model

Like other human organization, mission structures are, in
part, a product of their histories. In many instances,
denominations organized mission boards and sent out missionaries as part of the church's activity. This fits the
pattern of the sending churches in our first model. But
once abroad, the missionaries looked to missions already
there for an example of how to do the work, and imitated
the overseas patterns of the second model. In other words,
structurally the mission was part of the church at home, but
abroad the two were distinct (see Figure 5).

While this approach has often had a strong vision of the
church and church planting, and a stress on ministering to
the whole person, it faces at home the danger of losing the
mission vision, and abroad, the problems of transferring

responsibilities to the church. Moreover, like the second
model above, it makes a structural difference abroad between
the missionaries and the people that makes identification
with the people more difficult.

4. Post-Colonial Models

One of the greatest tasks now facing the church is to construct models for international church and mission relationships that have no vestiges of the colonial past. How do
we recognize the autonomy and equality of churches in different countries, and still build organizational structures
that will permit them to work together to accomplish the
work God has given them to do? How do we overcome cultural
differences, feelings of superiority, inequalities in wealth
and national loyalties in order to become one in Christ.
This oneness must find its expression not only in our
theology, but also in the structure of our interpersonal
relationships.

THE ORGANIZATION OF SOCIETIES AND CHURCH GROWTH

A third way of looking at social structures is to see how
societies as wholes are put together. What are the various
social groups and institutions within a given society, how do
these articulate with one another, and how does change occur?
Here, again, two or three illustrations can show best the application and usefulness of the concept.

1. Tribal Societies

In many tribes, social groups play an important role in the
life of an individual, more so than they do in our own
society with its strong emphasis on individualism and freedom. In a tribe a person is born and raised within a large
kinship group or lineage made up of all the male descendents
of some remote ancestor, plus all the families of these
males. To get something of a feel for this type of society,
imagine, for a moment, living together with all of your
relatives who share your last name, on a common farm, and
sharing responsibilities for one another. All the men one
generation older than you would be your "fathers" responsible
for disciplining you when you deviate from the tribal rules
and customs. All the women of that generation would be
your "mothers" who care for you. All in your lineage of
your own age would be "brothers" and "sisters," and all the
children of all your "brothers" would be your "sons" and
"daughters."

In some tribes, a lineage is made up of all the female descendents of a remote ancestress, together with their families. But, again, the authority of and responsibility to the group remains central in the life of the person.

Strong kinship groups in a tribe provide the individual with a great deal of security. They provide for you when you are sick or without food, support you when you go away to school, contribute to your purchasing a field or acquiring a bride, and fight for you when you are attacked. In turn, the group makes many demands on you. Your lands and your time are not strictly your own. You are expected to share them with those in your lineage who need them.

Important decisions in these tribes are generally made by the elders--the older men who have had a great deal of experience with life. This is particularly true of one of the most important decisions of life, namely, marriage. Unlike in our society where young people are all too ready to get married when they "fall in love" (analogous to "falling into a mud puddle?") without carefully testing the other person's social economic, mental and spiritual qualifications, in most tribes weddings are arranged by the parents. From long experience they know the dangers and pitfalls of marriage, and they are less swayed by the passing emotional attachments of the present. The parents make the match only after a long and careful examination of all the prospective partners. Love grows in these marriages as in any marriage by each partner learning to live with and to love the other.

Lineage and tribal decisions are also made by the elders. Family heads have their say, but they must comply with the decisions of the leaders if they want to remain a part of the tribe.

This type of social organization raises serious questions for Christian evangelism. Take, for example, Lin Barney's experience. Lin was in Borneo when he was invited to present the Gospel to a village tribe high in the mountains. After a difficult trek he arrived at the village and was asked to speak to the men assembled in the long house. He shared the message of the Jesus Way well into the night, and, finally, the elders announced that they would make a decision about this new way. Lineage members gathered in small groups to discuss the matter, and then the lineage leaders gathered to make a final decision. In the end they decided to become Christians, all of them. The decision was by general consensus.

What should the missionary do now? Does he send them all
back and make them arrive at the decision individually? We
must remember that in these societies no one would think of
making so important a decision as marriage apart from the
elders. Is it realistic, then, to expect them to make an
even more important decision regarding their religion on
their own?

Should the missionary accept all of them as born again?
But some may not have wanted to become Christian and will
continue to worship the gods of their past?

Groups decisions do not mean that all of the members of
the group have converted, but it does mean that the group
is open to further Biblical instruction. The task of the
missionary is not finished, it has only begun, for he must
now teach them the whole of the Scriptures.

Such people movements are not uncommon. In fact, much of
the growth of the church in the past has occurred through
them, including many of the first Christian ancestors of
most of the readers of this book.

2. Peasant Societies

The social organization of peasant societies is quite different from that of tribal societies. Here we often have
the weakening of extended kinship ties and the rise of
social classes and castes. Power is often concentrated in
the hands of an elite that is removed from the commoners.

We can turn to India for an illustration of how peasant
social structure influences church growth. Villages are
divided into a great many *jatis* or castes. Many of these,
such as the Priests, Carpenters, Ironsmiths, Barbers, Washer-
men, Potters and Weavers, are associated with certain job
monopolies. Not only does a person inherit the right to
perform his caste's occupation, he must marry someone from
within his own caste. A rough analogy would be for American
high school teachers to marry their children to other high
school teachers, for preachers to marry their children to
other preachers' children, and for each other occupation to
do the same. One can see, therefore, the need to begin
marriage negotiations early.

Castes are also grouped into the clean castes and the
untouchables. The latter are ritually polluting and their
touch, in the past, polluted clean caste folk who had to
take a purification bath to restore their purity. Consequently, the untouchables formerly had to live in hamlets

apart from the main villages, and were forbidden to enter the Hindu temples.

When the Gospel came, it tended to move in one of the group of castes or the other, but not in both. Some of the first converts were from the clean castes. But when many of the untouchables accepted Christ, the clean caste people objected. They did not want to associate with the folk from the wrong part of town. The missionaries continued to accept all who came and required that they all join the same church. Consequently, many of the clean caste people reverted back to Hinduism.

The problem here is not a theological one. Many of the high caste converts sincerely believed the gospel, and even today many are secret believers. It is a social problem. The high caste folk did not want to associate with the untouchables. Before we judge them, let us stop and look at the churches and denominations in America. In how many of them do we find a wide mixture of people from different ethnic groups and social classes? How long has it taken them to break down the last remnants of racial segregation? In how many of them have differences in wealth, social class and political power become unimportant in the fellowship and the operation of the churches?

The dilemma is that theologically the church should be one, but, in fact, people are socially very diverse. Moreover, they find it hard to associate closely and intermarry with people markedly different from themselves. Can we expect people to change their deep-seated social ways at the moment of their conversion--in other words, should we expect them to join the same church? Or is changing our social customs a part of Christian growth--should we allow them to form different churches with the hope that with further teaching they will become one? The question is similar to one many American churches faced: is giving up smoking or drinking alcohol or any other behavior defined as sinful essential to salvation, or is it a part of Christian growth?

There have been some in India who have held that the peoples' salvation is not tied to their joining a single church, and they have, therefore, started different churches for the clean castes and the untouchables. They have had a much greater success in winning people from the clean castes, but they have also faced a great deal of criticism from those who argue that this is contrary to the will of God.

URBANIZATION

The recent growth of cities has been phenomenal. In 1800 no
city in the world had a population of a million, and fewer than
twenty-five had more than 100,000 inhabitants. By 1950 forty-
six cities had more than a million residents. The New York
metropolitan area which had over fifteen million people in 1970
may reach twenty-two million by 1985 (Hiebert 1976:268-269).

This rapid urbanization of the world raises many questions
for those concerned with church growth. What is the social
structure of a city and how does this structure influence communication and decision making? How do changes take place in
the highly mobile and varied city society?

The social processes affecting church growth in tribal and
peasant societies are less evident in urban societies. Large
people movements in which people come to Christ on the basis
of group decisions, or in which the message is shared through
caste and kinship ties, seem almost absent. On the other hand,
there are new forces at work. City folk are often caught up in
rapid change. Their ideas are molded by mass media, educational
institutions and voluntary associations. Communication often
follows networks of people who are mutually acquainted. In
other words, a friend tells a friend, who, in turn, tells
another friend.

What methods should missions use in the city? So far no
clear-cut strategy has emerged. Mass media, friendship, neighborhood and apartment evangelism, large educational and medical
institutions and mass rallys have all been tried, and with mixed
success. There is no simple formula that will bring success--
there never has been. Building churches is a difficult and
long range task.

Cities also offer tremendous opportunity. They are the
centers for world communication, and the source from which
ideas spread to the countryside. One reason for the rapid
spread of early Christianity was its movement through the cities.
We desperately need to look more closely at modern urban dynamics
in order to understand how change takes place, and then to apply
these insights to today's mission planning.

7

Holism and the
Integrated Christian Life

The third concept we want to explore briefly is "holism."
Anthropologists take a comprehensive approach to the study of
human beings. They assume that no understanding of people is
complete without studying the full range of humanity. Just
because people think or behave in one way in a particular
society does not mean that they do so in all societies.

On one level this holistic approach has led to an interest
in the broad variety of human beings. Most scholarly studies
of people have dealt with "modern, civilized humankind." This
emphasis can be seen in the course offerings of American colleges. There are few courses on the literature of sub-Sahara
Africa, or of India, but a great many on Western literature.
The same bias is true in history, or music, or philosophy.
Anthropologists have emphasized the need to study people in all
parts of the world, at all times, and at all levels of society.
Their hallmark has been gathering data on nonliterate societies,
peasants, common folk and others who seldom have been objects of
scientific study.

Behind this effort is the assumption that any general theory
of humanity must account for the variety we see in human beings
and their cultures. Consequently, anthropologists make wide
use of the "comparative method" in which theories based on data
from one part of the world are tested against data from other
areas to test their validity.

But anthropologists are interested not only in human variety;
they are also concerned with human universals. Their discovery
of cultural differences, not only on the superficial level of

behavior and speech, but at the very fundamental assumptions and
perceptions of the world raises serious questions about all
human knowledge. If human languages are not based on the same
principles of thought, or if human reasoning is not universally
logical--in other words, if there are no human universals--how
is communication possible, and what does "knowledge" mean?
Consequently, one of the central questions facing anthropology
is what, if any, are the biological, psychological, or social
characteristics that are found in all males, all females, all
adults or all people? As the apostle Paul notes (I Cor. 15),
this is also a critical theological issue for Christians in
view of their doctrines of creation and salvation. We need to
face the questions raised by human variety and unity.

   Anthropologists are interested in a second approach to "holism," namely, in a comprehensive approach to the study of human
beings. It is this that will concern us here. The question is,
how can we get a complete picture of what it means to be human?

A COMPREHENSIVE MODEL OF HUMAN BEINGS

A person can be studied from many points of view. Each of these
adds to our understanding of one or another dimension of human
life. What are some of these viewpoints, and how can they be
integrated into a holistic model?

1. A Multiple Model Approach

   Anthropologists have taken a "multiple model" approach to
   the study of human beings. They have drawn heavily from the
   findings of other disciplines. This, in part, accounts for
   the broad scope of the field.

   People are physical beings. Their bodies consist of
   matter that is subject to the physical and chemical laws of
   nature. For example, a physicist can study that effects the
   rapid deceleration in an automobile accident, or the rapid
   acceleration in a space shot does to the body. He can also
   study it as a machine composed of levers such as arms and
   legs, and a data storing and processing system linked to
   sensory receptors.

   People are also biological beings, whose life processes,
   such as the assimilation of food and reproduction, follow
   basic biological principles. Diet, climate, aging, hormone
   balances and sexual differences are important factors in
   human life.

   People are psychological beings, who have conscious and
   unconscious drives, feelings, and ideas. In order to understand them we need to know how they think and respond to

stimuli. They are also sociocultural beings, who organize
families, groups and societies, and who create complex cultures.

To this the Christian adds that people are spiritual
beings, created in the image of God, and, though fallen in
sin, capable of experiencing Him and His salvation.

This willingness to use different models or ways of looking at human beings has both strengths and weakness. On the
one hand, it is impossible for anyone to master all our current knowledge of human life, and consequently fragmentation
results with scholars tending to specialize on a single point
of view. But on the other hand, this holistic approach does
provide a broad framework into which all our understandings
can be fitted. In this sense, anthropology is like a back-
pack frame onto which a great many different things can be
attached. But how is it possible to bring all our understanding of human beings into a single, broad analytical
scheme?

2. Pitfalls to Avoid

Two common pitfalls must be avoided in a search for an integrated model of humankind. The first of these is called the
"stratigraphic approach" by Clifford Geertz (Hammel and
Simmons 1970:50). This consists simply of stacking up the
various models, without relating them to each other. It is
simply to look at human beings as physical, biological,
psychological, sociocultural, historical and spiritual
beings, and to leave it at that.

But people are more than collections of body, soul and
spirit. The various parts within them interact in complex
ways to form a single person.

A second error is "reductionism," the attempt to interpret all observations by reducing them to a single level of
analysis. For example, we might try to reduce all human
activities to a biological explanation: to drives, needs
and instincts.

Obviously, a person is a physical creature whose body can
be analyzed in terms of physical equations, but he is more.
He has life, and this life cannot be reduced to purely
physical and chemical equations. Similarly, a person is a
biological being, but he also has "ideas" that cannot be
reduced simply to electrical impulses within the nervous
system. They are this, but they are more. If we want to
understand people, and, in fact, to formulate theories

ourselves, we must realize that at another level we must
perceive them as something more. Any young man knows this
when he says to his fiance, "I love you." He does not add,
"My heart rate is up fifty beats a minute, and my adrenalin
secretion is up twenty percent." To do so would be to lose
something of the original meaning.

On another level of analysis, societies are composed of
people, but they also exist apart from any particular set of
individuals. A college continues to exist even though the
current students all graduate and the professors retire. In
other words, social processes cannot be reduced completely
to individuals and psychological processes.

At each level of analysis, we become aware of certain
dimensions of what it means to be human, dimensions that
cannot be accounted for by lower levels of explanation.

One common danger of reductionism is that it defines the
essential nature of human beings in physical and biological
terms, and treats their social, cultural and spiritual
natures as superficial additions. An individual is seen as
a noble animal burdened with social and cultural and moral
restrictions. It fails to take into account the fact that
human beings are fully biophysical beings, and fully social
and spiritual beings. Religious reductionism, on the other
side, denies the biophysical and at times the psychosocial
dimensions of humankind.

3. A Holistic Approach to Human Beings

Any holistic approach to the study of humans must integrate
various models into a broader framework without the loss of
understanding that each model brings. Anthropology tries to
achieve this by accepting the various models and then by
showing how they interact with one another (see Figure 6).

For example, people's physical shapes obviously affect
the cultures they build. What would their houses, chairs
and automobiles be like if they were twenty feet tall?
What would their clothes be like if they had four hands?
On the other hand, their culture affects their physical
shapes. In Tongo, South Pacific, a woman is as beautiful
as she is fat, so a woman eats to maintain her shape. In
the U.S. a beautiful woman should be slim, so she diets to
maintain her shape.

It is not difficult to show that a person's biological
system affects him psychologically, and how both of these
affect his social relationships, and even his spiritual

responses. But a person's social and spiritual conditions
affect other areas of his life such as health and mental
balance.

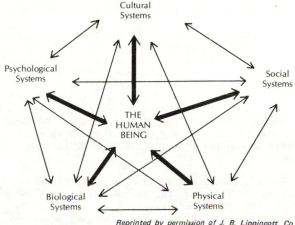

Figure 6. Anthropology seeks to discover the interrelation-
ships between various scientific models of the human being.

A synthesis must go beyond showing the interaction between
the various systems that make up human life. It must look
at the individual's response to the pressures and constraints
of these systems, and of his experiences, and how he alters
them in pursuit of his own goals.

4. A Holistic Approach to Culture

Just as we can view human beings from a number of perspectives, but must integrate them in order to get a complete
picture, so we can view cultures as made up of a number of
interrelated systems. Some of these cultural systems in
which anthropologists are particularly interested are economics, social organization, politics, aesthetics, and religion
and ideology.

Most human activities involve the allocation of resources:
land, labor, money, time, material possessions, food, friendship and so on. Many of these are material goods, and a
great deal of human effort relates to the acquisition and
use of them. But we also use a great many intangible

resources such as our time and affection. In using
resources, we calculate the gain and loss of various courses
of action, and seek to use the resources to reach our goals.
These goals may be comfortable living styles, new cars or
big bank accounts. Or they may be a desire to be a part of
the Kingdom of God--a desire that can cost us our lives.
For the anthropologist, economics is the use of any resource.

From this point of view it is clear that economics is a
dimension of much of life. It is the dominant factor in our
economic institutions such as shops, banks, stock markets
and industries. But it is also present in our other institutions: schools, political parties, governments, neighborhood clubs, families and churches. We cannot avoid making
economic decisions. Even an ascetic who rejects materialism
is making a decision regarding the use of resources, material
and nonmaterial. In one sense, then, people are economic
creatures and the institutions they build have economic
dimensions.

Human activities also involve politics--the use of power
such as coercion, wealth, status and gossip, and of leadership. Both power and leadership are involved in establishing goals, in mobilizing and allocating resources, and in
exercising control. Here again, we have institutions in
which the political dimension predominates, such as government, police, armies and political parties. But politics is
found in all human relationships and organizations.

Closely associated with politics are norms. All societies
have beliefs that define what is and what is not permissible.
These norms may be informal customs widely held, such as
eating with tableware in our culture. The violation of
these customs is considered simply a matter of bad taste,
and the culprit is socially rejected. Other norms are central to the values of the society, and their violation is
considered a sin. Both types of norms may be given religious
sanction or be codified into formal laws within the society.

Another dimension of human culture is aesthetics--the
appreciation of beauty. People are rarely content with a
purely utilitarian approach to life. Imagine what cultures
would be like if people did not decorate their pots and
baskets, embroider and dye their cloth, paint their houses
and hang jewelry of all sorts on their bodies. All of these
reflect the human penchant for self-expression and aesthetic
enjoyment.

Finally, people are concerned with meaning. Unlike animals, they are not content simply to live. They spend a

great deal of their effort in trying to understand and explain life. They construct explanatory systems such as religions, sciences and philosophies that provide this meaning.

Culture has all these dimensions. As we have seen, one or another of them may be dominant in any set of relationships or institution, but all are present whenever people interact.

IMPLICATIONS FOR MISSIONS

A holistic approach to human beings and to their cultures has some important implications for missions. Some of these will be touched upon here.

1. A Theology of the Universe

As we saw earlier, our conceptual maps, including our theologies, are deeply influenced by the basic assemptions our culture makes about the nature of reality. Frances Schaeffer (19) and Paul Tournier (1964) point out that western thought makes a sharp distinction between the natural and supernatural. The world of experience that can be explained by human reason by means of natural laws is considered natural. This means that supernatural beings, such as God, angels and demons, can be known only in supernatural ways--by miracles and visions. And even if we see these, we would probably try to explain them in natural terms, or go see our psychiatrist. For the most part, westerners do not live with the constant awareness that they live in a world inhabited by unseen beings.

This naturalization of the world has had some marked effects on western societies (Newbigin 1966). For one, it has created a crisis in morality. With the religious underpinnings of morality removed, there is no clear consensus on what is right or wrong. For another, it has created a crisis in meaning. Cynicism, terror and a search for meaningful alternatives are characteristic of modern western cultures.

On the other hand, looking at nature seriously has given us a great many insights into human nature and culture, and a technology that enables us to control the world, for good or for bad. And as secularism has spread around the world in the form of governments not committed to a particular religious point of view, the doors have been opened in many countries for a broader Christian witness.

In view of the growing discoveries of natural processes
Christians must develop a Biblical theology that takes into
account the whole of God's universe. If we continue to
make a sharp dichotomy, and ignore the natural dimension of
the world, our message will not be heard for people do live
in a natural world. But purely naturalistic explanations
have failed to provide meaningful answers to life. As Paul
Tournier notes (1964:145):

> "If it is true that the cause of catastrophes lies
> in the rift, which for several centuries now has torn
> asunder two inseparable realities, the material and
> the spiritual, in the individual as well as in society,
> then the cure can come only from their reintegration:
> Only God, who created man as body, soul, and spirit,
> can effect this harmonious synthesis in us and in
> society. Without him, we may be able somehow to
> co-ordinate our economic measures, our imaginative
> efforts, our intellectual conclusions, and our spiri-
> tual aspirations, but we cannot fuse them into an
> organic whole.

For Christians, the answer lies, in part, in the fact
that God created this universe. Therefore, we must take
both God and His creation seriously. To seek to understand
the natural world in its various dimensions is not to deny
God or His activity in it.

Missions needs a theology that encompasses all of life.
The world is looking not for a piecemeal answer to its
problems, but a total faith to live by. And we ourselves,
without such an integrated theology, leave large areas of
our lives outside the Lordship of Christ. The result is a
divided message. With our voices we proclaim a sacred
message of salvation. With our cars, planes and modern
technology we preach a secular message of modern science
and western culture.

2. A Theology of Humanness

A dichotomous view of humans depersonalizes them. A medical
doctor easily slips into treating only bodies, and psychia-
trists into treating only minds. Similarly, Christians
often have been concerned only with people's spirits, and
have looked upon the body and mind as necessary evils of
the present. The result has been a rejection of biological
processes, an anti-intellectualism, and an unconcern for
this present life.

But the Biblical answer to humanness is the incarnation--
in the fact that God Himself became a human being. During
His life on earth Christ ministered to people in all their
needs. In His death, He saved them not from their humanity,
but from sin. He made them new humans.

In missions this holistic view of man leads us to a
concern for the whole person. We are concerned with people's
salvation from sin and its devastating effects. We are concerned with hunger, sickness and ignorance, and their dehum-
anization of the individual. It is only when we take a
dichotomous view of the world that these concerns are set in
opposition to one another. How can we preach the Gospel and
stand untouched by people dying of famine and disease. Or
how can we provide for their physical needs and stand uncon-
cerned by their eternal destiny?

A holistic view of the person also leads to an awareness
of the intersystemic nature of human experience. A disease
can sap a person's strength and health. It can also affect
him economically by consuming his resources, or socially by
placing a burden on the family. It can create a sense of
spiritual depression that threatens his faith. On the other
hand, social problems in the home can lead to physical illness, and to spiritual and economic problems. And spiritual
conflicts can create social and physical tensions.

An awareness of this interrelationship between the various
systems within human beings helps us to avoid simplistic
solutions to human problems. If we cannot get along with
someone, the basic problem may be a spiritual one, in which
case a spiritual solution is ultimately needed. Or it may
be a biological one, such as a hormone deficiency, in which
case a medical answer is needed. Or it may be a structural
problem in which two individuals are put into a difficult
set of role relationships. In that case the solution lies
in a reorganization of relationships. For example, the
problems of relationships in the different mission models
we have already considered will be different simply because
their structures are different. The solution to our
problems is not always due to a single type of cause,
whether medical, economic, social, psychological, political
or even spiritual.

When problems arise we must deal with both the primary
cause and the side-effects. If a person is suffering from
illness created by spiritual conflicts, we must treat the
illness, but we must also seek to resolve the spiritual
problem. Similarly, if we are caught in a difficult work
relationship that leads to spiritual depression, we must

deal not only with the depression, but also the structure
of the relationship that brought it about. When we deal
with people and their problems, we must take all of their
systems into account.

Finally, to have a holistic view of humans contributes
to a whole and integrated life. We are called to worship
God, to minister to the world and to rejoice in the life
God has given us. We can sing and witness to God's glory.
The dichotomization of life into sacred and secular has
left little that is sacred. Little wonder, then, that much
of our life, and at times life itself, becomes meaningless,
even to many Christians. We need to recover a sense of the
wholeness, meaningfulness and joyfulness of a life lived in
all areas to the glory of God. Only then will be in harmony
with ourselves and with the world of nature that He created.

People whole in every sense of the term are particularly
needed in missions. The world is still citing the proverb,
"Physician heal yourself." People are looking not for those
who only preach healing, but those who have experienced it.
For many of them, the lives of the Christians they meet are
the only evidence of the power of God that they will ever
see.

Whole people are also needed in the needed because
pastors, missionaries and other leaders do serve as models
of Christian life for new converts. This is true even if
they reject the role of "Spiritual Father" and act as sign-
posts pointing to Christ. The media of communication has a
powerful message. A pastor often projects his personality
problems on the congregation. A missionary with a strong
need for the approval of others may build an empire by manipulating others. A leader afraid of the world can instill
this fear in his followers. And a mission organization
divided by tensions and bitter quarrels will give birth to
a church full of conflict.

The missionary must deal first with his own problems for
often the difficulties in the national church begin in him.
On the other hand, his joyous Christian life can spark a
similar response in the lives of his associates.

3.   A Theology of Culture

Just as we need an adequate theology of the world, and of
human beings, so also we need one of culture. Churches and
missions deal primarily with spiritual matters. But they
also have economic, social, political, aesthetic, and even
entertainment dimensions. To deny this is to deny what we
all know from personal experience.

Churches and missions desperately need a theology of power and of resources. This is true in their internal operations because they and their members must deal with questions of leadership, decision making, goals, money and property. A big share of a missionary's problems have to do with other missionaries and with his board. This missionary gets a higher salary than he, a finer house, or the newest car. The other one is always chairman of the important committees, or refuses to cooperate the way he should. And he himself rarely gets the recognition he should for the work he is doing. These feelings and uses of power and resources are accentuated abroad, for there a person is thrown into intimate relationships with people who are not of his choosing, and who, like himself, are often strong willed or they would not have been missionaries.

A theology of politics and economics is also needed by the church in its world mission. Today, as never before, the church faces questions of poverty, inequity, injustice and oppression. And the world is waiting to see the Christian's answer to them. Is it the maintenance of things as they are, or noninvolvement with people on the margins of society? Is it violent revolution challenging the world with its own power? Is it nonviolent revolution confronting the world with divine power? Or what is the Christian's answer? What was Christ's answer to power and wealth in His day, and is it still applicable today (see Yoder 1972)?

But the church needs a theology of power and wealth not only for the oppressed and poor, but also for the powerful and affluent. How does Christian faith express itself in the lives of those who are wealthy (and by world standards this includes most of us), and those who hold public office, or positions of leadership in the church?

The church needs a theology of society. What are the characteristics of Christlike relationships, marriages, families, communities and societies? How do we deal with differences of ethnicity, caste, class, race and culture? How can Christians take their stand on the basis of their faith when they are part of societies that often have anti-Christian norms?

We need a theology of creativity--of art, aesthetics, music, drama and literature--as well as a theology of recreation. As leisure becomes increasingly a part of modern life, how does the Christian use his time and energies creatively, and to the glory of God?

Finally, we need a theology of religion--not only of
what we believe, but also of rituals, symbols and institutions by which these beliefs are expressed and communicated.
What is a Christian marriage or funeral? What should the
structure of the church be? How should Christians live in
countries that are Communistic, autocratic or materialistic?
We need all of these theologies, for Christianity is not a
set of beliefs, but a set of beliefs that find their expression in a total way of living.

CONCLUSION

We have looked briefly at three anthropological concepts and
their relevance to our understanding of missions. There are a
great many more equally as useful that we cannot touch upon here.
Those thinking of entering missions should give serious consideration to studying mission anthropology, and of exploring its
insights further. They should also acquaint themselves with the
anthropological literature dealing with the people and the culture where they intend to serve.

This knowledge does not replace the message of the Gospel.
Nor does it give us a surefire formula for leading people to
Christ and building churches. Human beings are far to complex
to be reduced to simple equations. Moreover, the Christian is
not called to manipulate people. It is the work of the Holy
Spirit to win people to Christ.

But the study of people can help us to understand the human
dimensions of missions. God has chosen to build His kingdom in
and through the lives of people. To be aware of human processes
helps us to understand ourselves and our limitations. It also
helps us to deal with the problems of communication and human
organization. Above all, it helps us to understand and love
other people, particularly those who are so different from
ourselves.

Alicja Iwanska, a Polish anthropologist, in a discussion of
American value systems (Smalley 1967:245), noted that many of
them seem to divide the universe into three categories: scenery,
machinery and people. The first of these includes mountains,
plains, weather and features of the environment. Scenery serves
as a useful topic for casual conversations used to pass the time.
The second category, machinery includes anything used to do a
job--a tractor, car, pencil or toaster. So long as these are
needed and can be repaired, they are kept. Otherwise they are
discarded. The third category was people with their joys and
sorrows, successes and failures.

Her disturbing finding was that Americans (and they are not alone in this) often see others, such as American Indians and people abroad, as "scenery." As tourists they look at strange people with the same curiosity they show for new places and experiences. Moreover, they often see transcient labor such as Chicanos as "machinery." So long as these do the job, they are paid, but if they are too old to work, one has no further responsibility for them. It is only friends and relatives that are seen as truly human beings.

Our concern here is to begin looking at other people as humans, to be able to share our lives with them, and to share in their lives. But this concern is not new. It expresses only in part what we mean by Christian love. And to be a true missionary we must begin with love (I Cor. 13).

REFERENCES CITED AND SUGGESTED READINGS

ARENSBERG, C. M. and NIEHOFF, A. H.
  1964   *Introducing Social Change*. Chicago: Aldine.

GOODENOUGH, W. H.
  1963   *Cooperation in Change*. New York: Russell Sage
          Foundation.

HAMMEL, E. A. and SIMMONS, W. S., eds.
  1970   *Man Makes Sense*. Boston: Little, Brown and Co.

HIEBERT, Paul G.
  1976   *Cultural Anthropology*. Philadelphia: Lippincott.

LOEWEN, Jacob A.
  1975   *Culture and Human Values: A Christian Intervention in
          Anthropological Perspective*. South Pasadena: William
          Carey.

NEWBIGIN, Leslie
  1966   *Honest Religion for Secular Man*. Philadelphia:
          Westminster.

NIDA, Eugene A.
  1954   *Customs and Cultures: Anthropology for Christian
          Missions*. New York: Harper and Brothers.

NIEHOFF, A. H.
  1966   *A Casebook of Social Change*. Chicago: Aldine,
          Atherton.

SCHAEFFER, Francis A.
  1962   *Escape from Reason*. Downer's Grove, Ill.: Inter-
          Varsity Press.

SMALLEY, William A., ed.
  1967   *Readings in Missionary Anthropology*. Tarrytown, N.Y.:
          Practical Anthropology.

TOURNIER, Paul
  1964   *The Whole Person in a Broken World*. New York:
          Harper and Row.

  1966   *The Person Reborn*. New York: Harper and Row.

YODER, John H.
  1972   *The Politics of Jesus*. Scottdale, Pa.: Herald Press.

Part III

Historical / Statistical

Perspectives

on World Evangelization

Ralph D. Winter

Ralph D. Winter, author of Part III is Professor of the Historical Development of the Christian Movement of the School of World Mission at Fuller Theological Seminary. He is a graduate civil engineer from the California Institute of Technology, and has a doctorate in linguistics (with minors in mathematical statistics, cultural anthropology) from Cornell University. After his ordination as a minister of the gospel, he served as a missionary among Mayan Indians in Western Guatemala for ten years before joining the faculty of the School of World Mission. He is the author of *The Twenty-Five Unbelievable Years, 1945-1969* and the editor of *Theological Education by Extension* and *The Evangelical Response to Bangkok*. His interests and accomplishments range from historical and statistical studies to the improvement of reference tools for use in the study of the original texts of the Bible. He served as the Executive Secretary of the Northern Division of the Latin American Association of Theological Schools and as the first secretary of the American Society of Missiology. He is also known as the founder of the Summer Institute of International Studies and is the founder and director of the William Carey Library, a publishing house specializing in the area of mission strategy.

8

Seeing the task graphically

RALPH D. WINTER

Without apology, we see the entire world as the legitimate target of Christian expansion. This does not mean we envision forcing anyone to be a Christian, nor forcing anyone to change his language or his culture in order to become a Christian. This is not an institutional "triumphalism." We simply believe everyone has an equal right to knowledge of, and faith in, Jesus Christ. But if this is our goal, how are we doing?

HOW ARE WE DOING?

The first graphic clearly shows by an exact scale drawing the explosive growth of mankind during what was once predicted to be the "Christian century." The details are at the end of the article.[1] But you can tell by the unaided eye that the darkened (non-Christian) areas are getting larger, not smaller, and are bigger today than in the year 1900, and, at present rates projected, will be even larger by the end of the century. Bluntly, the number of people yet to be won in Africa and Asia has more than doubled since 1900 and will be more than tripled by the end of the century.

Ralph D. Winter is associate professor of missions at the Fuller Theological Seminary School of World Mission. He is a graduate of Caltech, Columbia University, Cornell University, and Princeton Theological Seminary. He served two terms under the National Evangelical Presbyterian Church of Guatelama as a fraternal worker of the United Presbyterian Church. He is the author of *Theological Education by Extension* and *The Twenty-Five Unbelievable Years, 1945-1969*.

This article is taken by permission from the January 1974 issue of EVANGELICAL MISSIONS QUARTERLY

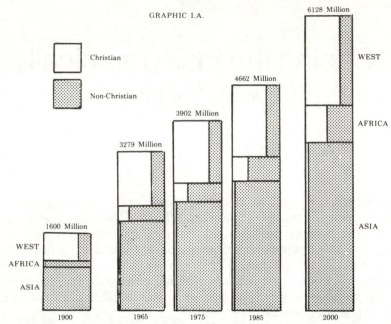

WORLD POPULATION GROWTH DURING THE "CHRISTIAN CENTURY"

However, first impressions may be misleading. The facts above have led some people to shout "Hopeless!" and then go on to propose that Buddhists don't really need to know Jesus Christ. (What would such people have said when there were only twelve disciples to do the task that Jesus left?) The other side of the coin is that while non-Christians in Africa and Asia have more than doubled since 1900 and will more than triple by the year 2000, the number of Christians in Africa and Asia is today *thirteen* times what it was in 1900, and by 2000 it will be 34 times as large.[2] The crucial factor is the difference in *rates* of growth. When we take *rates* of growth into account, as in the next graphic, we are not concerned simply by the fact that non-Christians are getting more numerous each year. Rather, we ask a much more important question: Just how fast are they growing? And, Is the rate of growth of the non-Christians faster than that of the Christians? What this means is that we mentally divide all the people of Africa and Asia into groups of one hundred and then ask, After one year of growth how many more than the original 100 are there?

The answer to this question is told in Graphic I.B. where

the very first pair of columns says this: "For every 100 non-Christian Africans there were 1.2 more at the end of a year (on the average, during 1900-1975), while for every 100 Christians there were 4.6 more!"[3]

For the same period we see Asian Christians growing at an average of 2.8 more each year per hundred Christians, while non-Christians grew by only 1.0 person per hundred. This, by the way, is called simple annual percentage growth. It is like interest on money in a savings account, and it is the easiest way to compare growth rates of two different groups of people.

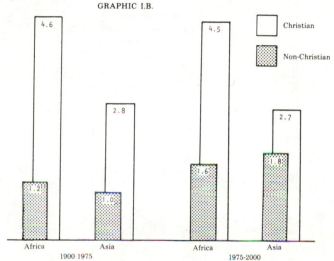

GRAPHIC I.B.

POPULATION INCREASE EACH YEAR PER HUNDRED PERSONS
(Christian growth rate exceeds that of non-Christians in both Africa and Asia
and does so during both periods—the latter based on present rates)

Note, however, that on the right half of Graphic I.B. our projections for 1975-2000 are not quite as striking a picture as on the left. During the entire first 75 years the Christians in Africa and Asia have been growing about three times as fast as non-Christians. But during 1975-2000 our estimates show the non-Christians increasing their rate of growth, and the gap between growth rates narrowing. In Asia, in particular, Christians are growing only 50 percent faster than non-Christians. The main point remains: While Graphic I.A. shows non-Christians truly exploding in sheer numbers, Graphic I.B. reveals the fact that the Christians in Africa and Asia are steadily catching up: they are on record as growing three times as fast during the last 75 years, and will likely continue to grow at least 50 percent faster in the next 25 years. If this is true, what is the discernible impact on the over-all population?

Graphic I.C. answers this question. It shows that in 1900 non-Christians out-numbered Christians 75 to one in Asia, and 28 to one in Africa. Today the same ratio is only 22 to one in Asia and 2.5 to one in Africa! Should present growth rates merely hold (not even increase), the picture in A.D. 2000 is definitely brighter. Are we going backwards? Not exactly![4]

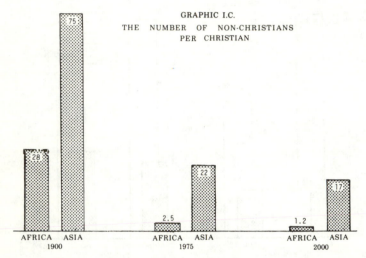

GRAPHIC I.C.
THE   NUMBER   OF   NON-CHRISTIANS
PER   CHRISTIAN

However, we must in all honesty admit that the growth picture in Asia is not what it needs to be. In order to see just what the problem is, let us take a closer look at the kind of people who are yet to be won.

WHO IS TO BE WON?

Winning people to Christ in Europe and America—in the Western world—where most people consider themselves Christians, is not a problem to be ignored. Every new generation has to be reevangelized, and hollow, nominal Christianity is a massive, urgent problem, even in the so-called mission lands, where unevangelized second and third-generation Christians are as nominal as the average citizen of the Western world. Big as this problem is, the task of winning non-Christian Asians and Africans is both far different and far larger. This is the task often referred to as the two billion who have never heard the name of Christ. For convenience, in Graphic II.A. we break these groups of people down into cultural rather than geographic categories.[5] Immediately three groups loom large. Most missionaries and most mission boards may hope that someone else will worry about the special problem of winning Muslims, Hindus, and Chinese, since these have historically been the most resistant to the gospel. But let's face it—these groups are by far the larger part of the task we face. There are now new insights regarding the reaching of these particular "resistant" peoples. But first let us avoid a common misunderstanding.

Current gloating over the emergence of the overseas "national churches" could easily lead us to suppose that we at least have a beachhead of Christians within each of these major non-Christian blocks. This is not exactly true. All of a sudden we have a reappearance of Jewish Christians among the Jews. But there are very few "Muslim Christians" or "Muslim churches" today. (The closest thing to this is the Christian movement resulting from SUM work in the Lake Chad area in Africa.) Chinese Christians are a tiny minority, and are isolated from the bulk of the Chinese by geographic, linguistic and cultural barriers. Most of the castes of India are not represented among the Christian denominations of that land. Ninety-five percent of the Christians come from less than 5 percent of the castes: this means that 400 million middle caste peoples in India cannot join any existing church without monumental social dislocation (the kind Paul didn't think the Greeks had to undergo).

Thus, the following graphic displays three mammoth fast-growing blocks, Hindus, Muslims, Chinese, that are *mainly beyond the reach of the ordinary evangelism of Christians reaching their cultural near-neighbors*. This horrifying fact means specifically that "native missionaries using their own language" can hardly begin to do this job. Recall also that most missionaries are not focused on any one of these three blocks of humanity. Yet in 1975 in these three blocks alone there will be roughly two billion people who will constitute 83 percent of the non-Christians in Asia and Africa.

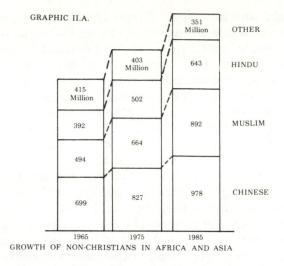

GRAPHIC II.A.

1965	1975	1985	
		351 Million	OTHER
	403 Million	643	HINDU
415 Million	502		
392		892	MUSLIM
	664		
494			
699	827	978	CHINESE

GROWTH OF NON-CHRISTIANS IN AFRICA AND ASIA

Graphic II.B goes on to show the amazing fact that the other 403 million non-Christians, who are 17 percent of the task, are the object of the attention of 38,000 missionaries who are 95 percent of the force. Meanwhile, the Hindu, Muslim, and Chinese blocks, some 1993 million people in all, are the object of the attention of only 5 percent of the missionary force. Please do not suppose that too many missionaries are devoted to the 403 million! The major lesson here is that we need to exert more effort on behalf of the bigger problem: if it is *reasonable* (and we believe it is) to send 38,000 missionaries (from all Protestant sources) to

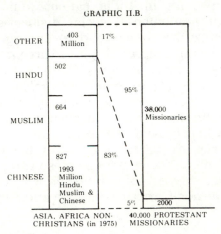

GRAPHIC II.B.

OTHER — 403 Million — 17%

HINDU — 502

MUSLIM — 664

CHINESE — 827 — 83%

1993 Million Hindu, Muslim & Chinese

95%

38,000 Missionaries

5%   2000

ASIA, AFRICA NON-CHRISTIANS (in 1975)   40,000 PROTESTANT MISSIONARIES

403 million people, then it is *unreasonable* to send only 2,000 to reach 1993 million. If we were to give the larger group equal effort per million, it would require 212,000 missionaries—almost 100 times as many as the 2,000 we are now sending!

But is this necessary? Yes. Can we do it? Yes. Will we do it? I don't know. We surely will not bestir ourselves if we are not convinced that it is both necessary and possible. Note in passing that the 38,000 working among the 403 million are extensively aided (and often even out-numbered) by national Christians working on an E-1 basis within those peoples. By contrast there is not any comparable internal evangelism going on at all among the 1993 million, with the possible exception, in part, of the Chinese. Surely in the Hindu middle-castes and in the Muslim world, there are virtually no internal allies. This fact greatly deepens the problem we face, and it is necessary to take a closer look at the full implications of it.

HOW "FAR AWAY" ARE THEY?

Our remarks just above lead us to spell out the problem of *cultural* distance. In Graphic III.A. we depict a typical village in India. Happily, thousands of villages in India today include Christians; nevertheless, there are still over 500,000 villages without any worshipping Christian group! Worse still, even where there is a church—note the cross—it is in most cases located in the ghetto of former "untouchables," in Telegu called *Palem*. The distance from this ghetto to the center of the village may be only half-a-mile *geographically*, but it is like 25,000 miles *culturally*. In this same sense, at least *80 percent of the non-Christians in the world today are beyond the reach of existing churches!*

Graphic III.B. portrays Acts 1:8, where Jesus uses an analysis that is not basically *geographic* distance. E-1

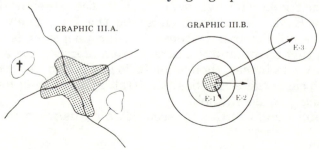

GRAPHIC III.A.   GRAPHIC III.B.

evangelism is ordinary evangelism, where you cross only the one barrier between the church and the world; and if there were no other barriers ordinary evangelism would be good enough. It would be good enough to pray that every church in the world would be warmly evangelistic in reaching out to its culturally near neighbors.

But there are other barriers. Jesus pinpointed a small community on the doorstep of the Judeans, called Samaritans with whom the Jews were not on speaking terms. They were culturally and ethnically *related* to the Jews, but their differences were significant enough to be considered an additional barrier. Call this E-2 evangelism.

Jesus then mentioned the whole rest of the world—" unto the ends of the earth"—where you don't expect any linguistic head start at all, no cultural affinity whatsoever. This is E-3 evangelism and is humanly speaking, the hardest kind.

Where there is a specific prejudice factor, the problem, whether in the E-1, E-2, or E-3 areas, may be so difficult that wise strategy will be to arrange for someòne to make the contact who is not the special object of prejudice. This is one reason why Christian witnesses *from a geographical distance* have always played so strategic a role in the expansion of Christianity down through history. In evangelism cultural distance is always more important than geographical distance, because cultural distance, whether it consists of linguistic difference or structured prejudice barriers, obstructs effective communication no matter how close the evangelist is geographically.

This is what is meant when we say that "crossing an ocean never made a missionary," or "you can go 18,000 miles but it's the last 18 inches that count." Geography is thus nearly irrelevant in such well known observations. But a brand new astonishing meaning for the same basic truth is the fact that the Christians who live next door to the Muslims in the Middle East, for example, may be the least likely to be effective missionaries to those Muslim people: it is the 18 inches that count, and if a person from afar can more easily cross that 18 inches, then so be it, it has got to be arranged. In such cases there may be little strategy in waiting for local Christians to do the job.

The full weight of this presses down on us when we recall

that the vast bulk (say 80 percent) of the non-Christian world is at the E-2 and E-3 cultural distance from every existing Christian. This fact in turn has profound implications for concrete arrangements in strategy.

WHAT WE MUST DO

In keeping with the concept of "body evangelism" we must not feel content—we can hardly feel our job is begun— unless people are brought into vital fellowship with other Christians. Once this is clear, there are four different categories of growth of the Christian movement which can usefully be distinguished, because *all four must take place.*

GRAPHIC IV

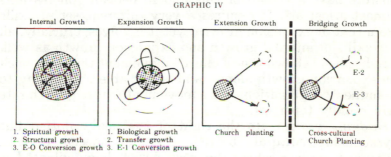

Internal Growth	Expansion Growth	Extension Growth	Bridging Growth
1. Spiritual growth	1. Biological growth	Church planting	Cross-cultural
2. Structural growth	2. Transfer growth		Church Planting
3. E-O Conversion growth	3. E-1 Conversion growth		

The first broad category of growth, *internal growth,* includes three quite different processes: (1) *Structural growth*[6]—the growth of internal structure, for example, the formation of a youth group; (2) The *spiritual growth* of the church community, and (3) *E-0 conversion growth*—the confirmation, the "evangelical experience" which, through E-0 evangelism (which crosses "zero" culture barriers) transforms mere members of the church *community* into *communicant* members. This kind of evangelism is very important but not the same as E-1 evangelism, where you are working across the cultural barrier between the church and the world. Thus *internal growth* does not include expansion of the church community but does refer to anything related to the development of life and health within the church. Internal growth makes sure both new and old persons in the fellowship are edifyingly related. In Japan this has been so great a problem that a high proportion of new Christians leave by the back door within two years.

Expansion growth expands the local church community. Hopefully, this expansion is the result of winning people from the community outside of the church. But it may also result from people coming from other congregations elsewhere. Lest these two mechanisms be confused with each other, or with a third, let us define the components of all three: (1) *Biological growth*—where an excess of births over deaths increases the size of the Christian community; (2) *Transfer growth*—an excess of believers transferring in (from other congregations) over the number transferring out, and (3) *E-1 conversion growth*—the excess of people outside the church being converted into the church over the number of those in the church who may revert to the world.

Extension growth is where new churches are planted. Few pastors have a vision for this and in certain spheres it is almost a lost art. It requires a very different set of skills from that of expansion growth; yet it involves, crucially, all the skills of internal growth and expansion growth as well. Studies have shown that a church movement that falls back on expansion growth alone—and is not able and willing to plant new congregations—is a movement whose growth rate will rapidly taper off.

Bridging growth—to the right of the heavy dotted line symbolizing cultural barriers—is that special case of extension growth where the new church being planted is made up of people who are sufficiently different from the kind of people in the mother church that they would be happier running their own church. This, according to our definitions, requires E-2 evangelism, or perhaps even E-3 evangelism. In other words, it requires cross-cultural communication in addition to all the other skills involved in the categories of internal, expansion, and extension growth.

Tough as this fourth category of growth is—it is the classical missionary task—it must be pointed out that all of our preceding charts suggest nothing less than that this task and technique is crucially necessary for the reaching of at least 80 percent of the non-Christian world in Africa and Asia. But, this *is* what we must do! Alas, how many missionaries are content to "let the nationals do it" in a social unit already penetrated, meanwhile overlooking pockets and strata in the same field which the nationals are not as able to reach as the foreign missionary! This is especially true when the "national church" unconsciously restricts the missionary to the limitations of its own

56676

immediate vision. These sobering thoughts introduce us to our final section.

HOW CAN WE DO IT?

At this point, we could easily give up. The task seems so vast, so distant culturally, so complicated to tackle. What can possibly be the vehicle of all this special effort? Two thousand years give us only one answer: the para-church structure. There is powerful evidence that while Paul *began* at Antioch, he did not simply work out of Antioch. He apparently employed a "missionary band" structure or an "apostolic team" structure borrowed from the Pharisaic proselytizing movement, just as he borrowed the Jewish synagogue structure for his local churches. Thus then and now we see both church and mission—two separate, very different structures which must both be considered normal.

This understanding is crucial for the immense task we face. Roman Catholic orders girdled the globe for well over 200 years *after the Reformation* with essentially no Protestant competition until William Carey broke the logjam and launched the mission that catalyzed the formation of a dozen other missions in the next two decades. In the ensuing 175 years Protestants in general have never quite become used to the para-church structure.

We must become much better acquainted with the subject, however, because successful world evangelization depends almost totally on the proper relation of the para-church mission structure to the on-going churches in both the sending and receiving countries.

Taking first the relation of missions to sending churches, Graphic V.A shows four common relationships. Since we hope and pray (and plan?) for all churches everywhere to be *sending* churches, these relationships apply just as well to overseas churches and their relationship to *their own national missions*. But we'll pick that up in a moment.

GRAPHIC V.A.

Type A Mission   Type B Mission   Type C Mission   Type D Mission

Lincoln Christian College

A *Type A Mission* is one that is (1) related to a specific church body; this is signified by the large circle; (2) administrated by that church through a board appointed by ecclesiastical processes; this is signified by the vertical bar on the left; and (3) funded by that church through a unified budget which discourages (or prevents) local churches from affecting the percentage going to the mission structure; this is signified by the vertical bar on the right and the *absence* of small arrows of relationship between the church and the mission.

A *Type B Mission* differs from Type A missions only in the elimination of the third characteristic mentioned. This type of mission raises its own support. It does not depend on a certain percentage of a church budget. Most Type A missions used to be of this kind.

A *Type C Mission*, such as the Conservative Baptist Foreign Mission Society, sustains a close relation to a church body (the Conservative Baptist Association) but neither its administration nor its budget are determined by the official processes of that church.

Type D Missions acknowledge no special relation to any specific church (although churches may choose to regard a certain Type D mission as their official expression in overseas work). All IFMA missions are of this type. By comparison, the EFMA includes all four types, and the DOM of the National Council includes mainly Type A structures.

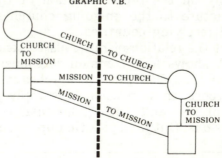

GRAPHIC V.B.

Graphic V.B. shows the additional dimensions of relationship once a mission has planted a "national church" across a cultural barrier. The two short vertical lines— Church-to-Mission—may be taken to imply any of the four cases in Graphic V.A.

Mission to Church. This relation may best be only temporary. Once a national church is able and autonomous it may choose to be related to a sister church directly rather than through a mission agency.

Church to Church. When a new national church is related directly to a sister church in a foreign land, this signifies full equality and maturity. This is why many U.S. churches have added a new office to handle these relations.

Mission to Mission. The tendency in some quarters is to phase out the older mission apparatus in favor of the church-to-church relationship. This is a profound mistake, since (as we have seen) the non-Christian world is not dwindling. Far better: encourage the national church to sponsor its own E-2 and E-3 outreach by means of its own mission initiative. This then allows the two mission structures to continue on, in relationship with each other, to complete the task of world evangelization.

If all churches are to become sending churches, they will be most effective only if they can express their energies through the mobile specific ministries carried on by dedicated mission structures. There are already more than 200 such agencies in the non-Western world. But there is still vast confusion both in the Western and non-Western world regarding the nature and destiny of the mission society. We need to be as concerned about the care and feeding of the mission structure as we are about the church structures.

Can we now "see" the task ahead? A relatively tiny trickle of missionaries from the Western world has, under God, produced over 200 million Christians in the non-Western world. Roughly half of these are in Africa, the other half in Asia. This is a significant achievement. It proves that Christianity, unlike any other religion, is truly universal. It provides an unprecedented base for what must, in the days ahead, be an unprecedentedly strong new push forward.

---

[1] *West* refers to all people of Western culture, whether in Europe, the Western hemisphere, Australia, New Zealand, South Africa, etc. For simplicity, all non-western peoples not in Africa are included here under *Asia*, such as those in Oceania, and New World aboriginals.

Graphic I.A. is drawn from the data in the following table which in turn is derived from Table IV in David Barrett's famous article "AD 2000: 350 Million Christians in Africa" in the January 1970 issue of the *International Review of Mission.* Note that he is calling *Christian* those who call themselves *Christian.*

This leaves Africa and Asia (as defined above) as the two large non-Christian continents. Also, since he gives world data for only the three yeas, 1900, 1965 and 2000, we have had to calculate the data for the intervening years 1975 and 1985, by using the average annual growth rate between 1965 and 2000.

Table VI.

	1900		1965		1975		1985		2000	
	NonCn	Cn	NonCn	Cn	NonCn	Cn	NonCn	Cn	NonCn	Cn
West	131	443	272	857	327	965	388	1101	500	1371
	.30 to 1		.32 to 1		.34 to 1		.35 to 1		.36 to 1	
Africa	114	4	231	75	282	116	337	181	417	351
	28.5 to 1		3.1 to 1		2.4 to 1		1.9 to 1		1.2 to 1	
Asia	896	12	1769	75	2114	98	2527	128	3297	192
	74.7 to 1		23.6 to 1		21.6 to 1		19.7 to 1		17.2 to 1	

Total Cn:	459	1007	1179	1410	1914
Total NonCn:	1241	2272	2723	3252	4214
Cn +NonCn:	1600	3279	3902	4662	6128

[2]These conclusions may be arrived at from the data in Table VI. For example, the number of African and Asian Christians in 1900 was 4 + 12 million, while today it is 116 + 98 million, or 13.375 times as great.

[3]Note that these rates are not the general biological growth rates for these areas of the world, nor are they the biological growth rates of specifically the Christian or non-Christian populations. In each case they consist of the biological rates plus (or minus) the effect of conversions from one group to the other.

[4]One of the rumors going around is simply, "The percentage of Christians in the world is getting smaller." This, it is said, is due to "the population explosion." We have seen that the percentage of Christians in Africa and Asia is markedly increasing not decreasing, despite the population explosion. Of this there is no question. How can people say that the overall number of Christians in the world is decreasing percentagewise? Easy: the great mass of Christians, nominal though they may be, has been in the Western world (defined in note #1). When Communism pulled a mass of these nominal Christians into nominal atheism there was a huge drop in the apparent number of Christians. At the same time Christians in Europe have been unable to win their children to true Christian faith. Finally, what Christians there were have decided on a zero population growth. What this does not mean, however, is that Christianity in the so-called mission lands cannot keep up with the very real population explosion in those areas of the world. There is where the crucial race is, and the presence or absence of population growth among Western Christians is not going to decide that issue.

[5]I am indebted for part of these data to the MARC office in Monrovia, California, but they must not be blamed for the guess work I have added in regard to other parts, growth rates, etc. Graphic II.B. cities 50,000 Protestant missionaries. This datum MARC offered to me in advance from their soon-to-appear *Mission Handbook: North American Protestant Ministries Overseas* (Monrovia: MARC, 1973).

[6]Alan Tippett has called this organic growth, because it involves the development of the internal structure of a social organism.

[7]Norman Cummings in a recent paper has presented this phrase as well as the underlying exegesis of the New Testament.

[8]A more extended discussion of this analysis, and many other characteristics of mission agencies, is found in a chapter entitled "Organization of Missions Today" in *Mission Handbook: North American Protestant Ministries Overseas* (Monrovia, MARC, 1973).

[9]An extended discussion of this diagram and this general subject is found in Chapter Seven, "Planting Younger Missions," in C. Peter Wagner, Editor, *Church/Mission Tensions Today* (Moody Press, 1973).

9

THE HIGHEST PRIORITY: CROSS—CULTURAL EVANGELISM

*Dr. Winter is Professor of
the History of the Christian Movement
in the School of World Mission at
Fuller Seminary, Pasadena, California
and Director of the William Carey
Library.*

PART I

In recent years, a serious misunderstanding has crept into the thinking of many evangelicals. Curiously, it is based on a number of wonderful facts: the Gospel has now gone to the ends of the earth. Christians have now fulfilled the Great Commission in at least a geographical sense. At this moment of history, we can acknowledge with great respect and pride those evangelists of every nation who have gone before us and whose sacrificial efforts and heroic accomplishments have made Christianity by far the world's largest and most widespread religion, with a Christian church on every continent and in practically every country. This is no hollow victory. Now more than at any time since Jesus walked the shores of Galilee, we know with complete confidence that the Gospel is for all men, that it makes sense in any language, and that it is not merely a religion of the Mediterranean or of the West.

This is all true. On the other hand, many Christians as a result have the impression that the job is now nearly done and that to finish it we need only to forge ahead in local evangelism on the part of the now world-wide church, reaching out wherever it has already been planted. Many Christian organizations, ranging widely from the World Council of Churches to many U.S. denominations, even some evangelical groups, have rushed to the conclusion that we may now abandon traditional missionary strategy and count on local Christians everywhere to finish the job.

This is why *evangelism* is the one great password to evangelical unity today. Not everyone can agree on foreign mission strategies, but more people than ever agree on *evangelism,* because that seems to be the one obvious job that remains to be done. All right! There is nothing wrong with evangelism. Most conversions must inevitably take place as the result of some Christian witnessing to a near neighbor, and that is evangelism. The awesome problem is the additional truth that most non-Christians in the world today are not culturally near neighbors of any Christians, and that it will take a special kind of "cross-cultural" evangelism to reach them.

Cross-cultural evangelism: The crucial need.

Let us approach this subject with some graphic illustrations. I am thinking, for example, of the hundreds of thousands of Christians in Pakistan. Almost all of them are people who have never been Muslims and do not have the kind of relationship with the Muslim community that encourages witnessing. Yet they live in a country that is 97 per cent Muslim! The Muslims, on their part, have bad attitudes toward the stratum of society represented by the Christians. One group of Christians has boldly called itself *The Church of Pakistan.* Another group of Christians goes by the name, *The Presbyterian Church of Pakistan.* While these are "national" churches in the sense that they are part of the nation, they can hardly be called national churches if this phrase implies that they are culturally related to that vast bloc of people who constitute the other 97 per cent of the country, namely, the Muslims. Thus, although the Muslims are geographically near neighbors of these Christians, normal evangelism will not do the job.

Or take the Church of South India, a large church which has brought together the significant missionary efforts of many churches over the last century. But while it is called *The Church of South India,* 95 per cent of its members come from only five out of the more than 100 social classes (castes) in South India. Ordinary evangelism on the part of existing Christians will persuade men and women of those same five social classes. It would be much more difficult — it is in fact another kind of evangelism — for this church to make great gains within the 95 other social classes, which make up the vast bulk of the population.

Or take the great Batak church in Northern Sumatra. Here is one of the famous churches of Indonesia. Its members have been doing much evangelism among fellow Bataks, of whom there are still many thousands whom they can reach without learning a foreign language, and among whom they can work with maximum efficiency of direct contact and understanding. But at the same time, the vast majority of all the people in Indonesia speak other languages, and are of other ethnic units. For the Batak Christians of Northern Sumatra to win people to Christ from other parts of Indonesia will be a distinctly different kind of task. It is another kind of evangelism.

Or take the great church of Nagaland in Northeast India. Years ago, American missionaries from the plains of Assam reached up into the Naga hills and won some of the Ao Nagas. Then these Ao Nagas won practically their whole tribe to Christ. Next thing, Ao Nagas won members of the nearby Santdam Naga tribe, that spoke a sister language. These new Santdam Naga Christians then proceeded to win almost the whole of their tribe. This process went on until the majority of all fourteen Naga tribes became Christian. Now that most of Nagaland is Christian — even the officials of the state government are Christian — there is the desire to witness elsewhere in India. But for these Nagaland Christians to win other people in India is as much a foreign mission task as it is for Englishmen, Koreans, or Brazilians to evangelize in India. This is one reason why so far the Nagas have made no significant attempt to evangelize the rest of India. Indian citizenship is one advantage the Naga Christians have as compared to people from other countries, but citizenship does not make it easier for them to learn any of the hundreds of totally foreign languages in the rest of India.

In other words, for Nagas to evangelize other peoples in India, they will need to employ a radically different kind of evangelism. The easiest kind of evangelism, when they used their own language to win their own people, is now mainly in the past. The second kind of evangelism was not a great deal more difficult — where they won people of neighboring Naga tribes, whose languages were sister languages. The third kind of evangelism, needed to win people in far-off parts of India, will be much more difficult.

Let's give labels to these different kinds of evangelism. Where an Ao Naga won another Ao, let us call that *E-1 evangelism*. Where an Ao went across a tribal language boundary to a sister language and won the *Santdam*, we'll call it *E-2 evangelism*. (The E-2 task is not as easy and requires different techniques.) But then if an Ao Naga goes to another region of India, to a totally strange language, for example, Telegu, Korhu or Bhili, his task will be considerably more difficult than E-1 or even E-2 evangelism. We will call it *E-3 evangelism*.

Let us try out this terminology in another country. Take Taiwan. There also there are different kinds of people. The majority are Minnans, who were there before a flood of Mandarin-speaking people came across from the mainland. Then there is the huge bloc of Hakka-speaking people who came from the mainland much earlier. Up in the mountains, however a few hundred thousand aboriginal peoples speak Malayo-Polynesian dialects entirely different from Chinese. Now if a Mainlander Chinese Christian wins others from the mainland, that's E-1 evangelism. If he wins a Minnan Taiwanese or a Hakka, that's E-2 evangelism. If he wins someone from the hill tribes, that's E-3 evangelism, and remember, E-3 is a much more complex task, performed at a greater *cultural* distance.

Thus far we have only referred to language differences, but for the purpose of defining evangelistic strategy, any kind of obstacle, any kind of communication barrier affecting evangelism is significant. In Japan, for example, practically everybody speaks Japanese, and there aren't radically different dialects of Japanese comparable to the different dialects of Chinese. But there are social differences which make it very difficult for people from one group to win others of a different social class. In Japan, as in India, social differences often turn out to be more important in evangelism than language differences. Japanese Christians thus have not only an E-1 sphere of contact, but also E-2 spheres that are harder to reach. Missionaries going from Japan to other parts of the world to work with non-Japanese with totally different languages are doing an evangelistic task on the E-3 basis.

Lastly, let me give an example from my own experience. I speak English as a native language. For ten years, I lived and worked in Central America, for most of the time in Guatemala, where Spanish is the official language, but where a majority of the people speak some dialect of the Mayan family of aboriginal languages. I had two languages to learn. Spanish has a 60 per cent overlap in vocabulary with English, so I had no trouble learning that language. Along with the learning of Spanish, I became familiar with the extension of European culture into the New World, and it was not particularly difficult to understand the life-ways of the kind of people who spoke Spanish. However, because Spanish was so easy by comparison, learning the Mayan language in our area was, I found, enormously more difficult. In our daily work, switching from English to Spanish to a Mayan language made me quite aware of the three different "cultural distances." When I spoke of Christ to a Peace Corpsman in English, I was doing E-1 evangelism. When I spoke to a Guatemalan in Spanish, it was E-2 evangelism. When I spoke to an Indian in the Mayan language, it was the much more difficult E-3 evangelism.

Now where I live in Southern California, most of my contacts are in the E-1 sphere, but if I evangelize among the million who speak Spanish, I must use E-2 evangelism. Were I to learn the Navajo language and speak of Christ to some of the 30,000 Navajo Indians who live in Los Angeles, I would be doing E-3 evangelism. Reaching Cantonese-speaking refugees from Hong Kong with the Good News of Christ would also be, for me, an E-3 task. Note, however, that what for me is E-3 could be only E-2 for someone else. American-born Chinese would find Hong Kong refugees only an E-2 task.

Everyone who is here in this Congress has his own E-1 sphere in which he speaks his own language and builds on all the intuition which derives from his experience within his own culture. Then perhaps for almost all of us there is an E-2 sphere — groups of people who speak languages that are a little different, or who are involved in culture patterns sufficiently in contrast with our own as to make communication more difficult. Such people can be reached with a little extra trouble and with sincere attempts, but it will take us out of our way to reach them. More important, they are people who, once converted, will not feel at home in the church which we attend. In fact, they may grow faster spiritually if they can find Christian fellowship among people of their own kind. More significant to evangelism: it is quite possible that with their own fellowship, they are more likely to win others of their own social grouping. Finally, each of us here in Lausanne has an E-3 sphere: most languages and cultures of the world are totally strange to us; they are at the maximum cultural distance. If we attempt to evangelize at this E-3 distance, we have a long uphill climb in order to be able to make sense to anyone.

In summary, the master pattern of the expansion of the Christian movement is first for special E-2 and E-3 efforts to cross cultural barriers into new communities and to establish strong, on-going, vigorously evangelizing denominations, and then for that national church to carry the work forward on the really high-powered E-1 level. We are thus forced to believe that until every tribe and tongue has a strong, powerfully evangelizing church in it, and thus, an E-1 witness within it, E-2 and E-3 efforts coming from outside are still essential and highly urgent.

Cross-cultural evangelism: The Biblical mandate

At this point, let us ask what the Bible says about all this. Are these cultural differences something the Bible takes note of? Is this something which ought to occupy our time and attention? Is this matter of cultural distance something which is so important that it fits into a Congress like this? Let us turn to the Bible and see what it has to say.

Let us go to that vital passage in the first chapter of Acts, so central to this whole Congress, where Jesus refers his disciples to the worldwide scope of God's concern — "in Jerusalem, in all Judea, and in Samaria, and unto the uttermost part of the earth." If it were not for this passage (and all the other passages in the Bible which support it) we would not even be gathered here today. Without this biblical mandate, there could not have been a Congress on World Evangelization. It is precisely this task — the task of discipling all the nations — which includes all of us and unifies all of us in a single, common endeavor. Notice, however, that Jesus does not merely include the whole world. He distinguishes between different parts of that world and does so according to the relative distance of those people from his hearers. On another occasion he simply said, "Go ye into all the world," but in this passage he has divided that task into significant components.

At first glance you might think that he is merely speaking geographically, but with more careful study, it seems clear that he is not talking merely about *geographical* distance, but about *cultural* distance. The clue is the appearance of the word *Samaria* in this sequence. Fortunately, we have special insight into what Jesus meant by *Samaria,* since the New Testament records in an extended passage the precise nature of the evangelistic problem Jews faced in trying to reach the Samaritans. I speak of the well-known story of Jesus and the woman at the well. Samaria was not far away in the geographical sense. Jesus had to pass there whenever he went from Galilee to Jerusalem. Yet when Jesus spoke to this Samaritan woman, it was immediately obvious that he faced a special cultural obstacle. While she was apparently close enough linguistically for him to be able to understand her speech, her very first reply focused on the significant difference between the Jews and the Samaritans — they worshiped in different places. Jesus did not deny this profound difference, but accepted it and transcended it by pointing out the human, cultural limitations of both the Jewish and the Samaritan modes of worship. He spoke to her heart and by-passed the cultural differences.

Meanwhile, the disciples looking on were mystified and troubled. Even had they understood that God was interested in Samaritans, they probably would have had difficulty grappling with the cultural differences. Even if they had tried to do so, they might not have been sensitive enough to by-pass certain differences and go directly to the heart of the matter — which was the heart of the woman.

Paul acted on the same principle when he sought to evangelize the Greeks, who were at an even greater cultural distance. Just imagine how shocked some of the faithful Jewish Christians were when they heard rumors that Paul by-passed circumcision, one of the most important cultural differences to the Jews, even Christian Jews, and went to the heart of the matter. He was reported to them as saying, "Neither circumcision nor uncircumcision is worth anything in comparison to being in Christ, believing in him, being baptized in his name, being filled with his Spirit, belonging to his body."

At this point we must pause long enough to distinguish between cultural distance and walls of prejudice. There may have been high *walls of prejudice* involved where Jews encountered Samaritans, but it is obvious that the Greeks, who did not even worship the same God, were at a far greater *cultural distance* from the Jews than were the Samaritans, who were close cousins by comparison. It is curious to note that sometimes those who are closest to us are hardest to reach. For example, a Jewish Christian trying to evangelize would understand a Samaritan more easily than he would understand a Greek, but he would be more likely to be hated or detested by a Samaritan than by a Greek. In Belfast today, for example, the problem is not so much cultural distance as prejudice. Suppose a Protestant who had grown up in Belfast were to witness for Christ to a nominal Belfast Catholic and an East Indian. He would more easily understand his Catholic compatriot, but would face less prejudice from the East Indian. Generally speaking, then, cultural distance is more readily traversed than high walls of prejudice are climbed.

But, returning to our central passage, it is clear that Jesus is referring primarily neither to geography nor walls of prejudice when he lists *Judea, Samaria,* and *the ends of the earth.* Had he been talking about prejudice, Samaria would have come last. He would have said, "in Judea, in all the world, and *even in Samaria.*" It seems likely he is taking into account cultural distance as the primary factor. Thus, as we today endeavor to fulfill Jesus' ancient command, we do well to be sensitive to *cultural distance.* His distinctions must underlie our strategic thinking about the evangelization of the whole world.

Evangelism in the Jerusalem and Judea sphere would seem to be what we have called *E-1 evangelism,* where the only barrier his listeners had to cross in their proposed evangelistic efforts was the boundary between the Christian community and the world immediately outside, involving the same language and culture. This is "near neighbor" evangelism. Whoever we are, wherever we live in the world, we all have some near neighbors to whom we can witness without learning any foreign language or taking into account any special cultural differences. This is the kind of evangelism we usually talk about. This is the kind of evangelism most meetings on evangelism talk about. One of the great differences between this Congress and all previous congresses on evangelism is its determined stress on *crossing cultural frontiers where necessary* in order to evangelize the whole earth. The mandate of this Congress does not allow us to focus merely on Jerusalem and Judea.

The second sphere to which Jesus referred is that of the Samaritan. The Bible account shows that although it was relatively easy for Jesus and his disciples to make themselves understood to the Samaritans, the Jew and the Samaritan were divided from each other by a frontier consisting of dialectal distinctions and some other very significant cultural differences. This was *E-2 evangelism,* because it involved crossing a *second* frontier. First, it involved crossing the frontier we have referred to in describing E-1 evangelism, the frontier between the church and the world. Secondly, it involved crossing a frontier constituted by significant (but not monumental) differences of language and culture. Thus we call it *E-2 evangelism.*

E-3 evangelism, as we have used the phrase, involves even greater cultural distance. This is the kind of evangelism that is necessary in the third sphere of Jesus' statement, "to the uttermost part of the earth." The people needing to be reached in this third sphere live, work, talk, and think in languages and cultural patterns utterly different from those native to the evangelist. The average Jewish Christian, for example, would have had no head start at all in dealing with people beyond Samaria. If reaching Samaritans seemed like crossing two frontiers (thus called E-2 evangelism), reaching totally different people must have seemed like crossing three, and it is reasonable to call such a task *E-3 evangelism.*

It is very important to understand the full significance of the distinctions Jesus is making. Since he was not talking about geographical, but cultural distance, the general value of what he said has striking strategic application today. Jesus did not mean that all down through history Samaria specifically would be an object of special attention. One Christian's Judea might be another Christian's Samaria. Take Paul, for example. Although he was basically a Jew, he no doubt found it much easier to traverse the cultural distance to the Greeks than did Peter, because unlike Peter, Paul was much better acquainted with the Greek world. Using the terminology we have employed, where an E-1 task is near, E-2 is close, and E-3 is far (in *cultural,* not geographical distance), we can say that reaching Greeks meant working at an E-2 distance for Paul; but for Peter it meant working at an E-3 distance. For Luke, who was himself a Greek, reaching Greeks was to work only at an E-1 distance. Thus what was distant for Peter was near for Luke. And vice versa: reaching Jews would have been E-1 for Peter, but more likely E-3 for Luke. It may well be that God sent Paul rather than Peter to the Gentiles partially because Paul was closer culturally. By the same token, Paul, working among the Greeks at an E-2 distance, was handicapped by comparison with E-1 "nationals" like Luke, Titus, and Epaphroditus; and, as a matter of evangelistic strategy, he wisely turned things over to "national" workers as soon as he possibly could. Paul himself, being a Jew, often began his work in a new city in the Jewish synagogue where he himself was on an E-1 basis and where, with the maximum power of E-1 communication, he was able to speak forcefully without any non-Jewish accent.

Let us straightforwardly concede right here that, all other things being equal, the national leader always has a communication advantage over the foreigner. When the evangelists went from the plains of Assam up into the Naga hills, it must have been very much harder for them to win Ao Nagas than it was for Ao Naga Christians to do so, once a start had been made. When the first German missionaries preached to the Bataks, they must have had a far greater problem than when the faith, once planted, was transmitted from Batak to Batak. E-1 evangelism — where a person communicates to his own people — is obviously the most potent kind of evangelism. People need to hear the Gospel in their own language. Can we believe God intends for them to hear it from people who speak without a trace of accent? The foreign missionary communicator may be good, but he is not good enough. If it is so important for Americans to have thirty translations of the New Testament to choose from, and even a "Living Bible," which allows the Bible to speak in colloquial English, then why must many peoples around the world suffer along with a Bible that was translated for them by a foreigner, and thus almost inevitably speaks to them in halting phrases?

This is why the easiest, most obvious surge forward in evangelism in the world today will come if Christian believers in every part of the world are moved to reach outside their churches and win their cultural near neighbors to Christ. They are better able to do that than any foreign missionary. It is a tragic perversion of Jesus' strategy if we continue to send missionaries to do the job that local Christians can do better. There is no excuse for a missionary in the pulpit when a national can do the job better. There is no excuse for a missionary to be doing evangelism on an E-3 basis, at an E-3 distance from people, when there are local Christians who are effectively winning the same people as part of their E-1 sphere.

In view of the profound truth that (other things being equal) E-1 evangelism is more powerful than E-2 or E-3 evangelism, it is easy to see how some people have erroneously concluded that E-3 evangelism is therefore out-of-date, due to the wonderful fact that there are now Christians throughout the whole world. It is with this perspective that major denominations in the U.S. have at some points acted on the premise that there is no more need for missionaries of the kind who leave home to go to a foreign country and struggle with a totally strange language and culture. Their premise is that "there are Christians over there already." With the drastic fall-off in the value of the U.S. dollar and the tragic shrinking of U.S. church budgets, some U.S. denominations have had to curtail their missionary activity to an unbelievable extent, and they have in part tried to console themselves by saying that it is time for the national church to take over. In our response to this situation, we must happily agree that wherever there are local Christians effectively evangelizing, there is nothing more potent than E-1 evangelism.

However, the truth about the superior power of E-1 evangelism must not obscure the obvious fact that E-1 evangelism is literally *impossible* where there are no witnesses within a given language or cultural group. Jesus, as a Jew, would not have had to witness directly to that Samaritan woman had there been a local Samaritan Christian who had already reached her. In the case of the Ethiopian eunuch, we can conjecture that it might have been better for an Ethiopian Christian than for Philip to do the witnessing, but there had to be an initial contact by a non-Ethiopian in order for the E-1 process to be set in motion. This kind of initial, multiplying work is the primary task of the missionary when he rightly understands his job. He must decrease and the national leader must increase. Hopefully Jesus' E-2 witness set in motion E-1 witnessing in that Samaritan town. Hopefully Philip's E-2 witness to the Ethiopian set in motion E-1 witnessing back in Ethiopia. If that Ethiopian was an Ethiopian Jew, the E-1 community back in Ethiopia might not have been very large, and might not have effectively reached the non-Jewish Ethiopians. As a matter of fact, scholars believe that the Ethiopian church today is the result of a much later missionary thrust that reached, by E-3 evangelism, clear through to the ethnic Ethiopians.

Thus, in the Bible as in our earlier illustrations from modern mission history, we arrive at the same summary:

The master pattern of the expansion of the Christian movement is first for special E-2 and E-3 efforts to cross cultural barriers into new communities and to establish strong, on-going, vigorously evangelizing denominations, and then for that national church to carry the work forward on the really high-powered E-1 level. We are thus forced to believe that until every tribe and tongue has a strong, powerfully evangelizing church in it, and thus an E-1 witness within it, E-2 and E-3 efforts coming from outside are still essential and highly urgent. From this perspective, how big is the remaining task?

Cross-cultural evangelism:
The immensity of the task

Unfortunately, most Christians have only a very foggy idea of just how many peoples there are in the world among whom there is no E-1 witness. But fortunately, preparatory studies for this Congress have seriously raised this question: Are there any tribal tongues and linguistic units which have not yet been penetrated by the Gospel? If so, where? How many? Who can reach them? Even these preliminary studies indicate that cross-cultural evangelism must still be the highest priority. Far from being a task that is now out-of-date, the shattering truth is that at least four out of five non-Christians in the world today are beyond the reach of *any* Christian's E-1 evangelism.

Why is this fact not more widely known? I'm afraid that all our exultation about the fact that every *country* of the world has been penetrated has allowed many to suppose that every *culture* has by now been penetrated. This misunderstanding is a malady so widespread that it deserves a special name. Let us call it "people blindness" that is, blindness to the existence of separate *peoples* within *countries*—a blindness, I might add, which seems more prevalent in the U.S. and among U.S. missionaries than anywhere else. The Bible rightly translated could have made this plain to us. The "nations" to which Jesus often referred were mainly ethnic groups within the single political structure of the Roman government. The various nations represented on the day of Pentecost were for the most part not *countries* but *peoples*. In the Great Commission as it is found in Matthew, the phrase "make disciples of all *ethne* (peoples)" does not let us off the hook once we have a church in every country — God wants a strong church within every people!

"People blindness" is what prevents us from noticing the sub-groups within a country which are significant to development of effective evangelistic strategy. Society will be seen as a complex mosaic, to use McGavran's phrase, once we recover from "people blindness." But until we all recover from this kind of blindness, we may confuse the legitimate desire for church or national unity with the illegitimate goal of uniformity. God apparently loves diversity of certain kinds. But in any case this diversity means evangelists have to work harder. The little ethnic and cultural pieces of the complex mosaic which is human society are the very subdivisions which isolate four out of five non-Christians in the world today from an E-1 contact by existing Christians. The immensity of the cross-cultural task is thus seen in the fact that in Africa and Asia alone, one calculation has it that there are 1,993 million people virtually without a witness. The immensity of the task, however, lies not only in its bigness.

The problem is more serious than retranslating the Great Commission in such a way that the peoples, not the countries, become the targets for evangelism. The immensity of the task is further underscored by the far greater complexity of the E-2 and E-3 task. Are we in America, for example, prepared for the fact that most non-Christians yet to be won to Christ (even in our country) will not fit readily into the kinds of churches we now have? The bulk of American churches in the North are middle-class, and the blue-collar worker won't go near them. Evangelistic crusades may attract thousands to big auditoriums and win people in their homes through television, but a large proportion of the newly converted, unless already familiar with the church, may drift away simply because there is no church where they will feel at home. Present-day American Christians can wait forever in their cozy, middle-class pews for the world to come to Christ and join them. But unless they adopt E-2 methods and both *go out after these people and help them found their own churches,* evangelism in America will face, and is already facing, steadily diminishing returns. You may say that there are still plenty of people who don't go to church who are of the same cultural background as those in church. This is true. But there are many, many more people of differing cultural backgrounds who, even if they were to become fervent Christians, would not feel comfortable in existing churches.

If the U.S. — where you can drive 3,000 miles and still speak the same language — is nevertheless a veritable cultural mosaic viewed evangelistically, then surely most other countries face similar problems. Even in the U.S., local radio stations employ more than forty different languages. In addition to these language differences, there are many equally significant social and cultural differences. Language differences are by no means the highest barriers to communication.

The need, in E-2 evangelism, for whole new worshiping groups is underscored by the phenomenon of the Jesus People, who have founded hundreds of new congregations. The vast Jesus People Movement in the U.S. does not speak a different language so much as it involves a very different life-style and thus a different style of worship. Many American churches have attempted to employ the guitar music and many of the informal characteristics of the Jesus Movement, but there is a limit to which a single congregation can go with regard to speaking many languages and employing many life-styles. Who knows what has happened to many of the "mods" and "rockers" who were won as a result of Billy Graham's London Crusades? On the one hand, the existing churches were understandably culturally distant from such people, and on the other hand, there may not have been adequate E-2 methods employed so as to form those converts into whole new congregations. It is this aspect of E-2 evangelism which makes the cross-cultural task immensely harder. Yet it is essential. Let us take one more well-known example.

When John Wesley evangelized the miners of England, the results were conserved in whole new worshiping congregations. There probably would never have been a Methodist movement had he not encouraged these lower-class people to meet in their own Christian gatherings, sing their own kind of songs, and associate with their own kind of people. Furthermore, apart from this E-2 technique, such people would not have been able to win others and expand the Christian movement in this new level of society at such an astonishing rate of speed. The results rocked and permanently changed England. It rocked the existing churches, too. Not very many people favored Wesley's contact with the miners. Fewer still agreed that miners should have separate churches!

At this point we may do well to make a clear procedural distinction between E-1 and E-2 evangelism. We have observed that the E-2 sphere begins where the people you have reached are of sufficiently different backgrounds from those of people in existing churches that they need to form their own worshiping congregations in order best to win others of their own kind. John, chapter four, tells us that "many Samaritans from that city believed in him (Jesus) because of the woman's testimony." Jesus evangelized the woman by working with great sensitivity as an E-2 witness; she turned around and reached others in her town by efficient E-1 communication. Suppose Jesus had told her she had to go and worship with the Jews. Even if she had obeyed him and gone to worship with the Jews, she would on that basis have been terribly handicapped in winning others in her city. Jesus may actually have avoided the issue of where to worship and with what distant Christians to associate. That would come up later. Thus the Samaritans who believed the woman's testimony then made the additional step of inviting a Jew to be with them for two days. He still did not try to make them into Jews. He knew he was working at an E-2 distance, and that the fruits could best be conserved (and additional people best be won) if they were allowed to build *their own fellowship of faith.*

A further distinction might be drawn between the kind of cultural differences Jesus was working with in Samaria and the kind of differences resulting from the so-called "generation gap." But it really does not matter, in evangelism, whether the distance is cultural, linguistic, or an age difference. No matter what the reason for the difference or the permanence of the difference, or the perceived rightness or the wrongness of the difference, the procedural dynamics of E-2 evangelism techniques are quite similar. The E-2 sphere begins whenever it is necessary to found a new congregation. In the Philippines we hear of youth founding churches. In Singapore we know of ten recently established youth break-away congregations. Hopefully, eventually, age-focused congregations will draw closer to existing churches, but as long as there is a generation gap of serious proportions, such specialized fellowships are able to win many more alienated youth by being allowed to function considerably on their own. It is a good place to begin.

Whatever we may decide about the kind of E-2 evangelism that allows people to meet separately who are different due to temporary *age differences,* the chief factors in the immensity of the cross-cultural task are the much more profound and possibly permanent *cultural differences.* Here too some will always say that true cross-cultural evangelism is going too far. At this point we must risk being misunderstood in order to be absolutely honest. All around the world, special evangelistic efforts continue to be made which often break across culture barriers. People from these other cultures are won, sometimes only one at a time, sometimes in small groups. The problem is not in winning them; it is in the cultural obstacles to proper follow-up. Existing churches may cooperate up to a point with evangelistic campaigns, but they do not contemplate allowing the evangelistic organizations to stay long enough to gather these people together in churches of their own. They mistakenly think that being joined to Christ ought to include joining existing churches. Yet if proper E-2 methods were employed, these few converts, who would merely be considered somewhat odd additions to existing congregations, *could* be infusions of new life into whole new pockets of society where the church does not now exist at all!

A discussion of the best ways to organize for cross-cultural evangelism is beyond the scope of this paper. It would entail a great deal of space to chart the successes and failures of different approaches by churches and by para-church organizations. It may well be that E-2 and E-3 methods are best launched by specialized agencies and societies working loyally and harmoniously with the churches. Here we must focus on the nature of cross-cultural evangelism and its high priority in the face of the immensity of the task. Aside from the Chinese mainland sector, the two greatest spheres in which there is a tragic paucity of effective cross-cultural evangelism are the Muslim and the Hindu. Our concluding words will center on these two groups, which in aggregate number well over one billion (1,000,000,000) people.

As we have earlier mentioned, a converted Muslim will not feel welcome in the usual Presbyterian Church in Pakistan. Centuries-old suspicions on both sides of the Muslim-Hindu fence make it almost impossible for Muslims, even converted Muslims, to be welcomed into the churches of former Hindu peoples. The present Christians of Pakistan (almost all formerly Hindu) have not been at all successful in integrating converted Muslims into their congregations. Furthermore, it is not likely to occur to them that Muslims can be converted and form their own separate congregations. The enormous tragedy is that this kind of impasse postpones serious evangelism along E-2 lines wherever in the world there are any of the 664 million Muslims. Far to the east of Mecca, in certain parts of Indonesia,enough Muslims have become Christians that they have not been forced one by one to join Christian congregations of another culture. Far to the west of Mecca, in the middle of Africa on some of the islands of Lake Chad,we have reports that a few former Muslims, now Christians, still pray to Christ five times a day and worship in Christian churches on Friday, the Muslim day of worship. These two isolated examples suggest that Muslims can become Christians without necessarily undergoing serious and arbitrary cultural dislocation. There may be a wide, new, open door to the Muslims if we will be as cross-culturally alert as Paul was, who did not require the Greeks to become Jews in order to become acceptable to God.

Vast *new* realms of opportunity may exist in India, too, where local prejudice in many cases may forestall effective "near-neighbor" evangelism. Indians coming from a greater distance might by E-2 or E-3 methods be able to escape the local stigmas and establish churches within the 100 or so social classes as yet untouched. It is folly for evangelists to ignore such factors of prejudice, and their existence greatly increases the immensity of our task. Prejudice of this kind adds to cultural distance such obstacles that E-2 evangelism where prejudice is deep is often more difficult than E-3 evangelism. In other words, scholarly, well-educated Christians from Nagaland or Kerala might possibly be more successful in reaching middle-class Hindus in South India with the Gospel than Christians from humble classes who have grown up in that area and speak the same language, but are stigmatized in local relationships. But who dares to point this out? It is ironic that national Christians all over the non-Western world are increasingly aware that they do not need to be Westernized to be Christian, yet they may in some cases be slow to sense that the challenge of cross-cultural evangelism requires them to allow other people in their own areas to have the same liberty of self-determination in establishing culturally divergent churches of their own.

In any case, the opportunities are just as immense as the task. If 600 million Muslims await a more enlightened evangelism, there are also 500 million Hindus who today face monumental obstacles to becoming Christians other than the profound spiritual factors inherent in the Gospel. One keen observer is convinced that 100 million middle-class Hindus await the opportunity to become Christians — but there are no churches for them to join which respect their dietary habits and customs. Is the kingdom of God meat and drink? To go to the special efforts required by E-2 and E-3 evangelism is not to let down the standards and make the Gospel easy — it is to disentangle the irrelevant elements and to make the Gospel clear. Perhaps everyone is not able to do this special kind of work. True, many more E-1 evangelists will eventually be necessary to finish the task. But the highest priority in evangelism today is to develop the cross-cultural knowledge and sensitivities involved in E-2 and E-3 evangelism. Where necessary, evangelists from a distance must be called into the task. Nothing must blind us to the immensely important fact that at least *four-fifths* of the non-Christians in the world today will never have any straightforward opportunity to become Christians unless the Christians themselves go more than halfway in the specialized tasks of cross-cultural evangelism. Here is our highest priority.

THE HIGHEST PRIORITY: CROSS-CULTURAL EVANGELISM
PART II

Let me now turn to the many hundreds of responses I have received from other participants in the Congress. I deeply value and intend to save every one of your papers that came to me. Practically all the questions either concerned the statistical *scope* of the task or the theological *nature* of the task.

Questions about the statistical scope of the task

Let us consider first the *scope* of the task. Figure 1 is an attempt to sum it up. Jesus said that no man builds a tower without first sitting down and calculating the cost. Here at this Congress we must sit down and assess the task of world evangelization.

CHRISTIANS	Western	Africa	Asia	TOTAL	
Nurture	120	40	40	200	
E-0 Renewal	845	76	58	979	
	965	116	98	1179	
NON-CHRISTIANS					
E-1 Ord. Ev.	180	82	74	336	-----13%
E-2, E-3, CC Ev.	147	200	2040	2387	-----87%
	327	282	2114	2723	
GRAND TOTAL	1292	398	2212	3902	

Figure 1

Note that the numbers above are all in *millions* of people in the world today. You will see I have first divided between those who call themselves Christians and those who do not call themselves Christians, and you will see in the column on the far right that the total number of Christians is 1179 million, and the total number of non-Christians is 2723 million.

I want you to think for a moment about this latter number — 2700 million. Do you notice that this is about one million people for each participant in this Congress? (This means that if each of you all had been busy and had won a million people on your way here, we would have been able to disband the Congress!) These two numbers, 1179 and 2723 are, of course, not precise counts except at a certain date — since the population clock tells us such numbers are constantly changing. For example, the number of Christians, 1179 million, is increasing by 70,000 each day we are gathered here. If we had an evangelism clock in addition to a population clock, it would register the number of additional Christians each minute. For example, from the opening of this Congress until now, four days later, the number of Christians in the world has grown more than a quarter of a million. If we had a really sophisticated clock, we could even record the fact that each day in practically every country of the world, the *percentage* of Christians is also increasing. I add these comments lest anyone shrink from the task of evangelizing the massive numbers of non-Christians in Figure 1. I don't want you to wonder if there is any hope of being successful in world evangelization. Dear brothers and sisters, we *are* being successful right now, and we surely have no *statistical* reason not to make definite plans here at this Congress to move ahead with Jesus Christ, Lord of History, to finish the task of world evangelization.

In other words, the numbers in the last column are only apparently static. They do not show the fact that we are constantly gaining in the Christian percentage in all columns, that is, in the Western World, in Africa, and in Asia. (Australia and Latin America are included in the Western World; the Pacific I am including in the Asia column.)

You will now note that both the Christian and the non-Christian populations have been further divided. The Christian group is divided into the committed Christians, who need nurture; and nominal Christians, who need renewal. Then the non-Christians are also divided in two groups, this distinction being the heart of my whole presentation: those who can be reached by ordinary, near-neighbor evangelism (which I have called E-1 evangelism); and those who are beyond a significant cultural frontier, *whom we can only reach by cross-cultural evangelism,* that is, who may wish to exercise their biblical right to self-determination in establishing a separate cultural tradition of regular worship and fellowship. In a word, they are people at a sufficient cultural distance so that we cannot necessarily expect them to join existing Christian churches. Their existence calls for special cross-cultural evangelism, and constitutes the major technical obstacle to world evangelization.

In Figure 2 you see the quantities and distinctions mentioned in Figure 1 now visualized with the spaces drawn to scale. For example, the four numbers down the right side of the large, vertical rectangle — 200, 979, 336, 2387 — are the same numbers we have just seen in the last column of Figure 1. The first two numbers are those who call themselves Christians, requiring nurture and renewal. Then you'll notice a dark line running across the rectangle, and the two categories below this line are the non-Christians — the 336 million who can be reached by the ordinary

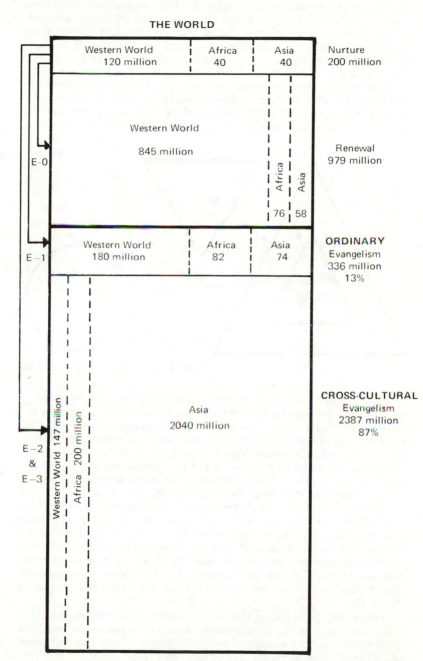

Figure 2.

evangelism of Christians reaching out to their cultural near-neighbors, and 2387 million who are not within the range of the ordinary evangelism of any Christian congregation — people who require cross-cultural evangelism (E-2 or E-3). Note that according to these estimates, 87 per cent of the non-Christians are in the cross-cultural category. Before leaving this diagram, note that most of the people needing renewal are in the Western World, while the people needing cross-cultural evangelism are mainly in Asia. This fact helps to account for the instinctive difference between the way most Western Christians think about evangelism and the way people involved in cross-cultural evangelism think about evangelism.

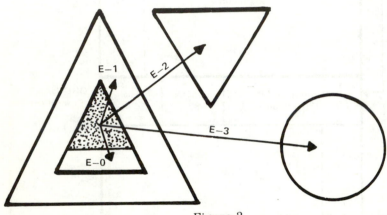

Figure 3.

Now let's look at Figure 3. Here you see a small triangle representing the Christian community, from which four arrows emerge. One arrow, labeled E-0, is aimed into a sector within the Christian community. This is the winning of nominal Christians to personal faith and commitment — the "evangelical experience." This E-0 evangelism involves just as much a spiritual experience as E-1, E-2, or E-3 evangelism, but there is no cultural distance involved — hence the zero. The arrow labeled E-1 goes out of the church into the culture within which the church is at home, the only barrier being the "stained-glass barrier" between the church and the world. People in this area, if converted, will feel at home in existing churches. However, the E-2 arrow reaches outside this culture into a similar culture that is nevertheless sufficiently different to make the founding of separate congregations desirable to act as a base for effective outreach to others in that same culture. The E-3 arrow involves similar church-planting implications, but reaches out to a totally strange culture (the circle).

I hope this doesn't seem too complicated. It is a help when looking at any country or region of the world to size up the situation by making a rough estimate of the number of people in each of these five categories which the diagram in Figure 3 gives us: First, there are the committed Christians (shaded area) who are the only active agents you can count on to do the work. Next there are the four kinds of people who are not committed Christians and who are either at a 0, 1, 2, or 3 cultural distance away from the committed Christians. Following this scheme, you can divide the people in a small town into these five categories. Or you can make estimates of the number of people in these five categories for a whole country. This seems to be helpful to size up the task.

I have done this by way of example in the diagrams in Figure 4. The first three diagrams are for three different sections of the non-Western world, where from left to right there is a progressively greater number of committed Christians. (In these diagrams I have not distinguished between the E-2 and E-3 areas because they are both cross-cultural evangelism and therefore usually require founding new churches.) The fourth diagram — the Western World — shows the close comparison between the South Pacific and Western World. In both cases a high proportion of the people are at least nominal Christians, and this means the need for cross-cultural evangelism internal to the regions may not seem so important to people in these areas.

Figure 4.

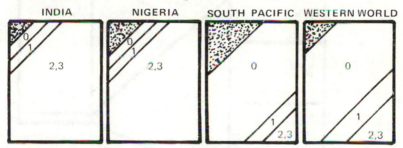

On the other hand, India and Nigeria are more typical of all the rest of the world, and that is why cross-cultural evangelism is of the highest priority in the non-Western world. Let me repeat that although there are a lot of Christians in India, this must not obscure the fact that most of the people in India are at a *cross-cultural* distance from any Christian congregation whatsoever.

In Figures 5 and 6, unlike in the table in Figure 1, we have divided the total world population first into Western and non-Western spheres. In Figure 5 you'll notice the statistics from the first column of the earlier table, where the Western world is divided between Christian and non-Christian — 965 million Christians and 327 million non-Christians. Note that the 10,000 missionaries working in the Western world (mainly Europe, North America, Latin America) are focusing almost all of their efforts on the nominal Christian sphere while only a fairly small percentage, according to my estimates, are really concentrating on people who do not consider themselves Christians (E-1, E-2, and E-3). This is not surprising, because the majority of Westerners are nominal Christians. Things are very different in the non-Western world, as we see in Figure 6. There for simplicity we have divided all the non-Christians into four groups — Chinese, Muslim, Hindu and "other." The bottom three layers represent three virtually untouched blocs of humanity, amounting to 1993 million people.

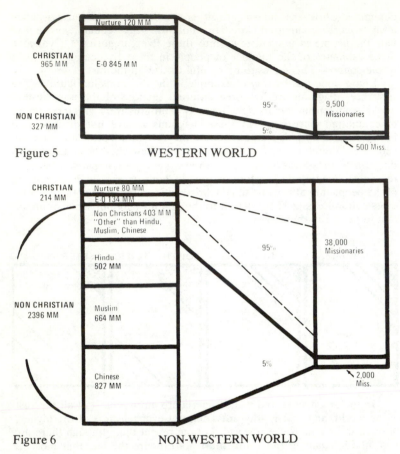

Figure 5   WESTERN WORLD

Figure 6   NON-WESTERN WORLD

Let us think prayerfully for a moment about these three groups. A few minutes ago we noted that there are roughly one million non-Christians in the world for each participant here. If our Congress participants consisted of people whose gifts and calling were focused proportionately on all non-Christians in the world, would we not have to have here one participant for each million in each of these groups? This means we would have to have 502 people here specializing on reaching the 502 million non-Christian Hindus. These would have to be cross-cultural specialists, on the whole. We would also have to have 664 people here specializing on reaching the 664 million Muslims. They too would have to be almost entirely cross-cultural specialists, since only tiny numbers of Muslims can be won by local Christians living in their areas who try to reach them by ordinary evangelism. (Parenthetically, let me observe that the Muslim group, which is already immense, is growing at a biological rate almost double that of the Chinese, and that if present rates continue, there will be more Muslims than Chinese within about ten years.) Moving on to the Chinese, proportionately to represent the 827 million non-Christian Chinese would require at this Congress 827 people specializing on the task of reaching them. In the case of the Chinese there are millions of Christian Chinese to help in the task, but even so, the Chinese are so split up by dialects, social distinctions, and highly significant clan differences that most of this task is E-2 rather than E-1, and thus mainly a cross-cultural problem as with the other two major blocs.

Now note something very significant. As in the case of the Western world, most of the cross-cultural workers are focusing their efforts on nurture and E-0 evangelism connected with the Christian community. The number of Christians in the non-Western world (214 million) is the sum of the Africa and Asia columns in the previous table, that is 116 + 98. Again by merging the columns, there are 80 million committed Christians in the non-Western world, whose nurture soaks up a very large proportion of the energies of both Christian missionaries and national church leaders; there are also 134 million nominal Christians who take up practically all of the rest of the efforts. It is only a guess, but it is safe to say that 95 per cent of all missionaries deployed in the non-Western world are focusing their efforts either on communities that claim to be Christian or upon non-Christian peoples in the immediate environment of the Christians, these latter probably being mainly the 403 million non-Christians in the "other" category in this chart. That leaves only a tiny percentage of cross-cultural workers to deal with the three major blocs of non-Western non-Christians. Brothers and sisters, this is a grim picture. The task to be done on the left is big enough, but precisely where the cross-cultural task is the largest, the cross-cultural workers are the fewest.

For example, the number of effective evangelists winning middle caste and upper caste Hindus (well over 400 million people) are very few indeed, and the number of effective cross-cultural evangelists winning Muslims are very few indeed. While there may be proportionately more cross-cultural workers who are reaching out to non-Christian Chinese, these would mainly be in Taiwan. But even in Taiwan most missionaries and national leaders are absorbed with the needs of the Christian community. This is not to begrudge the "interchurch" exchange of E-3 workers. *The danger is that we may easily deceive ourselves concerning the proportionate weight of personnel that is going to the evangelism of non-Christians.* This is so important to understand that we must use an extended illustration of this whole matter of the statistical scope of the task of cross-cultural evangelism. Since I have already said a good deal in my original paper about Pakistan, let me build on that situation.

The rough proportions in Pakistan are similar to the diagram in Figure 4 for India. In Pakistan there are proportionately fewer Christians than in India, but they number well over one-half million (out of 70 million). The Christian community today is the product of a great people movement and spiritual revival over a half-century ago, but there are very few people living today who were brought to Christ in that movement, and the churches of Pakistan by now have a sizeable proportion of their own members who need to be won by E-0 evangelism to personal spiritual obedience to Christ. The really surprising thing is why the E-1 sphere is so small. A country of 70 million people where there are 500,000 Christians does not on the face of it seem likely to be a place where near-neighbor evangelism would have relatively small significance. Why can't the 500,000 Christians just reach out to their near neighbors and win them to

Christ? This is the crucial question. The answer is that 99 per cent of the Christians have a Hindu (not Muslim) cultural background, whereas 97 per cent of the non-Christians in Pakistan are Muslim. In the north you have scattered communities of Christians (just as in India, most Christians are in separated, isolated areas, almost like ghettos), but their *physical* separation from so many of their countrymen does not remotely approach the significance of their *cultural* isolation.

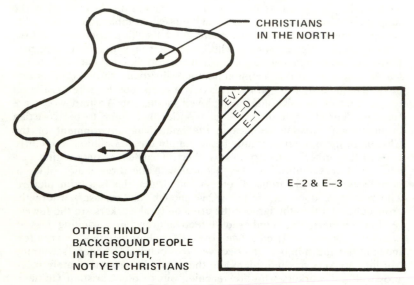

Figure 7. PAKISTAN

Thus, from the beginning of the revival movement in the north over fifty years ago until the present time, almost never has a Muslim joined a Christian church, while hundreds of thousands of former Hindus have become Christians. Although the church in Pakistan has a large E-0 population of nominal Christians, it is continuing to win some remaining Hindus to Christ through E-1 evangelism. On this basis, how soon will the church run out of Hindus to convert? In the northern part of the country, where most of the Christians are, practically all of the non-Muslim people of Pakistan are already at least nominally Christian. Curiously, there are almost a million people of Hindu background yet to win, but they are in the South, hundreds of miles from the main body of Christians. While it would be relatively simple for these Christians to do evangelism in the South (only a geographical distance away), the Christians are very, very distant from their Muslim neighbors. Why? Because there is a very pronounced cultural distance between the cultural tradition represented by the church and the cultural tradition represented by the Muslims.

Let us be more specific. Both Muslims and the (Hindu-background) Christians in the North speak Urdu. But they don't speak exactly the same kind of Urdu. A Muslim can tell either by listening or by reading that the religious language of the Christians comes from the originally Hindu minority in his country, and he has monumental prejudices about this difference. The Christians, on the other hand, while they don't hate the Muslims, don't feel it is necessary to make a special translation of the New Testament into the religious language of the Urdu-speaking Muslims, even though there are more than 30 million Urdu-speaking Muslims alone! Feelings of suspicion between the two communities are so great that an occasional Muslim convert does not feel at home in any of the Christian congregations. Christians have not yet made an effective effort nor even drawn up speculative plans for the development of worshiping communities drawn wholly from the Muslim tradition. This is only natural, in a way, because the Christians come from a stratum of society which has for centuries been impoverished and virtually enslaved. The Christians even yet are barely struggling to their feet economically. Their resources, their education, their evangelistic imagination does not readily stretch to radically new ways of evangelizing the Muslims — especially not to ways that will allow the Muslims the kind of liberty in Christ which the Gospel guarantees them.

The situation in Pakistan both illustrates the immense scope of the need for cross-cultural evangelism, and also moves us into the theological dimension of the problem. To that dimension we must now turn.

Questions about the theological nature of the task

First briefly let me say a word to those who asked, in effect, "Will not the allowance of indigenous life ways lead us into syncretism?" Michael Green has already answered this for us in his excellent discussion of flexibility without syncretism. I might add a personal note that as a Western Christian, I grew up without realizing that Easter Sunrise services could easily revert to their original paganism if Christians attending them do not see and sense a Christian meaning in them. The very word *Easter* comes from a Teutonic spring goddess of fertility called *Eostre*. The same is true of Christmas. We have all fought to maintain Christ in Christmas, since Christmas is also originally a pagan holiday that was taken over by the early church. (Romans gave gifts to each other on December 25th long before Jesus was born, and for that matter, Jesus may have been born in June, not in December.) Briefly, in employing pagan words and customs, we must be careful to make sure that the whole counsel of God is constantly taught and understood.

The main theological question, raised more often than any other, is so profound that I feel I must devote my remaining time to it. The question was stated in many ways in your response papers, but is basically this: "Will not our unity in Christ be destroyed if we follow a concept of cross-cultural evangelization which is willing to set up separate churches for different cultural groups within the same geographical area?" It is only with humble dependence upon the Holy Spirit to honor the Word of God above the secular influences to which we all are subject that I dare to proceed with a perspective which I myself could not understand nor accept until several years ago. I was brought up in the United States, where for many people integration is almost like a civil religion, where such people almost automatically assume that eventually everyone will speak English and really shouldn't speak any other language. To me cultural diversity between countries was a nuisance, but cultural diversity within a country was simply an evil to be overcome. I had no thought of excluding anyone from *any* church, (and I still do not), but I did unconsciously assume that the best thing that could happen to Black, White, Chicano, etc., was that they all would eventually come to the White, Anglo-Saxon, Protestant church and learn to do things the way that I felt was most proper.

Following this kind of American culture-Christianity, many missionaries have assumed that there ought to be just one national church in a country — even if this means none at all for certain sub-groups? Such missionaries, in all earnestness, have assumed that the denominational pluralism in their own home country is simply a sin to be avoided. They have assumed that *Southern* Baptists aren't necessary in *Northern* India, even though, as a matter of fact, in Boston today most of the Anglo churches have been sitting around waiting for the Arabs and the Japanese to come to their churches, and it has taken Southern Baptists to go into Northern United States and plan Arab churches, and Japanese churches, and Portuguese churches, and Greek churches, and Polish churches, right under the nose of hundreds of good-willed Anglo churches which have been patiently waiting for these people to assimilate to the Anglo way of life. With one or two fine exceptions, the Anglo churches, with all their evangelistic zeal, simply did not have the insight to do this kind of E-2 and E-3 evangelism.

For my own part, after many years of struggling with this question, I am now no less concerned than before about the unity and fellowship of the Christian movement across all ethnic and cultural lines, but I realize now that Christian unity cannot be healthy if it infringes upon Christian liberty. In terms of evangelism, we must ask whether the attempt to extend, for example in Pakistan, an external form into the Muslim culture is more important than making the Gospel clear to such peoples within their own culture. Can we not condition our desire for uniformity by an even greater desire for effective preaching of the Gospel? I personally have come to believe that unity does not have to require uniformity, and I believe that there must be such a thing as healthy diversity in human society *and in the Christian world church*. I see the world church as the gathering together of a great symphony orchestra where we don't make every new person coming in play a violin in order to fit in with the rest. We invite the people to come in to play the same score — the Word of God — but to play their own instruments, and in this way there will issue forth a heavenly sound that will grow in the splendor and glory of God as each new instrument is added.

But some of you have said, "OK, if that is what you mean, what about the Apostle Paul? Did he set up separate congregations for masters and slaves?" I really don't know. I don't think so. But that does not mean that didn't happen. In a recent monograph by Paul Minear entitled *The Obedience of Faith*, the author suggests that in Rome there were probably five separate congregations of Christians, who numbered a total 3000, and that Paul's letter to the Romans was written actually to a cluster of churches in the city of Rome. He also suggests that these churches were very different from each other, some being composed almost entirely of Jewish Christians, and others (the majority) almost entirely of Gentile Christians. "Instead of visualizing a single Christian congregation, therefore, we should constantly reckon with the probability that within the urban area were to be found forms of Christian community which were as diverse, and probably also as alien, as the churches of Galatia and those of Judea." But whatever the case in Rome, Paul in his travels was usually dealing with the phenomenon of house churches, where whole households, masters and slaves, quite likely worshiped together. We cannot believe he ever separated people. However, we do know that he was willing to adopt in different places a radically different approach, as he put it, "for those under the law and for those not under the law." When, for example, he established an apparently non-Jewish congregation among the Galatians, it was obviously different, perhaps radically different from that of the Jewish congregations elsewhere. We know this because Jewish Christians followed Paul to the Galatians and tried to make them conform to the Jewish Christian pattern. Galatia is a clear case where it was impossible for Paul to submit simultaneously both to the provisions of the Jewish Christian way of life and at the same time to the patterns of an evidently Greek (or perhaps Celtic) congregation.

Paul's letter to the Galatians, furthermore, shows us how determined he was to allow the Galatian Christians to follow a different Christian life-style. Thus while we do not have any record of his forcing people to meet separately, we do encounter all of Paul's holy boldness set in opposition to anyone who would try to *preserve a single normative pattern* of Christian life through a cultural imperialism that would *prevent* people from employing their own language and culture as a vehicle for worship and witness. Here, then, is a clear case of a man with cross-cultural evangelistic perspective doing everything within his power to guarantee liberty in Christ to converts who were different from his own social background.

This same thing is seen when Paul opposed Peter in Antioch. Peter was a Galilean Jew who was perhaps to some extent bi-cultural. He could have at least been able to understand the predominantly Greek life-style of the Antioch church. Indeed, he did seem to fit in until the moment other Jewish Christians came to the door. At this point Peter also discovered that in a given situation he had to choose between following Jewish or Greek customs. At this point he wavered. Did he lack the Spirit of God? Did he lack the love of God? Or did he fail to understand the way of God's love? Peter did not question the validity of a Greek congregation. Peter had already acknowledged this before his Jewish compatriots walked in the door. The point was that Peter was pained for others to know him as one who could shift from one community to the other. What this means to us today is quite clear. There were in fact in the New Testament period two significantly different communities of believers. Peter was regarded the apostle to the circumcision and Paul to the uncircumcision. Peter identified more easily with the Jews, and no doubt had a hard time explaining to Jews his experience at Cornelius' household, namely his discovery that Greek congregations were to be considered legitimate. Paul, on the other hand, was able to identify more closely with the Greek congregations. They were perhaps eventually his primary missionary target, even though in a given locality he always began with the Jews.

One clue for today is the fact that where Paul found some Christians to be overscrupulous about certain foods, he counseled people in those situations to abide by the stricter sensibilities of the majority. However, it is always difficult to make exact parallels to a modern situation. The

New Testament situation would compare more easily to modern India today were it the case that the only Christians in India were Brahmins (and other members of the middle castes) with their highly restrictive diet. Then we would envision Brahmin Christians finding it hard to allow the less restrictive meat-eating groups to become Christian; but the actual situation is very nearly the reverse. In India today it is those who eat meat who are Christians, and the problem is how to apply Paul's missionary strategy to this situation. In regard to food restrictions, it is as though the Brahmins are "under the law," not the present Christians. In this situation can we imagine Paul saying, "To those under the law I will go as under the law if by all means I may win some"? Can we hear him say as an E-2 or E-3 evangelist, "If meat makes my brother offended, I will eat no meat"? Can we hear him defending worshiping groups among the Brahmins against the suggestion *or expectation* that they should change their diet or join congregations of very different life-style in order to be accepted as Christians? Against the accusation that he was dividing the church of Christ, can we hear Paul insist that "in Christ there is neither Jew nor Greek, low caste nor high caste"? Is this not the actual force of his oft-repeated statement that these different kinds of people, following their different cultural patterns, are all equally acceptable to God? Was he really announcing a policy of local integration, or was he insisting on the equality of diversity?

Note very carefully that this perspective does not enforce (nor even allow) a policy of segregation, nor any kind of ranking of Christians in first- and second-class categories. It rather guarantees equal acceptability of different traditions. It is a clear-cut apostolic policy against forcing Christians of one life-style to be proselytized to the cultural patterns of another. This is not a peripheral matter in the New Testament. True circumcision is of the heart. True baptism is of the heart. It is a matter of faith, not works, or customs, or rites. In Christ there is freedom and liberty in this regard — people must be free either to retain or abandon their native language and life-style. Paul would not allow anyone to glory either in circumcision or in uncircumcision. He was absolutely impartial. He was also widely misunderstood. Paul's problem ultimately was in gaining acceptance by the Jews, and it was Asian Jews, possibly Christians, who pointed him out in the temple and thus finally caused his martyrdom for his belief in the separate liberty of the Greek Christian tradition. Let no one who seeks to be a missionary in the tradition of the Apostle Paul expect that working between two cultures will be easy to do. But he can take heart in the fact that the hazards of the profession are more than justified by the urgent missionary purposes of the cross-cultural evangelist.

If, for example, a cross-cultural evangelist encourages members of a Brahmin family to begin worship services in their own home, does he insist that they invite people from across town to their very first meeting? On the other hand, any Brahmin who becomes a Christian and who begins to understand the Bible will soon realize, whether it was entirely clear before or not, that he now belongs to a world family within which there are many tribes and tongues — indeed, according to the Book of Revelation (Rev. 7:9), this kind of diversity will continue right down to the end of time. When the cross-cultural evangelist allows the development of a Brahmin congregation, he is not thereby proposing Brahmin segregation from the world church. He is not suggesting that the Brahmin Christians shun other Christians, but that Brahmins be included within the world church. He is merely affirming their liberty in Christ to retain those elements of their life-style that are not inimical to the Gospel of Christ. He is not increasing their alienation. He is giving them the Word of God which is the passkey to the ultimate elimination of all manner of prejudices, and is already signing them into a world Christian family which embraces all peoples, tribes and tongues as equals.

Now, I regret that this subject is so delicate, and I would not embark upon it if it were not so urgently significant for the practical evangelistic strategies which we must have if we are going to win the world for Christ. I would not even bring it up. Yet I must say I believe this issue is the most important single issue in evangelism today.

Many people asked me what I meant by the strategic value of the establishment of youth churches. It is important to realize the youth situation is highly parallel to the situation we have just discussed. It is by no means a case where we are suggesting that young people not be allowed in adult services. We are not suggesting segregation of the youth. Youth churches are not ends, but means. We are not abandoning the thought that young people and older people should often be in the same service together. We are merely insisting, with what I pray is apostolic intuition, that young people have the freedom in Christ to meet together by themselves if they choose to, and *especially if this allows them to attract other young people who would likely* not come to Christ in an age-integrated service.

I will, however, freely admit that this strategy may unintentionally make it appear that we are setting aside goals of unity for goals of evangelism. This in fact is not the case. It is quite the opposite: we are willing to do evangelism in the highly divided world in which we live, believing wholeheartedly that in the long run the working of the Holy Spirit through true evangelism is the only way to melt down the high walls of prejudice and thus produce unity where none at all existed before.

Some have warned that this kind of culturally sensitive evangelism will lead to ghetto churches. I suggest rather that it will go to ghetto situations and eventually bring those isolated people into contact with others in a rewarding and enriching way. Where there are already ghetto churches all around the world that are isolated from their neighbors, this may not be the fault of the original evangelists, but of the nurture in succeeding years. If the Gospel begins in a ghetto, it should not end there. Rival street gangs may more easily be brought together by being brought to Christ separately. The initial evangelist does not add a ghetto to the church; he takes the church to the ghetto. People from that ghetto are then automatically present at the next city-wide Christian meeting. The efforts of the Billy Graham Crusades must be seen in this light not as an optional, but as an essential, beautiful, and permanent part of God's ultimate uniting strategy. There must, in fact, be annual city-wide and regional Christian festivals whether or not Billy Graham can personally be there. There must be many other contacts between Christians of all kinds between such annual meetings. Yet we must yield to the fact that God allows the family and the local congregation and even whole denominations to speak different languages and to express their faith in different linguistic and cultural traditions. But woe to such self-determining Christians if this liberty in Christ becomes understood as a basis for superiority or isolation. Why? Because, as Paul said, "In Christ there is neither Greek nor Jew, nor Barbarian, nor Scythian, nor bond nor free, nor male nor female."

It is a curious fact that the kind of culturally sensitive evangelism I have been talking about has always been acceptable wherever people are geographically isolated. No one minds if Japanese Christians gather by themselves in Tokyo, or Spanish-speaking Christians gather by themselves in Mexico, or Chinese-speaking Christians gather by themselves in Hong Kong. But there is considerable confusion in many people's minds as to whether Japanese, Spanish and Chinese Christians should be allowed or encouraged to gather by themselves in Los Angeles. Very specifically, is it good evangelistic strategy to found separate congregations in Los Angeles in order to attract such people? Do Cantonese-speaking non-Christians need a Cantonese-speaking congregation to attract them to Christian faith and fellowship? If you talk to different people, you will get different answers. In my opinion, this question about evangelistic strategy in the forming of separate congregations must be considered an area of Christian liberty, and is to be decided purely on the basis of whether or not it allows the Gospel to be presented effectively to more people — that is, whether it is evangelistically strategic. Some go as far as granting separate *language* congregations, but hesitate when the differences between people are social and non-linguistic. Somehow they feel that people may be excused for meeting separately if their language is different, but that the Gospel urges us to ignore all other cultural differences. Many people are literally outraged at the thought that a local congregation would deliberately seek to attract people of a certain social level. And yet, while no one should be excluded from any church under any circumstances, it is a fact that where people can choose their church associations voluntarily, they tend to sort themselves out according to their own way of life pretty consistently. But this absolutely must be their own free choice. We are never suggesting an enforced segregation. Granting that we have this rich diversity, let us foster unity and fellowship between *congregations* just as we now do between *families* rather than to teach everyone to worship like Anglo-Americans. Let us glory in the fact that the *world* Christian family now already includes representatives of more different languages and cultures than any other organization or movement in human history. Americans may be baffled and perplexed by world diversity. God is not. Let us glory in the fact that God has allowed different life-styles to exist in different forms, and that this flexibility has been exercised throughout history. Let us never be content with mere isolation, but let us everlastingly emphasize that the great richness of our Christian tradition can only be realized as these differing life ways maintain creative contact. But let us be cautious about hastening to uniformity. If the whole world church could be gathered into a single congregation, Sunday after Sunday, there would eventually and inevitably be a loss of a great deal of the rich diversity of the present Christian traditions. Does God want this? Do we want this?

Jesus *died* for these people around the world. He did not die to preserve our Western way of life. He did not die to make Muslims stop praying five times a day. He did not die to make Brahmins eat meat. Can't you hear Paul the Evangelist saying we must go to these people within the systems in which they operate? True, this is the cry of a cross-cultural evangelist, not a pastor. We can't make every local church fit the pattern of every other local church. But we must have radically new efforts of cross-cultural evangelism in order to effectively witness to 2387 million people, and we cannot believe that we can continue virtually to ignore this highest priority.

10

THE WORLD CHRISTIAN MOVEMENT
1950-1975: AN INTERPRETIVE ESSAY
Ralph D. Winter

In 1975 anyone expecting to live to the year 2000 or even to 1984 would have had to take a very hard look at the unique developments of the 1950-to-1975 period. For the previous two centuries observers with increasing consternation had begun to predict dire events in the future owing to the giddy pace of the acceleration of history. But, by 1975, the voices of doomsday prophets had become a roar, and, at the time, the oil crisis only seemed to confirm man's worst fears. This was a period—if there ever had been one—in which an interpretative treatment of the development of the Christian movement would have to be done, in Latourette's words, "in relation to the total story of mankind." In doing this, a number of traits of the period stood out.

In the first place, during the 1950 to 1975 period the Western world under-went the most astonishing contraction of political empire that had ever been seen in history in so short a period of time. Shortly before the middle of the century, Western man had completed a gradual buildup of control over the rest of the world that was itself unprecedented. But while that control had been achieved during several centuries of time, the collapse of the Western colonial empires took place within the 1945-to-1969 period. Yet this is merely to speak negatively. Positively: never before had so many new nations come into being so suddenly.

In the second place, no account of this period could fail to take note of the great increase in what had been already a noticeable acceleration of history, an increase which distinguished this particular quarter of a century from any other in all the annals of human history. The acceleration that was noticed was only in part because people could travel faster, communicate more readily, and thus collaborate more efficiently. It was in great part because there was a startlingly greater number of people on earth to make things happen. During this twenty-five-year period the *gain* in world population was as great as the entire population of the world in 1875. In the United States, specifically, the total number of human years lived out during the entire nineteenth century was equalled by the same number of people-years for only the fifteen-year period 1960 to 1975. The United States had 5.3 million people in 1800, and, after a very slow buildup for most of the next hundred years, had 76 million by 1900. But by 1960 there were 180 million, and by 1975, 214 million.

But this was not all. Not only was the world population enormously greater—and this meant that history would inevitably seem to speed up simply because there were each year massively more human beings delving, tussling, working at a given time—but an even greater factor in increased acceleration was the fact that in certain parts of the world (the so-called oil-consuming nations) a sudden and immense amount of labor saving, time saving, and effort multiplying had taken place. The almost unbelievable result was that while, as we have seen, United States citizens expended as much human effort between 1960 and 1975 as they had in the nineteenth century, the work performed (measured by Gross National Product adjusted for inflation) during the entire nineteenth century was equalled in just the two years 1973 and 1974.

In the fourth place, no previous twenty-five-year period in history had witnessed so many technological advances. It had been said that the period covered five revolutions and three renaissances. Whatever was intended by that statement, it was during this quarter of a century that the atom was tamed and the cybernetic revolution became prominent in the meteoric rise of the computer. It was the era of jet planes, earth satellites, moon landings, and unmanned travel within the solar system. Microelectronics brought amazing changes including the transistor radio, which found its way to the furthest reaches of the earth. Many of these new achievements remarkably enhanced the spread of Christianity.

In the fifth place, however, while the economic and technological development of the whole world had been a prominent goal for many years, by 1975 it had become clear that there was really no solution, no possible answer to the "rising expectations" of the majority of the population of the earth for development along Western lines. It became plain to all that economic development in the so-called underdeveloped nations was constantly being outrun by the population explosion in those same nations. Thus arose the widespread concern for limitation of population. But before any solution for overpopulation was discovered, it became clear that the Western way of life itself would be unworkable if extended even to the existing, unexpanded world population. If the average American used up twenty-two tons of mineral resources per day, it simply wasn't possible for such a way of life to become standard for all mankind. Neither was anything remotely like the United States diet something other nations could copy. Senator Hatfield remarked in 1975 that "we can get 667 pounds of protein from one acre of soybeans, but we can only get nine pounds of protein from one acre cultivated in feed grain for cattle." Most nations could not afford to use up seventy-four times as much land in order to get animal protein instead of vegetable protein. Thus it turned out that the Western way was sustainable only by a very inefficient use of land for a very few people. By 1975, the impossibility of the orderly continuation of the pattern of past development had become dreadfully obvious.

In the sixth place, a phenomenon somewhat similar to the increasing inefficiency of land use was the increasing inefficiency in the use of fuel to obtain Western man's vastly increased productivity. Just as an animal protein diet was a highly inefficient exploitation of land, in parallel fashion in 1975 United States citizens, in order to produce as much in *two years* as in the entire nineteenth century, were using as much oil in *two months* as was consumed in the entire nineteenth century. That is, fifty times the productivity cost six hundred times as much oil.

In the seventh place, toward the end of this period, Western man finally discovered with acute embarrassment that the Western World itself had become almost irretrievably dependent—"umbilically dependent" was the phrase—upon a single, rapidly shrinking resource: oil. This was one of the main reasons the Western way of life could not be extended to the rest of the earth, but it was also why such a lifestyle could not be perpetuated even in the West at anything like the 1975 level. This sudden awareness threatened that at some future date Western man might appear not as the pioneering technological benefactor of all the earth, but as the bandit that broke into the storehouse and plundered all the world's energy resources before the bulk of mankind had had a chance to enjoy its share. People in 1975 feared that world oil consumption continuing to rise at 1973 rates would exhaust all known reserves in twenty-one years, and that the United States, if it were to use only its own oil, would run out by 1981. Alternative energy sources were believed to be costly, hazardous, delayed, and uncertain, while foreign sources of oil were also uncertain if only because prohibitively expensive.

Thus in early 1975 the outlook for Western man and his way of life was suddenly very bleak. But the hungry, exploding populations of Asia and Africa faced ever so much more serious dangers. Mesarovic and Pestel in *Mankind at the Turning Point: The Second Report to the Club of Rome* described a nearly inevitable scenario in which the number of children dying per year would rise from 10 million to more than 40 million by the year 2000. Probably at no time in the twentieth century had man's achievements loomed smaller in proportion to the real problems he faced. At no time was there greater need for the best possible international understanding. At no time were the values and perspectives of the Christian faith more widely shared. Never before in history had the nations of the world as great a sense of obligation toward each other; superficial though this attitude might be, it was a feeling stemming from the remarkable record of selfless service that had been performed by Christian missions.

In 1975, the world in many ways seemed to be passing into a post-Western period. Would this be a post-Christian period as well? Hopefully the presence of the Christian movement in the world could make a considerable direct and indirect contribution in the troubled times ahead. The movement itself was not in decline. The number of Protestant missionaries from North America more than doubled between 1950 and 1975 and so did the number of mission agencies. The net increase in the number of Christians in the non-Western world by the end of this period was far larger than the total number of Christians in the non-Western world at the beginning of the period. That is to say, in the non-Western world, Christians increased by 140 percent while the general population increased by only 42 percent. Another way to visualize the growth rate of the Christian movement in the non-Western world in 1975 would be to picture at least one thousand new churches opening their doors each Sunday. But we are anticipating the study that follows.

THE WESTERN WORLD

The two areas Latourette spoke of as "traditional Christendom" and "the Larger Occident" are really a single cultural sphere often called the Western world which, for the sake of space, can be discussed as a single unit. One reason this can be done is that during the third quarter of the twentieth century much of this whole area was undergoing the same series of experiences in regard to the breakdown of centuries-old established relations between civil governments and Christian institutional structures.

Thus, the most useful generalization about what happened to Christianity in the Western world between 1950 and 1975 is simply that it continued (and even speeded up) its gradual, painful withdrawal from entrenched legal and cultural establishment. This complex process of disestablishment—and we use the term more broadly than is customary—began much earlier and seemed to move much faster in America. Nevertheless, even as late as 1975 religious properties still escaped taxation in America. Similarly, in Russia, despite the violent disestablishment that occurred in the Communist revolution, the former state church still retained significant cultural influence. But everywhere in the Western world in both Protestant and Roman Catholic areas, and in both

Communist and non-Communist areas, the trend was relentlessly and probably irreversibly away from a Christianity possessing any political power of establishment which could conceivably force its forms upon a whole populace. Latourette stressed that Communism was not the only force hastening the process of disestablishment; he also felt that Communism and the process of disestablishment were partially products of Christianity, even though they might also be anti-Christian.

Thus, while the Communist movement represented the most extensive, single organized force in the trend to disestablishment, it drew much of its inspiration from the social concerns growing out of the Evangelical Awakening in Britain, where it was born amidst the labor pains of the industrial revolution. The Methodist class meeting, borrowed perhaps from the Brethren of the Common Life, was a forerunner of the Communist cell, and the Communistic emphasis on confession also stemmed from Methodism. Going further back in history, Communism's stress on "people governments" and the rights of the people could hardly be distinguished from any number of earlier, more obviously Christian, revolutionary movements such as Wat Tyler's Rebellion, the Bundschuh Revolt, the Peasants' War, etc., except that in these earlier movements the Bible had been appealed to as the source of revolutionary perspective. Since Marx, Engels, and Lenin apparently felt that the Church was forever on the side of the bourgeoise, they saw the rising up of the masses as inevitably requiring the destruction of the Church and, for safety, the elimination of the religion and theology behind the Church. Yet such goals were to some extent incidental to the more profound cause of Communism, the liberation of man—a concept which in turn is a cluster of ideals almost entirely stemming from Christianity. But could such ideals survive as fruits when once separated from their Christian roots? Elton Trueblood felt not and called the society with this kind of secular vision "a cut-flower civilization."

It is not surprising, therefore, that in the 1950's and 1960's many people in the Western world, especially in the United States, confused the somewhat academic tension between capitalism and Communism with the larger issue of Christianity versus atheism. But according to Latourette, even the latter tension did not best describe the major process unfolding in the Revolutionary Age. As Christianity was becoming disestablished, many of the surface evidences of this disestablishment—declining registration of Christians in Germany, declining statistics of baptisms in the areas of state-church traditions, and even declining perfunctory attendance in some of the older church traditions—did not by any means signal the exhaustion of the energy and vitality of the Christian movement. Again and again in Latourette's writings, and in our own observations of the Western world, we are forced to distinguish between the admittedly widespread evidences of the decline of the Christian establishment and the springing up of a vast plethora of new movements, contrasting sharply with the decline of the settled Christian past.

It was, for example, in 1818—early in Latourette's Revolutionary Era—that American churches in Connecticut were finally and dramatically cut off from state support. At that time the eminent church leader, Lyman Beecher, sincerely predicted the fatal demise of the United States Church, only to contradict himself ten years later with relief and exultation when the newly emerging "voluntary church" tradition seemed to offer more hope than ever before for continuity of vigor and vitality despite the absence of the older forms. For Europe, it was under Hitler that German congregations had briefly to face the necessity of direct local support of their pastors when state support was slashed or withdrawn completely. Then for more than a quarter of a century after World War II, the Church in East Germany had to survive in the face of intense opposition by the state. Even earlier in Russia, as we have seen, the Christian movement had proved itself capable of surviving the most extreme opposition of an atheistic government. But the loss of establishment apparently did not mean the emergence of a "post-Christian era."

The thrust of Latourette's blunt, earnest prediction in the 1950's that the use of the phrase "post-Christian era" was "hasty and naive" was eminently confirmed by 1975. A specific case might be the East Germany we have just mentioned. The Protestant community—consistently penalized for church involvement—dropped from 80 percent to 60 percent of the population, and by 1975 there were perhaps at the most only one million people (6 percent) who could be called highly committed Christians. Yet cautious observers suggested that this committed minority was probably larger than at any previous time. Students in Christian groups at the universities of Dresden and Leipzig numbered in the hundreds. It was not uncommon for groups of young people numbering more than one thousand suddenly to materialize for worship and Bible study, coming from all parts of East Germany but especially from the south, brought together by word of mouth alone. The famous Dom (cathedral) across from the Imperial Palace in East Berlin was being reconstructed by the end of the period. A small group of Communist-leaning pastors existed for a time, but had disappeared by 1975.

Thus, for all their trouble, the leaders of the totalitarian Communist regime had through diligent oppression apparently done no more damage to the Christian movement than had the benign neglect of the non-Communist governments in other parts of Europe and the Western world in the same period.

In both the East and West, from Russia west to Australia, the overarching phenomenon was the accelerated disestablishment of the Christian movement. Where was this massive process leading?

Clues to the future could perhaps be seen in the New World where the transformation was more advanced. "The shot heard 'round the world" at the outbreak of the American Revolution had an immediate effect in France but was then heard all down through the Americas. Mainly in the New World the reverberations almost instantly furthered the disestablishment of churches that were for the most part already heading that way. Thus, the churches in the United States were much more extensively disestablished much sooner than in Europe, even though between 1950 and 1975 events were still taking place that further disestablished Christianity even as a semi-official faith. In 1962, the Supreme Court made unlawful even the voluntary recital of a non-denominational prayer written by the New York State Board of Regents. In 1975, the California State Court of Appeal ruled that "the three-hour closing of state offices on Good Friday is unconstitutional and an 'excessive governmental entanglement with religion.'" That same year the California State Legislature appointed a Buddhist priest as chaplain, a move profoundly significant in the disestablishment process. Nevertheless, legal disestablishment meant cultural disestablishment only for a time. Church membership was 6 percent of the population at the time of the American Revolution, but was over 60 percent by 1975.

Latin America, at first glance, may have seemed to many Protestants an area of unrelieved and seemingly permanent Roman Catholic establishment. But by 1975, any such illusions were well-nigh completely shattered. As a matter of fact, the disestablishment of Christendom in Latin America had begun most emphatically over one hundred years earlier as country after country declared its independence both from Europe and from the Church in the years that followed the American Revolution to the north. What had confused Protestants was the apparently close, continued association of the Roman Catholic Church with the various governments. Yet the famous Concordat between the Spanish crown and the Vatican did not consolidate the power of the Vatican in Spain so much as it consolidated the power of the Spanish crown over the Church, and the same shift was true for the Colombian Concordat signed after the wars of independence. Such concordats did mean a continued, prominent role for the Church, but the Church now became subservient to the state—a development which we can see only as the first step in our larger concept of disestablishment. In Mexico, for example, the power of the state over the Church allowed the state eventually to seize all the properties of the Church and progressively to disenfranchise it in many other ways. Legal proscriptions of Roman Catholic activities in Mexico long antedated and perhaps even guided similar measures taken later in Russia by the Bolsheviks as the new era of the USSR came to constitute an even more determined and relentless disestablishment of the Church. In the constitutions of most Latin American countries for over a century there had been provision for both freedom of, and freedom from, religion.

Nevertheless, despite such striking handicaps and limitations, the Roman Catholic Church was able to survive at least as a cultural tradition, and especially following Vatican II it adopted in many places an outright anti-government posture which aligned it with the masses and the downtrodden. Meanwhile, vigorous new thinking, especially in Latin America, championed a "theology of liberation" which boldly assumed the very institution of the Church to be secondary to the larger will of God in society.

Even more estranged from the institutional Roman Catholic tradition were the rising Protestant and Pentecostal movements which flourished in the anti-clerical atmosphere. Pentecostalism was especially prominent in Brazil and Chile, but by 1975 had become a significant force from Mexico to Argentina. Thus Christianity in various forms represented a vigorous and vital element in almost every sector of Latin America despite the fact that the older institutions of the Church by 1975 were more completely disestablished than ever before.

Nevertheless, these traces of final, legal disestablishment in the Western world were accompanied by abundant evidence that legal establishment as such was by no means essential—nor perhaps even desirable—for the best interests of the Christian movement. In America where disestablishment had gone beyond the same process in Europe, it was discovered that when the churches were thrown on their own initiative, this allowed and perhaps even encouraged the development of many striking signs of vitality.

For example, in the 1950's and the 1960's in the United States, and especially in the 1960's as the Vietnam war was escalated, anti-establishment feelings and sometimes militancy were shared by a major sector of the population. Profound doubts about big government and all the established institutions threatened the main-line denominations along with the civil structures. Anti-war dissent bred anti-establishment dissent of many other varieties. The drive for racial integration was in some respects overtaken by the drive for black power, and then brown power, and Indian power, and female power, and youth power, and gay power, and led to a vast convulsion of self-determining subsections of society. The task of assimilating these cause groups into the orderly processes of civil and ecclesiastical government meant a good deal of trauma for many of the ecclesiastical structures which tried hardest to respond to their voices. In the process, the disestablishment of inherited Christian structures seemed to be accelerated, although by 1975 the greatest intensity of most of these storms seemed to have passed.

Meanwhile, a vast profusion of new movements had gained strength. The youth counterculture, which earlier had spurned the entire array of established structures including the Church, had to a considerable extent become the mainspring behind the Christian vitality in the so-called Jesus People movement, which at one extreme was manifested in so radical a movement as the widely reported Children of God, but was also a force behind a new mood and considerable new strength in many traditional seminary student bodies. Of the more than 250 new missionary agencies formed in the period, a significant group were almost exclusively the product of the youth movement, and many more made room for youth divisions; "short-termers" became a third of all missionaries from the United States. Young people, long conspicuous by their absence in both European and mainline church congregations, now became prominent in dozens of unanticipated ventures, both in Europe and in America, which bypassed traditional channels but clearly expressed genuine Christian vitality. One major youth mission originating in the United States, Operation Mobilization, discovered British and Continental young people to be so much more receptive that it virtually abandoned further recruitment in the United States. At the same time the voice of youth became increasingly heard in traditional structures as well, and was characterized by an unprecedented sensitivity to the new common concerns about ecology, hunger, and social justice. But while the most populous American state, California, elected as governor at 37 Edmund G. Brown, Jr., a man who was in his twenties during much of the Vietnam war, it was by 1975 unheard of for there to be any comparable reliance upon youth for formal leadership in the major denominational traditions.

The largest single Christian structure, the Roman Catholic Church, could be the object of a special study of the process of disestablishment. We have briefly touched on it in our references to Latin America, and will be referring to it below in the section on Asia and Africa. For the Roman Catholics, the central event of the third quarter of the twentieth century was clearly Vatican Council II. In a physical sense, this event was simply a four-year-long series of consultations between some two thousand bishops from the world wide domains of the Roman Catholic Church. It was the result of the inspired genius of an elderly man who was elected virtually as an interim pope. Yet in launching this council, Pope John XXIII opened a window which might never be fully closed again.

As a result, in a hundred ways this major ecclesiastical tradition achieved a massive, breath-taking adjustment to modern times—the untranslatable *aggiornamento* in Italian. Pope John's more conservative successor, Pope Paul VI, qualified and tempered but also implemented willingly or unwillingly many of the gains. Long overdue was a readjustment of Roman Catholic theology to the unwaning prominence of the Bible in the Christian movement, a readjustment of Roman Catholic structure to the nearly universal acceptance in the modern world of democratic governmental structure in place of a monarchial pattern of authority, and a readjustment of the Roman Catholic official stance towards Protestantism. In regard to the latter, it seemed that the new attitude of some Catholics simply included Protestantism with other non-Christian religions, welcoming both Protestants and Buddhists on the same ground. But in a new and healthy way, the Catholic charismatic movement fused Protestant, Evangelical, and Pentecostal patterns of informal prayer and worship with a new emphasis on the Bible, including in some quarters in the United States experiments in Christian community living that went beyond the casual fellowship so characteristic of United States church life.

Thus by 1975 in the Western world Christianity was less and less the legally or culturally established religion. In its nominal form it had lost much of the automatic respect it may have had in an earlier era. At the same time, voluntary structures were carrying forward a great deal of what seemed to be, over all, increased vitality in the Christian movement.

THE NON-WESTERN WORLD

In 1975 one of the essential differences between the Western and the non-Western worlds insofar as Christianity was concerned was the fact that with some notable exceptions (e.g., the Syrian tradition in India and the Oriental Orthodox Churches in the Middle East and Ethiopia), the Christian movement was relatively young and accordingly less well established in the non-Western sphere. As we have seen, churches in the West were increasingly *disestablished,* while in the non-Western world the churches were to a much greater extent what we may call *unestablished*—that is, they had for the most part not yet attained either a legal or a cultural monopoly. Furthermore, as the nineteenth and twentieth centuries wore on, a significantly increasing percentage of the missionaries working in the non-Western world originated from within the new variety of American disestablished churches of which we have already spoken, and thus tended to implant in non-Western countries that same new type of Christianity which neither sought nor expected to become established. For example, despite the popular stereotype of missionaries being backed by colonial governments, it is likely that as early as 1910 a majority of Protestant missionaries were at work in lands in which their home governments had no control, and this general absence of either government or cultural support tended to modify the very nature of the churches being planted.

We are not surprised therefore to find that by 1975 the overall character of the Christian movement in the non-Western world was extensively different from its Western counterpart. Many Western observers of the so-called younger churches in the non-Western world were so impressed by the unusually high quality of commitment they found overseas that they suggested there ought to be a "reverse flow" of missionaries from the younger churches to help in the work of renewal in the West. This was surely to be welcomed. Ever since Henri Godin and Yvan Daniel had written *La France, Pays de Mission?* the awareness of the need to consider traditional Christendom a mission field had grown apace, and the electrifying phrase of the World Council's new Division of World Mission and Evangelism, "Mission in Six Continents," had become the dominant perspective by 1975.

On the other hand, it would not have been entirely true to suggest that all non-Western Christians belonged to tiny, unestablished, committed minorities any more than to have maintained that all Western Christians belonged to vast nominal masses whose Christianity virtually came with their citizenship. Estimates for 1975 indicated, very roughly, that only about 120 million out of a total of 965 million Western Christians could be considered significantly disestablished, while 80 million out of a total of 214 million non-Western Christians were considered disestablished or unestablished. That is, the ratio was about 1 to 8 in the Western World and 3 to 8 in the non-Western World.

Reminding ourselves that we are speaking of a much broader type of disestablishment than the narrow and technical, conventional meaning of the term, the distinction here drawn is not intended to be invidious but descriptive. We have spoken of Christian communions possessing "legal or cultural monopolies" upon a citizenry, and have suggested that the third quarter of the century witnessed an accelerated shift from an established Christian tradition to a non- or dis-established Christian tradition. While the one form declined, the other was rising. Here is the paradox of weakness and strength referred to in the title of Chapter 60. Here is the distinction the absence of which allows such widely differing assessments of the state of Christianity in the modern world. Here is a perspective which prepares us to evaluate the uniqueness of the Christian movement in the non-Western world. However, our discussion will first turn to the Middle East, which is in some ways a halfway step to the rest of the non-Western world.

The Middle East

Thanks to Alexander the Great, who took Hellenism as far as India, and to Mohammed, whose forces held western Switzerland for over two centuries and parts of Spain for over seven, there was a great deal of inter-penetration between Europe and the Middle East. Furthermore, the Judeo-Christian heritage was by definition a blend of the Indo-European and the Semitic. As a result, the Middle East constitutes a fairly small step away from the Western cultural tradition. We are not surprised therefore to find that the life of the Christian movement in that area has been basically the confrontation of various human traditions, all of which have kinship at some point in the literate past.

In 1975 there were sixteen different kinds of older, culturally established Christian traditions in the Middle East. These groups were in most cases minority enclaves within the overwhelming context of the Muslim tradition, existing as battered survivors of centuries of turmoil. Yet, if North Africa and Ethiopia were included as part of the Middle Eastern museum of the ancient churches, there were by 1975 still nearly 17 million in the various sub-populations of the total Christian community, comprising 7 percent of the whole area, but 77 percent of Cyprus, half the population in Lebanon, 37 percent of Ethiopia, 13 percent of Egypt, 10 percent of Jordan, 9.8 percent of Syria, 5 percent of Sudan, and 4 percent of Iraq. Christians comprised 1 percent or less in all the other countries in this area—Morocco, Algeria, Tunisia, Libya, Turkey, Iran, Saudi Arabia, and the smaller Arabian States. The vast majority of these 17 million Christians represented the tenacious continuation of ancient churches—one million Eastern Orthodox, 13 million Oriental Orthodox (i.e., non-Chalcedonian), and roughly 100,000 Assyrian Church of the East ("Nestorian"), all of whom were at least *culturally* established if not in all cases *legally* established. Then there were almost two million Catholic Christians (of eight different traditions) that recognized the Pope as their supreme authority. These too could be considered culturally established. This left less than one million Protestants and Anglicans who to some considerable extent reflected the characteristically disestablished posture of the Evangelical tradition, but these constituted only 5 percent of the 17 million Christians, and were thus only one-third of 1 percent of the general population of the area.

Curiously, although the scattered elements of this latter group were only tiny minorities wherever they were found, nevertheless because they were relatively committed and were backed by churches in the West, they had a truly immense impact in the area, especially in education and public health.

Between 1950 and 1975 the entire area was drastically shaken by the further withdrawal of colonial forces, by internal revolutions, by wars and tensions with Israel, and in 1974 by the stunning impact of the unexpectedly vast new oil wealth of some of the states. All this turmoil affected the churches in the area. Immediately after withdrawing from Vietnam, the French were determined to hold onto Algeria, but in the ensuing conflict, over a million Algerians lost their lives, and an equal number of French, Spanish, and other foreigners, almost all nominal Roman Catholics, withdrew from Morocco, Algeria, Tunisia, and later Libya.

The impact of the twenty-five-year period on the actual numbers of Christians in the area was extremely difficult to determine, not for the lack of knowledge in 1975 but for the lack of precise figures for the number of Christians in the 1950's with which to make comparisons. Numbers Latourette was forced to quote as estimates diverged so widely from quantities accurately known for 1973 that it was virtually impossible to do more than offer several fairly general observations. By 1950, as colonial protection of the minorities was gradually withdrawn, the Christian populations in the area along with some of the other minorities had been in many cases tragically decimated by nearly genocidal aggression against them in Turkey, Syria, Iraq, and Iran. In the following twenty-five years, however, except for the plight of Christians among the West Bank Jordanians and the southern Sudanese, adversities of this sort were not so extensive. Generally speaking, the Christian communities were able to consolidate and to grow at least as fast as the general population, and thanks to a careful statistical study of the entire area sponsored by the Near East Council of Churches and conducted by Norman Horner, by 1975 there was detailed knowledge of the size and vast complexity of the constituent elements of the 17 million Christians to whom we have referred. Future studies of the area could build on these statistics and keep in closer touch with the growth and life of these churches.

It would be inaccurate to leave a depressing picture of the weakness and division of the Christian movement in the very region where Christianity first began. On the contrary, note the genius of the Eastern Orthodox tradition, for example, that created "autocephalous" branches comprising different ethnic and language communities. The vast bulk of the Christians in the area had early parted ways with the Greek tradition in refusing to accept the Chalcedonian Creed, but their autonomy within their own separate traditions was to a great extent in keeping with the autocephalous concept and was a surprising testimony to the resilience and flexibility of a Christian faith that embraced a widely disparate group of peoples whose diversity was, after all, not created by Christianity but in fact surmounted by it, even if imperfectly. Here was vivid proof that Christianity does not blot out ethnic and cultural uniquenesss, but to an incredible extent is a preserver of such distinctions, even as emigrants from the Middle East carried their distinctive faith with them to other lands. The acid test would be whether ethnic and cultural traditions calling themselves Christian would be known by their love for one another and for all men. Early Protestant attempts to work within and for these ancient churches usually resulted eventually in small Protestant communities outside them. It was a promising fact in 1975 that the Near East Council of Churches, originally a council of missions, was able to number the Antioch Patriarchate of the Syrian Orthodox Church as a member.

In this connection a broad generalization might be hazarded. On the one hand, the Western Roman Catholic tradition developed a monolithic ecclesiastical umbrella that spanned many culturally diverse peoples. But para-ecclesiastical movements such as the Friars and Clerks Regular (e.g., Jesuits) constituted live options for the expression of internal diversity. Such structures by their very nature were voluntary options and thus "unestablished" in the way we are using that word. On the other hand, the Orthodox churches developed decentralized autonomy for each of the ethnic and cultural entities in their region, but possessed very thin overall unity and seriously lacked the profusion of voluntary options presented in the West by the Catholic orders. Protestants, Anglicans, and Western Catholics in modern times brought to the Middle East additional competitive ecclesiastical options, perhaps unintentionally; but they also brought a profusion of non-conflicting para-church structures, ranging from Sunday schools and youth movements of evangelizing societies to major (Catholic) orders. By 1975 it appeared as though these secondary elements in the Western presence were inspiring similar initiatives in the Orthodox churches, especially in Greece and Lebanon. One very influential renewing force which spanned several churches and countries was the Movements of Orthodox Youth, which provided from its ranks the new, young Greek Orthodox Archbishop of Cyprus when Archbishop Makarios was made president of the country. Movements like this had profound implications for renewal and unity in the world of these ancient churches.

Overshadowing all discussion of the Christian movement in the Middle East was the colossus of Islam. It is not our specific purpose to describe non-Christian movements, but it is for several reasons necessary to pause briefly to reflect on the nature and role of Islam. As president of Egypt, Nasser could say, "Islam recognizes Christians as brothers in religion and brothers in God." Contrary to widespread belief among Christians, when Islam overran the Middle East centuries ago, the enforced conversion of Christians to Islam was by far the exception rather than the rule, and nothing in Muslim history approaches the ugliness of the militant opposition to Islam mounted by the warriors calling themselves Crusaders when Europeans fought back five centuries later. Reflections like this are necessary to clear the air.

However, only the most profound reorientation in our Christian thinking about Islam will avoid a harsh and artificial contrast between Islam and the various types of Christianity co-existing in the same area of the world. In some respects Islam was simply one more movement stemming from Judaism and Christianity. The missionary-theologian Arend Th. van Leeuwen suggested that just as Hellenic Christianity resulted from Paul's application of the Christian message to the Greek cultural sphere, so Islam was to a great extent the adaptation of Jewish Christianity into the Arab world. He claimed, in fact, that some forms of Orthodox Christianity in Ethiopia differed more from what the Western world understood by Christianity than did Islam. Whatever the case, the assumption that Islam was as different from Christianity as, say, Hinduism was a gross misunderstanding and perhaps hampered the possibility of Christian growth where Islam was dominant. Nevertheless, by 1975 it was clear that the relatively tiny presence of Western missions in the Middle East had opened a doorway of contact with the Western world which had spectacular influence. A handful of colleges and universities won over a high percentage of the entire new leadership of the area at least to Western science, technology, manners, and morals. This did not produce a Christianized stratum of society in the religious sense, but it did build an enormously significant bridge of understanding across which better religious communication could take place.

By 1975 Islam was the second largest of the world's religions, having about half as many adherents as Christianity. We have already seen Communism as an outgrowth of Christianity; it was far more obvious that Islam was also an outgrowth of the Judeo-Christian tradition. Van Leeuwen would even add that the scientific and technological revolution was still another outgrowth of Christianity. Thus we see that in one way or another the impulse that can be traced back to Jesus had flowed out across the world in the form of the Protestant, Catholic, and Orthodox forms of Christianity proper, plus the various "outgrowths" of Communism, Islam, and science and technology, such that virtually the entire planet had by 1975 been profoundly altered, indirectly at least, by the Gospel of Christ. If to formal Christianity, constituting one-third of mankind in 1975, we were to add the adherents of the profoundly theistic and ethical religion of Islam, constituting one-sixth of mankind, we would find that half of all people on the planet were at least nominal adherents of faiths that recognized Jesus in a very special way. Meanwhile, the other half of mankind was subject to massive cultural, intellectual, educational, medical, political, and moral influences which stemmed from Christianity more than from any other single source.

These statements are not meant to imply that Christians conceived their task to be finished once people had been influenced in the ways we have described. Indeed, Christians would consider the task only begun. Rather, the purpose of such statements is to integrate the massive extent to which the influence of the life of one man has already encompassed the world, and to note the extent to which future efforts have a tremendously significant foundation on which to build. Islam in particular, now that its heartland had come into unbelievable wealth, was by 1975 undergoing the most rapid transition into modern ways, meaning mainly Western ways, and was surely a phenomenon urgently requiring profound, new theological reinterpretation from Christian and Islamic scholars alike.

AFRICA

As we shift our vision to Sub-Saharan Africa, we realize immediately how much further from the Western world we are moving culturally speaking. Unlike the area of the Middle East, North Africa, and Ethiopia which we have just surveyed, in 1975 Sub-Saharan Africa offered no comparably long-standing points of contact with the Western world except in those limited areas that were Semitic or Muslim. The advance of Christianity in Africa in the nineteenth and twentieth centuries thus initiated an abrupt confrontation and interpenetration of cultural systems that were utterly distinct from each other. As a result, the rising interest in the 1970's in the development of African theology raised issues far more profound than did the relatively minor variations involved, for example, in the development of a Latin American theology, a development to a great extent within Western culture. The only parallel in Western experience to the immense impact of Christianity on non-Semitic Africa was the impact a millennium earlier of Latin, Greek, and Celtic Christianity on the pagan tribes of northern Europe—a series of events so far back in history that in the 1970's the lessons seemed not to be readily recoverable.

Between 1950 and 1975 over a century of serious occupation of Africa by colonial nations was abruptly ended. By 1975 forty-one African countries had been granted their freedom and had become members of the United Nations, leaving only a handful of African countries to continue under colonial rule. The largest single sector of these populations were under Portugal, which either partially or fully withdrew from each sector by the end of the period. Speaking in historic terms, a more sudden and complete collapse of external control could hardly have been imagined. Many predictions turned out to be false. Organized Communism was not able to fill the vacuum. Even a man like Kenyatta, whose accession to power was assumed to be equivalent to introducing Communism to Kenya, turned out to be much more pro-Christian and anti-Communist than the reverse. Westerners assumed that the new nations could not manage themselves politically, but the record by 1975 did not involve any instabilities which had not already bedevilled Western countries from the beginnings of the modern nation states. Even the marked trend to dictatorship and totalitarian police states was unfortunately not altogether different from the conditions in many Western countries. As for civil wars in the absence of the colonial powers, leaders in the Nigerian civil war drew comfort and even military guidance from the American experience. The inevitable attempts of resource-rich portions of countries to form separate nations, as in the case of mineral-rich Katanga in Zaire and oil-rich southeastern Nigeria, were direct parallels to the inclination of the cotton-rich American South to rule its own affairs as a separate country.

On the other hand, not everything paralleled contemporary Western experience. In the African nations the dominant social patterns inherited from the colonial era even if relatively secure were nevertheless relatively superficial. Christianity was in many ways becoming culturally established and increasingly nominal. Here the parallel was perhaps with fourth-century Rome when Christians had only recently gained government backing for schools, hospitals, libraries and, most important, public worship. Between 1950 and 1975 as the African states burst into independence it was inevitable that there would be in some measure a resurgence of the cultural substratum. Following the colonial period of nominal Christian ascendance, would a "Julian the Apostate" appear and attempt to reinstate the pagan tradition?

In Chad the Christian movement had brought no effective substitute for the important and impressive indigenous "rites of passage" at puberty, and in 1974 the government sponsored the widespread reintroduction of African puberty ceremonies, even for highly Westernized government officials in adult life, some losing their lives in the austere practice. On the other hand, in Tanzania tribal dress was suppressed in the interests of national unity. But in Zaire in the interests of African "authenticity," beginning in 1972, the government ordered the people to drop European for African names, banned religious youth organizations, church periodicals, and radio programs, seized control of elementary and secondary schools (the vast proportion church-run), and replaced religion courses and wall decorations with teachings that tended to present the president as a saviour. In 1974 Christmas was henceforth to be eliminated in favor of a

June independence celebration, and key theological seminaries were notified of closure at the end of the school year. In December of that year, according to one report, the state press agency announced that the nation's single political party "must henceforth be considered as a church and its founder a messiah." Kwame Nkrumah had already attempted to transfer devotion to the state and to himself in Ghana. He too had problems with the continuing influence of the churches, but was overthrown in 1966.

Christianity and its schools had virtually singlehandedly produced the new leadership of the African nations. But where state power was held by one tribal group and threatened potentially by the leadership of another, the church within the second group often became the enemy of the state. In such a situation, educated leaders of the wrong tribe, as often as not pastors, might be slain by the thousands, as in Burundi. In Uganda, although Muslims constituted only 6 percent of the population, the military dictatorship was held by a Muslim; and Libyan oil money, perhaps with the hope that the number of Muslims could be increased, seemed to provide an external source of power to a government so despotic as to be reminiscent of Caligula's reign. This fact by 1975 might have held grave forebodings for the strong Roman Catholic and Anglican communities in that country had they not constituted two-thirds of the population.

The overall picture in Sub-Saharan Africa seemed to imply that the power of the Church would go unopposed only if it supported political governments, or at least avoided conflict with them. Governments were sometimes rattled by the existence of a pluralism of churches which, though friendly to each other, did not support a centralized church administration for all varieties of Christians. Russia for a long time had attempted to bundle all Protestants under a single Baptist umbrella, and during World War II Japan had attempted the same in the formation of the Kyodan. In Zaire all Protestants were forced into a single council, and in Ghana Nkrumah had moved in the same direction. In Africa, however, the ethnic sub-stratum constituted a mosaic exceedingly more diverse than in Japan, or in the Western world, and the result was an increasingly unmanageable diversity. In particular, what were called the African Independent Churches became prominent. The phrase referred to denominations born in Africa outside missionary initiative. Latourette was well aware of the significant growth of the African Independent Churches even by 1950 (p. 1437). According to estimates by David Barrett, while mission-founded churches were still the majority Christian pattern in less than four hundred denominations, the number of Independent Church denominations had increased by 1975 to five thousand (one thousand in 1950) with a total membership of 7 million adherents (one million in 1950). This kind of church grew about 40 percent faster than the Christian movement in general, which itself grew twice as fast as the population in most areas. The phenomenon of Independent Churches was found in thirty-four African nations and 290 different tribes. Some of these churches were quite orthodox in their theology, others so unorthodox as to have within their midst a "divine" person. Yet each called itself Christian, and most of them looked upon the Bible as their sacred book.

Some observers felt Africa was descending into a chaos of cults. Latourette, had he been alive, would probably have rejoiced cautiously at the luxuriant spontaneity, the apparent overall vitality of a Christian movement which continued despite (perhaps because of) all the tumult of the times. Christianity had not created the immense African diversity but did ultimately bring to it a common denominator. One of the most outstanding indigenous movements, the church resulting from the work of Simon Kimbangu, by 1975 numbered well over one million members, mainly in Zaire, even in the most cautious estimates. Its desire to join the World Council of Churches and its acceptance by that body in some ways hinted that the diversity of the Christian movement worked ultimately for unity rather than disunity.

Between 1950 and 1975 no African nation adopted Christianity as a state religion, and by early 1975 the legal establishment of the Ethiopian Orthodox Church was increasingly tenuous. The prevailing mood did not seem to lead toward a European type of church establishment. For one thing, in most countries Roman Catholic, Anglican, and Protestant traditions were all well represented, and it would have been unlikely that any one tradition would become established in the political sense. Furthermore, even Roman Catholic missionaries from the United States (and certainly all other missions from the New World) arrived without any desire or expectation of becoming established, as noted previously. This was not to say, however, that Christianity was not increasingly established in the cultural sense in many (if not most) African nations south of the Sahara. One significant factor postponing the nominality so often associated with establishment was the continued rapid growth by conversion and the continued high percentage of people in many churches who had elected to become members of the church as adults, especially in the newer and Independent Churches. Even so, by 1975 second- and third-generation Christians dominated the leadership of many denominations, and a remarkable phenomenon called the East African Revival played an important role in renewal. Originating in an Anglican area in the 1930's, it was a movement that deliberately held its meetings outside normal church hours and offered an additional option of fellowship and openness beyond normal church membership. By 1975 it was found in most of East Africa and neighboring countries, touching more than one million lives, and did not show any signs of decline.

This movement and literally hundreds of other para-church phenomena vitally contributed to the overall health of the Christian movement. There was a tendency in the 1960's and 1970's, as the colonial officials disappeared from Africa, for it to be assumed in some quarters that the Western mission agencies also had no further role. A proposal by John Gatu, an East African church leader, for a "moratorium" on Western mission personnel and funds was widely discussed in the 1970's and its meanings and merits were as widely misunderstood. His proposal was eminently reasonable for many situations where a well-founded national church—somewhat parallel to a national political entity—needed to function entirely on its own power. He did not intend his proposal to wipe out all the initiatives of a para-ecclesiastical nature, much less divert attention from population elements that were not yet Christian. On the other hand, while his own church was prepared to send missionaries, very few African denominations had organized their own mission boards. A major exception was the Evangelical Churches of West Africa, which by 1975 had established an autonomous board under which over two hundred Africans served as missionaries.

In any case, the very discussion of a moratorium highlighted the fact that by 1975 the dominant voices in church leadership in Africa (not only in the Independent movement but in the churches which were the direct result of mission agencies) were duly empowered African church leaders. For example, Latourette noted that there were in 1952 only four African Roman Catholic bishops. By 1975 the Roman Catholic Church had consecrated 129 African bishops, 22 African archbishops, and 5 African cardinals. The change in the Protestant sphere was comparable even though not so easily summed up. Christianity, as a movement, was clearly out of the control of the West.

In no other continent during the 1950-to-1975 period had Christianity made a greater apparent advance. Yet the future was not clear. Some signs threatened serious cultural backlash. In many places nationalism seemed to conflict with the power and presence of the Christian churches. Islam was a rising force with new prominence and potential power owing to the oil wealth in its heartland countries. But in 1975 in Sub-Saharan Africa, Christianity was by far the most widespread, potentially unifying religion and was uniquely influential in the formation of most of the other social and cultural forces deriving from the West.

ASIA

By the time Christianity in the 16th century first penetrated to the Far East in force, Asia was by no means a sea of animism as uncontested by any other "higher" religion, as was Sub-Saharan Africa. For the greater part of the first sixteen Christian centuries there was no effective sea route to Asia from Europe, and

Christian missionaries sent overland accomplished relatively little that endured except for the Syrian Orthodox presence in South India. Prior to modern times, Islam had greatly expanded under Muslim rule in many parts of India and even in Southeast Asia. Buddhism, a Hindu reform movement, early had a special appeal where Hinduism was strong, and in expanding into other areas had the advantage of being a religion which originated in the very heart of Asia rather than at its geographically distant Western edge like Christianity and Islam.

Furthermore, when Western colonial powers began to take over many parts of Asia, the two great Protestant colonial powers, the British and the Dutch, never seriously sponsored mission work as did the Portuguese, Spanish, and French. Thus by 1900 Christianity in Asia numbered only 9 million adherents, constituted mostly by the nominal Roman Catholic communities in the Philippines and Indochina. By 1975 Christians had grown to more than 80 million, at an average growth rate of three times that of Asia in general, but this number was still a modest presence compared to the 285 million Muslims just in that part of Asia east of Pakistan. Furthermore, depressed classes in certain parts of India were rapidly becoming Buddhist, and Islam, while not at this time actively missionary in India, had the potential backing of the new wealth of the Middle East. The development of an Islamic way of life—an Islamic basis for civil government—was the serious concern of the new Islamic state, Pakistan, during the entire 1950–1975 period. Nevertheless, neither Buddhism nor Islam possessed a mechanism of outreach remotely comparable to that which had been mounted by Christians in the West and carried to the Far East following the development of sea travel in the sixteenth century. Even so, not until the nineteenth century did the Protestant movement begin participating seriously in this effort, and it was not until the twentieth century that the major growth of Christianity took place.

Between 1950 and 1975 the vast new energy of an industrialized West eclipsed all previous influences on a relatively passive East despite the simultaneous collapse and withdrawl of the formal colonial government apparatus. By 1975 Christianity possessed literally thousands of centers of outreach, mostly new in the twentieth century, which meant that while it was still overshadowed in sheer numbers in most of Asia by the earlier advances of Buddhism and Islam, its overall presence was no longer tenuous but in fact remarkably influential.

On the other hand, its future was by no means assured. One great handicap to a continuation of Western mission efforts was the widespread assumption that the evangelism and missionary outreach of the younger churches, once firmly established, would be relatively automatic. On the contrary, churches in India, for example, showed little ability to evangelize non-Christians. As missionary leadership from the West declined, the churches moved rapidly to co-existence with Hinduism. The vast bulk of what evangelistic efforts there were was evangelism of existing now-nominal Christians. Many of the older missions interpreted the missionary task as "helping the younger churches" rather than communicating the Gospel to unbelievers. Since the main drive of both nation and Church in the post-colonial years was to get rid of foreign domination, the churches showed little ability to use their foreign servants in pioneer evangelism. Consequently huge numbers of the citizens of India, Pakistan, and latterly Bangladesh, growing larger every year, were left untouched. The burgeoning cities, rapidly filling up with immigrants from the countrysides, did not blossom with thousands of new congregations as happened in Africa and Latin America. The main churches remained tied to the cantonments, where the British had lived in the colonial period, and until the mid-1970's few new churches were established in the urban developments which proliferated all over India. On the other hand, in almost no area of India did Christians decrease in their percentage of the population; indeed, they generally increased slightly more rapidly. In the Hill Provinces of northeast India by 1975 Mizoran had become 98 percent Christian, Meghalaya 50 percent Christian, and Nagaland 80 percent Christian.

A word of caution is necessary in regard to these references to percentages of Christians in a given area of the world. For example, of what great value is it to note that the percentage of Christians in Asia was 4 percent or a little more in 1975? As with all averages, there might actually have been no specific area whatsoever where that percentage was actually true. On the one hand, at least a third of the Christians in Asia were those nominally Christian peoples in the Philippines, where practically everyone was Christian but where neither Roman Catholics nor Protestants would claim very many truly committed Christians. On the other hand, there were vast sectors of India, and perhaps virtually the whole of the People's Republic of China, where there was little Christianity, if any, in terms of known numbers of formal adherents. Meanwhile, there were specific areas of Asia where there were not only a large number of Christians, constituting a high percentage of the population, but in fact there was a great deal of fresh, young, vital Christianity. This was spectacularly true in northeast India, as we have mentioned, but was also true for many areas of Indonesia. Burma was not a Christian country, but in northern Burma the vast proportion of the population was Christian. Thailand was not a Christian country, and yet there were areas where there was a strong, virile Christian witness. Roman Catholic Christians had survived in large numbers in South Vietnam, and although the Protestant movement was small, it was healthy and had more than a quarter million adherents, exercising an influence which was considerable. In Hong Kong one out of every ten people was Christian. In Japan a very small proportion of the population, far less than Asia's average, was formally related to Christian churches as such, but more than half of all the marriages taking place in Tokyo followed the Christian pattern. In Japan well over 75 percent of the people answering a government census which asked, "Who is the greatest religious leader in history?" answered "Jesus Christ." In many respects, Korean Christians represented the strongest Christian community in Asia. Over half of all the Protestant theological students in Asia were Koreans studying in one of the many large seminaries there. While only one out of one hundred in the rural areas of South Korea was Christian, one out of ten in the cities was Christian, and one out of seven in the capital city of Seoul. One out of three of the lower-level government officials was Christian, and the proportion of Christians was even higher, close to half, in both the army and the upper echelons of government.

Thus where Christianity had taken root, it had often grown spectacularly. It had proven that it could flourish on almost any soil. But there were many places where it had not taken root at all. It had not necessarily favored any class of society but had demonstrated its ability to give substantial meaning and hope even to the lowest levels of society. In the areas of medicine, in education, and in sacrificial social amelioration, the Christian movement had worked almost without competition.

A few final comments about the meaning of Christianity within so vast a population as Asia, in view of the limitations of space, can perhaps best be focussed on the three largest ethnic-religious groups of non-Christians: the Muslims, the Hindus, and the Chinese. In 1975, by one estimate, they numbered roughly 650 million, 500 million, and 820 million respectively, or about three-fourths of all Asians. It was illuminating to see the potential relationship of the Christian faith to these three major cultural spheres as a parallel to certain new developments in the relationship between Christianity and the Jewish tradition.

In the 1960's and the 1970's there had been increasing interest in certain Christian circles in the possibility that Jews might become "Christians" without calling themselves Christian and without assimilating themselves to what is perhaps basically a Hellenic Christian tradition in the West. "Jews for Jesus" had become well known, although the phrase actually referred to a number of different attempts to reach Jewish people without tearing them out of their cultural tradition. Meanwhile many voices counselled that all evangelistic efforts be given up with regard to the Jews, a view which Gerald Anderson successfully challenged (*Missiology, An International Review*, Vol. II, No. 3). "Messianic Judaism" was the phrase used to refer to the desired result of most of the attempts new in the 1970's and late 1960's, not all of them successful. But it was probably true that the most sensitive attempts along this line avoided many of the admittedly objectional elements of evangelism as it had been practiced toward the Jews in earlier periods.

Of great significance, however, was this approach to the Muslim tradition. The acceptability of the Christian message among the Muslims was hindered by ill-will retained from the age of the Crusaders. There was also the fact that Christianity had approached the Muslims almost invariably from a Hellenic base. The apostle Paul had felt that he should be a Greek to the Greeks and a Jew to the Jews. He might just as well have suggested that he be a Muslim to the Muslims. It was not beyond reason to suppose that Muslims might become truly believers in Jesus Christ as Saviour and Lord without calling themselves Christians, even as the "Messianic Jews" did. Theoretically then what was needed was for the Muslims to become believers without having to abandon their Muslim language and culture. For the most part this was not possible in those areas where the only Christian contact the Muslims had was with enclaves of Christians who had been there for centuries and who represented differing racial, linguistic, or cultural traditions. For Muslims to have to shift from one culture to another, even to a "Christian" culture, seemed to be the kind of proselytism which the Apostle avoided and which all future missions ought assiduously to avoid.

A similar barrier existed to Christian efforts among the Chinese. The very earliest missionaries had felt that the Chinese language and culture could become a vehicle for the Christian faith without, for example, the necessity of destroying the strong cultural traditions in China involving a continuing and abiding respect for one's ancestors. Later missionaries were required by the Pope to reject this inheritance. Communism did everything possible to demolish this trait, and so did the bulk of Protestant missionaries. By 1975 there were fascinating possibilities in recent thinking being done by both Protestants and Catholics with regard to the relations of Chinese to their ancestors and the ways by which Christian truth could be made meaningful to them. Was it possible to encourage the Chinese to adhere to the meaning of the first commandment, that no one but God must be worshipped, and at the same time allow them to honor their elders as is enjoined in the fifth commandment? In early 1975 there was hope that a new era of leadership by Chou En-lai might somehow offer new opportunities for Christian witness in China. This very possibility encouraged a thorough rethinking of the approach.

One of the great practical obstacles to Christian growth in India was the fact that most Christians there—the main exception being the Syrian tradition—

came from the depressed classes, earlier called "untouchables." This fact demonstrated to India more graphically than anything else could have the phenomenal power of the Christian faith to transform and uplift. Yet it also tended to seal off the Christian movement within certain social classes. A few voices were raised in defense of a deliberate "second front" into the higher strata of the former caste system. Asked what receptivity there might be for Christianity on the part of the 500 million middle-caste peoples of India, one Indian leader suggested that at least 100 million of these people would become Christians if it were possible for them to do so without abandoning their entire social inheritance. Yet many Western Christians tended to believe that social evils, seemingly perpetuated by the traditional social structures, could be conquered only by displacing those structures. By 1975 Christian denominations and larger associations bridged many social barriers and impressively demonstrated the unity of all men in Christ; nevertheless, at the same time relatively few local congregations spanned great cultural distances. Many social groups had church traditions within them, but the majority of more than one thousand middle-caste groups, constituting at least 80 percent of the population, had as yet no branch of the Christian Church represented within their communities.

Yet Christian unity across all cultural distances, prejudice barriers, and political boundaries was an accomplished fact in Asia, and the same could be said for other regions of the world, and indeed the world itself. This uniting dimension of the Christian movement was one of its major contributions to international understanding as well as being one of the essential features of Christianity itself. As such it is a fitting subject with which to conclude this interpretive essay.

DIVERSITY AND UNITY

Curiously, during the 1950–1975 period, Christianity as a movement became strikingly more diverse and at the same time remarkably more unified. Its greatest diversity was displayed in Africa, especially in the vast profusion of African Independent Churches, which have already been mentioned. On the other hand, this same period was the era of the World Council of Churches, of new, friendlier attitudes between Catholics and Protestants following upon Vatican Council II, of a remarkable series of local, regional, and world evangelistic crusades and congresses, and finally of the emergence of the neo-pentecostal charismatic movement which by 1975 had penetrated all major Christian traditions.

The diversity was itself unique. Christianity as it expanded across the world displayed the capacity to become clothed in the language and culture of all peoples accepting it, and at the same time to bind those diverse peoples into fellowship with other Christians in other parts of the world. This characteristic was not so well known, nor so widely appreciated, prior to the 1950-to-1975 period, despite the fact that the shift from Semitic to Hellenic culture was one of the central dramas of the New Testament. For example, it was not until Vatican II in the 1960's that the Roman Catholic Mass was extensively translated into other languages, although for Protestants the translation of the Bible had long been a principal task of missions. Nevertheless, the effect of missions had generally been to uplift and enhance the local cultures in which they worked— despite the widespread stereotype to the contrary. Widely diverse types of Christianity were the inevitable result, but that diversity surprisingly did not imply isolation or disunity; rather, it contributed a new richness and renewing balance to the entire world movement.

It was true that centuries earlier as the Roman Empire and later Western Europe had become nominally Christian, wars continued between the nominally Christian peoples of that region, right down to World War II. But the reappearance in modern times of significant movements of relatively disestablished Christianity injected a new and unifying element that became quite powerful by the twentieth century. One of the most significant manifestations of the trend toward this new type of voluntary Christianity was constituted by the various student initiatives at the turn of the century: the college division of the YMCA, the Student Volunteer Movement for Foreign Missions, the various Student Christian Movements, the World's Student Christian Federation, etc. These movements almost immediately leaped ancient barriers, and the impact of this new generation of committed students upon Christian unity world-wide was permanent and incalculable. Latourette had noted that these students, soon church leaders, raised money from the Allied Nations to support German mission efforts during World War I. One of them, J.H. Oldham, made the decisive suggestion at the table of the Treaty of Versailles which prevented expropriation by the Allies of German mission properties. While this new impetus did not prevent World War II, it had by that date forged unbreakable bonds of fellowship and collaboration across warring lines in an unprecedented way (p. 1378). An outgrowth of these student movements had been the trail-blazing World Missionary Conference of 1910. An usher at that conference, William Temple, thirty-two years later (1942) was crowned Archbishop of Canterbury amidst the ruins and deep mood of depression following the Battle of Britain. His oft-quoted remarks at that ceremony (p. 1390) appropriately had as their immediate background the Tambaram (1938) meeting of the International Missionary Council, which had once again demonstrated the long-standing working unity of foreign mission agencies and overseas national church leaders participating in the highly diverse cutting edge of Christianity as it expanded in the non-Western world, a unity which was finally to be realized in the more nominally Christian European and American homeland as the World Council of Churches was formally founded in 1948.

The aftermath of all the students' high-minded aspirations through the 1950–1975 period was a complex and in some ways perplexing story. Voluntary societies, whether denominational or interdenominational, had blazed the trail in the realm of cooperation and in explorations of unity, hoping to renew the older ecclesiastical structures in the process. The resulting ecumenical movement was a gradual transition from the initiatives of para-church structures to the greater and greater prominence of duly constituted church leadership, a phenomenon parallelling in many ways the long-standing process whereby the Catholic order structures had across the centuries lent leadership to the ecclesiastical hierarchy of the Western Roman tradition. In twentieth-century Protestant experience, however, the very voluntary structures which had created the ecumenical movement lacked the centuries of experience and mutual understanding characterizing the abbot-bishop, order-diocese relationship, and gradually gave over and virtually gave up their life to the churches they loved and served. Thus the dozens of councils founded by John R. Mott (and others) around the world generally moved from being consultations between leaders of active voluntary societies to being meetings of leaders of churches—structures passive by comparison. As that happened, the International Missionary Council became increasingly based not on such voluntary societies at all, but (indirectly) on churches (through its national and regional councils) just as the World Council of Churches was (directly) based on churches. The eventual merger of the two organizations in 1961 was in many ways a logical step. The International Missionary Council thus became the Commission on World Mission and Evangelism of the World Council of Churches, the first meeting of which then took place in Mexico in 1963, the second meeting in Bangkok in 1972–1973. At the Bangkok meeting, of the 326 who gathered, 20 percent were World Council and regional council staff, 50 percent were denominational officials, 15 percent theologians, 7 percent Roman Catholic observers, and only 8 percent missionaries or mission directors.

Thus it was equally clear that in the great transition we have described a growing vacuum resulted where once the para-church structures—the voluntary societies—had long held the greater part of the initiative. Let us look at India as an example. The National Christian Council of India, in its decisive constitutional change of 1956, excluded all entities other than churches from direct representation and thus became functionally, from then on, simply a council of churches. But no adequate provision was made or envisioned for continuing consultation specifically between voluntary societies, either (*a*) those working in India from abroad, or (*b*) those springing up in India and working in India and/or abroad. (By 1975 there were at least two hundred societies of the latter category.) The resulting vacuum was filled in part by the Evangelical Fellowship of India, which allowed both churches and voluntary societies as members.

To complicate the picture, in 1974 there appeared the Federation of Evangelical Churches of India, the largest member of which, at its founding, was the St. Thomas Evangelical Church, which had in 1961 separated from the Mar Thoma Church. This new structure was for its member churches presumably a substitute for the National Christian Council. Yet, theoretically, a denomination in India could belong simultaneously to the National Christian Council, the Evangelical Fellowship and the Federation of Evangelical Churches as well as to the East Asia Christian Conference (in 1974 renamed Christian Conference of Asia), the World Council of Churches, and the World Evangelical Fellowship. In many cases a church could have regional, national, and international confessional linkage as well, for example with the World Alliance of Reformed Churches, the Lutheran World Federation, the Baptist World Alliance, etc. By contrast, a non-denominational Indian voluntary society could belong only to the Evangelical Fellowship and the World Evangelical Fellowship, and in neither case would the specific role of a society, as distinct from a church, be the dominant concern of the unifying structure. In 1974 the Asia Missions Association was proposed for establishment in 1975. Related to it, hopefully, would be various national associations of Asian-based voluntary societies in mission.

This was still only part of the picture since unity was not expressed merely by the existence of unifying councils, fellowships, and transdenominational voluntary societies (such as the YMCA, the Overseas Missionary Fellowship, the American Bible Society, etc.) Many other types of gatherings also brought Christians together. Beginning· in 1966, one society in particular, the Billy Graham Evangelistic Association, sponsored a number of "congresses" on evangelism, which drew representative leaders from a very wide spectrum of the Protestant world. Two of these, Berlin 1966 and Lausanne 1974, were world-level gatherings, the latter spawning a Continuation Committee which in 1975 organized regional committees pledged to the promotion and coordination of evangelism in all six continents.

However, despite the many avenues of unity briefly mentioned, the resulting mechanisms of consultation not only worked for unanimity in some matters but also brought to light seriously different perspectives. Structures of unity, operated by human beings, sometimes tend, against all good intentions, to be monolithic in viewpoint in given subject areas at a given time. Even some denominational structures, in the period under study, tended perceptibly to be fountains of singular emphases, not merely forums of the diverse views of their constituencies. In this respect Protestant and Orthodox communions suffered for the lack of the wide variety of decentralized initiatives represented by the Catholic orders; better said, the Protestant tradition spawned eventually a large variety of mission sodalities, to use the technical term, but Protestant attempts towards unity had not by 1975 achieved any regular, structural way for the churches and the para-church structures to work in constant, responsible reference to each other.

A second area of dispute related to the profound, ultimate question of the destiny of human diversity. In the United States by 1975, owing significantly to the emergence of the Black Power drive for ethnic self-determination, the goal of either racial or cultural integration was for many a thing of the past, and the dominant mood was to allow for and abide all kinds of diversity. This mood ran counter to all forms of imperialism or paternalism or interference, but tended logically to suggest virtual isolation instead. This was not a Christian concept of unity—which assumed interdependence, not independence—yet in an age of new-born nationalism it was difficult to turn away from the new voices pressing for disengagement. An extreme case of the new emphasis stressed mission *in* six continents in place of mission *to* six continents, since it virtually outlawed the sending of missions from one country to another unless, conceivably, the sending structure were internationalized so as at least partially to disguise the national origins of workers from foreign lands.

Yet despite the relative confusion of many clashing views, there seemed to be by 1975 an appreciably greater mutual understanding on the part of all the varied participants. Never before had so many different sectors of the world Church been so well acquainted, so well on the road to even better insights both into self-understanding and into appreciation of the true nature of a multi-cultural world family of faith.

The United Nations gathered together all of the diversity of humanity. But bitter enmities and non-speaking relationships existed in its corridors from the very beginning and without noticeable abatement across the years. Christian circles, on the other hand, gathered people from as wide a spectrum of humanity and did not have anything like the barriers to understanding between them. Furthermore, the success of the movement toward Christian unity was not based on a simple watering down of beliefs and giving up of distinctions, but was in the earliest instances, proposed and carried forward by those members of the world Christian community most committed to their own Christian beliefs, namely the missionaries.

There was a time when Christians fought each other with seeming impunity in much the same way that warring factions within the world Communist movement often found themselves in opposing political polarizations. As late as World War II, Christian nations were locked in massive conflict. Russia and the United States were allies against a country which had contributed much to the Reformation heritage dominant in the U.S. By 1975 there still seemed no hope of resolving the conflict between nominal Protestants and nominal Catholics in Northern Ireland. In the same way, some of the most profound rivals on university campuses were different factions of Communist sympathizers.

Yet, while Christians could not readily find major distinctions between nominal Christian nations and non-Christian nations, there was, nevertheless, no parallel outside of Christendom either to the degree or to the quality of cooperation between Christians. In 1975 consultation, fellowship, and collaboration went on at local, national, regional and world levels in dozens, even hundreds, of ways as Christians conferred, planned and moved earnestly together in worship, conference and united action. It could truly be said that being a Christian in 1975 guaranteed one a profoundly sincere welcome in more countries, among more peoples, in more places than would result from any other allegiance, whether religious, political, ethnic or professional.

SUMMARY

By 1975 Christianity had clearly outpaced and was continuing to outgrow all other religious movements in global size and influence. Insofar as this achievement was largely one of an established nominal membership, along with other older nominal religious movements, Christianity had little power to contribute to the larger human community, and its lukewarm witness in some cases even contributed to its own decline. Insofar as Christianity was able to be manifested in forms that allowed for its highest ideals to be enacted and expressed, it displayed an active, transforming energy which could be traced in the background or the context of a great proportion of the high-minded men and women of integrity in countless circles throughout the world of 1975.

Certainly, in view of the tragic stresses planet earth was sure to face in the days ahead, the developing world unity of the Christian movement could become not only an important aspect of the greatest religious movement in the world but conceivably an essential resource in an ever more necessary civil world community of coordinated action against the age-old problems of hunger, famine, war, and pestilence. By 1975 such goals did not seem more achievable than they had at any earlier time—in some ways less possible. Whatever might come of optimistic hopes for man, it was clearly the hope of the Christian that there might be peace on earth, good will towards all men.

Part IV

Crucial Issues

in Missions Tomorrow

Donald McGavran is well known around the world as perhaps the foremost missiologist today. He is the founder of the church-growth school of thought, starting an Institute of Church Growth in Eugene, Oregon and then becoming the founding dean (and now dean-emeritus) of the School of World Mission at Fuller Theological Seminary. Over the years he has done vast research on the growth of the church in all six continents and is the author of numerous books, among them *Bridges of God, How Churches Grow,* and *Understanding Church Growth.* He is the editor of the *Church Growth Bulletin* and writes extensively. He has always maintained that "in most questions decisions should be made on the basis of the unshakeable ground of God's revelation in the Bible and in Jesus Christ, our Lord."

Alan R. Tippett is Professor of Missionary Anthropology of the School of World Mission at Fuller Theological Seminary. He is an ordained minister of the Methodist church of Australia and spent over twenty years as a missionary in the Fiji Islands. He is perhaps the world's leading authority on animism. He has written extensively in the fields of missiology and anthropology, his most well-known title being *Solomon Island Christianity* by Lutterworth Press, which is acclaimed as a classic by leading missiologists and anthropologists alike. Other widely read books include *Church Growth and the Word of God* (Eerdmans), *Peoples of Southwest Ethiopia* (William Carey Library), *People Movements of Southern Polynesia* (Moody Press) and *Verdict Theology in Missionary Theory* (William Carey Library). He is an extremely careful researcher who brings unusual anthropological insight into all he writes.

Dr. Tippett was the founding editor of *Missiology: An International Review* and writes extensively in that magazine, *Evangelical Missions Quarterly, The American Anthropologist* and other scholarly and popular journals.

Roger Greenway, author of chapter 13, "Urbanization and Missions" was for some years a missionary in one of the huge metropolitan areas of the world--Mexico City. He has a doctorate in the field of Urban Studies from the University of Iowa. At present he is the General Secretary of the Board of Foreign Missions of the Christian Reformed church.

Edward Murphy, the author of chapter 14, "Guidelines for Urban Church Planting", was an Overseas Crusades missionary in Latin America for twelve years, serving first in Argentina, and then as the field director in Colombia. He is currently the associate executive director of Overseas Crusades, responsible for its Division of Ministries. He received his M.A. in Missiology at the School of World Mission and is working on a doctorate in the same field. At the same time he is a visiting professor at Biola College. His book, *Spiritual Gifts and the Great Commission* was published in 1974 by the William Carey Library, and articles by him appear in *Christianity Today, Evangelical Missions Quarterly,* and *Missiology: An International Review.*

11

Introducing Crucial Issues in Missions

by

DONALD McGAVRAN

THE CRUCIAL ISSUES in tomorrow's missions described in this book by the twelve authors must be seen in the light of today's terrain. Several features dominate the landscape. Consciously or unconsciously, those carrying out mission adjust to this terrain their convictions, programs and judgments of what is feasible and right. After all, it is here that God has placed them.

FIVE NOTABLE FEATURES OF TODAY'S TERRAIN

THE RETREAT OF WESTERN EMPIRES

The feature of the landscape which, perhaps, most affects missions is that, politically and militarily, *Euro*pe and Ame*rica,* which we shall conveniently call Eurica, have departed from *Af*rica, Latin Ame*rica* and *Asia,* which we shall call Africasia. Whereas in 1940 the nations of Eurica ruled most of Asia and Africa; today, with the exception of Angola and Mozambique, the nations of Africasia are entirely self-governing. While individually no Africasian nation except China has much military might, and except for Japan few have economic power, collectively they form a formidable block which some people call the Third World. In Africasia, the Western, erstwhile imperial, nations are notable by their absence. The fact is so well known that it needs no illustration. The West *has* retreated.

A COMPLEX PLURALISTIC SOCIETY

The second prominent feature of the terrain is that of many radically different religions living in friendship and equality. It is unpopular today to think in terms of one true religion and the others all false, for men tend to believe that each people has a right to its own ideas of God and its own religion. The common assumption is that all religions are what man thinks of God and, because each man has a right to his opinions, each religion is about equally true. If it is "true for you," that is all that matters. As anthropologists explore the complexities of various cultures, many conclude that all cultures are equally good and bad. Cultures are merely ways of acting which please certain men. It is, so some anthropologists teach, immoral to try to change the glorious culture of any ethnic unit. It is theirs. What right has anyone to alter it? Since the world view—or religion—is part of culture, a vast religious relativity billows out behind the science of anthropology. Such relativism is the anthropological form of scientism.

William Hocking in the early thirties taught that the era of church-planting was over and that the era of the reconception of religions, each standing in the presence of others, had begun. He held that actively aiding such reconception and zealously refraining from conversion evangelism was the form mission should take. While one may doubt whether this form is permitted to Christians, no one can doubt that a pluralistic world sees a great deal of reconception of religions going on. This feature of the landscape vitally affects missions in both theory and practice.

THE BATTLE FOR BROTHERHOOD

Christians have always believed in the brotherhood of man under the fatherhood of God. But today (when multitudinous have-not segments of world society have become politically powerful and marvelously vocal) the affluence of Eurican

Christians and their smug acceptance of it seem terribly sinful to the sensitive among them. Former imperial powers are
seized with a guilty conscience at the depth of poverty and
ignorance of their erstwhile subjects. Christians in North
America—white and black—agree that the depressed and
backward position of the blacks is a stench in the nostrils of
God; He will not tolerate it. At all costs equal opportunity,
schooling and recompense—in short, full integration—must
go forward at full speed. Nothing, they hold, must interfere
with the achievement of brotherhood now.

SECULARISM AND SCIENTISM

Secularism dominates the land we live in like snow-crowned
Ranier dominates the great port of Tacoma. More and more
people live as if there were no divine dimension to life; man
is held to be all-sufficient. If secular man thinks of God at all,
he considers Him as some vague First Cause, Totality, or the
Ground of Being. Scientism reinforces the idea that the laws
of nature rule supreme, and God neither does nor can interfere with them in any way. Hence, prayer is useless, except
maybe as self-hypnotism. A thin deism, which at best considers God as the prisoner of His creation, becomes the dominant form of Christianity. Rationalism and existentialism are
fashionable. New hermeneutics distorts the Bible to bring its
teachings into line with the new look. Life becoming one-
dimensional becomes also meaningless. Erosion of faith in the
sovereign God makes some Christians believe that all that
really counts is human action. The way of salvation taught by
the apostles, compared with "salvation" offered by the "green
revolution," seems vague and insubstantial. Jesus Christ as
"Saviour," some say, seems scarcely credible to modern man.
Faith in the immortal soul grows dim. The resurrection of
the Lord Jesus becomes merely a mythic way of saying that
when men believe on Him, it is *as if* He were present and aiding them. Some churchmen insist that mission is to "all of

'life," meaning that physical life must be improved. They precisely do not mean that mission should emphasize the immortal soul.

HITLERIAN FALLOUT

This feature of the landscape looms larger for German Christians than for others, but it affects millions all over the world. The deliberate killing of six million Jews, the snuffing out of freedom, and the fact that the orthodox churches did not furiously oppose Hitler have produced in many German Christian thinkers a tremendous guilt complex. They hold that the church—busy about its own life and wedded to its doctrines—failed to do God's will. From now on, they believe, the world will not listen to Christians when they say God is love. It will demand that they live a life of love. To those Christians in positions of leadership in the years 1930 to 1945, the twenty million or more who died in World War II, the several hundred thousand who died in Hiroshima and Nagasaki, and those who died in the following years of slaughter, all create a conviction that a different kind of Christianity must be developed to make this kind of happening impossible for evermore.

MINOR FEATURES

Minor features of the terrain, such as the following three, also influence missions: *Fear of manipulating men* has been created by the awesome power of calculated and callous persuasion using computers, chemicals, and mechanical means such as subliminal suggestion. Communist brainwashing and high-pressure sales campaigns make men do what others want done. As a result many men recoil from all persuasion. Permissiveness becomes the right style in life. *A sudden realization of the enormous extent of suffering* has flooded Eurica, brought close by television and seen against the confident assumption that no one ought to suffer. Earthquakes, starvation, the ravages of drugs, and the horror of refugee camps ought not to be. *Simultaneously nature is being controlled as never before.* Diseases are being wiped out. The power of the atom has been unlocked. During the 1971 exploration of the moon, Gulf Oil told several hundred million television viewers that atomic fusion is just around the corner. Inevitably multitudes ask, With abundant power at hand, what need of God? Why propagate speculations about ultimate questions when the really constructive thing to do is for men to manage global resources? Forget God. Stress development. Some such attitude as this is a well-known feature of the landscape.

BALEFUL EFFECT ON BIBLICAL MISSIONS

SOME DEFINITIONS

By biblical missions I mean those carried out primarily by messengers of the church sent specifically that men might repent of their sins and turn from idols to serve the true and living God. Biblical missions or missionary missions proclaim Jesus Christ as divine, and the only Saviour, and encourage men to become His disciples and responsible members of His church. Such mission is the God-given task of the church and is enjoined on all generations of Christians till Christ returns. The mandate does not change.

How mission is carried out, however, does change mightily from culture to culture and from year to year. It is effected by each phase in a denomination's history. When small and weak, the denomination carries out mission in one way; when large and powerful, in another.

To those who argue that the missionary mandate itself has in these fast-moving days been abrogated, or that it applied when Europe ruled the world, but does not in a family of free nations, I reply that I well understand what they are saying but believe they are mistaken.

At a seminary meeting some years ago, a group of enthusiastic ecumenicists were discussing the future. "As the nineteenth was the century of missionary expansion, so the twentieth and twenty-first are going to be centuries of a great uniting of the scattered fragments of the church. Missions are now over. Church union has begun." Believers in missionary missions hold such opinions to be either irresponsible or sub-Christian.

The duty of *the church* is, of course, much wider than missionary missions. It includes doing justice, loving kindness and walking humbly with God. In their spheres of influence, Christians should—and do—make every aspect of life sweeter. They are better mothers and fathers, wives and husbands, sons and daughters, neighbors and citizens. They teach better, manufacture better, and legislate better. They are redeemed souls in human bodies. They are the body of Christ in the world—salt and light, joy and peace. They are also sinners constantly confessing their sins, being forgiven, and making new starts. The church, but not the mission, touches all of life. The mission has its specific sphere of activity—the communication of the gospel. The missionary society is not the church, even as the surgeon is not the hospital. The mission plants church after church which, when established, touch every aspect of life, including both propagating the gospel and changing the culture so that it conforms more to God's will.

THE MAIN FEATURES OF THE TERRAIN ENDANGER MISSION

Dean Glasser maintains that Christians "are confronted anew with the significance with which He [Jesus] regards the task of preaching the Gospel of the Kingdom, discipling the nations, baptizing converts and teaching them what it means to bear His yoke." To biblical missions thus conceived, the main features of today's terrain present terrible dangers, which we briefly discuss one by one:

The retreat of Western empires is commonly interpreted as a retreat of Great-Commission missions. This danger has many faces. Some nationals, mistaking missions for Eurican governments, say the day of the missionary is over. He is an anacronism. Mistaking mission guidance (at no cost to Afericasian churches) for government control (entirely at the cost of the ruled colony), some nationals demand that the missionary society turn over its moneys and personnel. Missionary societies, also, mistakenly consider turning the whole country over to nationals and getting back to Eurica as the modern form of mission. They exclaim, "Let national Christians carry on whatever evangelization is proper in their countries. We are going home." The sending churches in Eurica feel that their nations are no longer empires but merely small countries among many other small countries. "It is not our task to win the world to Christ," they say. "In missions let us avoid all triumphalism. The servant church is the correct ideal." As this erroneous assessment of the situation gains ground, conversion missions appear to be a somewhat outmoded enterprise.

In pluralistic society, men easily conclude that all religions are about equally true. All are ways to God. All are "true" for their own believers. All are good adjustments to reality and are culturally right. Pluralistic societies incline to religious relativism as water runs downhill. The danger has many faces and threatens mission on many fronts.

The infallible Word of God becomes just one of many scriptures—the way in which Jews and early Christians perceived God. Jesus Christ becomes not "the only begotten Son of God" but one of many fine founders of religions—the eldest in a vast family of brothers. The inevitable result is that the basic reason for Christian missions disappears. If God is available to men in salvic power through many incarnations and religions, there is no need to reconcile men to God in Christ.

The battle for brotherhood displaces missions. Many sensitive Christians today argue—erroneously, I believe—that till brotherhood among all colors and races becomes an accomplished fact, no one will listen to the proclamation of the gospel. Since white Christians hold themselves aloof from men of other colors, proclaiming Christ is rank hypocrisy. Even the less sensitive tend to feel that justice has been so outraged, that the highest priority in Christian action must be to establish brotherhood. "The most effective missions," said a minister recently, "is vigorous action on the side of the oppressed masses of mankind. No more proclamation of Christ. The day cries aloud for our being Christlike in our relationship to other men."

Thus the discipling of the nations is pushed off the stage, while action to achieve justice and brotherhood leaps into the spotlight. Many leaders of missionary societies feel the need for brotherhood so keenly that they are prepared to use the apparatus of missionary missions—the income, goodwill, buildings, organization, salaried staff, and the missionaries themselves—not to reconcile men to *God* in the church of Jesus Christ, but to fight behind Che Guevara, battle for land distribution, and rectify the wrongs of hundreds of years. They have, in effect, hijacked the plane of missions which for a hundred years has been dedicated to bringing the nations to faith and obedience to Jesus Christ, and are taking it to Jordan to fight the battles of the refugees.

It is essential to see the distinction between the church doing such things on budgets and with organizations created for social action of this sort—which is good—and the missionary society doing them—which is bad. The missionary society was created for the specific task of discipling the nations.

Secularism quietly seduces missions. Concerning the good goals toward which Christianity has been working, secularism says in effect, "The goals are good. We seek them not because God desires them, but simply because they are advantageous." Every Christian goal—except enlisting men and women as baptized followers of Christ—is adopted and promoted by secularists. The programs are the same—the same schools, hospitals, agricultural demonstration centers, leprosy homes, and social actions—but all are done as if convictions concerning the Bible and the Lord were matters of small import. Secularism is also called humanism.

Humanism has become the real religion of vast numbers of men—Buddhists, Hindus, Muslims and Christians. The welfare of the physical body and the visible society becomes the only welfare worth striving for. The power of man to create the good world is worshiped and adored, while all supernatural religion is suspect. The miracles recorded in the Bible are "of course, simply fables."

This thinking greatly afflicts the church as she carries out biblical missions. Many Christians think it more honorable to run a hospital than an evangelistic enterprise and strongly advocate hospitals which say nothing about the Saviour and refuse to "take advantage of helpless people to make theological profit of them." They hold it more constructive to dig wells and distribute heifers than to baptize believers and multiply congregations. The growth of the church earns their particular scorn. To them the only really valid mission is humanization.

This is the danger to which Peter Beyerhaus speaks in chapter 2 and from which he guards world mission in such an effective way. The famed Frankfurt Declaration plays a significant part here.

Hitlerian fallout emasculates Christians. Christians become paralyzed by guilt, forgetting that God forgives denominations (churches) as well as individuals. Curiously, as Beyerhaus says in passing, while guilt keeps them from multiplying Africasian congregations, it does not prevent them from multiplying fertilizer factories or hydroelectric plants there.

In his gracious chapter entitled "Salvation Now," Arthur Glasser recounts the way in which Christian leaders, reflecting on the fact (?) that in "Germany those who were pre-occupied with dogmatical purity lined up with Hitler, while those who did not so believe withstood him," has led to wide-spread skepticism concerning dogmas and to a wholehearted embracing of good works interpreted as God's real mission. Since Dr. Glasser examines this danger and exposes this fallacy, I do not comment on it at length. That it widely threatens Christian leaders is evident. Within the last two years a most eminent executive secretary of a large and famous missionary society wrote an article to the effect that after the American aggression and savagery in Vietnam, it would be a hundred years before anyone in Southeast Asia would listen to the gospel! And this in spite of the fact that during the very years of the American involvement in the defense of freedom in Vietnam, hundreds of thousands of Chinese, Indonesians, Taiwanese and Koreans have been not merely listening to the gospel, but accepting Christ and becoming Christians. In those very years, for the first time in history, over a hundred thousand Southeast Asian Muslims have become Christians.

The sins of countries in which Christians are in a majority seem so heinous to some Christians that they embark on furious crusades to atone for them. Each crusade becomes *"the* mission of the church," and the propagation of the gospel is assigned a very low priority. One can understand the emotional tumult which dictates such behavior while disagreeing heartily with its theology and deploring its effect on the discipling of the multitudes perishing in a famine of the Word of God (Amos 8:11).

The combination of features increases the danger. One time Daniel Boone was exploring the wilderness which later became Kentucky. Suddenly he stumbled on a mother bear with cubs, trod on the tail of a rattlesnake, and saw a hostile redskin slipping an arrow into his bow. An even more threatening combination of dangers now confronts missionary missions. The several forbidding features of the landscape *combine* to make travel difficult. Some missions are bogged down.

Each feature of the terrain exists not in isolation but in combination, with each supporting and reinforcing the other. Religious relativism is encouraged by secularism. Withdrawing missionaries under the mistaken assumption that Western nations should retreat from gospel proclamation in Africasia is hastened by the guilty conscience caused by Hitlerian fallout. This combination makes sincere and reasonably intelligent Christians devise hermaneutics which run directly contrary to the plain meaning of Scripture. Seeking a path congenial to the religious relativism and rationalistic secularism which dominate the scene, they interpret the Bible in a way which destroys its primary purposes. It is the combination which makes missionary societies and sending churches give the bread which perishes in place of that which men eat and live forever. The combination of dangerous features of the terrain creates the *Zeitgeist*. "Hemmed in by these swamps and precipices, this desert and that river," men say, "standing still and being Christians where you are—this new way of mission is the only possible way. It is right, whether men believe in Christ or not. We live in the age of the atom. Who knows whether belief in Jesus Christ is necessary or not." Some even maintain that "in this new world a non-evangelistic form of mission is the best way of obeying Christ."

WHAT SHALL CHRISTIANS SAY TO THESE DANGERS?

The crucial issues in tomorrow's missions discussed in this book, together with many not discussed, must be seen against the whole landscape—not merely against its unfavorable features.

Christ's mission of "making known the way of salvation to all men and incorporating in His body, the church, those who are being saved" will be here long after Christians have passed this terrain and left these features behind them. But in the next three decades the threats and dangers described will probably continue. What shall we say to them?

GREATLY OVERESTIMATED

Perhaps the first thing the missiologists in this volume say concerning the dangers of the terrain is that they have been exaggerated. Popular writers, vying for the attention of the public, have outdone each other in horrific descriptions. They have created an entirely false expectation of disaster. Our missiologists do not share the pessimistic outlook which charterizes prophets of doom. We well know the problems, but have there not always been problems? The religious relativism of today does not begin to be as dangerous to the kingdom of God as was that of the first three centuries. And the power of the church is so much greater than it has ever been. Is it not a little ridiculous for the largest, wealthiest church in history—the church in six continents—which has seen few martyred for their faith, to maintain tearfully that the dangers are really very great? The United States spends twenty-one billion dollars a year for alcoholic drinks, and a billion more for cat food! Can anyone suppose that the American church which spends a third of a billion a year for overseas missions is overdoing it? Is that sum not really only a beginning? A small part of what we shall one day spend? Should not the church in six continents increase missionary sendings? And press on, proclaiming to all men that Christ is the wisdom and the power of God?

MANY FAVORABLE FEATURES OF THE TERRAIN

It would be a first-class error to determine our Christian duty while looking at the dangerous features of the terrain, for there are also dozens of encouraging and favorable features. One of these is *the enormous number of earnest Christians in the world today*. If it were not for scores of millions of these and for hundreds of thousands of faithful churches, how truly hopeless and depraved the world would be! The advanced state of Christian nations is commonly attributed to the fact that they are mechanized, educated, and advanced in science and technology. But these things in themselves neither would have been born nor would bring about great good. That in their administration Christians are playing notable roles is a large part of what decreases their harmful effects and increases their benefits.

Another favorable feature of the terrain is the *increased understanding of the mind of Christ* among Christians and increased determination to reform society in a more Christian mold. Social customs and conditions, antithetical to the teachings of our Lord, which to our Christian forebears seemed an uneradicable part of life, now are recognized as sub-Christian. Slavery, poverty, ill health, and racial prejudices which once were accepted are now being attacked left and right. True, the curse of drink—to which may be attributed not only a hundred thousand needless deaths each year in the United States, but also untold shame and suffering—is temporarily triumphant, but it too is still challenged by courageous Christians and it too will be banished from Christian nations.

A third feature of the terrain most favorable to Christian missions is the *mounting conviction that God wills the growth and multiplication of churches of Jesus Christ.* After World War II this basic Christian conviction was eclipsed for nearly two decades, but now it is moving out of the shadow into the sunlight.

A fourth favorable feature is constituted by the *tremendous turnings to Jesus Christ.* True, these are not going on in every nation, and some segments of the population in every nation have set their faces like flint against the good news, but the tide toward Jesus is so great that without fear of contradiction one can affirm that never in the history of the world have there been more people hearing about Christ and accepting

Him. Never has there been more vigorous and widespread growth of His churches.

A fifth and most favorable feature is *the rising tide of revival and renewal*. The divine fire is graciously touching the church in many places and accomplishing more in half a day than ministers and missionaries can in half a lifetime. In answer to earnest prayer for infilling, the Holy Spirit is descending on His church and empowering it to be righteous, do justice, and rejoice in the Lord. A vast dedication of life at all levels is going on in the race-and-culture-transcending household of God, giving promise of new reservoirs of power for the many tasks which God, the righteous Judge, assigns to His servants.

EVEN UNFAVORABLE FEATURES HAVE FAVORABLE ASPECTS

It would be another first-class error to fail to observe that each difficult feature of the terrain has a balancing factor which aids missionary mission. The moon dust, which sensational writers feared might be fifteen feet deep and drown whoever landed in it, turned out to be so solid that the moon jeep made tracks only half an inch deep. The dust was there, but so well packed that it made for smooth riding! Just so, each of the dangers of our day is there, but in God's hands it turns out to advantage the propagation of the gospel.

Western empires *have* retreated. The British army is no longer quartered in cantonments all over India. The officers of the Royal Bengals no longer play polo on the maidan. The Dutch army remains in Holland, not Indonesia. Africasian nations have seen China imprison British newsmen, *fedayeen* hijack and destroy planes—without Eurica firing a gun in protest. Truly an abject retreat. But, in God's mysterious providence, while the military might of Eurica has retreated, its culture and technology have never been so accepted. Country after country adopts the cultural trappings of the West—from high-rise apartments to fighter planes, from compulsory education to curled hair. Agricultural advances, sparked by fertilizers and improved seed, are so numerous that, despite the enormous growth of population, famine is years away.

A vast new receptivity toward innovations, a willingness to learn, and a readiness to experiment with new forms of government and to adopt new ideologies are apparent. Sometimes they favor Communism, sometimes Christianity, and sometimes new syncretistic religions. In India where, in British days, idolatrous popular Hinduism (the religion of 95 percent of the people) was seldom questioned and reformed Hindu sects made scant way, educated Indians are today rejecting it. The bawdy, irresponsible doings of the gods recounted in many Hindu scriptures now seem incredible to them. Fifty years ago, to become Christian was "to espouse the religion of our conquerers"; today the new generation, which has grown up in free India, has seldom seen a white man and thinks of Christianity as one of India's religions, which indeed it is. During the rule of Holland in Indonesia, it is doubtful whether a hundred thousand Muslims could have turned to the Christian faith; but twenty years after the Dutch left and becoming Christian was no longer unpatriotic, a hundred thousand Muslims were baptized. The fact of the matter is that political and military Eurica has retreated, but cultural and religious Eurica has advanced throughout the world.

Or consider pluralistic society—many religions living in friendship and equality, with its corollary that each people should practice its own religion and live in its own culture.

This does pose a very considerable danger. Careless Christians, ill-founded in their faith, can say as they skirt this swamp, "After all, why impose our faith on others? They have their religion which is good for them."

Pluralistic society, however, also presents a very great opportunity. Curiosity about Christianity pervades Africasia. Campus Crusade reports that university students welcome

opportunities to talk about Jesus Christ and many profess
the desire to receive Him. Bible correspondence courses flourish, and Christian radio is listened to with avidity. Those who
become Christians are not boycotted. Semi-Christian sects
are arising which regard the Bible as their sacred book, and
meet to worship Jesus Christ. In India, a Hindu high school
principal, Subba Rao, found out through a thrice-repeated
dream that when he prayed in the name of Jesus for sick
men to be cured, the Lord Jesus often cured them. Mr. Rao
threw out his idols and urged people to believe in Jesus
Christ. True, he warns them not to be baptized or to join
existing churches, but his Bible study groups look very like
unstructured Christian congregations.

Since the military and political retreat of Eurica, men can
become Christians without appearing to be antinational. Since
their countries so desperately need power, Christ's claim to
give them power is heard gladly. True, millions are not bat-
tering down the gates of Zion to get into the church. In most
places to become a Christian is still difficult. The individualistic pattern of becoming Christian which ages of stiff resistance
to the Christian faith has made normal, still makes "becoming
Christian" seem like action traitorous to the family and thus
holds back multitudes. Nevertheless, it can be safely said
that no era in the history of the world has ever been more
widely favorable to the multiplication of Christian churches
as this pluralistic world.

Third, consider the battle for brotherhood, its attendant
guilty conscience, and its use of resources given for missionary mission, for advancing the cause of racial equality. Massive reallocation of mission resources is no doubt a danger.
Most missions come to the edge of that precipice and some
of them may slip over it.

Yet, the battle for brotherhood is being won and it is a
good battle to win, for nothing could say more eloquently to
the pagan world of both Eurica and Africasia that Christian-

ity is highly relevant to the crying issues of each age. The battle is going well because of Christian churches. They are not doing as much as they ought, that is true, but they are doing very much more than would be done were they not there. The steady action in favor of equal treatment for all men—black and white, brown and yellow—is being fueled by the Christian consciences of ordinary church members in school administrations, supreme courts, legislative halls, publishing companies, television corporations, and neighborhoods— black and white.

As the battle is won, large numbers of missionaries from the brown and black and yellow segments of the church will launch out in gospel proclamation. The won battle is validating and will validate the good news.

Furthermore, the battle won in Eurica will encourage unnumbered millions of the depressed in Africasia to fight for brotherhood. In Japan live four million Ettas, a very depressed segment of the population. In Africa live many "slave tribes" against whom ruler tribes discriminate. In India the seventy million members of the excluded castes are pressing up into education and fresh air—and the higher they get, the more they demand real equality. Increasingly all these see that only in Christianity does their *religion* assure them that they are equal before God and man. In Latin America the masses are turning toward Communism, believing that it will "give" them equality and justice. If this does come in, it probably will not give them land and good wages. But even if it should, the deepest levels of brotherly behavior are forever beyond Communism, for it does not believe in God the Father. The masses will turn to the Master.

In short, the battle for brotherhood, in the long run, advantages the spread of the gospel and the discipling of the nations. It is perhaps less a danger than a built-in advantage.

What shall we say about secularism? And the truly terrific danger of a weak, deistic Christianity, rampant rationalism, erosion of faith in the sovereign God, abandonment of faith in the soul and the resurrection, and consequent emphasis on mere humanism? No one can underestimate the forbidding nature of this part of the terrain. And yet, Christians must not imagine themselves the only ones afflicted. Secularism erodes Christianity, it is true, but it erodes other religions far more. It is secularism which makes the Hindu elite so scornful of the elephant-headed, ten-armed, monkey-faced and long-tailed gods of the traditional pantheon.

As secularism spreads, a huge vacuum of faith develops. When faith in the Divine diminishes, life becomes meaningless and societies break down. Men turn to astrology and demon worship; spiritual hunger increases, and spiritual thirst rises. Men begin to listen to news about the bread of heaven and the water of life. The Jesus People on the West Coast of America are flourishing among the very youth who sought life in LSD, pot and speed. Vacuum of faith is camouflaged by increase in physical well-being, national affluence, and a rising gross national product, but it is there. If not filled by Christianity, it will be filled by new religions of all sorts. Indeed, it is being filled by these religions in areas where the fervor to multiply churches of Jesus Christ grows dim. Christians are called, then, to proclaim Christ and lead men to become His responsible disciples in a world where secularism is making men increasingly hungry for just this good news.

As for the Hitlerian fallout, its heyday has already passed; it is a temporary phenomenon. Those who plan mission strategy on the basis that guilty Eurica has lost the privilege of preaching the gospel are running from a dust devil which comes whirling across a plowed field but will disappear before getting to where we stand. The German pastors and ministers who filled responsible posts in the thirties and thus were, perhaps to some small degree, responsible for not opposing Hitler, are now at least seventy years old. They have carried their guilt for twenty years and have been heard, but they are soon going to meet God the most merciful, who will, I am inclined to think, assure them that their guilt was not as great as they had imagined. As the new generation of Christian leaders in Eurica reads its Bible and receives its marching orders from the Lord, it is much more likely to hear "Go, disciple the nations" than "Sit, and blame yourselves and your fathers for their sins."

Horror of manipulating persons? Yes, they must not be manipulated; but as most ministers and missionaries can testify, there is much more chance of the people manipulating the minister than of his manipulating them. The church is *not* the totalitarian state; is is not likely soon to be powerful enough to persuade and manage men. Furthermore, persuasion and counterpersuasion are life. It would be a dull world in which no one ever persuaded anyone else.

The enormous extent of suffering? Yes, the world has always been a suffering world. We hear about it today. Much suffering is caused by an ingrained love of evil—what theologians call "original sin." The best men do has an unfortunate way of turning sour. Far from disproving the need for missionary mission, the suffering of the world cries aloud for heart transplants—excising these hearts of stone and substituting for them hearts of flesh.

"The control of nature and the miracles of technology are so great that God is no longer either necessary or credible. We can do everything for ourselves, thank you." We reply, "Indeed?" The temptation of pride besets man. Even while he fears the hydrogen bomb, he spends billions to develop limitless power for atomic fusion, believing with all his heart that if only he has enough electricity, and heat in the winter, and coolness in the summer, and dollars on payday, and cars in the garage, everything will be all right. Such convictions are the very stuff out of which conversions occur—the miry clay from which God lifts man. They are the ground on which men, seeing the bankruptcy of the natural life, turn to Jesus

and take His yoke on them. To see multitudes voicing this
pride is the best possible invitation to men indwelt by the
Holy Spirit to tell them of the Saviour.

THESE CHAPTERS AND THIS TERRAIN

The following chapters are written by men intimately in
touch with today's terrain. They have grown up in the midst
of these swamps and have looked over the edge of these
precipices, so they write as moderns. But they also write as
Christians. They are picking their way among these bogs and
mountains, but their eye is fixed on the unchanging mandate
of the everlasting God. In their hand is the compass of an
infallible Bible, *and they are finding a way through*. They believe that Christian mission, which for 1,940 years has been
bringing the *ethne,* the families of mankind, to faith in Jesus
Christ, is going to continue doing just that. God wills it.

However, since they are picking their way carefully between the mountains and forests, through which God has
caused our path to lie, they talk a great deal about adjustments to present conditions. The road to world evangelization twists and turns to find solid ground and favorable
grades, to avoid the canyons and to wind its way through the
mountain passes. The twelve authors are in favor of good
works, but oppose substituting them for belief in Christ. They
are—perhaps a bit fanatically—in favor of the cultures of
men, but they believe that cultures reach their optimum development as they are transformed according to the divine
pattern revealed in the Bible.

The writers of these chapters may not refer to the features
of the terrain to which I have called attention. Yet they are
aware of them and are pointing out ways in which Christian
mission can carry out its God-given task while adjusting to
these temporary obstacles. Diversions in direction they hold
are permissible, but only if the long-range goal is steadily
pursued.

The long look characterizes the chapters of this book. We are describing aspects of Christian mission which will be here till our Lord returns. Till He comes, His church will be baptizing men in the triune name, teaching them all things He commanded, and multiplying churches of Jesus Christ. These —the most potent ingredients of a just social order—will, in turn, both multiply other churches and work that God's loving and just rule may extend more and more widely among the nations.

Drs. Beyerhaus, Glasser, Tippett and King address themselves to key theological issues which today confront Christian missions and threaten the propagation of the gospel. If anyone would understand basic, contemporary issues, he must read Arthur Glasser on "Salvation Now," Peter Beyerhaus on "The Kingdom, Humanization, and Mission," Alan Tippett on "The Holy Spirit and Responsive Populations," and Louis L. King, eminent Foreign Secretary of the Christian and Missionary Alliance, on "The New Shape." Nothing in this book is more contemporary and up-to-date than these brilliant essays.

Drs. Tippett, Mbiti and Kwast address themselves to certain anthropological opportunities and dangers which pluralistic society presents to Africasians and Euricans propagating the Christian faith across cultures. It is essential in such propagation to respect cultures, to affirm that they contain much that is good and must be preserved, and to deny that "the advance of Christianity is over the dead cultures it conquers." Equally truly, it is essential to remember that Christ is the only begotten Son of God, the Word who was in the beginning with the Father, through whom everything was made, and before whom all men and all cultures will be judged. The everlasting God has chosen to give His revelation to men in the Bible which passes from culture to culture, purging each of them repeatedly as new light breaks from it. It purges all cultures—Christian, partially Christian and non-

Christian alike. Since it purges twentieth-century Christianity in a way it did not purge seventeenth-century Christianity, it also purges twentieth-century Bantu religion and Marxist religion as their adherents come to believe on Jesus Christ.

How can Christianity purge and yet not destroy? How can a culture become Christian without being destroyed? To be specific, what parts of the Christianity practiced by those citizens of India, who have turned to Christ from an idolatrous culture, *must be transmitted* by Indian missionaries to Indonesian converts from Islam, and what parts *must be abandoned* as not of the essence of Christianity? This last question is usually asked in Eurican terms: What portions of the Christianity they knew in their homelands must Eurican missionaries transmit, and what portions must they abandon as accretions of Western culture? But to ask the question that way confuses matters because the guilt complex of Eurica so heavily colors the answers. The men writing to the anthropological issues are addressing themselves to various aspects of the puzzle just set forth.

"The Practical Issues"—Part III of this book—are also set in the forbidding terrain which is today. The mountains of the moon, which Scott and Irwin* traversed in their moon jeep, are no more dangerous to human beings than the features I have described are to Christian mission. In this particular combination of plains, mountains and bogs, if the mandate of Christ is to be carried out, specific actions have to be taken. They have theological and anthropological aspects, but primarily they are practical tasks. For example, in chapter 9, I argue that societies committed to the propagation of the gospel are essential. They must not turn from the task to which God called them; they must know they are *missionary* societies. Those who support them must be sure that the

---

* James B. Irwin is a devout Christian. He left on the moon photographs of a banner bearing the signatures of 700 people praying for him, of his church, and of its slogan, "Things Happen at Nassau Bay Baptist Church."

prayer and money they dedicate to the propagation of the gospel will go to the discipling of the nations.

The easy and fallacious argument that "quality" is a mysterious value which exists in a vacuum entirely apart from quantity is being employed these days to denigrate all evangelism. Evangelism is stigmatized as "numberolatry." Winning men to Christ is selfish; church growth is self-aggrandizement. In a scintillating essay, Ralph Winter discusses this curious but influential error, and argues for recognizing that quantities frequently measure qualities.

Presenting the gospel to great crowds, as Dr. George Peters so well points out, has been part of the Christian church's program since the beginning. Its modern form—great-campaign evangelism—is being greatly blessed of God during these decades. How to employ it more effectively is a crucial issue today. Dr. Peters helps us to see what must be done. His chapter—especially its concluding few pages—is "must reading" for all leaders of mission.

The rush to the city is transforming populations. Most men in the future are likely to constitute, not a peasantry but an urban proletariat. Therefore it is of highest importance that the church perfect forms of evangelism which will establish cells of Christians (units of God's peace and light, churches of God indwelt by the Holy Spirit) throughout the towns and cities of today and tomorrow. Dr. Roger Greenway, speaking out of years of experience as a missionary in Ceylon and Mexico City, contributes a luminous chapter on "Urban Evangelism." Not the least of its values is that it records an evangelistic campaign of several years' duration in which seminary professors and their students did multiply churches.

The Rev. Edward Murphy, Executive Secretary for Latin America of Overseas Crusades, out of twelve years' experience in city evangelism in Argentina and Colombia, writes the fine chapter entitled "Guidelines for Urban Evangelism." He argues that such evangelism must do much more than reach the cities and proclaim the gospel. It must seed the cities—inner cities and suburbs, barrios and wards, high-rise apartments and shack towns, beautiful sections and ugly sections—with congregations, assemblies of God, fellowships of disciples, call them what one will. Each of them is what Oscar Cullmann calls "an eschatological phenomenon . . . constituted by the Holy Spirit." Each—no matter how humble and how partial—is a sign that Christ has instituted the new age. The redemption of the cities depends on urban evangelism.

CONCLUSION

As readers turn to the following chapters, I hope they will share the excitement with which we view missions tomorrow. We believe, with the late Cardinal Agaganian, head of the Propaganda Fide in Rome, that the missions of the last two centuries are but a prologue to the drama about to unfold. The very fact that by and large only the primitive peoples have been discipled, means that the tremendous populations of secularists, materialists, Hindus, Muslims, Marxists, Buddhists and others have yet to turn to the Lord and be saved. The great age of missions is about to begin. Africa south of the Sahara is even now in the midst of a march to Christ so huge that by the year 2000 there will be well over 200 million Christians there—David Barrett estimates there will be 357 million. Great turnings of Asian populations are going on and will accelerate. As to Latin America, Stephen Neill says in his *History of Christian Missions,*

> In South America the growth of the Churches numerically in the last fifty years has been startling; there is no sign that their evangelistic vigor and their eagerness to witness are declining . . . it seems certain that this type of Christianity will be one of the dominating influences in Latin America as it emerges out of political confusion and economic distress into calmer and more settled existence. It is no exag-

geration to say that "Protestantism is the most powerful and transforming spiritual influence in Latin America today."[1]

Perhaps this is the feature of today's terrain which is most germane to missions tomorrow.

Note

1. Steven Neill, *History of Christian Missions* (Grand Rapids: Eerdmans, 1965), p. 567.

12

THE HOLY SPIRIT AND RESPONSIVE POPULATIONS

by
ALAN R. TIPPETT

"The Holy Spirit and Responsive Populations" looked harmless enough when the title was given to me. What subject would be more natural in a symposium of this kind? The business of Christian mission is to seek conversion responses, and certainly in the final analysis this is the work of the Holy Spirit.[1] However, on deeper reflection, the title brings together two much-debated issues in current missionary theory and theology, both with serious consequences in the existential missionary situation. I shall discuss first the *fact* of responsive populations so that we may understand the conversion phenomena to which the theology of the Holy Spirit is to be applied.

Responsive Populations

Why *populations,* one may ask, why populations and not *persons*? In this context the word *populations* directs one to the non-Western world of extended families, clans, tribes, castes and age-grades, where whole villages may represent precise ethnic entities, and where such groups may elect to turn from animism to Christianity as total units at one precise point of time. This kind of religious movement may be positive *toward* Christianity or negative *away from* it. For purposes of differentiation we may describe the former as a *people movement* and the latter as a *nativistic movement*. Spiritually they are direct opposites, but psychologically they comprise almost identical dynamics. When we speak of "responsive populations" we are thinking of large homogeneous units of people who, once they have made their decision, act in unison. Many peoples have become Christian in this manner; indeed, most parts of the world where Christianity is solidly entrenched were originally won from paganism in the first place by people movements. A decade ago the debate on the validity of this kind of conversion complex was quite heated. Today the people-movement idea is more widely accepted by evangelical missionaries and strategists because it is better understood. Many of its critics still speak of it wrongly as *mass movement*. Church-growth writers, however, have been working on people movements for years and have resolved the basic problem by means of the term *multi-individual* to describe the phenomenon. This came into use about 1962 and has been written up at length in statements which demonstrate its anthropological and theological validity.[2]

CHURCH-GROWTH AND PEOPLE MOVEMENTS

Church-growth writers have also engaged in considerable research with respect to the use of group structures in "the transition from animistic to Christian forms" in the process of church-planting.[3] Generally this has been well received by both anthropologists and nationals. Side by side with this, some new dimensions, and warnings, have been developed about the *indigenous church concept* to make it more theological and more realistic on the practical level.[4] Likewise Bavinck's idea of *possessio*[5] has been appropriated and given a little more depth[6] by tying it in with the notion of the *functional substitute*. The concept relates to the *permanence of culture change* when the social group accepts it, and speaks especially to *directed* change and therefore is significant both in anthropology and mission. The cultural ramifications of functional substitution in church-planting has been discussed by this writer on the theoretical level,[7] on the existential level with respect to data from Fiji[8] and the Solomon Islands[9] and as a principle to be allowed for in planning church-planting.[10] These ideas bear on the handling of people movements and have been well received by Christian nationals who have known this type of experience. The development of this concept permits the preservation of many cultural features in the church being planted—thus a more indigenous church emerges from the beginning because it allows for the congregation acting as a multi-individual group. At the same time it is a safeguard against syncretism—a long-standing criticism against some group movements. The people-movement idea is thus culturally acceptable and Christian mission can be undertaken with a minimum of cultural disruption and a maximum of indigenity.

The character of missionary role has changed, but there must be a *continuing* missionary role. Now that the era of the old mission-station approach[11] has virtually given way to a new era of partnership with, or fraternal-worker service in, indigenous churches, there is no other feasible option before the Christian mission in communal and tribal societies, but that which is commonly called "the church-growth approach." The church-growth viewpoint is anthropologically based, indigenously focused and biblically orientated. It is certainly not, as some superficial critics have maintained, mere statistical "denominational extension," although the church-planting may be denominationally serviced.

THE THEOLOGY OF PESSIMISM AND PEOPLE MOVEMENT

The missionary strategists who nonchalantly reject church growth as an adequate approach to mission are usually conditioned by a *theology of pessimism*. This may be universalist or liberal or even conservative and still be pessimistic. This pessimism may spring from any one of three causes:

1. The wartime experiences of Christianity driven underground in Europe and the philosophical adjustments demanded by existence in the oppressive situation.

2. The current frustration and despair because of the encroaching secularity, the scientific agnosticism, the selfish individualism and permissiveness, the multi-individual rejection of the establishment, including institutional religion, and the frequently articulated idea that the church is fighting for its survival.

3. The experience of nongrowth in the resistant mission fields, where after a century or more of our foreign missioning, there has been created only a small, foreign church, worshiping in English, French or German instead of the vernacular, with our own foreign denominational structure, content to remain dependent on foreign funds and leadership, and who (if they have produced any leaders of their own) will be so foreignized as to be seen as foreigners by their fellow countrymen.

Many of the vocal theologians of today, and likewise many makers of mission policy, are victims of one or more of these factors, so that we do not wonder at the cloud of gloom and pessimism over everything*; and the futile attempts at reevaluating missionary philosophy to meet these conditions. The error here lies in the assumption that the *whole* world

---

* The manner in which missionary policy can be influenced by the background of home officials came home to me some years ago when I was researching an African situation where a rapid conversion intake was suddenly stopped. Eventually I discovered that a missionary from India, who had been in a location where he had seen extremely small and slow growth, upon retirement was given a portfolio with authority over this African tribal situation. He had demanded that, as missionary staff did not permit further intake, the men on the field *consolidate* the existing gains, and let the accessions not begin again until the personnel was adequate to handle the movement. It never did get started again. Thus, a responsive movement had been sealed off, and a community which might have been won whole was left half Christian and half pagan.

is resistant: that there are no ripe fields waiting for harvest anywhere. This error is tragic.

It is tragic because it accepts a wrong criterion. The idea of mission (i.e., bringing peoples to discipleship in terms of accepting the name of Father, Son and Holy Spirit) is not determined by the physical and social conditions that cast the gloom about us, but by the word of the Lord. He said that all power was now given Him, that His followers were to make disciples of all nations, and that He would be with them to the end of the world. If you accept that word, the implication is that mission in these terms goes on to the end. The idea that "the world sets the agenda" is true only in one sense. There is another sense in which it is false. That the needs of the world should or should not claim our attention is not argued; what is argued is that the Great Commission has not been withdrawn.

It is tragic because it is a wrong evaluation of the world situation. This view presupposes there are no responsive populations and no doors wide open. It overlooks hundreds of communities in Africa, in Latin America, in Indonesia and New Guinea, and bypasses what has really been happening in these postwar years. Dr. Winter, a provocative church-growth historian, realist and yet an optimist, pointed out in *The Twenty-Five Unbelievable Years: 1945-1969*:

> The church in Korea grew more in the years 1953-60 than it had in the previous sixty years. The church in Sub-Sahara Africa more than tripled from thirty to ninety-seven million. In Indonesia at least fifty thousand Moslems became Christians. . . . The South India Conference of the Methodist Church in the face of persecution grew from 95,000 to 190,000 members. The Presbyterian Church in Taiwan between 1955 and 1965 engaged in a "Double the Church Campaign" concluded it successfully. In Latin America, largely due to ceaseless and effective personal evangelism on the part of the Pentecostal family of Churches, Protes-

tants grew from about 1,900,000 in 1945 to at least 19,-
000,000 in 1970. In Brazil alone, by 1970, new congregations of the evangelical variety were being founded at the
rate of three thousand per year.[12]

The battle is by no means lost. If the church has her back to
the wall in some places it is certainly not so in others—even
if it means that the responsibility of the church is being taken
away from the West.

*It is tragic because a theology of pessimism can never
handle these responsive population opportunities.* The great
majority of these people movements have beeen husbanded
by Christians with a simple, biblical faith of a conservative
type and spirit of optimism. Another factor which frequently
comes to notice in church-growth case studies is the way missionaries explain nongrowth as due to their "being in resistant
fields" and being quite convinced that this is so; while comparative analysis reveals that the Pentecostals or some neo-
pagan religious movement is going ahead by leaps and
bounds. We find the growth may be Baptist here, Methodist
there, Presbyterian over yonder, but I have never found
growth in a church or society clouded with a theology of
pessimism. There have always been a vibrant missionary
drive, a clear goal and a simple clear-cut faith.

Those pagan movements which are bounding forward in
our day are frequently using the techniques of evangelical
Christianity, and they indicate that people are open for religious change and probably looking for it. For a century or
more Christians have been striving to win the American Indians. Some are Christian, usually where they got caught up
in revivals or people movements. Now, before our eyes, 45
percent of the Navahos are reported to be involved in the Peyote Cult. It may be that missionaries have used the wrong
methods. It may be that few have learned the Navaho language. It may that they have offered a foreign church. It
may be that the white man's poor relations with the Indians

through history was too great an obstacle. But we can never say Indians are now resistant to religious change. No one who has investigated the spread of peyote among them can say that. We are surrounded by winnable peoples in locations we call resistant.

It is tragic because it is satisfied with something less than the best. As long as we are in the world as Christians, being there and finding God's presence there, merely "witnessing" by our presence, or "being faithful" and engaging in dialogue with men of other faiths—the theology of pessimism leaves it there. To strive to bring the pagan to a decision for Christ, what church-growth theory calls *verdict theology,* is to create a *dialogical crisis,* and this is frowned on. This attitude of "if you cannot bring men to decision, then come to terms with them and co-exist" is certainly not scriptural. It eliminates the existential cross of the disciple of Christ from his ministry in the world. We turn to a missionary theologian who came from people-movement experiences in New Guinea, whose opinion was that:

> Today we have a Christianity that shies away from suf-
> fering, which still goes on dreaming of a Christianized world,
> appeals to the rights of man and the freedom of conscience
> and wants to put them into operation; all this in order to
> escape suffering and to make that suffering impossible in-
> stead of recognizing her call to suffer. Suffering does not fit
> into the Church's need for security nor into the modern
> philosophy of men.[13]

Vicedom's book throughout is one which realistically faces up to the confrontations of the Christian with the world, and sees the mission of the church in the world and "the congregation as the point of breakthrough for the Holy Ghost in the world" with a responsibility to lead men in the world to commitment.[14] In a smaller book he described down-to-earth events which showed converts being formed into congregations by people-movement patterns.[15] Here is the Holy Spirit at work on a responsive population, and here is a book which fits in with the church-growth case studies. His *Mission of God* reacts against the theology of pessimism because the defeatism of the latter has no way of dealing with people-movement responses and therefore ignores them.

To recapitulate to this point, I have claimed that the fields open for mission are not as resistant as often imagined, that the people who await the gospel should be seen as large groups—tribes, peoples, populations—that they may be expected to turn Christian as social groups, that from these multi-individual people movements we may expect indigenous churches—formally cultural, rather than denominational extension. I have also pointed out the current theology of pessimism that controls much missionary policy-making, and I find it a wrong criterion, a wrong evaluation of the world situation, unable to handle the responsive situations, and less than scripturally prescribed in that it avoids responsibility to which we have been called. Against all this the Bible calls us to a theology of encounter and does not promise any escape from a way of the cross. Nevertheless, we are encouraged to go forward with expectation and optimism, knowing that ultimately victory will be with the Lord. It is important that we *recognize the existence of responsive populations.* Anthropology has taught us much about how to handle them, but this is not enough, we have to bring ourselves into tune with the Spirit of God and put ourselves under His direction.

THE HOLY SPIRIT

The other dimension of our title is the Holy Spirit. Some Evangelicals still relate cross-cultural missions to their own Western conversion requirements. They cannot see a people movement as "under God." I have known some Western missionaries to refuse to harvest a field "ripe unto harvest," and even in one case to hold off people at gunpoint when they came as a tribe to burn their fetishes and thus demonstrate their change of heart. These missionaries wanted them to come one by one, against their tribal cohesion. Church-growth literature has not bypassed this problem; it is one of the most recurring themes. The multi-individual conversion pattern has been examined on a basis of its New Testament precedents and prototypes, and usually Evangelicals who take the trouble to follow through the relevant passages are soon convinced that multi-individual people movements are quite biblical.

In my earlier writing I have been mostly concerned with simply demonstrating that many types of people movement are found in Scripture, and that these may therefore be presumed to have been "under God." But one can go further. These movements, which followed social structure, were under the specific direction of the Holy Spirit and the biblical writers have said so. It was only when I began following them as a theme through the book of Acts that this recurring feature struck me. I had studied the Holy Spirit as a doctrine. I had been instructed in His role in conversion, in the life of faith, in the church and its ministry and so on. When I thought of the Holy Spirit I tended to recall certain specific passages of Scripture, but the Spirit as a recurring feature of the episodes of church expansion was a belated realization. I had read about this in Roland Allen but it had not registered until I discovered it for myself:

> Missionary work as an expression of the Holy Spirit has received such slight and casual attention that it might almost escape the notice of a hasty reader . . . it is in the revelation of the Holy Spirit as a missionary Spirit that the Acts stands alone in the New Testament. The nature of the Spirit as missionary can indeed be observed in the teaching of the gospels and the epistles; but there it is hinted rather than asserted. In Acts it is the one prominent feature. . . . Directly and indirectly it is made all-important. To treat it as secondary destroys the whole character and purpose of the book.[16].

In this essay I am concentrating on a single aspect of the work of the Holy Spirit, namely *His relationship with responsive populations, with the winning of human communities to Christ.*

The mission to the world to which our Lord called His followers was built on *the prototype of His own mission to the world.*[17] This is clearly stated in John 17. His coming to this world, as the nativity stories in Luke show, was charged with the power of the Spirit (Lk 1:35; Mt 1:18, 20). Even those persons associated with the nativity complex received the Spirit—Elizabeth, Zacharias, Simeon (Lk 1:41, 67; 2:25-26). The Spirit was at the Lord's baptism (Mt 3:16; Jn 1:33), His temptation (Lk 4:1) and with Him throughout His ministry (Ac 10:38). Jesus Himself lived in the power of the Spirit and accomplished His mission to the world in that power. It was in the same power that He commissioned the apostles both before (Mt 10:20; Jn 17:18) and after the resurrection (Mt 28:19), promising them the resources of the Spirit, a promise He had made on other occasions for other purposes also (Jn 15:26; 16:13). Not only are we sent *as He was sent* into the world, but we are to teach what He taught (Mt 28:20) and love as He loved (Jn 15:12, 13:15). The Spirit was clearly with Jesus during His lifetime (Mt 3:16; Mk 1:10; Lk 3:22; 4:1; 10:21; Jn 1:32; 3:34; Ac 1:2), and in this power He achieved His mission on earth (Mt 12:28; Lk 4:14-15, 18 ff.; Jn 3:34, etc.). Furthermore, He took His stand on a basis of prophecy related to the Gentile world mission (Mt 12:18 ff. and Lk 4:18; cf. Is 42:1-4; 61:1-2).

So Jesus taught His followers to interpret His own mission to the world as a prototype for, and a prelude to, their own. Quoting the Scriptures, He claimed the Spirit (Lk 4:18), and the gospel writers who reported what they remembered of Him certainly declared that the Spirit was with Him. *Thus for their mission to be built on the prototype He had pro-*

vided, there had to be an event something like Pentecost. The mission of the apostles presupposes the *availability* of the Spirit as a source of power. An intellectual or social Christian "mission" without the power of the Holy Spirit is invalid because an essential ingredient is missing. When Jesus gave His own model for mission it implied the power and activity of the Spirit.

There is one other thing to be noted about this prototype of our Lord—one other implication besides the availability of the Spirit: He also implied the *importance of the social group.* If we are to relate the Holy Spirit to responsive groups, as distinct from individuals, we must pause here for a moment. We have emphasized Jesus' dealings with individuals and, of course, He was deeply concerned with individuals. But our Western individualism has closed our eyes to the fact that individuals belong in groups. Jesus was moved by the individual without *a group,* the individual *isolated from his group,* and the joy and salvation of the healing of a leper or a demoniac was not merely a matter of physical restoration but that *now he belongs.*[18] He could go back to the group from which he had been alienated and tell them what the Lord had done to him (Mk 5:19). This is the point of the three parables in Luke 15: the isolated one now belongs again; the lost sheep is no longer lost; the lost son is home again. Jesus' concepts are *collectives*—folds and flocks (Jn 10:16). Even when He deals with individuals He has the total group in mind. The episode with the woman of Samaria is a good example of this: Beyond the woman, Jesus saw the group to which she belonged. He sent her back into the village (Jn 4:16), knowing she would talk (vv. 27-30). He saw Sychar as a field ripe unto harvest—a responsive population (v. 35)—and He was quite right, for many of the Samaritans of that city believed on Him (vv. 34-43). When He preached the gospel to the poor and deliverance to the captives, though this may have been directed to an individual at times, I believe He was speaking here of collective man—the communities that He desires to restore. Jesus concentrated His ministry on groups like the publicans and sinners, village groups, occupational groups (Lk 15:2; Mk 2:16; Jn 1:24, etc.), He sent His disciples to households and villages (Lk 8:1; 10:5, 8-9, etc.) and the Great Commission is in terms of ethnic units within ecumenicity.

Therefore, from among the features of Jesus' model for mission I have selected two only for this article: (1) the presupposition of the availability and the activity of the Holy Spirit as the source of power, and (2) the implication that the human group is a thing to be preserved, that the isolated individual needs to be restored to the place where he belongs, and that groups are winnable. Thus the two elements of the subject assigned to me for this article are both found to have been clearly articulated in the mission of our Lord Himself. As He Himself determined what the apostle's model for mission was to be, this surely ought to be valid for us today. Pessimistic theology has to be rated against this model.

NEW TESTAMENT CHURCH-PLANTING

Our Lord gave us to understand that the Holy Spirit would be operative within the Christian mission (Mk 13:10-11). We also have the word that He operates to the end, together with both the witnessing church and convert (Rev 22:17). The whole sweep of church history lies between these points.

Pentecost itself, the historic happening when the Spirit was manifestly given to the waiting apostles, was followed by their first missionary proclamation (Ac 2). The proclamation was in terms of trinitarian action. The audience was reminded of the promise of the Spirit (v. 33) which was not, in reality, offered to a wider audience than the apostolic band (v. 38). This is verdict theology—repentance and response. Three thousand souls is a people-movement figure (v. 41). These converts were baptized together and immediately consolidated into a physical fellowship, as Jesus bound together the disciples. Thereafter in their travels they left behind little social groups as Jesus Himself had left in Sychar. Thus the churches or fellowships, with doctrine, fellowship, breaking of bread and prayers, began to grow organically from the very start (v. 42). They went from house to house and praised God (vv. 46-47), and their numbers grew day by day. Although this was a strong people movement that went on day after day, it was not a mass movement, for the biblical recorder speaks of *"every soul"* (v. 43).

In the following chapter the lame individual was cured, but the incident was used by Peter as a subject for a sermon to the total group. This sermon to the people (men of Israel) involved an encounter with a select group (4:1), and imprisonment. Asked by their judges to give an account of themselves, they spoke of the Holy Spirit (v. 8). Peter spoke at length and they were released with warning. Subsequent preaching and healing and fellowship led to another outpouring of the Holy Spirit (4:31). The movement had grown so much that by Acts 6 it was out of hand and murmurings arose. The church was already bicultural. Under the leadership of the twelve, the community was called together and the multi-individual group operated as decision-maker. The ideas put forward by the leaders were ratified by the populace (vv. 3-5), new roles were created, and men were appointed—further organic growth. The three criteria for this position were "honest report, full of the Holy Ghost and wisdom." One of the appointees was a proselyte. They were ordained by the laying on of hands. As a result of this organic growth under the Spirit of God, a number of priests joined the community. This phase of the people movement was terminated, as far as the written record shows, with the death of Stephen, whose message was rejected in spite of the fact that he was full of the Holy Spirit (7:55). He had pointed out plainly to his audience that they were resisting the Holy Spirit (v. 51).

This episode is a bridge to the story of Paul after a series of rural incidents. Word came to Jerusalem of interest in Samaria. We might call it a *mood of inquiry,* or a readiness to listen to the gospel (8:14), and so John and Peter were sent there. As yet there was no spiritual movement, no outpouring of the Spirit (v. 16); but after prayer directed to this end (v. 15), they of Samaria also shared the experience (v. 17). This gift of the Spirit was so manifest that a local magician wanted to buy it, as animist magicians trade their secrets to this day. Thus the early church was alerted to a danger and given a useful piece of instruction. The preaching extended through the villages (v. 25).

We are now introduced to Philip who was directed to Gaza to meet the Ethiopian and lead him to Christ, under the guidance of the Spirit (vv. 29-38). Subsequently the Spirit led him away to Azotus and the cities of Caesarea (v. 40), leaving the convert to take the gospel to the nation where he had great authority (v. 27). Also from the Petrine narrative we have the people movements at Lydda and Saron where whole villages ("all that dwelt at") turned collectively to the Lord. Peter was itinerating. There were already Christians at Lydda and he visited them for pastoral encouragement. These movements were sparked off by a healing miracle (9:32-35), as also happened at Joppa (vv. 36-43). In the following chapter Peter was with Cornelius at Caesarea, whither he had been called. Cornelius had "called together his kinsmen and near friends" (10:24) and they were many (v. 27). Peter witnessed (vv. 39-41), that is, he shared his experience, and the Holy Spirit fell on those who heard (v. 44). This extended-family conversion in the Gentile community surprised those "of the circumcision," but the converts were baptized because they had received the Holy Spirit (vv. 44-48).

All this demonstrates that Jesus led the apostles to expect expansion from Jerusalem, to Judea, to Samaria, to the uttermost parts of the earth when they had received the Holy Spirit (1:8). One of the reasons for this diffusion is found in chapter 11. Persecuted converts scattered to Phoenicia, Cyprus and Antioch and preached to the Jews of the dispersion. However, at Antioch some of those who had come from Cyprus and Cyrene preached to Grecians, and "a great number" believed (11:19-21). Barnabas, who was sent from Jerusalem to investigate it, rejoiced at the expansion of the Christian community, exhorted them to faithfulness, and went to Tarsus for Saul, whom he brought along in order to help him with instruction for a whole year (vv. 22-26). He knew of Saul's conversion and of his powerful testimony among the Jews at Damascus (9:22).

The Pauline missionary experiences are similar to those already summarized. The Holy Spirit was always active, some movements were quite extensive, and groups of converts were formed into congregations. From this point as the gospel spread in the Graeco-Roman world we meet house-churches (Ro 16:11; Phile 1). Lydia was baptized together with her household (Ac 16:15), as was the Roman centurion in the same city (v. 33). Paul preached to the household and obtained a group response (vv. 30-34). The word *all* appears three times in these verses, with respect to his preaching to all, and all believing and all being baptized. It is a good picture of the total multi-individual group. In chapter 18 there is the house of Crispus, the chief ruler of the synagogue, all of whom believed and were baptized (v. 8). The household was the social unit, the small group which made its own decisions at the level of personal religion as distinct from national loyalty.

In Acts 19 is recorded the disturbance which Demetrius the silversmith caused. The previous episode reveals why the craftsmen were so alarmed. Verses 17-20 record a strong movement away from the magical arts to Christianity in Ephesus. It must have been a large and significant movement (because of the implications of the passage). The magical books and paraphernalia were worth 50,000 pieces of silver, and they were destroyed by burning, as animists burn their fetishes upon conversion as an ocular demonstration of their change of faith: belief, confession, demonstration—the regular pattern.[19] A people movement among the magicians brought a counterdemonstration among the craftsmen whose trade was in jeopardy; it was a movement on the basis of occupation. People movements in occupational classes or castes may reach a great size, as for example, Xavier's movement among the fishermen in India.

To Paul's experiences at Antioch, Philippi and Ephesus we could add those at other places. Each place had its own uniqueness. In Asia Minor he began in the synagogues and presented a study arising out of the history of Israel as a stepping-stone to Christ (Ac 13:14 ff.). Sometimes he had Jews, proselytes and Gentiles who responded (vv. 42-43), but organized opposition from the more envious Jews made these would-be converts less stable. In Iconium also, Jews and Greeks both believed (14:1). Paul now identified the troublemakers as "unbelieving Jews" (v. 2), but before departing from the district he ordained elders in the churches he had planted, so the organic church grew (vv. 22-23).

At Rome it was quite different. This Christian community emerged by migration growth. Merchants, soldiers, craftsmen and others moved into the capital along the network of Roman roads. Many of them met in Rome in private homes and secret places; they were even found in the household of Caesar. From Romans 16 it is apparent that Paul knew many of them before they had gone to Rome. Their names are often Greek or Roman—craftsmen, kinsmen, fellow prisoners. Eventually he reached the capital himself and, although a prisoner, he lived for two whole years in his own house, receiving all who came, preaching the kingdom, teaching of the Lord Jesus (Ac 28:30-31). A similar ending is used in his letter to Rome, in which the preaching of Jesus Christ was made manifest to all nations (16:25-27). Where better than at Rome! From the Scriptures he wrote to Rome, "I will confess to thee among the Gentiles, and sing unto thy name . . . the God of hope fill you with all joy and peace in believing, that ye may abound in hope, through the power of the Holy Ghost" (15:9, 13).

To sum up this biblical unit, two things stand out clearly: (1) the activity of the Holy Spirit in the New Testament church-planting, and (2) the operation and approval of the Spirit in the conversion of social groups. The control of the Christian mission by the Spirit may be seen in His initiation of mission (Ac 1:2; 13:2, 4) and His deployment of it (16:6-7). As the blessing and power of the Spirit were promised the mother of our Lord when the incarnation was announced for His earthly mission (Lk 1:35), so the same blessing and power of the Spirit were manifested in the mission of the apostles (Heb 2:3-4). The New Testament church was planted by the apostles, through group-movement patterns, by the power and under the direction of the Holy Spirit. The church grew from a recurring spiritual experience that brought conversion responses to multi-individual communities upon their receiving of the Spirit. Where they did not respond, this was said to be "resisting the Spirit."

THE SPIRIT IN THE GROWTH PROCESS

Essential to the possibility of the idea of Christian mission is the existential reality of a discrete fellowship group. We call this the church, though it has other biblical names—the flock, the body, the fellowship, the household, the temple, the priesthood, all of them corporate groups into which converts are to be incorporated (1 Jn 1:3).[20] The Bible does not bind us to any single structural form for the church (either cultural or denominational), but it does commit us to a group of some kind. Our Lord formed the apostles into a group in His lifetime with the precise intention of leaving it behind in the world after His departure: a fellowship of those sharing the kingdom experience, says Bowman, the remnant called out by the Messiah.[21] He promised them the Holy Spirit, using another term, the Paraclete, who would dwell within them, and whom the world could not know (Jn 14:16-18). He would remain with them after the bodily departure of our Lord (16:7). He would be their Teacher as Christ had been (14:26), and both the Paraclete and the disciples would bear witness to Christ in the world thereafter (15:26-27). This small body of material in John's gospel, where this word is used, is addressed to the disciples collectively. Jesus sees them as a group whom He sends back into the world to represent Him there. The burden of this gospel is *witness to Christ* (20:31): witness for a verdict of acceptance. Yet, it recognized the possibility of rejection (1:11). Acceptance (i.e., believing) means power to become sons of God (1:12) and gives one a place in the fellowship group and assurance of the presence of the Comforter, which means a peace that the world cannot give (chap. 14).

John 14 takes us far beyond the other religions, for it shows Christ as the only way to the Father (v. 6). It is thoroughly trinitarian and therefore will allow no dialogue which eliminates the uniqueness of the Son and seeks a compromise on the basis of God and Spirit. It shows the Christian's spiritual separation from the world no matter how much his ministry may be in it. The world cannot receive the Paraclete (v. 17) or mediate His peace (v. 27).

Jesus brought the disciples together and made them a fellowship that they might stand together and support each other. In a good deal of the New Testament teaching that calls for Christian maturity and growth in grace, the collective form, as the idea of "perfecting the saints," is used.

Ephesians 4:11-12 shows both the perfecting and organic growth expected of the church. If we look forward we find the church as a body fitly joined together, with every part working effectually so that the body edifies itself in love (v. 16). If we look back we find we are instructed to keep the unity of the Spirit in the bond of peace, for there is one body and one Spirit (vv. 3-4). Here is diversity in unity. Here is the multi-individual group. This is possible only in the presence and power of the Spirit.

The moral living and virtues that are expected of converted Christians, either of individuals or groups, are also possible only in the presence and power of the Spirit. This is the Spirit who witnesses with our spirit that we are sons of God by adoption and heirs of Christ (Gal 4:5-7; Ro 8:8-17). Through the Spirit the Christian man has his spiritual gifts (1 Co 12:13; Ro 5:1-5). His Christian graces are sometimes described as the fruit of the Spirit (Gal 5:22-23; Eph 5:9). Thus it is the Holy Spirit which enables the church to be the church ministering the life and love of Christ to the world, in New Testament times and today.

One of the features of the New Testament church which may be traced to the work of the Spirit, quite apart from the service ministry and the mutual edification within the fellowship, was the vital experience of *power, joy* and *faith,* which Hunter calls *the concomitants of the Spirit's presence.*[22] You will find men described as "full of faith and of the Holy Spirit" (Ac 6:5, NASB; 11:24, etc.), and these terms, with *joy* and *power,* cluster together in the record. These concomitants of the Spirit give a zest and thrust to the group. When the Holy Spirit falls on a group, that group becomes transformed. It is this new dynamic that gives the group outreach and makes it witness, and leads to what Roland Allen called "spontaneous expansion." In my case studies of the planting and growth of the church in the south-central Pacific, and in the archival documents on which I have worked for years, I have invariably found this to be true of the great people movements to Christianity.[23] The narrative vibrates with power, joy and faith, in spite of the persecution and military pressure from enemy groups.

Another concomitant of the Spirit's presence which I have found in the island records is the assurance of the ultimate triumph in glory with God. This was a radiant and exciting experience and was certainly associated with the work of the Spirit. The apostle Paul spoke of the earnest of the Spirit, the Spirit being, as it were, a pledge and a promise of more to come, a foretaste of glory for Christians to enjoy here on earth (2 Co 1:22; 5:5; Eph 1:13-14). This also for the island converts was a matter "to be told abroad" and shared. They communicated it with power by dialogue, by dancing, by chanting and proclamation. It was part of the excitement of the people movements. As Green points out, the power of the Holy Spirit was for the New Testament church a "guarantee of the coming Kingdom," and "eschatology and mission were irrevocably united in the person of the Spirit."[24]

The church in the New Testament was not supported and controlled from some overseas board or other foreign-sending body. True, a missionary program went out from Antioch, but the churches stood on their own feet from the beginning, and were indeed themselves missionary churches. Without organized training programs and seminaries, how did the early preacher get his message? Without our printed resources, Bible and commentaries, how did he know what to proclaim? The message was certainly preached with power. Jesus had led them to expect that the special role of the Spirit would be to teach them all truth (Jn 14:26) and to testify of Christ (15:26), and they were to bear witness of what they had learned from being with Him (v. 27). Paul (1 Co 2:13; 1 Th 1:5), Peter (1 Pe 1:12; 2 Pe 1:18-21) and John (1

Jn 5:6) all speak of the role of the Holy Spirit in revealing the message of truth and life.

To sum up the role of the Holy Spirit in the growing process of the church, we have seen first that there must be a physical entity we call the church, a discrete group. This has been preserved and nourished by the Spirit since the departure of Jesus to the Father. From the Spirit the fellowship group has a peace the world cannot give and an experience the world cannot share. The operational pattern of the group is to have members mutually supporting each other, building each other up in virtue and service. United and diverse, they are a multi-individual group. All this is possible only in the power of the Spirit, from whom we have also the gifts of the Spirit and the fruit of the Spirit, which enable us to operate as the body of Christ in the world. Other concomitants of the Spirit are power, joy and faith, which frequently occur together and are features of the church in times of spontaneous expansion, a fact borne out also in history. These are often accompanied by a strong eschatology with assurance. Eschatology and mission unite in the person of the Spirit. The message which is preached with power is that revealed and verified by the Spirit. These are the features of a church growing at the qualitative level of what McGavran calls *perfecting* in church-growth theory.[25]

RESPONSIVE POPULATIONS TODAY

Not all populations are responsive. Fields *come* ripe unto harvest. The harvest time has to be recognized, and harvesters have to be sent in at the correct season. A discussion of how fields ripen is another subject, but what happens to a crop which is not harvested when it is ripe goes without saying. In this essay I have argued that many ripe fields exist, some of which are large and promise an abundant harvest. Responsive populations should mean many people movements and great numerical church growth. Identifiable groups are waiting to be won for Christ. When the group responds, a congregation has to be created, preferably with the same structure as the group itself. Those responsible, as the stewards of the ingathering, need common sense, humility, anthropological understanding, and a strong personal faith to be good stewards; but, above all, they need obedient submission to the Holy Spirit, without whose power and blessing there could be no mission at all.

Also related to our subject, but worthy of separate treatment of its own, is the subject of the thousands of new churches (denominations) emerging all over Africa. A large body of literature is growing, and this discloses the wide range of religious ferment in Africa.[26] Some of these movements seem to be quite heretical, others quite conservative as far as their Christianity goes, others are boldly experimental. All are intensely enthusiastic. Neither is this religious ferment limited to movements that are Christian or syncretistically Christian. Some relate to the other faiths and some are quite new-pagan. Neither is this confined to Africa. In Japan there are Soka Gakkai and many other movements, the statistical rise of which may be set off against an inverse fall in Christian baptismal intake figures of the traditional churches, dating from about 1957. The greatest Christian growth is among groups little known in the West, such as the Spirit of Jesus Church. What I am saying as I draw this chapter to a close is that great multitudes which no man can number are currently either modifying their religious position or changing their religious affiliation. Viewing the matter on a world scale, there probably never has been such a period in history when such a large percentage of the world's peoples have been so open for religious change. Far from being a secular age, it is intensely religious, even in our Western cities. This dynamic situation calls for reevaluation of missionary techniques, and a deployment of men and resources so that missionary thrust is directed where the populations are most likely to be responsive. But having said that, the thrust must carry religious conviction, it must meet both the physical and spiritual needs of man in society, it must have power, joy, peace and vitality, it must not make individual converts into religious and social isolates, but bind them together into a fellowship community. All this can only be done under the direction of the Holy Spirit. As Starkey has said, "The most striking purpose of the Spirit's advent . . . is to be found in his gift of community."[27] I see no hope for the way of individualism in our modern world. The individual must feel he belongs. The interacting, multi-individual aspect of the community must be brought to maturity. Nearly all the basic problems of human society spring from carrying the interests of the individual too far so that they deny the rights of the neighboring individual. Individuals belong in context and the context requires balance— loving one's neighbor as oneself. All this has a superb backing from the anthropology of communal society, but this is theory. The theory has to come to root in real-life situations. The world needs not merely a world understanding, but understanding in all the cohesive subunits that make up the various levels of human society. For us in mission this means the local churches at grass-roots level, the fellowship groups which are the body of Christ, ministering His mind, and service, and love and mission in their neighborhood. In the last analysis, it is here that the church grows or does not grow. You can take a Christian fellowship group and study it anthropologically as an institution, and see "how it ticks," but if you carry your research to the ultimate conclusion you will have to admit that there is still one element which registers in your data but cannot be explained in human or processual terms. I call this the *noncultural factor*. It is, of course, the Holy Spirit. He is at work. Anthropologically I know how the church ticks, but another factor has to be introduced before the ticking is regulated as it should be. Given the current mood for religious change, and considering the missionary program in such a responsive population, I see no better way of handling the situation than by planting Christian fellowship groups that fit the local social structure and encouraging the people to pray for the gift of the Holy Spirit. If such a group is both indigenous in character and filled with the Spirit, and the religious mood of the location is innovative, we may expect a spontaneous expansion of the church. This is the regular pattern of people movements, and God has most certainly blessed it.

Notes

1. For the place of the Holy Spirit in church-growth theory and theology, see Donald McGavran, "Authentic Spiritual Fire," *How Churches Grow* (London: World Dominion, 1959), pp. 55 ff.; and Alan R. Tippett, "The Non-cultural Factor," *Church Growth and the Word of God* (Grand Rapids: Eerdmans, 1970), pp. 42 ff.
2. See Tippett, *People Movements in Southern Polynesia* (Chicago: Moody, 1971), pp. 251-61, 338; and "Religious Group Conversion in Non-Western Society" (Research in Progress Paper No. 11, School of World Mission, Pasadena, 1967); McGavran, *Understanding Church Growth* (Grand Rapids: Eerdmans, 1969), pp. 296-315.
3. For example, see Tippett, *Solomon Islands Christianity* (London: Lutterworth, 1967), pp. 269-85.
4. Tippett, *Verdict Theology in Missionary Theory* (Lincoln: Lincoln Christian College, 1969), pp. 126-41; and McGavran, *Understanding Church Growth,* pp. 335-53.
5. Johan H. Bavinck, *An Introduction to the Science of Mission* (Philadelphia: Presbyterian & Reformed, 1964), pp. 179-90.
6. Tippett, *Verdict Theology . . .,* pp. 105-6.
7. Tippett, "Initiation Rites and Functional Substitutes," *Practical Anthropology* 10, no. 2 (March 1963).
8. Tippett, "The Integrating Gospel" (Bound ms. School of World Mission, Pasadena, 1958).
9. Tippett, *Solomon Islands Christianity.*
10. Tippett, *Peoples of Southwest Ethiopia* (South Pasadena, Calif.: William Carey Library, 1970).
11. McGavran, *Bridges of God* (New York: Friendship, 1955), chap. 5; Malcom R. Bradshaw, *Church Growth Through Evangelism-in-Depth* (South Pasadena, Calif.: William Carey Library, 1969), p. 27.
12. R. D. Winter, *The Twenty-Five Unbelievable Years: 1945-1969* (South Pasadena, Calif.: William Carey Library, 1970), p. 67.
13. G. F. Vicedom, *The Mission of God* (St. Louis: Concordia, 1965), p. 139.
14. Ibid., p. 93.
15. Vicedom, *Church and People in New Guinea* (London: Lutterworth, 1962).
16. Roland Allen, "Pentecost and the World" in *The Ministry of the Spirit,* ed. David M. Paton (Grand Rapids: Eerdmans, 1962), p. 21.
17. This theme is the subject of Tippett's "His Mission and Ours," a bound manuscript at the School of World Mission in Pasadena, Calif., 1960.

18. For the church-growth theology of belonging, see Tippett, "The Convert and His Context" and "Belonging and the Process of Incorporating" in *Church Growth and the Word of God.*
19. Tippett, "Religious Group Conversion. . . ."
20. Tippett, *Church Growth and the Word of God,* pp. 58-61.
21. John W. Bowman, *The Intention of Jesus* (Philadelphia: Westminster, 1943).
22. Archibald M. Hunter, *Paul and His Predecessors* (Philadelphia: Westminster, 1961), pp. 92-93.
23. Tippett, *The Christian: Fiji—1835-67* (Auckland, N.Z.: Inst. Printing & Pub. Soc., 1954).
24. Michael Green, *Evangelism in the Early Church* (Grand Rapids: Eerdmans, 1970), p. 273.
25. McGavran, *Bridges of God,* pp. 13-15.
26. See Bengt Sundkler, *Bantu Prophets in South Africa* (New York: Oxford U., 1961); Harold W. Turner, *African Independent Church* (London: Oxford, 1967); G. C. Oosthuizen, *Post-Christianity in Africa* (Grand Rapids: Eerdmans, 1968); and D. B. Barrett, *Schism and Renewal in Africa* (New York: Oxford U., 1968).
27. L. M. Starkey, Jr., *The Holy Spirit at Work in the Church* (Nashville: Abingdon, 1965), p. 23.

13

URBANIZATION AND MISSIONS

by
ROGER S. GREENWAY

"THE WORLD UPSURGE in urban populations is one of the most outstanding revolutions of the modern epoch."[1] As demographers, sociologists and economists everywhere are turning their attention to this phenomenon of urbanization, men concerned with missions must ask themselves what this means for the spread of the gospel. Missionary strategists cannot afford to ignore this worldwide movement to the cities.

Urbanization is one of the most important aspects of worldwide social change today. Changes are occurring with such unprecedented speed and with such far-reaching consequences that a constant reappraisal of missionary strategy is required. If the gears of missions are not shifted to keep up with social change, God-given opportunities for discipling the nations will be lost. This is unquestionably true with respect to the migration of the masses to the city. At the beginning of the twentieth century only about 13 percent of the world's population lived in the cities and 87 percent in rural areas. But by the end of the century the situation will be completely reversed. By then 87 percent of all people will reside in urban areas. Obviously the rural-orientated missionary patterns of past decades will be largely obsolete in the years ahead.

Table 1 World's Urban Population Compared to World's Total Population, 1800—1950 (Population figures given in millions.)						
		Cities of 5,000 and over		Cities of 20,000 and over		Cities of 100,000 and over	
Year	World Popula- tion	City Popula- tion	Percent of World Population	City Popula- tion	Percent of World Population	City Popula- tion	Percent of World Population
1800	906	27.2	3.0	21.7	2.4	15.6	1.7
1850	1,171	74.9	6.4	50.4	4.3	27.5	2.3
1900	1,608	218.7	13.6	147.9	9.2	88.6	5.5
1950	2,400	716.7	29.8	502.2	20.9	313.7	13.1

Source. United Nations, Economic and Social Council, Economic Commission for Latin America, Preliminary Study of the Demographic Situation in Latin America, E/CN. 12/604 (New York: United Nations, April 23, 1961), p. 31

THE WORLDWIDE PICTURE

ASIA

"The sheer rapidity of urban growth," says Paul Abrecht, "is one of the most astonishing and awesome aspects of the whole social change in Asia, Africa, and Latin America. It is both the cause and the effect of that change, and a measure of its depth."[2]

Asia's "teeming millions" are today, in increasing numbers, *urban* millions. Think for a moment of the great urban centers located in the Asian-Pacific area:

Karachi .... 3 million
Calcutta .... 5 million
Bangkok .... 2½ million
Saigon .... 1½ million
Puson .... 1½ million
Seoul .... 4 million
Tokyo .... 11 million
Osaka .... 3 million
Yokohama .... 2 million
Nagoya .... 2 million
Manila Gr. .... 3 million
Singapore .... 2 million
Sidney .... 2½ million
Djakarta .... 3 million

Metropolitan Tokyo is greater than half the population of Canada, and the first ten cities of India equal half the population of Britain. Our century began with only eleven cities with a population of over one million, but today there are more cities than that in Asia alone, which claim populations of more than a million.

A glance at any newspaper will tell you that the decisions which make the headlines regarding Asia and the Far East are made in their cities. The centers of political power, education, and mass media invariably are located in the cities. Christian leaders need to take these facts into account as they consider what strategy they should follow in world missions during the last third of this century. The decisive battles for the souls of men will be fought not in the jungles, or the mountains, but in the teeming cities.

AFRICA

The worldwide trend toward an urban culture, writes John Dilworth, is sweeping over the vast continent of Africa. "The city has become the focal point attracting hundreds of thousands of young people into its orbit, and its neon lights and technological wonders fascinate whole populations, even where the majority still live in the villages. The number of city dwellers [in Africa] increases literally daily."[3] Christian missions, however, tend to concentrate their efforts on the traditional rural population which has been thought to be more receptive to Christianity. There is something irrational about this, for the educational activities of Christian missions have been one of the major factors in the orientation of young people toward city life. Young people in Africa were first introduced to urban ways in the Christian schools, but when they reached the city they were left "high and dry" as far as the church is concerned. Missionaries have been slow to realize the challenge of African cities. This area of the world is a prime example of the rural orientation of Christian mission work.

Writing about urbanization in West Africa, Kenneth Little states that

> in the last twenty years the population of Nigeria has increased at an estimated rate of 1.5 per cent annually and with the control of epidemic diseases and improvement in maternity and child welfare, this trend should continue. However, so far as urbanization is concerned, the census figures leave no doubt that migration is the principal factor. Thus, no less than 58 per cent of the population of Lagos consisted in 1950 of people born elsewhere, while from figures provided in the Ghana census (1960) it may be estimated that only 25 per cent of the population of the city of Takoradi, about 40 per cent of the population of Sekondi, some 37 per cent of the population of Kumasi, and some 47 per cent of the population of Accra are of local origin. In 1948, over one-half the population of Takoradi and 36 per cent in the case of Accra had lived in those towns for less than five years. While in Ghana, as a whole, more than two-thirds of the urban inhabitants have been in the towns concerned for less than five years.[4]

Of significance for Christian evangelism is Little's comment that rural-urban migration creates a far-reaching network of social and other ties between the town and the hinterland. When people move from the farm to the city it does not necessarily mean a permanent separation between them and their kinfolk who have stayed behind. On the contrary, there is a constant coming and going of visiting relatives, traders, seasonal workers, and others, and this keeps the lines of communication open between the urban migrants and their rural kin. This means that new ideas and practices, including new religious beliefs acquired by the newcomers to the city, are transmitted to the countryside. In Africa, as everywhere else, towns and cities set the pace for society as a whole, and ideas and movements which have their base in the urban center quickly diffuse themselves over a much wider area.

LATIN AMERICA

Missionary leaders involved in Latin America should take careful note of what has been happening in that part of the world. "Latin America," writes Benjamin Higgins, "is more urbanized than the world as a whole. The proportion of the urban population was 39 per cent in 1950 and 46 per cent in 1960. During the 1950's the absolute increase in Latin America's urban population seems to have been about double the increase in the rural population."[5] In another recent study, the *Centro Lationamericano de Demagrafia* (CELADE) estimated that 51 percent of the population of Latin America is presently found in the urban areas, and that for 1975 an estimated 56.5 percent will be urban.

Another remarkable feature of the urban picture in Latin America is the fact that the urban population is often concentrated in one or two large cities, and the next towns in size are usually very much smaller. The large towns and cities, moreover, are growing faster than the small ones, with the result that the urban population structure in Latin America is "top-heavy" and tending to become more so every year. Most Latin countries are right now in the most dynamic and critical stage of the urbanization process. In one lifetime we are witnessing a colossal shift of population which will transform Latin America from a primarily rural to a primarily urban continent. What this means for Christian missions deserves most careful consideration.

OVERCOMING FRUSTRATION

By and large, Christian churches are not multiplying in the great cities of Asia, Africa and Latin America as they should be, or could be. Despite the volumes of literature being produced on the subject of urban ministry in the United

States of America, relatively little of it is useful as far as planting churches in non-Western cities is concerned. Studies are needed on how to evangelize urbanites so *that living churches eventuate and proliferate.* The literature on urban evangelism eminating from North America shows such over-riding concern with urban social problems that it is not helpful in church-planting evangelism in Africasia. The impression is given that urban ministries everywhere can and should change urban structures. Social problems exist, to be sure, and American Christians—who are numerous and powerful in American cities—must face them squarely with all the resources at their disposal. But as we consider the Christian mission in the great urban centers of the Third World,—where evangelical Christians are very few—we should see that the task is first of all kerygmatic. Modern Ninevahs need to hear and obey the gospel, but first there must be some Christians!

An effective urban thrust, however, will require a large degree of openness and flexibility on the part of the evangelizing agency. The emerging urban expression of the church may startle some people. It may do away with some time-worn practices such as large, expensive buildings, somber organs and robed choirs. The emphasis may fall upon the neighborhood fellowship, informal Bible study, folk music and complete lack of clericalism. Jarring as some of the changes may be, they may more closely resemble the churches of Asia Minor in apostolic times than the sophisticated organizations we commonly call churches today. The crying need is for greater openness and sensitivity on the part of Third World churches as they seek to meet urban newcomers with their very pressing needs.

It is lamentable that precisely in this area the historic churches are especially weak. In his study of the African situation, John Dilworth reports that when new migrants "encountered loneliness and other difficulties in the city, they found little comfort in the orthodox Churches and turned for help to one or other of the Healing or 'spiritual' Churches. Here they find a more intimate sense of community, attention and special prayer and ceremonies are devoted to their individual problems!"[6] Dilworth is referring, of course, to the indigenous, Pentecostal-type of churches which account for the majority of urban Christian groups throughout the world. The Pentecostal forms of worship—with drumming, dancing and handclapping in Africa, and with guitars, wind instruments, and loud "Gloria al Señor" in Latin America—offer more release and relaxation to the troubled urban migrant than do the imported forms of worship of traditional denominations. Frustrated in their efforts to really reach the masses, many orthodox churches have settled for some form of social service through their established institutions and have left the multiplication of urban churches to the Pentecostals. The secretary for Latin America of one of the oldest and largest denominations said recently in Mexico City that except for the program which will be described later in this chapter, he did not know of a single church-planting enterprise being carried on by traditional denominations in Latin American cities. "Most churches," he said, "have written off the urban masses to the Pentecostals."

Credit should be given where credit is due, and in this case it goes to the Pentecostals who have indeed proven to be more responsive to the needs of new urbanites than have their older sister churches. The Pentecostalists have moved out among the receptive displaced masses with their simple message of the Christ who both saves and heals. They accept the slum dwellers where they are, with all their problems and frustrations, and provide them with a circle of religious fellowship where people count as individuals. Amid the whirlpool of urban life, the new urban immigrant discovers in the local Pentecostal church the face-to-face contact and sense of belonging which he can find nowhere else in the cold unfriendly city. The Pentecostal emphasis upon group prayer and divine healing touches some of his greatest personal needs. The unsophisticated sermons are rich in verbal symbols which convey the gospel to the unlettered far better than the high-toned rhetoric of the educated pulpit. Despite all their advantages, the traditional churches have not yet come close to matching the Pentecostals in their penetration of the urban masses.

The task of reaching the great cities for Christ need not, and should not, be left to the Pentecostals alone. "The clear implication," writes William L. Wonderley, "is that the church today has a responsibility, as never before in its history, to meet these culturally 'displaced persons' in their place of need and help them in their hour of transition to discover those values which alone can enable them to keep a sense of human dignity and to weather the storm of cultural change."[7] To do this, however, the traditional churches will have to move out of their middle-class shells and find out what the people on the fringes of urban society are really like. They will have to walk through the mud and the filth of their streets, climb their stairways, and sit in their homes. Amid the stench and the flies and the wailing children, they will learn what the needs and anxieties of these people are, and they will sense how the gospel can be made the most relevant thing in the world for their lives.

These things cannot be learned at a distance. Direct personal encounter with the realities of urban slums is required. Churches and missions with enough passion for souls to leap the cultural gap will discover a sea of humanity, weary and heavy laden, whom the Lord would have us call to His rest. If what God is doing in the world at large means anything to the church today, it should be clear that the phenomenon of urbanization is the work of God in preparing great multitudes of people for evangelization and the planting of tens of thousands of new churches.

MEXICO CITY EXPERIMENT

In January, 1968, an experiment began in the Mexico City area with teams of students from the *Seminario Juan Calvino* and, later, from the *Instituto Cristiano Mexicano*. Both schools are related to traditional Reformed and Presbyterian denominations, so we may consider this an experiment not only in urban evangelistic methodology but also in the adaptability of historic churches to the challenge of cellular multiplication in a Third World urban situation.[8] Mexico City is representative of the many great cities of the Third World that have experienced rapid urbanization in the last few decades. The 1970 census shows a total of over eight million in the metropolitan area, with an annual growth of over half a million. The sprawling slum communities which surround the city give ample testimony to both the rate of urbanization and the incapability of the present city to absorb such an influx of rural-urban migrants.[9] As we began our urban evangelistic efforts, natural instinct caused us to avoid the slums. We tended toward the paved streets and the better neighborhoods. It was not until later, after we had discovered the amazingly high degree of receptivity in the *colonias* (colonies) of the newer migrants, that we began to direct our major efforts in their direction.

The theory which we set out to test was this: that the simple method of house-to-house visiting by trained and highly motivated young people would be the key to establishing neighborhood churches which would form meaningful fellowships of Christian witness and service.[10] Our method would consist of intensive visiting in selected areas of the city where, as far as we knew, no Protestant church was established. We would sell Bibles and New Testaments from house to house, give a verbal testimony to the gospel wherever we could, and we would seek out families that would allow us to begin Bible classes in their homes. We hoped that in this way we would be able to establish *iglesias hogareñas* (churches which meet in houses) in each neighborhood.[11]

Before going on to tell about the results of this experiment in Mexico City, something should be said about the missionary ideology which lay at the heart of our effort. This ideology, quite frankly, has shaped every stage of our urban program. Both the goals and the methods have been determined by it. We have taught it to our students and we have continually used it to test each phase of the program. Simply stated, it is this: that the organized local church is the God-ordained institution for the corporate worship, witness, and fellowship of Christians. The church is as important to Christians and to Christianity today as it obviously was to Paul in the first century. In order to make a Christian impact on society as a whole, you first of all need born-again Christian people who are obedient to the Word of God. They in turn should be organized into churches, not just big, central churches serving people from all parts of the city, but local, neighborhood churches where parents and children together can meet with their neighbors for instruction, fellowship and worship.[12] With this ideology behind us, we set out to experiment in church-planting in the sprawling megapolis that is Mexico City.

"Nothing succeeds like success," they say, and it would be easy to write only about the areas of the city where we have been successful in planting healthy growing churches. But to limit our report would be misleading. Our churches-in-houses approach has been hounded by the inavailability of houses with adequate space. Our teams have spent days and weeks in neighborhoods where we seemed to get nowhere. We have managed to organize some promising groups only to see them evaporate before our eyes. Sometimes we have come home so tired and discouraged that we wondered if we were following the right procedure at all. The truth is that we have failed in almost as many places as we have succeeded.[13] Certain neighborhoods proved to be virtually in-penetrable; others showed only moderate receptivity. Some left us thinking that only a divine visitation could break down their resistance to the gospel.

In this connection, we want to single out the great apart-ment complexes as an area which to us posed almost insur-mountable difficulties. In many of the apartment buildings tenancy regulations forbid the holding of religious services, which makes occupants reluctant to allow any kind of gather-ing, especially if there will be singing that can be heard in the next apartment. Visiting is not easy either, for there are guards at the entrances and "peep holes" in the doors. More-over, the desire for anonymity seems to make many apart-ment-house residents particularly resistant to any personal contact. We have visited every home in four of Mexico City's largest apartment complexes, and we managed to hold meet-ings for some weeks in two of them. But in neither case were we able to organize a permanent congregation.

Great apartment buildings, now a worldwide phenomenon, are characteristic marks of urbanization. In Mexico City our strategy has largely failed to reach either the wealthier homes or the apartment dwellers, so it is our feeling that these two segments of society require a very specialized approach. With the erection of every new *condominio* and apartment com-plex, the need for such a strategy grows more urgent.

Success in church-planting came for us in Mexico City in the neighborhoods composed of ground-level, upper-lower and lower-middle-class homes. Considering the time and ef-fort involved, these are the areas which show the greatest re-sults. In the Colonia Pedregal Carrasco, for example, after only three weeks of Sunday morning house-to-house visiting, we had Bible classes started in three different homes.[14] That was in March, 1969. The first formal service was conducted on April 17, and within six months the group had built a humble chapel on a piece of land provided by one of the members, was contributing regularly toward the erection of a larger chapel, and was taking on the characteristics of a responsible, self-perpetuating church.

In varying degrees but with basic similarities, we have experienced results like these in a dozen different parts of Mexico City. This has led us to believe that the densely populated fringe *colonias* are the most receptive to the gospel. A large percentage of these people, though not all of them, to be sure, are new immigrants to the city. In the newfound freedom and independence of the urban environment they can decide for themselves whether they wish to continue to follow the traditional religion or whether they will give the new way at least a hearing. In these neighborhoods the man or the lady of the house comes to the door when the evangelist knocks. You meet the whole family in their home situation.[15] Face-to-face contact with both parents and children soon establishes the visitor as one who is known and is trusted, and as one who is interested in the family and its needs. House-to-house visiting, concern for the family as a unit, clear testimony to the gospel, Bible instruction in the home: that has been our formula, and *it has worked*.

CASE HISTORY OF A NEW CITY CHURCH

On Sunday afternoon, March 13, 1968, five students sat huddled around a map of Mexico City in our living room. It was decided to make our next target the Colonia A. Lopez Mateos, a heavily populated area of the city just east of the airport. It was originally settled by squatters, but through the patronage of the wife of the late president of Mexico, after whom the *colonia* was later named, the squatters had been given some assurance that they could retain the land.[16] A government school was under construction. After prayer and a hymn we loaded the station wagon with Bibles and tracts and headed for the *colonia*. We covered every home in the area, working in teams of two. My nine-year-old daughter was my companion. To relieve the shock of a towering *gringo* appearing at the door, I have found that taking along a son or daughter is quite effective. The sight of the child and father together removes the suspicion and hostility toward foreigners which one naturally can expect to find. The only wrinkle on this particular afternoon was a troublesome drunk who followed us for several hours.

My notebook shows the following entry for that day:

> Door-to-door visiting in the Col. A. Lopez Mateos. Excellent response. Three homes invited us to hold services. We will begin in the home of a "sometime" Presbyterian woman next Wednesday night.

The reference to the "sometime" Presbyterian points up an important factor to be found not only in this *colonia* but in almost all our new city churches. Roughly two-thirds of the members were Christians before we contacted them. Half of these were members of Protestant churches either in some other part of the city or in their village before moving to the city. The other half is composed of persons converted through some form of mass evangelism (Bible distribution, radio, correspondence courses, tracts) but who had never joined a church. The final third is made up of new Christians won to the Lord through the personal work of the students and the services they conduct in the homes. However, we prefer to hold services, not in the homes of these very new people, for that can be risky, but rather in the home of a family that already has made some form of Christian commitment.

An interesting sidelight on the beginning of the work in the Col. A. Lopez Mateos is the fact that when we began we knew just one person living there. He was a retired Presbyterian pastor. We had hoped that he might open his home for services and for this reason we visited him first. However, while on the one hand he greeted us warmly, he rebuffed our suggestion of evangelizing the *colonia* and beginning services.

"It can't be done," he told us. "These people are too hard; they will never accept the gospel." As we went down the street, selling Bibles to his very own neighbors, the elderly pastor stood in his doorway watching us. He was a classic example of "limited expectations."

For four months we held services on Wednesday nights in the home of the Presbyterian woman. She was very poor, having been abandoned by her husband, and neither she nor her young son had been to church for several years. We equipped their two-room house with four benches for the services, and they were always dusted and in order when we arrived. Before the service began each Wednesday night we generally spent an hour visiting in the neighborhood. In addition, student teams continued to work the area on Sundays, inviting people to the Wednesday night services. My notebook shows that at one time, in the month of May, when the attendance had dropped sharply the previous week, we revisited the entire *colonia* with a team of ten students, searching for new families. It was on that particular occasion that two new families were contacted who eventually became the leading families in the church.

Records show that the attendance wavered between fifteen and twenty during the first few months. The entry in my notebook for April 24 states: "Growth continues but the rains are now hindering attendance. The unpaved streets are all mud." All mud they were indeed. On several occasions my station wagon was buried in mud down to the axles and the students had to literally lift the vehicle out of the ruts. During this period we began the services rather late in the evening because the men in the area had to take two or three different buses in order to get home from work. They arrived home late, and therefore, in order to get the men as well as the wives and children, we began the services late and continued until 9:30 or even later. We usually showed a Bible filmstrip at the close of the service and that kept the children both awake and quiet until the end.

The main part of the services consisted in learning and singing new hymns and choruses, Bible teaching and preaching, and prayers for the sick and for those with special problems. No rigid order of worship was followed, though quite naturally a certain routine was gradually fixed. Opportunity was always given for questions to be asked, and if anyone had something special to say, he was free to stand up and address the group. Offerings were taken right from the start, and it was always explained that we would keep this money on behalf of the group until they themselves could erect a chapel building. Records of the weekly offerings and attendance were carefully maintained in both the mission and the school office.

A faithful nucleus began to appear by the month of May, and by the middle of June we felt that it was time to turn this young church over to a Mexican pastor. On June 26, we introduced Mr. and Mrs. Santos Galan to the group and explained that while we would still visit them from time to time, Mr. Galan would now be in charge of the affairs of the congregation. From that day on Mr. Galan, who is employed by the World Home Bible League in Mexico City, became the volunteer pastor-evangelist of the church. At about the same time the services were changed to Sunday and the members began looking for larger facilities.

By the beginning of 1969, the Colonia A. Lopez Mateos Church was renting a large room for their services. In the month of May a "steering committee" was elected from among the members. Mr. Galan prepared a large sketch of the church building they hoped to erect and this was hung on the wall near the entrance for everyone to see. While, on the one hand, the strength of the congregation was evidenced by the large proportion of complete families and men in attendance, there were also some internal problems involving members who had formerly been Pentecostals. Severe attacks were made by the Jehovah's Witnesses, who hoped to take away some of the new Christians. The Seventh Day Adventists also tried to get something started but were largely unsuccessful. Two adult members, however, did leave the church and joined the Pentecostals.

Baptisms of whole families together has been the general rule. Upon occasion, baptism has been immediately preceded by a marriage ceremony since some couples had not been legally married before. The men are almost all employed in factories or in construction, or work in small businesses. The women are all housewives, though one operates a small store in the front part of her house. The biggest gap is in the teen-age group. But since nearly all the members are parents with small children, this problem will probably disappear in a few years.

Sunday school is now held at 11:00 each Sunday, followed at 12:00 by a worship service. Almost all the members attend both. The average attendance stands between seventy and eighty, and some remodeling had to be done recently to facilitate the increasing attendance. Thursday night services continue to be held for the main purpose of attracting new families who normally would not interrupt their Sunday outings or visits to relatives by coming to church.

Two major steps have been taken very recently. First, the Colonia A. Lopez Mateos Church has obtained a loan of $3,-200.00 from our board of missions to buy the property which they are now renting and begin the construction of a church building. Second, they themselves have begun a mission in an adjoining *colonia*. It so happened that a family of the church moved to this new area and, finding no evangelical church there, immediately invited Mr. Galan to begin services in their home. There is every reason to believe that before long this very young church will have a daughter in the Colonia Arenal, and both Mr. Galan and a team of our students are working hard toward that end.

If the Colonia A. Lopez Mateos in Mexico City can be considered a kind of urban laboratory, and our evangelistic efforts there can be regarded as a laboratory test of planned action resulting in church-planting, then we may have something here that is significant not only for Mexico but for urban centers throughout Afericasia. It has been shown how urban masses can be effectively evangelized in their own neighborhoods and how new churches can be established among them. What is more, it has been demonstrated that Christians from traditional denominations, if they are willing to adapt, can do the job.

Here lies an important point. As Henry D. Jones has pointed out, this is not the task of the missionary alone. *It is primarily the task of the church in each nation.*[17] Churches and seminaries throughout Asia, Africa and Latin America need to be aroused to confront an urbanized people with the claims of Christ in a meaningful way. The rapidity of worldwide urbanization demands a reorientation of missionary strategy in which church workers, both foreign and national, catch the vision and share the responsibility.

Notes

1. United Nations Economic and Social Council, *Preliminary Study of the Demographic Situation in Latin America* E/CN. 12/604, (Apr. 23, 1961), p. 30.
2. Paul Abrecht, *The Churches and Rapid Social Change* (New York: Doubleday, 1961), p. 149.
3. John Dilworth, "The Growing City," *African Ecclesiastical Review* 10, no. 4, (Oct. 1968), p. 321.
4. Kenneth Little, *West African Urbanization: A Study of Voluntary Associations in Social Change* (London: Cambridge U., 1965), pp. 19-20.
5. Benjamin Higgins, "The City and Economic Development" in *The Urban Explosion in Latin America,* ed. Glenn H. Beyer (Ithaca, N. Y.: Cornell U., 1967), p. 118.
6. Dilworth, p. 328.
7. William L. Wonderly, "Urbanization: The Challenge of Latin America in Transition," *Practical Anthropology* 7, no. 5 (Sept.—Oct., 1960).
8. The Seminario Juan Calvino and the Instituto Cristiano Mexicano are related to the Board of Foreign Missions of the Christian Reformed Church and the Iglesia Presbiteriana Independiente of Mexico.
9. It has been observed that the slums of Mexico City are not, in fact, as wretched as those of Caracas, Lima, or Sao Paulo. For vivid accounts of the life of the urban masses, see Oscar Lewis' books, *Five Families*

(New York, Basic Books, 1959) and *Children of Sanchez* (New York: Random House, 1961). The setting of these books is in Mexico City, but they apply throughout Latin America and into other continents as well.

10. For a most stimulating booklet on the use of students in evangelism, see A. Clark Scanlon's *Church Growth Through Theological Education,* published in Guatemala in 1962.

11. By "churches" we mean congregations of baptized believers who meet regularly in a given place for worship, and who both corporately and individually seek to proclaim the full message of the gospel to their community. This, we believe, is the New Testament understanding of the local church.

12. This preference for neighborhood churches as over against central churches whose membership is drawn from many different parts of the city presupposes the social and economic situation of most city dwellers outside the more advanced countries such as the United States of America. In areas of the world where comparatively few people have cars and where bus travel is difficult and uncertain, the need for neighborhood churches close at hand is all the more important.

13. "Failed" here is used relatively. The fact must not be forgotten that even in the areas where we were unable to establish a church, many people were brought into contact with the gospel and eventually may become members of a Christian church.

14. See *Church Growth Bulletin* 6, no. 3 (Jan. 1970), for a fuller description of this project.

15. The main problem, as I see it, with the so-called "Industrial Evangelism" approach is that it generally fails to involve the whole family as a unit in Christian worship and fellowship. When asked: "What about the wives and children?" a well-known advocate of industrial evangelism in Great Britain is quoted as saying: "We leave them to the churches." Very well. Churches are what we aim to establish. We want the whole families, both fathers, mothers, and children, for both practical and theological reasons.

16. The development of this *colonias* appears to have followed to the letter what Richard M. Morse calls the "Spanish municipal tradition." Commenting on the historical parallels between the growth of modern urban slums and early Spanish traditions, Morse says: "It is not far-fetched to say that the Spanish municipal tradition is vigorously perpetuated in today's squatter invasions, which may recapitulate all the ingredients of a town-founding by a conquistador's band: careful staging and role allocation; solicitation of patronage from a powerful political figure; legitimation of the claim by planting of lags and strategic publicity; meticulous distribution of building lots; common resistance to low-echelon police; discrimination against later settlers; formation of a committee of *vecinos;* mutual-aid arrangements; a gridiron layout with provision for plaza and common facilities; erection of community chapel, school and council house; priority for legalization of land titles; efforts to create a channel for claims and grievances to the highest political authority, even the president or his wife" (Richard M. Morse, "Recent Research on Latin American Urbanization: A Selective Survey with commentary," *Latin American Research Review* 1, no. 1 (Fall, 1965), p. 61.

17. Quoted by W. Stanley Rycroft and Myrtle M. Clemmer, in *A Study of Urbanization in Latin America* (New York: Commission on Ecumenical Mission and Relations, the United Presbyterian Church in the U.S.A., 1963), p. 135.

14

GUIDELINES FOR URBAN CHURCH-PLANTING

by
EDWARD F. MURPHY

SINCE DR. GREENWAY, in his splendid chapter on "Urbanization and Mission," has described so adequately the worldwide spread of urbanization, my task is to emphasize the tremendous evangelistic opportunities and to suggest guidelines for urban discipling. My work for the last dozen years has been evangelism in the great cities of Argentina and Colombia. Out of scores of evangelistic campaigns and thousands of evangelistic conversations I present aspects of the task which are of vital importance to all ministers, missionaries, and lay Christians who seek to obey the Great Commission in the cities of our time.

SOCIAL CONSEQUENCES OF URBANIZATION

William L. Wonderley, in a review of that shocking book, *Five Families* by Oscar Lewis, says:

> . . . urbanization presents almost unbelievable problems of adjustment for millions in Latin America who have left their Indian, peasant, or small-town backgrounds because of land shortage or in search of a more modern way of life, only to find themselves alone and near the bottom of the socio-economic scale in the big, unfriendly cities.[1]

Urban migrants become culturally displaced persons. Coming mostly from close-knit face-to-face societies, the impersonal atmosphere of the big city produces a terrible loneliness. There is a breakdown of the social ties that formerly gave life its meaning, for families break up and friendships that have endured for generations are severed. Having once been part of a homogeneous unit, and now finding himself a nobody, one out of an agglomeration of unrelated individuals, the new urban dweller loses his sense of security.

Furthermore, his value system takes a terrible shaking. Family, home, neighbors, the church and other loyalties were once highly regarded. In the city, with its money economy and ruthless materialistic philosophy of life, these allegiances are gradually eroded and his entire value system undergoes a transformation. Stripped of his former moral stimulation and higher value system, the urban migrant finds that his life is little more than a battle for existence and a constant struggle to hold down a job. He vainly tries to find a decent place to live and to earn enough money to feed his growing family.

During the first ten or fifteen years of the life of the urban migrant the common social consequences of rapid urbanization are devastating. Yet, they often produce a receptivity to the gospel that would not exist under normal circumstances. The authors of *Latin American Church Growth* affirm that

> the current wide-spread migration to the city, with concomitant changes in labor and wage patterns, is more likely to render people responsive to the Gospel than to make them resistant. The areas of urban expansion throughout Latin America are uniquely open to the evangelical message.[2]

THE IMPORTANCE OF PLANTING NEW TESTAMENT CHURCHES IN CITIES

The present wave of urbanization (just a foretaste of what is to come) provides a church-growth potential never seen since, perhaps, the days of the early church. At whatever cost, we must restructure our missionary strategy to step into this open door of opportunity. Allocation of both personnel and funds must be made in the light of the opportunity for church-planting that world urbanization presents to world missions. Both theological and sociological factors support this conviction.

THEOLOGICAL FACTORS MAKING GROWING CITIES PRIME FIELDS FOR CHURCH-PLANTING EVANGELISM

The mission of the church is "to give every person in the world an opportunity to say 'yes' to Jesus Christ."[3] Obviously we must seek persons where they are. In the past, men lived largely in the rural areas and in the small face-to-face communities, the towns and villages scattered across the world. All this is now rapidly changing with the move to the cities.

In Latin America as a whole, "The projected growth rates for urban population between 1960 and 1975 are three times those for rural populations. For the South American countries these rates are 67 and 22 percent respectively; for Mexico and Central America, 85 and 26 percent."[4]

The world in general presents other examples of the rush to the city. Tokyo's population was eleven million in 1966. By the end of this century, it will contain over thirty million people.[5] By that time perhaps half of the world's population will be living in huge apartment complexes.[6] *The church must evangelize the cities to be theologically sound.*

A second theological factor has to do with responsiveness. We are told in the Scriptures that, while the whole world is to be evangelized, we are to give priority to "the fields white unto harvest" (Mt 9:35-38; Jn 4:1-42). That is, *the strategic people are the responsive people.*

Generally speaking, recent migrants who live in the working-class suburbs of the great urban centers are responsive to the gospel.

The acculturation which characterizes . . . urbanization provides good opportunity for church growth based on personal conversion. The old structured nature of family life gives way to a more open stance toward life, which in turn necessitates new values of discipline, education, family relationships and social contacts. . . . The introduction of these new elements is altering the old fabric of Latin American life. . . . The fast-growing indigenous churches with their urban base and lay orientation have particular appeal to the new urban dweller. In them he finds opportunity to belong to a group whose activism fits his new-found sense of personal power. The positive evangelical message helps answer his questions concerning the new society in which he finds himself. . . . As urbanization increases, so the opportunities for evangelical growth also increase. As the evangelical churches multiply themselves in the opportunities presented by social change stemming from urbanization, they can influence the direction that the urban masses will follow. *Only as they multiply themselves, however, will they have any such influence.*[7]

This, written of Latin America, is true of many cities in all six continents.

SOCIOLOGICAL FACTORS MAKING CITIES SIGNIFICANT FOR EVANGELIZATION AND CHURCH-PLANTING

The influence of the rapidly growing cities over the life of the undeveloped nations is an important sociological factor. Large cities are the centers of government, transportation, education, industry, communication, religion and, in short, of all the essential areas of life. Though this is seen in most nations, it is much more in evidence in the underdeveloped, emerging nations. An amazingly high percentage of the population lives in or near the state or national capital. This makes urban evangelism more potent than rural evangelism, for the whole life of the nation can be influenced by multiplying churches in major cities.

The transiency of responsiveness is another factor. As we have already seen, the newer city dwellers are in a state of tremendous social flux. McGavran says that the migrating city dwellers have been jolted out of old adjustments and set social, political, economic and religious patterns and are searching for better, truer and more satisfying ways of life. This *searching,* the first step in any journey that finally leads to God, is evidence that the Holy Spirit is at work.

Yet the period of responsiveness is usually very limited. "Specific cases of urban church growth in Mexico City, Bogota and Belo Horizante indicate that it takes a rural migrant a decade or two to adjust to the new urban situation. During such a period of adjustment, he is responsive; we must act quickly if we are to act effectively."[8]

The rapid growth of heterodox sects in the growing urban centers, sometimes excelling that of all the evangelical churches combined, is a third factor. In most of these urban centers, spiritism, Jehovah's Witnesses, and Mormonism are rapidly multiplying. For example, during the past few years in the city of Cali, Colombia, the Mormons have gained more adherents than those gained by all evangelical churches in the city combined. Christians must "act quickly if they are to act effectively."

GUIDELINES FOR URBAN CHURCH-PLANTING

Having considered the cities—the setting in which evangelization takes place—we now propose certain principles to govern and direct the evangelism done. These will be presented under three headings: theological, sociological, and methodological.

THEOLOGICAL GUIDELINES

A theology of harvest. Much urban evangelism is intended to be little more than seed-sowing. This will not do. God has sent us to reap a spiritual harvest. It is not enough to distribute literature, use radio and TV to proclaim the gospel, and organize evangelistic crusades, visitation evangelism, and open-air preaching. Such efforts must be seen as only the first step in the evangelism cycle. New Testament evangelism brings men to Christ and *incorporates* them in New Testament churches. Anything less is sub-Christian. Churches and missions must *intend* church growth.

A theology of discipleship. The Great Commission speaks of making disciples, not just converts (Mt 28:19-20 in the original Greek). A disciple is one who believes in the doctrine of his teacher and follows him. The idea of following Christ is implicit in the word *disciple.* Professions of faith, therefore, that do not produce followers of Christ do not represent the New Testament concept of evangelization. Those who "accept Christ" but do not follow Him are not true Christians. Much of our evangelization so overemphasizes "the saving work of Christ" and so ignores His lordship that we continually produce non-Christian Christians. Thus the "spontaneous multiplication of the Church"[9] dies with the falling away of the first converts.

A theology of the church. The purpose of the incarnation was at least twofold: Jesus came "to seek and save that which was lost" (Lk 19:10). He also came to "build [His] Church" (Mt 16:18). The two are completely interrelated. When men are saved, they must immediately become church-related. This means they must become members of local churches which, as Louis King has said, are societies "in which man is perfected [and] God is glorified."[10]

The church glorifies God. As a true theist, this is my deepest desire: that God should be glorified. The church perfects man. As a true humanist, this is my deepest desire: that man should be perfected. Therefore to extend the church to the ends of the earth is the most important task and the highest privilege that God has given to Christians.

Church-planting, therefore, must have priority over other

forms of Christian service, and is must be the rule by which we evaluate every aspect of mission. A valid theology of the church demands multiplying churches in cities.

A theology of indigenous churches. Much is being written about indigenous churches. Most missions strive to make their churches self-supporting, self-governing and self-propagating, for it is felt that in this way they will be true indigenous churches.

It is important to bear in mind, however, that a local church can practice these three "selfs" and still be far from truly indigenous. Such churches are "indigenized" but not indigenous, since they have been structured according to Western, traditional Protestant patterns, not local, native patterns. They are still foreign, even if they are guided by national pastors.

What is required is a theology which, while cleaving to the Bible, takes culture seriously. The worship patterns, self-image of the church, its hymnology, and its concepts of its structure and leadership must all be *harmonious with the culture of the people who are being discipled.* These practices must be formed by Scripture in light of local culture. Therefore church planters must, from the very beginning, allow the emerging church to take its own form and shape, express its theology and life in its own way, in concepts meaningful to the local believers. It is essential, of course, that all of this be in accordance with scriptural truth.

A theology of responsiveness. As we evangelize the great urban centers, experimentation and investigation will enable us to discover which sectors are responsive to the gospel and which are resistant. The theological truth must be grasped that the responsive must be favored in church-planting evangelism. Those who want to be liberated have a higher priority than those who resist their liberators.

So important was a theology of responsiveness to our Lord that He told His disciples that they should let responsiveness determine the "where" of their church-planting mission. Where people persistently rejected their message, the disciples were to "shake the dust off their feet" in judgment against them and pass on to more responsive peoples (Mt 10:14; Mk 6:11; Lk 9:5). That the early church understood what Jesus meant by these words is evident by Paul's action described in Acts 13:43-52 and 18:1-6.

SOCIOLOGICAL GUIDELINES

The personality of each city or urban center. We must know the city we are attempting to evangelize, for every city has its own personality. Los Angeles is different from Indianapolis; Buenos Aires is even more different from Quito, and Tokyo still more from Mexico City. There is no substitute for careful investigation before we attempt church-planting in any urban center. We must become thoroughly familiar with the major sociological, anthropological and church-growth studies available which deal with the urban center in question.

The cultural mosaic of the urban center. In *Church Growth and Christian Mission,* McGavran compares the general population of a city to a great mosaic. He says, "Each piece of the mosaic is a society, a homogeneous unit. It has its own way of life, its own standards, degree of education, self-image and places of residence."[11]

All of these factors, and many more, affect the responsiveness of each subculture or part of the mosaic. Its degree of responsiveness, in turn, should guide us in our church-multiplying mission. Let me illustrate by citing the case of Cali, Colombia, where I spent many years in missionary service.

Cali is booming. Its population has doubled during the past ten years to almost one million people. It is one of the fastest-growing cities in the Western world, yet Cali is not one but at least eight different cities.[12]

The first Cali is the inner city. It is, almost 100 percent, a business area. Very few people live there.

The second Cali is composed of the semibusiness residential barrios, completely surrounding the inner core of the city on the north, south and east. It is a stagnant area. Here is found the market, surrounded by a vast red-light district and barrios of the middle-lower class.

The third Cali is found directly west of the inner city and separated from it by the Cali River. Running both north and south and nestled between the river and the foothills of the western range of the Andes Mountains are found the largest middle-and-higher class residential barrios.

The fourth part of our mosaic is lovely Santa Terresita and adjoining barrios. Composing one of the newest residential sectors of Cali and built on the lower foothills of the Andes Mountains, it is filled with hundreds of higher-middle to higher-higher class families.

The fifth Cali spreads south of Santa Terresita for miles. It is made up of dozens of middle-middle class to higher-middle class barrios. We will call it San Fernando, the name of its principal barrio.

Our sixth Cali is located south of Santa Terresita and west of San Fernando, also occupying the foothills of the western range of the Andes. Rising to quite a height, it is visible for miles throughout the valley. These hills are covered with several lower-class barrios where some 50,000 people dwell. The barrios were formed by invasions of homeless families who simply moved in and took over the land. We will call this piece of the mosaic Siloe after its most prominent barrio. Siloe is a world in itself and is unlike any other sector of the city. It is important to observe that some residents of Siloe have moved up the social ladder and could be considered lower-middle class.

The seventh Cali comprises the middle-middle-class areas

north and east of San Fernando. We will call it Alameda after its most prominent market area.

The eighth Cali is the largest in the area, the most populated, and the most strategic for church-planting. It is composed of the dozens of working-class barrios, which are rapidly expanding, being fed by continuous migrations from all over Colombia. The city is completely surrounded by these barrios which are multiplying so rapidly it is impossible to provide them with sanitary facilities, water, and power.

What does all this have to do with church-planting in Cali? Much, for churches grow in society, among men, not in vacuum tubes. If we desire to plant indigenous churches in Cali which can continue to grow and multiply, where should we plant them? By seeing Cali not as one, but as eight, we can begin probing to find which is the most responsive and shows the greatest promise for rapid church multiplication.

Many missions engaged in church-planting in Cali, though sincere, have been largely ignorant of the mosaic of the city or have chosen to ignore its significance. Some have tried to plant churches in the inner city, where few people live. Others have tried to raise up churches in the stagnant semibusiness-residential areas surrounding the inner city. It has been difficult going, and these congregations show little growth. Others have deliberately chosen the middle-class barrios and find their churches growing very slowly. It is important to observe that the fastest-growing churches in Cali and those which multiply themselves are in the working-class barrios.

If a church or mission desires to plant more rapidly multiplying churches in Cali, where should they evangelize in light of these observations? The answer is clear. It should concentrate on the eighth Cali. Dozens of small-house churches, churches meeting in rented buildings or under thatched roofs, can and should be established all over this eighth Cali. It is a great city.

What a difference it would make in the direction of the

social revolution now sweeping the lands of the younger churches if the great masses of migrating lower-class peoples moving to the cities would find vigorous evangelical churches established in the areas where they are going to take up residence. This could be the greatest single factor in the spiritual transformation, moral regeneration and social uplift of these masses.

The strength of living relationships in growing urban centers. Christians from the Western world are strongly individualistic. We act independently from our friends, and even from our families. This is not true, however, in the lands of the younger churches where family and friendship ties are very strong, and people like group action and group decision. This fact can become either our friend or foe in the spread of the gospel. If we seek individuals, calling them to come out of their groups, it will be our foe. If we attempt to win to Christ whole families or geographical, occupational or friendship groups, it will become our greatest ally.[13]

The local church can become the ideal functional substitute for the group-belongingness lost after migration from the rural or face-to-face communities. Dr. Eugene Nida has written,

> These people need to experience a kind of fellowship which is even more satisfying than what they have known in the community as a whole. If people can be taught the meaning of the new fellowship in Jesus Christ and what the new community of saints can and should mean, they can be brought into a type of fellowship which will be not only satisfying, but creative. . . . The Protestant Church has a very special ministry [in the urban environment], for it can help to create effective, mutually beneficial social groups in the midst of the impersonal environment, and thus meet people's basic needs for fellowship.[14]

For this to occur, it is necessary that the convert move into

a church in the company of a group of his fellows. Thus he
will not have to suffer a second social dislocation coming
soon after the social upheaval incurred in his migration to
the urban area.

Church multiplying can be a mission venture. Missionaries
can still be effective church planters in the lands of the younger churches. The myth that the day of the missionary church
planter has now passed is substantiated neither by the facts
nor by Scripture.

In most of the lands of the younger churches there remain
vast areas with few evangelical churches. In their great urban
centers, huge sections are either without any local church at
all or are served by one or two small struggling churches.
Missionaries with an apostolic gift can move into these unevangelized areas and raise up indigenous New Testament
churches. Two things must always be kept in mind, however.
(1) If national denominations already exist in the area, their
support and blessing must be sought. Simply to move in,
ignoring the churches already laboring there, is religious imperialism. (2) All converts must immediately be organized
into indigenous local churches. These new churches must be
brought into a living relationship with the other evangelical
churches found in the area, for to hold them aloof from the
rest of Christ's body is a violation of Scripture, a sin against
God, and evidence of spiritual pride and sectarianism.

Church multiplying can be a younger church venture. As
soon as a church is planted, it must in turn plant more. This
is what is meant by "the spontaneous expansion of the
church"—God's blueprint for world evangelization.

The chain of continuous church-planting too often breaks
after the first few are established. A paternalistic relationship
is formed between them and their spiritual fathers, and these
churches become sealed off from their community. They

continue dependent upon the mission, missionaries, or national pastors who become substitutes for the missionary.

Many churches complain that they do not have the necessary financial resources nor the highly trained leaders necessary for further church expansion. This is unscriptural. A new church, experiencing the power of the Holy Spirit and motivated along New Testament lines, can multiply cells of believers without dependence on missionaries or ordained ministers. The early churches did not depend on foreign missions for financial aid before planting more churches. Neither did the apostles import ordained men from Jerusalem or Antioch to pastor the hundreds of new churches being planted all over the Roman Empire. Pastors were found within the churches themselves. Local men gifted by the Holy Spirit, were given on-the-job training by the apostles and other leaders, and thrust out to work.

One of the most thrilling experiences of such church establishment is now in progress in El Salvador, Central America, under the guidance of the Assemblies of God. In 1953 the Assemblies had 3,940 baptized church members in that country. After a period of waiting on God, the Holy Spirit sent a refreshing revival. Bible institute students, pastors and laymen began evangelizing and planting churches everywhere—in homes, in the ranchos of humble believers, and in rented halls. By 1966 the baptized membership had increased to 13,000. Sunday school attendance went up from 3,356 to 30,-000. Even so, in 1966 only 1 percent of the population of El Salvador was attending one of the Sunday schools of the Assemblies of God.[15] Tremendous potential for growth remained.

The organized churches multiplied from 78 in 1954 to 313 in 1968. Their annex churches, called "whitened harvest fields," increased from 200 to over 1,000.[16]

This remarkable growth has been basically the work of laymen and Bible institute students, not highly trained nationals or missionaries. With very little formal education these men, gifted by the Holy Spirit, and trained on the job by their leaders, who themselves had little academic preparation, have become instruments in God's hand to carry forward a notable church multiplication. This is one of God's blueprints for world evangelization.

Church multiplication can be a joint venture of a younger church and a foreign mission. The younger church can provide gifted church planters, while the mission gives some financial backing. It is helpful if church planters are on the same social and educational level as the people among whom they labor. The Christian and Missionary Alliance followed this procedure in a high-potential area of Colombia. The result was one of the finest examples of spontaneous church multiplication seen in Colombia during the past few years.[17]

The reverse plan also produces good results. The younger church provides guidance and financial assistance while the mission provides a church-planting missionary. The Central Presbyterian Church of Cali, Colombia, in cooperation with the Cumberland Presbyterian Mission follow this procedure in a working-class barrio. The church rented an old home in Barrio Popular and the mission sent in a church-planting missionary released from all other responsibilities. He was specifically commissioned to *raise up a church in Barrio Popular*. St. Mark's Presbyterian Church is the result. It continues now under a national pastor trained by this fine missionary, and is continually multiplying itself in Cali.

METHODOLOGICAL GUIDELINES: HOW ARE CHURCHES PLANTED?

Now to the "how" of urban church-planting. Four basic methods are bringing good results: evangelistic crusades, visitation evangelism, the extension program of existing churches, and planting by students of Bible institutes and seminaries.

Prolonged evangelistic and Bible-teaching crusades. These

have proven effective ways of establishing growing churches in a short period of time in the urban complexes of the Third World. Two important factors must be kept in mind: (1) The purpose of the crusade is not mass evangelism. *It is to found New Testament churches—churches which will reproduce themselves—in a short period of time.* (2) The strategy involved is that of continuous, vigorous evangelizing and systematically instructing new converts until a local church is born.

Dr. Melvin Hodges, Latin American Field Director for the Assemblies of God, says this was the main method that led to the remarkable multiplication of churches in El Salvador, already referred to. He cites the growth of the churches in the capital, San Salvador, as an example. In 1956 there was only one church in the city, with a membership of less than one hundred. That year an open-air evangelistic campaign was held.

> Crowds of approximately 3,000 attended nightly. At the end of two and a half months, 250 new converts had been instructed and were ready for baptism. Six weeks later, an additional 125 converts were baptized. Instead of trying to hold all these people in one congregation . . . the city [was divided] into twelve sections. A call was made for workers to take charge of new meeting places. Some . . . were Bible school students, others were men who had had outstation experience. . . . Each was assigned to a section. . . . At the end of one year there were 12 new churches in the city and a combined total of approximately 1200 in Sunday school. Yet, the story does not stop there. For these churches have continued to grow and extend their influence in establishing new churches. In 1964, eight years later, there were 27 Assemblies of God churches, with 200 outstations [branch churches] in the city and surrounding areas. In the city alone, combined Sunday school attendance was fluctuating between 7,000 and 9,500.[18]

The same procedure was followed by the Four Square Gospel in a remarkable church-planting movement in Guayaquil, Equador. Wayne C. Weld in his book *An Equadorian Impasse* comments,

> At the close of the six-week campaign a baptismal service was held with 30,000 in attendance. Fifteen hundred were baptized in a river in Guayaquil. *The instruction for these baptismal candidates was given during the campaign.* It was discovered that by 9:00 p.m., when the evangelist was already well into his message, people were still coming. Therefore the main message was set back, and [first] an associate gave a message of instruction on the Christian life. . . . Those who attended every night received more pre-baptismal instruction than many candidates ever do. The pattern successful in Guayaquil was followed for planting churches in other areas.[19]

Shorter evangelistic and Bible-teaching crusades. When there already are a few believers living and meeting in the area to be evangelized, a shorter crusade can be very effective. The strategy is to concentrate on winning those persons with whom the believers enjoy a living relationship. This rather than the gathering of unrelated individuals is the effective method.

The author has had considerable experience in this type of church-founding in Colombia. A case in point would be the request in 1965 that Overseas Crusades help a Mennonite Brethren missionary and a group of eleven believers begin a church in Barrio Villa Colombia in Cali. In just a few nights of evangelistic emphasis, there were over one hundred professions of faith. These people were immediately given studies in the Christian life. I was present when most of them gave their first public testimony of their new faith. Ninety-five percent were either relatives or friends of the original eleven believers. Within a few months most of these new converts were baptized and a vigorous church was formed. This church continues to evangelize and grow in this working-class barrio.

Church-planting through extension programs of existing churches. In most cities responsive to the gospel, some churches have already been planted. True, many are sealed off and introverted. Others, however, need only a little stimulus to launch an effective church-planting program in the surrounding barrios.

Once again, the remarkable church-planting ministry of the Assemblies of God in El Salvador has lessons to teach us. As we have noted, the organized churches multiplied from 78 to 313 between 1957 and 1967, and their branch churches grew from 200 to over 1,000 during the same period of time. Their strategy has been to make each church responsible to bring to birth a daughter congregation. Laymen, gifted by the Holy Spirit and trained by the pastors of the sending churches are the church planters. Hodges writes,

> Churches have so consistently followed the pattern of establishing other churches through their work, that in some areas the mother churches find themselves completely surrounded by daughters. For example, in the area within a thirty-mile radius of Santa Ana, there are at least 100 established churches. This is partly the work of Bible school students, but mostly it is a development of local church outreach.[20]

Visitation evangelism church-planting. At least two different approaches to visitation evangelism are leading to successful church-planting in urban centers:

1. *Visitation without living contacts.* This is usually exploratory, to find which areas show the greatest potential for church-planting. First, an area is mapped out for house-to-house visitation. Second, believers going two by two offer Christian literature to each home. Third, being alert to anyone who shows interest in the gospel, they find homes willing to open for a weekly Bible study. These then become evangelistic cells or even house churches.

Ernie Poulson describes the success his students are having

in Singapore with this type of evangelism and church-planting. For a couple of years they have regarded each high-rise apartment house with its 1,000 residents as a parish—a small town—and have tried to plant a congregation in each. Their best "apartment house church" has eighty members, most of them new Christians, and contributes about $1,000 Singapore ($330 U.S.) per month for the Lord's work. He writes,

> More than half a dozen such churches have emerged as a result of intense door-to-door evangelization within multi-story apartment buildings. In some instances, services have been held in the flat of a believer. At least three worshipping groups are housed in a ground-floor shop. During the week [the church] is used as a kindergarten, the fees of which pay the rent. Other congregations have been helped in the initial stages by an older sponsoring church or by a group of concerned individuals.[21]

2. *Visitation of living relationships.* The gospel flows best over living bridges, the channels of family and friendship. Visitation evangelism directed to relatives and close friends of Christians can produce exciting results.

One large evangelical church in Buenos Aires had an interesting experience along this line. A dynamic, soul-winning pastor encouraged his members to visit every apartment in the large apartment complexes in the nearby barrios. Thousands of pieces of literature were distributed and hundreds of visits were made, but there was almost no fruit. The pastor then tried a different approach. Knowing that one of his most faithful church members lived in one of those apartment complexes, he encouraged her to win her friends to Christ. Over a short period of time this lady won forty-five of her neighbors to the Saviour. Her friendship with these people was the bridge over which the gospel moved. The relatives and close friends of the forty-five new Christians should prove even more responsive.

In the city of Armenia, Colombia, a woman living in a

small apartment complex was converted during one of the first nights of a crusade. She invited a few of her neighbors in nearby apartments to attend the meetings the following night. They also were converted. By the end of the crusade all twenty-two persons living in her apartment area came into a living relationship with Jesus Christ. Once again, friendship ties formed the bridge over which the gospel moved.

Bible institute and seminary church-planting programs. Bible institutes and seminaries have been established in many large urban centers, and their students represent one of the greatest resources for church-planting. Furthermore, such on-the-job training is the best way of discovering which students have received the spiritual gifts necessary for leading ongoing churches. If for this reason alone, Bible institutes and seminaries should engage their students in systematic church-planting in their own and nearby cities.

Roger Greenway's chapter in this book tells of just such church-multiplying by seminary students and missionaries in Mexico City. The instance is particularly significant because it is done by the staid orthodox Christian Reformed of Grand Rapids, Michigan. To those inclined to believe that city evangelism can only be done by new and ardent branches of the church universal, I say, "Look at the Christian Reformed in Mexico City."

Melvin Hodges states that the same thing is happening in El Salvador. The mission has established

> an aggressive Bible school program which trains both doctrinally and in evangelistic methods, such as literature distribution and outstation work. Many students are actively engaged in church planting. . . . Because students play such an important part in establishing churches, the school has now been moved to the capitol, San Salvador, to provide this new sphere to activity.[22]

CONCLUSION

The growing cities in the lands of the younger churches are among the most strategic and important mission fields in the world. In the new emphasis given to urban church-planting, we must not merely "reach" the cities, not merely sow seed there, but *must multiply congregations and cells of Christians on a magnificent scale.* Both nationals and missionaries should be trained in the complex and exciting task of establishing churches which will continuously reproduce others. It is of the greatest importance to recognize that *the strategic people are the responsive people.* Since the most responsive seem to be the working classes, the barrios where they live should be recognized as the fields of highest priority. May God usher in a day of church-multiplying in the great cities of the world.

Notes

1. William Wonderley, "Urbanization, the Challenge of Latin America in Transition," *Practical Anthropology* (Sept.—Oct. 1960).
2. W. R. Read, V. M. Monterroso, and H. A. Johnson, *Latin American Church Growth* (Grand Rapids: Eerdmans, 1969), p. 280.
3. Edward Dayton and John A. Klebe, "PERT, Newest Tool for Mission," *World Vision* (Oct. 1966), p. 10.
4. Read et al., p. 243. Quoting Frank Bonilla, "The Urban Worker" in *Continuity and Change in Latin America* (Stanford, Calif.: Stanford U., 1964), pp. 186-205.
5. Akiri Hatori, discourse given at the World Congress on Evangelism, (Berlin, 1966). From notes taken by the author.
6. Ibid.
7. Read et al., pp. 241-43.
8. Read et al., p. 274.
9. Roland Allen, *The Spontaneous Expansion of the Church* (Grand Rapids: Eerdmans, 1964).
10. Louis L. King, *The Church's Worldwide Mission,* Wheaton Congress, ed. Harold Lindsell (Waco, Tex.: Word, 1966), p. 18.
11. Donald McGavran, ed. *Church Growth and Christian Mission* (New York: Harper & Row, 1965), p. 71.
12. Various statistical reports published in Colombia.
13. Eugene Nida "Culture and Church Growth" in *Church Growth and Christian Mission,* pp. 94-96.
14. Eugene Nida, "The Relationship of Social Structure to the Problems of Evangelism in Latin America," *Practical Anthropology* (Mar.—Apr. 1958).
15. Melvin Hodges, "Spiritual Dynamics in El Salvador," *Evangelical Missions Quarterly* (Winter, 1966), pp. 80-83.
16. Edward F. Murphy, *Preliminary Essentials for Producing Growing Churches in Latin America* (Bogota, Columbia: Latin American Congress on Evangelism, 1969), pp. 20 ff.

17. Murphy, "How a Dead Church Came to Life," *Evangelical Missions Quarterly* (Fall, 1969), pp. 41 ff.
18. Hodges, pp. 80-83.
19. Wayne C. Weld, *An Equadorian Impasse* (Chicago: Evangelical Covenant Church of America, 1968), pp. 61-63.
20. Hodges, pp. 80-83.
21. E. N. Poulson, "Every Thirteen-Story Building a Parish," *Church Growth Bulletin* (Jan. 1970), pp. 45-46.
22. Hodges, pp. 80-83.

Part V
Church/Mission
Tensions Today

The three chapters in this section are all reprinted by permission of Moody Press from the book entitled *Church/Mission Tensions Today* published in 1972. Each chapter bears a biographical note about its author at the bottom of the first page. Each author is still in the position he held at the time the original book was printed.

C. Peter Wagner began his missionary career working with jungle Indians in Bolivia. When he left the field fifteen years later he had become involved in a number of other different kinds of work including his responsibility as Associate General Director of the Andes Evangelical Mission. He was also vitally involved in innumerable tasks, forces and new developments throughout Latin America. He was one of the early exponents of theological education by extension, has authored many books, later became Executive Director of the Fuller Evangelistic Association, Associate Professor in the School of World Mission, member of the Lausanne Committee for World Evangelization both of the North American Committee and the executive committee at the world level. He is known as one of the most articulate writers, speakers and interpreters of the global task of world evangelization.

No easy formula for mission/church relationships
can be developed which may be applied anywhere
and at any time. Even among missions and
churches of the same denomination, historical
and geographical factors often determine varying
patterns of relationships. In an incisive way,
Warren Webster pinpoints these time-space fac-
tors, as he calls them, and shows how flexibility is
required to face contemporary mission/church
problems. Some of Webster's observations on
the traditional "indigenous church" theories of mis-
sion will be of special interest to readers.

15

MISSION IN TIME AND SPACE

by WARREN WEBSTER

"The Mighty One, God the Lord, speaks and summons the earth from the rising of the sun to its setting" (Ps 50:1, RSV). "The God of the *whole earth shall he be called*" (Is 54:5).

The Bible is a missionary book from cover to cover. In Genesis we read of a time past when God made all things. In Revelation we read of a future time when all things shall be made

---

WARREN WEBSTER is General Director of the Conservative Baptist Foreign Mission Society, under which he served in literature and linguistic ministries among Muslim and Hindu peoples for fifteen years in West Pakistan. Extensive travels throughout the Muslim world and Orient have given him a broad perspective on mission activities in that part of the globe. A graduate of the University of Oregon and Fuller Theological Seminary, he also holds the D.D. degree from Conservative Baptist Theological Seminary. Dr. Webster's writings have made him much appreciated as an evangelical missiologist, and he has lectured on missions at Fuller Theological Seminary and Gordon-Conwell Theological Seminary.

new. And in between we follow the outworking of God's purposes in time and space.

The universal range of divine concern for the whole created world permeates the Old Testament as well as the New and is seen in two dimensions:

The temporal or historical dimension—"to the end of the age."

The spatial or geographical dimension—"to the end of the earth."

In a context bounded by these dimensions, contemporary mission/church relations find their meaning and substance.

Historical and geographical factors have influenced the Christian world mission from its inception. At the midpoint of redemptive history, when the Word became flesh midway between East and West, the Mediterranean world had been prepared religiously, politically and linguistically for the coming of Christ. Forces were at work that contributed greatly to the early growth and spread of the Christian message. It was neither the first time nor the last that God used the interplay of historical and geographical realities to effect His purposes.

CHRISTIAN AND SECULAR HISTORY

The rise of Islam in the seventh century A.D. offers an example of external factors affecting the spread of Christianity. Sitting astride both land and sea routes to the Orient, Islam formed an immense barrier between Western Christendom and the Far East. For more than a thousand years repeated attempts to penetrate this barrier largely failed. As a result Christian influence moved northward and westward in the Christianization of Europe. The expansion of Christianity in Asia and the launching of the modern missionary movement had to await finding a way to circumvent the barrier of Islam through the discovery of an all-sea route to India and China. In the process, North and South America and sub-Saharan Africa were also discovered, thus opening vast new mission fields in addition to Asia. The very historical forces which impeded Christian missions at one point actually contributed to a new and greater outburst of missionary expansion.

Dr. Kenneth Scott Latourette in his book *The Unquenchable Light* traces the ebb and flow resulting from such interaction of Christian and secular history. From the time of Christ to the twentieth century he sees four major waves of Christian advance, alternating with periods of stagnation or recession. However, he notes that each successive recession has been progressively briefer in duration and each ebb period has produced forces leading to a fresh advance of the Christian faith which has carried the influence of Jesus Christ to a new high point in the total life of mankind.[1]

While we cannot predict that this ebb and flow must inevitably be the course of the future, we know that "The Great Century of Christian Advance" (A.D. 1800-1914) established the body of Christ as a worldwide reality for the first time in history. The presence of the church throughout the world is one of the great facts of the twentieth century. As Bishop Stephen Neill has observed, "In the twentieth century one phenomenon has come into view which is incontestably new—for the first time there is in the world a universal religion, and that the Christian religion."[1a] At the beginning of the 1900s the promise of the risen Christ that "repentance and forgiveness of sins should be preached in his name to *all* nations" (Lk 24:47, RSV) was nearer fulfillment than ever before.

The era of the two great world wars which followed was a time of mixed spiritual advance and decline. If, overall, the forces of spiritual regression appeared to dominate, it may have been the briefest and most short-lived ebbing of the Christian tide to date. The very events which seemed so foreboding on the political scene actually prepared the way for a new outburst of Christian vitality in quite unexpected places.

COLONIALISM AND MISSION

Ralph Winter in his book, *The Twenty-Five Unbelievable*

Years, chronicles the postwar era from 1945 to 1970 as a generation that witnessed four hundred years of Western colonial expansion rolled back like a rug.[2] Prior to the end of World War II most of the non-Western world was under Western domination of one type or another. Twenty-five years later, 99.5 percent of non-Western countries were independent.

This political "retreat of the West" led many observers to conclude that the fate of Christianity would ultimately parallel that of European colonialism. This viewpoint as set forth by Professor K. M. Panikkar, a prominent Hindu philosopher and historian, maintains that Christianity is nothing more than an epiphenomenon of Western political expansion and as the West retreats politically, so also will the Christian faith. While this may have been Panikkar's hope as a cultured Asian who rejected Christianity, it has not been borne out in the intervening period. In the past "twenty-five unbelievable years" the church of Jesus Christ has grown significantly in nearly every area from which Western colonial powers retreated. It is now more evident than ever that the growth of biblical Christianity is not dependent upon Western political presence and power.

While it cannot be denied that the modern expansion of Christianity and the spread of Western civilization have gone on at the same time, they have not always gone hand in hand, and their relationship is not a simple one of cause and effect. Some critics allege that Christianity is, and always was, the handmaiden of imperialism. This is a widely current falsehood which deserves to be labeled for what it is. In many places the mission of the Christian church has spread in spite of, rather than because of, Western diplomatic and commercial interests whose representatives have often impeded the spread of the gospel, both through direct opposition and through personal lives that sometimes reflect the worst rather than the best of Christian culture. The East India Company, for example, initially did not want missionaries in the East at all and exerted strenuous efforts to keep them out of its territories in India and elsewhere. In Java, the Dutch colonial rulers decided not to permit the Christianization of the Muslim inhabitants of the island and for over two hundred years almost nothing was done to take the gospel to the Javanese. Now in free Indonesia the church is growing dramatically in areas from which it was largely excluded by Western colonial rulers. Similarly, British colonialists prohibited missionary work in Malaya. And in recent years in at least one Asian country American government representatives proved a bigger hindrance to the importation of Bibles than the local Muslim officials.

In place after place the gospel has spread in spite of this opposition of vested interests in the West. Today in independent nations of Asia, Africa and Latin America, evangelical churches are growing faster, with deeper roots, than they did during the era of Western dominance, which is evidence that the church is not the servant of colonialism and that its mission is not a form of religious imperialism.

NATIONALISM AND MISSION

In reflecting on an era when the Christian world mission was too often identified with colonialism and Western culture, it seems necessary to separate the life-giving kernel of Christian truth from the culturally colored shells which embody and carry the seed. In proclaiming Christ as the Saviour of the world, both mission and church need to distinguish clearly between the gospel and Christianity.

The gospel is God's gracious provision of salvation through Jesus Christ to all men in every age and clime who submit themselves to Him in faith and trust. Christianity, on the other hand, is the human response to the gospel. The gospel is the power of God unto salvation—divine, pure, universal in its application. Christianity is the local expression of the gospel as it takes root in the soul and in the soil of a given place. The gospel message is universal. Christianity is often compounded with provincial customs, local tradition and human fallibility. While we can say with Paul that we are not ashamed of the gospel of Jesus Christ, we may sometimes be embarrassed by things that go on under the banner of Christendom. Apparently this is what one Asian student meant when he said, "We want your Christ, but we do not want your Christianity."

Nationalistic pressures have encouraged the "rediscovery" of indigenous church patterns in this century. While the principles of "self-government, self-support and self-propagation" are necessary disciplines for a church learning to develop its own character in the face of political and cultural nationalism, some leaders, both missionary and national, have made the mistake of looking upon the establishment of indigenous churches as the end and goal of missions and the final answer to nationalistic pressures. The fallacy of this, however, became apparent when some churches became so indigenous, so nationalistic, that they no longer had room for anything foreign, including missionaries and Christians of different racial and national origins.

While it is right for a people to want to stand on their own feet religiously as well as politically, there is a point where nationalism and the church must part company, for the church cannot be itself when imprisoned in the framework of a narrow nationalism. While churches must take root in the soil as well as in the soul of a people, they must also learn to see their relationship to other believers in Christ who is the Head of the church.

Mission and church both need "a new grasp of the biblical truth that the church is the 'people of God' an elect race, composed of people out of all nations, transcending all nations and races."[3] The body of Christ which ultimately includes men of "every tribe and tongue and people and nations" is by definition supranational, supraracial and supracultural though locally it may be largely national, racial and cultural.

From the biblical standpoint, a truly Christian church is not one without a foreigner in it, but one in which a believer is treated like a brother; or more precisely, one in which all believers—without distinction of nationality, race or cultural background—fellowship as members one of another in the household of God. This understanding of the essential oneness of all the people of God was what enabled an African churchman to say with deep spiritual insight in the face of rampant nationalism, "We do not want an African church, we want a Christian church in Africa, a church which is truly missionary and in which there is neither black nor white."[4]

The Christian answer to divisive nationalism and the false brotherhood of Communism lies neither in patterns of dependence nor of independence, but in the recovery of that interdependence in the one Spirit which marked the New Testament churches. In the biblical interdependence of both younger and older churches lies the future of the church's mission to the world.

GEOGRAPHY AND CHURCH GROWTH

Not only *historical* considerations influenced church growth and mission/church relations, but *geographical* factors have played a bigger role than is often realized.

The factor of accessibility to the Christian message has often determined the timing and sequence of Christianization. But the religious distribution of mankind has even more profoundly affected the growth and success of Christian missions. While in the last century and a half men have come to Christ from every culture and climate, from every religious background as well as from every major language family, the movement to Christian discipleship has by no means been of equal dimensions from all religions.

The great ingatherings into the church from pagan backgrounds—virtually all the major people movements—have been from among basically animistic peoples. This was true in times past of the "conversion" of northern Europe and the Christianization of Latin America. It remains true today of the rapid spread of Christianity in Africa and most significant Christward movements in Asia. All are among peoples whose basic religious patterns have been animistic, however much influenced by contact with the major ethnic religions of Buddhism, Hinduism and Islam.

In Indonesia, which has the world's largest Muslim population, there is a growing Christian community of approximately ten million people, but more than 90 percent of these have come into the church from Indonesia's sizable animistic minority. On the island of Sumatra where Batak tribesmen ate the first two missionaries who visited there a century ago, there are now indigenous Batak churches with their own ministry and institutions and over a million members—all former animists or their descendants.

The notable church growth reported from Korea and Taiwan in this century have taken place primarily among people with animistic beliefs, however much influenced by traditional national religions.

The progress of the church has been much less marked where the majority of people are adherents of one of the major ethnic religions. "In fact," Nida and Smalley report, "in no major pagan region in the so-called 'missionary world,' apart from the aboriginal areas, has Protestant missionary work gained more than one per cent of the population."[5] This is true of the Muslim world, long known for its resistance to the Christian gospel. In West Pakistan three-quarters of a million Protestants and Catholics comprise slightly more than 1 percent of the total population, but fewer than one-tenth of 1 percent of Pakistan's Christians have come out of Islam.

In Japan where Buddhism and Shintoism are strong, Protestant Christians after a century represent less than one-half of 1 percent of the population. In Thailand less than one-tenth of 1 percent of Thai Buddhists have become Christians, and the picture among Burmese Buddhists is similar, although there are more than 200,000 Christians among the hill tribes of Burma—all formerly animists.

In India fifteen million Protestants and Catholics comprise 2 to 3 percent of the population and might appear to be the exception to Nida and Smalley's statement about accessions to

Christianity from the lands where ethnic religions predominate. But on closer study, it is evident that most of India's Christians have come as a result of people movements from the scheduled castes or outcasts whose religious beliefs and practices have more in common with animism than with philosophical Hinduism. In India's state of Nagaland, between Assam and Burma, Christianity has spread to the point that all of its 850 town and village communities are reported to have both a church and a school, and 60 to 70 percent of its 500,000 people claim to be at least nominally Christian. It is doubtful that any other state or province in Asia (with the possible exception of Roman Catholic areas in the Philippines) has a higher percentage of Christian population. But the Naga believers formerly were animists—some of them headhunters—just a couple of generations ago.

By way of contrast, the accessions to the Christian faith in India from Hinduism's upper castes, while not entirely lacking, have been almost microscopic in comparison.

The significance for world missions of geography as it relates to the distribution of established ethnic religions and of responsive animistic peoples is quite evident. The success of different churches and missions in various parts of the world frequently owes less to their theological and methodological distinctives than to the responsiveness of the people to whom they have gone, and their readiness for change at a given point in history. Baptists, Methodists, Anglicans, Lutherans, Pentecostals and Roman Catholics have all shepherded large group movements into their churches—and all from basically, or formerly, animistic peoples.

In the long debates over missionary principles and "the indigenous policy" many protagonists have failed to see that the policies of Roland Allen, Alexander Hay or Donald McGavran, which apply well to growing Christian movements from among responsive peoples, do not necessarily work in the same way when applied to static or resistant situations. When people are coming to Christ in great numbers as part of a homogeneous movement, the so-called "indigenous principles" give helpful direction in guiding and broadening the movement. But where there is no movement or where conditions are not right for responsiveness, a doctrinaire application of so-called "indigenous principles" has seldom, if ever, been adequate to elicit such a response.

Because large group movements into the church come from responsive (largely animistic or previously Christianized) peoples, they call for a different structuring of mission and of mission/church relations than the much slower growth of the church among more resistant peoples (often found in the major ethnic religions).

DENOMINATION BY GEOGRAPHY

There is another direction in which mission-church relations have been influenced by geographical considerations. In the history of modern missions when societies for the proclamation of the gospel multiply to the point of competition and rivalry, Protestant missions generally attempted some type of cooperation known as *comity* in terms of which participating missions agreed to work in well-defined geographical areas which did not overlap or duplicate the outreach of others.

This meant, however, that in many places congregations grew up which had no choice in the matter of denominational affiliation. Where Methodists began work, people became Methodists. When one of those families migrated to an area assigned to another mission they might become Baptists or Presbyterians overnight, but for the most part comity agreements tended to perpetuate sectarianism on a regional basis— "denomination by geography."

In time, national Christians became increasingly sensitive to the fact that the particular distinctives of their group often owed less to personal conviction than to the accidents of geographic location and comity agreement. Not infrequently younger churches began to express impatience and dissatisfaction over being "united" to fellow denominationalists thousands of miles away while being discouraged from close fellowship with believers of another communion across the river, or even across the street. Comity, the younger churches say, may relate to missions as missions, but it has little meaning for the church as the body of Christ which cannot be contained or divided by lines on a map. It is not surprising that where national churches have outgrown dependence on missions they have sought to expand their circle of fellowship with other Christians on national, but interdenominational, lines, rather than through extending international, but purely denominational, ties. It has been observed that "whatever the historic justification of denominationalism in European Christendom, it represents an irrelevant pattern for the younger churches which cannot be made indigenous, because it is not rooted in the gospel nor related to the soil in which these churches exist."[6] This undoubtedly has been one of the factors behind church-union movements among Third World churches. It may also help explain why some of the fastest-growing and most virile Christian groups in Asia, Africa and Latin America today are spreading along indigenous lines largely outside the historic denominational churches.

In any event, one of the present tensions in mission/church relations revolves around attempts to undo or to transcend artificial patterns of "denomination by geography" through the discovery of a biblical unity in which all who are "sons of God through faith in Christ Jesus" (Gal 3:26, NASB) come to experience their relationship one to another in the household of God.

THE "HOME BASE" IS EVERYWHERE

Both church and mission now find themselves in an age when the body of Christ is more broadly planted and more deeply rooted among more peoples than ever before in history.

One corollary of the church's presence in virtually every land is that the home base for mission is everywhere—wherever the church is found. Now that the church has become a worldwide fellowship, the "home base" of missions can no longer be thought of as one or two countries in the West. Even if it were possible (and it manifestly is not) for the Christians of one country to evangelize the world, from a biblical perspective it would work an irreparable loss upon the churches in other lands who are also commanded to "go and make disciples."

There may have been a time when people thought of the mission field as something "out there," equated with "dark continents" and "regions beyond." Now we see more clearly that the work of mission is not simply a matter of crossing geographical frontiers, but rather of discipling men and women on the frontier between faith in Christ and unbelief, wherever we find it. As such, the true missionary frontier—the conflict with paganism—runs through every land.

This points up the importance of church and mission cooperating in every nation to bring the whole gospel to the whole world. The establishing of indigenous churches is no longer seen as an adequate end and goal of biblical missions *unless* such churches become "sending" churches in, and from, their own milieu. The New Testament knows nothing of "receiving" churches which are not also in turn to be "sending" churches. To this end the founding of national mission societies and the entrance into mission of national churches on every continent are cause for profound gratitude and continued encouragement. If Western nations and institutions are on the decline, Eastern nations, and the churches rooted in them, are bridging the gap. We are beginning to see churches in Japan, as well as in Taiwan, Korea, the Philippines, Indonesia, India and elsewhere accepting the missionary responsibility which of necessity lies upon the church in every place, not just in Western lands.

Partnership, Not Paternalism

While Christianity did not spread simply as an accompaniment of Western political expansion, the spirit of the colonial era not infrequently influenced Christian missions in directions that were frankly paternalistic. Today, among nations that are free and independent, the key word for mission/church relationships is *partnership,* and new patterns are emerging along biblical lines which offer hope for spreading the gospel of Jesus Christ more widely than ever before in history.

In an effort to lead Evangelicals in the West from a precolonial to a postcolonial understanding of mission, Dennis Clark in his book *The Third World and Mission* proposes a number of major policy changes for a new and creative partnership between "sending" churches, missionary societies and the growing churches of the Third World. He envisions the transfer of all major policy-making for Third World ministries from Western bases to the nation and region concerned. He also advocates the multiplication of leadership training centers, communications consortiums and evangelistc teams—in all of which nationals would lead and direct the program with a minority of Western colleagues.

Further proposals recommend the dismantling of all foreign mission compounds and the breaking up of concentrations of foreign mission personnel (with the possible exception of pioneer base camps in primitive areas). For "sending" churches who still think "West is best" the author pleads for an embargo on exporting Western ecclesiastical disputes and cultural taboos to the new churches of the Third World. Having talked with Christian leaders in some fifty nations, he notes the heavy-handed influence of home boards and churches which often try to control field policies from a distance without firsthand knowledge of the situation.

Partnership for mission in the '70s requires that Third World believers be free "under God and led by His Spirit" to determine what is best for the evangelism of their people, even if it means dumping tracts, tapes and techniques from the West. They must also be free under the Holy Spirit to choose and follow their own accredited leaders and not simply those hand-picked by missionaries.

A Philippine representative at GL '71 observed that too often in the past, mission/church relationships have resembled the proverbial "horse and rabbit stew" supposedly mixed in "equal" proportion, that is, one horse to one rabbit! The present decade requires almost everywhere a greater "partnership of equality and mutuality."

Another delegate at GL '71, Arsenio Dominguez of the Christian Nationals' Evangelistic Commission, outlined four principles for church and mission leaders in the '70s:

1. Work with national colleagues in such a way that they do not appear as tools of the West.

2. Avoid those things that could suggest new believers have taken up a white man's religion.

3. Seek to minimize disfavor on the part of Third World governments.

4. Structure ministries in such a way that the gifts of national believers are brought into prominence.

Worldwide "partnership in obedience" among believers will accomplish what we cannot do separately. The key is not simply better ecclesiastical structures, but transformed attitudes and relationships based upon partnership, not paternalism.

THE END OF THE CHRISTIAN MISSION

It seems fairly certain, as far as we can interpret history, that the Western orientation of the world is rapidly coming to an end. However, this need not in itself pose a threat to the Christian world mission.

One of the striking characteristics of the Christian faith has been its repeated ability to survive the passing of an era and an order of which it once seemed to be an inseparable part. This has been in evidence ever since the decline and fall of the Roman Empire which was survived by the very faith it once sought to destroy. In a similar way the Christian church outlived the darkness of the Middle Ages and outlasted the Renaissance and the Age of Reason. The Christian message spread during an era of exploration and discovery. It adapted to the changing demands of the industrial revolution and gained strength. In this century, the Christian hope continues to spread despite the rise of Communism, the advent of the atomic age, and the inauguration of space travel.

In an era of "wars and rumors of wars" marked by the two greatest conflicts in world history, the church of Jesus Christ has demonstrated the vitality not only to survive but to expand. While the church may have lost ground during this time in some areas where it was once strong—most notably in Europe —this is no new phenomenon. Elsewhere the postwar years have seen a fresh extension of the church into half a dozen countries that had previously been "closed lands" with neither believers nor Christian churches. The modern record of rapidly growing churches has often—as in Indonesia and the former Congo—been one of triumph through tragedy, and transformation through testing.

In the twentieth century, for the first time in history, it can be truly said that the sun never sets on the church of Jesus Christ. With the possible exception of the Mongolian People's Republic, there does not appear to be another independent nation on earth in which the church of Jesus Christ is not represented. Samuel Moffett of Korea reminds us:

> Even where there are no organized churches, even where missionaries are turned away with guns and Christianity is a forbidden faith, you will find Christians. Perhaps only one, two, a handful, perhaps only foreigners, but they are there, and they belong to the oldest and strongest world-wide fellowship the world has ever known, the people of God, the Church of Jesus Christ.[7]

The great missionary fact of the present day is that *"the Church is there. . . . ,* the Body of Christ in every land, the great miracle of history, in which the living God himself through his Holy Spirit is pleased to dwell."[8]

It is estimated that in the last 180 years more people have become Christians and more churches have been planted than in the previous 1,800 years of church history. In the last 60 years Protestants are said to have multiplied 18 times in the non-Western World.[9] Due in part to the population explosion, the number of professing Christians is greater than it ever has been before.

Untwisting Statistics

We frequently hear, however, that church growth is not keeping up with biological growth, so that while the *number of Christians* in the world continues to increase, the *Christian percentage* of world population has been steadily declining from about one-third in 1940 to less than 30 percent today, with an expectation that it may not be more than 16 percent by the year 2000. Since many began to question these pessimistic prognostications, a group of former engineers and systems analysts in the missionary enterprise went to work to check out the figures and concluded they are based largely on false premises and poor arithmetic. In this connection Stephen Neill recently observed that

> for the first time an attempt has been made to arrive at a scientific estimate, based on population figures supplied by the United Nations and on the best available statistics from Christian sources. . . . It appears that in the past the Christian percentage has been overestimated, since the population of China, almost entirely non-Christian, is now held to be larger than was earlier supposed. When the necessary corrections have been made, the conclusion is reached that the *percentage has been slowly increasing* since the beginning of the century, *is slowly increasing* and *will continue to increase;* so that, if present trends continue, it will in the year 2000 stand higher than ever before in the history of the world. What is a little startling is that at that date less than half the Christians will belong to the white races.[10]

While the Lord of history is sovereign, and no man can say what must happen tomorrow, we know from Scripture that the

God of the whole earth is at work in this age calling out a people for His name which ultimately will embrace some "from every tribe and tongue and people and nation" (Rev 5:9, NASB).

It has been said repeatedly that the day of missions is coming to an end. This is nothing new. The Bible says the same thing. But rightly understood, the end of the mission will be the end of history as we know it.

Many students of the Word and world events believe that in the closing interplay of Christian and secular history there will be one final ebbing of the faith—perhaps the briefest, yet most intense, recession to date—marking the advent of Antichrist and preliminary to the triumphal appearance of the coming King. This is to be followed by the greatest wave of spiritual advance ever seen, when "the kingdom of the world has become the kingdom of our Lord" (Rev 11:15, NASB) and "the earth shall be filled with the knowledge of the glory of the LORD, as the waters cover the sea" (Hab 2:14).

Whatever the precise sequence of eschatological events, it is clear that in God's program the geographical and historical are integrally related. When our Lord commissioned His disciples to go "to the ends of the earth" (the spacial dimension), He promised to be with them "to the end of the age" (the temporal dimension). He also declared that the gospel of "repentance and forgiveness of sins should be preached in his name *throughout the whole world,* as a testimony to all nations; and *then the end will come"* (Lk 24:47; Mt 24:14, RSV).

This is the divine program for church and mission in time and space. The historical culmination awaits the geographical fulfillment. The end of the age awaits the completed proclamation to the ends of the earth. The indications are that the "Omega point" of history is nearer than it has ever been before.

In this day of opportunity it devolves upon church and mission everywhere to move forward together in discipling men and nations—to make history, not just read about it!

NOTES

1. Kenneth Scott Latourette, *The Unquenchable Light* (New York: Harper, 1941), chap. 9.
1a. Stephen Neill, *A History of Christian Missions* (Baltimore: Penguin Books, 1966), p. 559.
2. Ralph D. Winter, *The Twenty-Five Unbelievable Years* (South Pasadena, Calif.: William Carey Library, 1971).
3. Henrik Kraemer, *A Theology of the Laity* (London: Lutterworth, 1958), p. 157.
4. Lesslie Newbigin, *Is Christ Divided?* (Grand Rapids: Eerdmans, 1961), p. 22.
5. Eugene Nida and William Smalley, *Introducing Animism* (New York: Friendship Press, 1959), p. 59.
6. *An Advisory Study* (New York: COEMAR, 1962), p. 37.
7. Samuel H. Moffett, *Where'er the Sun . . .* (New York: Friendship Press, 1953), pp. 4-5.
8. Neill, p. 576.
9. R. Pierce Beaver, *From Missions to Mission* (New York: Friendship Press, 1964), p. 63.
10. Neill, *Call to Mission* (Philadelphia: Fortress, 1970), p. 79.

*The "syndrome of church development" is a dan-
ger inherent in missionary work that has not
been stressed in evangelical missiological writings
in recent years. C. Peter Wagner in this final
chapter contends that if this syndrome can be
avoided both the mission and the church will be
healthier. He proposes that ultimate mission
objectives be stated, not so much in terms of
the church, as of the "fourth world," and gives
some specific recommendations for implementing
these principles.*

16

MISSION AND CHURCH IN
FOUR WORLDS

by C. Peter Wagner

Few readers are likely immediately to understand the significance of the term "four worlds" in the title of this chapter.
It may be one of the first times it has been used in print, since
the "fourth world" is a relatively new term currently being
popularized by a small circle of missiologists.

C. Peter Wagner is Associate Professor of Latin American Affairs
in the Fuller Theological Seminary School of World Mission and also
Executive Director of the Fuller Evangelistic Association. Before as-
suming these responsibilities he spent sixteen years as a missionary in
Bolivia under the South America Mission and the Andes Evangelical
Mission, most recently as Associate General Director of the AEM.
Mr. Wagner holds the B.S. from Rutgers University, the B.D. and
M.A. from Fuller Theological Seminary, and the Th.M. from Princeton
Theological Seminary. Some of his most recent books include *Latin
American Theology, The Protestant Movement in Bolivia, A Turned-On
Church in an Uptight World, An Extension Seminary Primer* (with
Ralph Covell), and *Frontiers in Missionary Strategy*.

"Third World" is now in common use, however, and is found in several of the other chapters in this book. Although some think the concept is condescending (which are the "first" and "second" worlds, anyway?), it nevertheless is quite useful. It refers to those countries, most of which are below the thirtieth parallel north, populated by the black, brown and yellow races, and struggling against almost impossible odds toward an elusive goal sometimes called "development." Africans, Asians and Latin Americans, together with some minority groups closer to home, share a world view which has many common elements. They feel that history has been unkind to them, that they have been exploited by colonialist and imperialist ambitions of the more affluent nations, that current world policy has cleverly stacked the cards against their attaining a truly just portion of the world's goods, and that present international trends are widening, rather than closing, the gap between the rich and the poor nations.

The Third World nations have to a large extent also been those called "mission fields" and evangelized by Christian missionaries from the first two worlds. When missionaries speak loosely about the "national church" they usually mean those newer churches which are emerging in the Third World. Some missions have stated that their goal has been to plant churches, *indigenous* churches if you will, in the Third World. It is the contention of this chapter that this stated goal, while perhaps innocuous on the surface, is nevertheless in the final analysis truncated. It is good as far as it goes, but it does not go far enough.

By articulating the goal in terms of the church alone, missions may end up betraying their own nature. In the beginning, most missionary visions are focused on the world from which disciples are to be made rather than on the church, which at the very beginning does not yet exist. By their nature missions fulfill their mission primarily in the world. In chapter 1, Jack Shepherd rightly stresses that the proper missionary formula is God-church-world. We must grant that one of the noble, and indeed necessary, results of a successful mission in the world is a church. But if the missionary task is considered accomplished because a church now exists, the original missionary vision has been lost. Note that the *final* element in the formula is the *world*. Disciples are made, not in the church, but in the world.

At this point, the term "fourth world" may be helpful. The "fourth world" embraces all those peoples who, regardless of where they may be located geographically, have yet to come to Christ. In that sense, the fourth world is the top-priority objective of missions.

This pushes the statement of the goal of missions one notch further than the indigenous church. The indigenous church may become a great and dynamic instrument for the continued push toward the fourth world, but it is an unfortunate fact that in some cases it has instead become a hindrance to the discipling of the fourth world.

Therefore, the proper objective of a mission is not merely the establishment of a church, but ideally of a *missionary* church which is in turn moving into the fourth world. If the mission has somehow been unsuccessful in transmitting its own missionary vision to the new church, it has not lived up to its best potential and highest calling.

STUNTED OBJECTIVES STUNT GROWTH

Much more conscious effort needs to be dedicated to clarifying today's missionary objectives than missionary strategists have been willing to invest in the past. To consider the church as an end in itself rather than an instrument for "making disciples" in the fourth world is to adopt a stunted objective. Stunted objectives will sooner or later stunt the fulfillment of the Great Commission.

The primary objective of missions needs to be distinguished from secondary or intermediate objectives. What are some of these intermediate objectives? As we list them, let us state clearly that just because they are intermediate, they are neither bad, inferior nor superfluous. If you live in New York City and want to drive to Pennsylvania, for example, you have to go through New Jersey. While you are moving through New Jersey you are glad to be there, but you are not satisfied with staying there if your goal is Pennsylvania. New Jersey is only an intermediate objective.

Some intermediate missionary objectives include a larger number of workers, an increased budget, more activity in sending and receiving churches, excellence in ministerial training, spiritual revival, culturally relevant liturgy and music, translation of the Scriptures, distribution of certain quantities of Christian literature, wide dissemination of the gospel message through the mass media, the manifestation of social concern, etc. As *intermediate* objectives, all the above and many more good things that missionaries and churchmen do can be very useful in accomplishing the *ultimate* objective of making disciples. If this distinction is kept clear, possibilities of continual, healthy church growth will increase.

A mature church is often another helpful instrument toward making disciples. Certainly, once disciples are made they must gather together in congregations (whether inside or outside of the institutional or more traditional churches is not relevant here) in order to share the *koinonia* or Christian fellowship so necessary for Christian nurture and qualitative growth. But while the church *should* be a help toward the task of reaching into the fourth world and making disciples there, it often is not. In this sense the church can be thought of as the automobile that takes you from New York City to Pennsylvania. If it is in good mechanical condition, it is a great help; but if the carburetor plugs in Jersey City and the transmission goes out in Newark, the car turns out to be a hindrance and you realize you would have accomplished your objective of reaching Pennsylvania better if you had taken the train.

JESUS PEOPLE

As everyone knows, some churches have plugged carburetors, so to speak. They are ineffectual in reaching the fourth world and need to be bypassed. One does not have to go to the Third World to find examples, although they abound there as well. Right here at home we have a abundant supply of churches which have become introverted and centripetal. They give little thought and energy to the task of reaching the fourth world. In the 1960s, for example, a large segment of the fourth world gathered together on the West Coast of the United States in the hippie movement. Most of the "national churches" (the U.S. "establishment" in this case) were either hostile, indifferent, or incapable of reaching this curious fourth world group in an effective way. They didn't know what to make of the psychedelic drugs, the free sex. and the Eastern mystical religions.

Because the "national church" could not or would not make disciples among these street people does not mean that the Spirit of God allowed them to be forfeited. He raised up agencies outside the established church (call them "missions" in our context), such as the World Christian Liberation Front in Berkeley and the Jesus People Movement in Los Angeles. These new "missions" did not worry about protocol, comity, or the agenda of the established church. They moved ahead with such evangelistic methods as coffee houses, street meetings, *Hollywood Free Papers,* baptisms in the ocean, and Christian communes, which predictably were little understood by the establishment. They wore beads, let their hair grow out, played guitars and went barefoot. As a result, many of the "national churches" did not even want these "missionaries" to attend their services. They said, in effect, "Missionary, go home!" Here, right at home, we witnessed "creative tensions" between the mission and the church.

Although many United States churches still have not accepted this freewheeling new missionary movement, the trend —at least on the West Coast—is toward reduced tensions and more mature recognition of the all-important fact that the supreme task of both establishment and counterculture is winning the fourth world. Therefore, a mutual appreciation is developing, based on the recognition that God can use each of the groups to make disciples in different segments of the fourth world.

CHARISMATIC MOVEMENT

Just one more example from home base before returning to the Third World. Let's move from the counterculture to the middle class.

During the 1960s the United States "national churches" were to a large extent in the doldrums. They were plugged-carburetor churches which were not fulfilling the Great Commission even in their own communities. Again, the Spirit of God raised up a force of "missionaries" which did not meet the approval of most "national churches." In this case the majority of these "missionaries" were good church members who had become frustrated and restless because of the introversion, nominality and ineffectiveness of their churches. They did not form a counterculture; they formed a "charismatic movement."

This charismatic movement startled the leadership of the established churches in much the same way that missions startle the leadership of some of the newer churches in the Third World. They could not understand why these "missionaries" held their meetings in living rooms rather than in church halls. They were revolted by some of the unusual liturgical practices of the charismatic movement. They questioned the validity of baptisms in private swimming pools. Some churchmen shouted "Missionary, go home!" so loudly that their churches split. But others, more wisely, made the adjustments necessary to harness the pulsating spiritual vitality of this new "mission" for the renewal of the church and the evangelization of the fourth world.

These contemporary examples of church-mission tensions, of course, are not unusual in the history of Christianity. Anyone who turns back the pages of church history with this in mind can notice that it has been a recurring pattern. God has been raising up Jesus People and charismatic movements under other names through the centuries. The Waldensians and the Lollards, the Pietists and the Methodists, the Conservative Baptists and the Assemblies of God, the Student Volunteer Movement and Campus Crusade, the Christian and Missionary Alliance and the Sudan Interior Mission—all are examples of "missions" which formed because their own churches had become ineffective for winning certain segments of the fourth world.

It must be recognized that sometimes the carburetor can be repaired and a stalled church can once again become effective in the fourth world. Most Evangelicals in the United States are aware of the "evangelism explosion" in James Kennedy's Coral Ridge Presbyterian Church in Florida and of the "body-life evangelism" of Ray Stedman's Peninsula Bible Church in California. Churches like these complete the picture I am attempting to paint. Some churches are effective evangelistic instruments, while others are not.

BACK TO THE THIRD WORLD

This brief flashback into our own homeland church-mission tensions is designed to clarify our thinking concerning parallel church-mission tensions in the Third World. Across the board, Christian churches in the Third World are no different from those at home. Some will effectively reach the fourth world; some will not.

But missions, if they are true to their nature and their calling, *must* keep their objective as the fourth world. This must be the starting point of church-mission policies. The effective evangelization of the fourth world must remain, Gibraltarlike, the objective of missions.

Effective evangelism of the fourth world will make multitudes of disciples and baptize them into the church. But as long as there are more people to win out there in the fourth world, these churches that have been formed under the blessing of God do not constitute the final objective. If the whitened field holds ten thousand bushels of wheat, a five-thousand-bushel harvest is not enough. The harvesters would be foolish to allow the fascination of five thousand harvested bushels tempt them to shut down their combines and begin to manufacture bread, spaghetti and breakfast food before the harvest is completed. The Lord of the harvest would call them "wicked and slothful servants."

This is why missions which turn from evangelism to church development do poorly. True, the church needs some help. The wheat that has been harvested needs to be stored in elevators if it is to be preserved. The newborn infant needs milk and its diapers changed. Missions which neglect this basic nurture are irresponsible. But missions which allow the emerging church to absorb so much attention and energy that the push into the fourth world is slowed down or stalled are worse than irresponsible. They are unfaithful to their calling from God.

LET THE NATIVES EVANGELIZE

"We now have a national church," some missionaries say. "Let the natives do the evangelism. We will now teach the Bible to the Christians, help them raise better crops, improve their hygiene, train their pastors, and teach them modern evangelistic methods. Since they speak the language better than we do, since they know the culture, since they are the right color, they now become responsible for the fourth world. We have done our job." In other writings I have called this severe fallacy in missionary strategy the "syndrome of church development." I would not keep stressing it if my experience had not confirmed that it is such a widespread and devastating error in the thinking of both contemporary missions and national churches.

Missionaries who fall into the syndrome of church development are often rather deluded. They unwittingly operate under the false assumption that they can do almost everything better than national Christians. They feel they can preach better sermons, they can organize more active church programs, they can lead choirs and play instruments better, they can teach Sunday school classes better, they can build better buildings, write better tracts, teach better seminary classes, they can start youth camps and youth centers, they can write constitutions and administer denominational offices with supreme efficiency. On top of all this, they are free—the church doesn't have to pay a cent for all this service. Sometimes, in fact, the missionaries are able to obtain sums of outside money that enlarge the church treasury rather than take from it.

But these missionaries, somehow, don't feel they can evangelize better than nationals!

The above may border on a caricature, but it is close enough to much current missionary mentality to raise a warning flag for discerning missionaries and churchmen. All the different activities involved in the syndrome of church development are good in themselves, and at one time or another a missionary may help the church by participating in them. But they are only temporary. A mature church can handle all of them. As men like Roland Allen and Henry Venn saw years ago, the less the mission gets involved in these internal affairs of the church, and the quicker the church itself assumes responsibility for these things under the Holy Spirit rather than under the missionary, the better for both mission and church. But even when the ideal is reached and the new church fully and effectively handles all its own internal affairs, neither the church nor the mission is relieved of its responsibility toward the fourth world.

SETTING PRIORITIES

Whereas for a time this concept was neither articulated nor accepted in evangelical missions, some hopeful signs of progress are appearing. In a remarkable editorial entitled "Our

First Priority," Joseph McCullough of the Andes Evangelical
Mission reflects the trend in his own group:

> Evangelism, once again, will be the primary thrust of the
> Andes Evangelical Mission. Reaching the unreached has
> always been our objective as a pioneer mission. But somehow
> with the growth of a strong national church, we began to
> think that the responsibility for evangelizing belonged to this
> church. Our task would be to carry on the training program
> of Bible schools, seminaries, and other church-supporting
> ministries such as literature, radio, youth centers, camping,
> Bible conferences, and so forth. . . .
>
> In a new way, however, we believe the Lord would have us
> direct our attention and efforts to direct evangelistic oppor-
> tunities. As missionaries we need to set the example and pace
> for the national churches and pastors. Our responsibility is
> to keep moving out to the cutting edge of the work. As new
> churches are planted, we will continue to break new ground
> rather than limit our efforts to organizing and training.[1]

One might ask whether missions like the Andes Evangelical
Mission have the *right* to establish such priorities. Should they
not have asked the national church to make the policy statement? Should not the nationals decide whether they want doctors, radio broadcasters, seminary professors, primary school
teachers, chicken farmers, basketball players, Bible translators,
airplane pilots, printers—or (perhaps) evangelists and church
planters? Are not missions which seem to go above the head
of the national church in setting their priorities in the fourth
world arrogant and domineering?

No more so than the Jesus People movement which moved
into the West Coast fourth world without seeking the advice
and consent of the established churches their parents belonged
to. Nor than the horseback circuit riders of the Wesleyan
movement who perhaps "arrogantly" penetrated the British
fourth world without the approval of the national (Anglican)
church. The fact that some of our present-day missionary or-
ganizations· do the same thing cross-culturally does not alter

the principle that when God raises up a group of His servants and gives them the missionary vision of making disciples in the fourth world, this vision is never required to be brought under the control of the established church, no matter whether this church is found in the first, second or third worlds. The Protestant effort in Latin America, for example, began and flourished despite the protests and persecutions of the Catholic established church.

Having said this, however, it is necessary to point out immediately that the best of all possible situations is complete harmony both in thought and action between church and mission. This seems to be the situation, for example, that Ian Hay describes in chapter 11 of this book. Both the Sudan Interior Mission and the Evangelical Church of West Africa have kept their vision fixed on the fourth world. As a result, the harvest in West Africa is being gathered with top efficiency.

WEST CAMEROON

As all missionaries are aware, this kind of harmony between church and mission does not always develop. Take a recent situation in neighboring West Cameroon, for example. The remarkable good growth of the West Cameroon Baptist Church, beginning in 1950, stalled with a plugged carburetor in the period 1955-60. One of the reasons was an overenthusiastic policy of indigenization on the part of the mission. Apparently losing its vision of the fourth world, the mission thought that the withdrawal of missionary personnel engaged in evangelism and church-planting would hasten the indigenization of the church. Evangelism became the responsibility of the church, no longer that of the mission. With indigenization taking higher priority than the fourth world, the syndrome of church development was in full swing. Commenting on the situation, Lloyd Kwast says, "This complete withdrawal from evangelism by the mission was without doubt an excessive move and hurt the growth of the Church."

Earlier in this book, Robertson McQuilkin has stated that

"the church universal has an obligation to all people outside of Christ and may not attempt to discharge this responsibility by delegating it to representatives who are not fulfilling it."

At Green Lake, Louis King warned strongly against what we are calling the syndrome of church development. He stated that as a *first principle* in mission/church relationship, "missionaries refrain from accepting administrative functions in, and forego imposing their plans upon, the church."[3] Without using the term "fourth world," King asserted that "the mission's relationship with the church is primarily at that point in which the church is engaged in witness and mission to the non-Christian world outside its door."[4]

George Peters adds his voice to reinforce these principles. He believes that missions, properly conceived, are neither mission-centered nor church-centered. While they are "church-based" they are also "world-faced." One of his diagrams presented at Green Lake represented the mission of the church as a bow shooting an arrow called "missionary thrust" toward the world. The two equal sections of the bowstring were labeled "sending church" and "receiving church."[5] On the church-development syndrome, Peters says,

> The energies of the sending church must not be spent in perfecting church structures, drafting constitutions, exercising church discipline, and superintending institutions. The goal of missions is not the structural and institutional life of the church community, but the proclamation of the gospel to those who do not confess Jesus Christ as Lord and Savior.[6]

SECONDARY ISSUES

Once the matters of the fourth world as the primary objective of missions and the syndrome of church development are cared for, the other issues involved in mission/church relationships really become secondary. The New Testament gives us no inspired structure for mission/church relationships. Fusion, modified fusion, dichotomy, modified dichotomy, unilaterality, functional partnership, parallelism—all are options with more or less validity according to the circumstances and according to the degree they help or hinder the fulfillment of the Great Commission.

Certain geographical areas of the world, certain ethnic temperaments, certain historic backgrounds, certain backlogs of failures or successes in mission/church experiments, certain ecclesiastical conditions, or a myriad of other circumstances might combine on one field in such a way that fusion of mission and church is the most acceptable alternative. But an entirely different combination of these same factors might recommend parallelism on another field.

It is a mistake to commit a mission to a certain preconceived principle of relationship with the national church without regard to the local circumstances. By doing this, a mission can all too easily forfeit its opportunity to evangelize. Some missions, committed to an inflexible policy of indigenization, have disbanded their missionary organization and assigned their missionaries to the newly formed national church. There is nothing wrong with this procedure per se, if by doing so the total outreach to the fourth world becomes more effective. But if the church loses its own evangelistic vision and tells the mission that it prefers radio technicians and community development experts to evangelists and church planters, the mission should reconsider the relationship. If contracts have been signed and the church is stubborn, probably the mission will have to look for other fields if it is to continue faithful to its call to make disciples of all nations.

In a widely circulated article, Donald McGavran warned the delegates to Green Lake not to "betray the two billion." By the "two billion" McGavran means what we mean by the fourth world. He said that "church-mission relationships have little importance in themselves. They are important chiefly if they enable effective discipling of men and ethne to take place."[7] Pragmatic considerations, based on the biblically centered imperative of fulfilling the Great Commission, will determine the best mission-church relationships for a given time and place.

ASKING THE RIGHT QUESTION

Is the day of the missionary over? Now that there is a strong indigenous church in Upper Zax, are there any more missionaries needed there? Do the Upper Zaxonian Christians want any more missionaries?

These are all *wrong* questions, but they are frequently being asked in church circles in the sending countries today. Sometimes they cause confusion and unnecessary tension between missionaries and their sending churches.

All should be clear that the day of the missionary will not be over until the present age ends. When Christ gave the Great Commission to make disciples of all nations, He added the reassuring promise that He would be with His servants to the end of the age (Mt 28:20). This was not only a promise but also an indication of the duration of the Christian mission. Missions must continue until Christ returns.

The bulk of this chapter has been dedicated to the issue raised in the second hypothetical question above. The existence of a strong national church in Upper Zax, in the United States, or in West Africa does not regulate the need for more or fewer missionaries, unless the missionaries have fallen into the syndrome of church development. We will not labor this any further.

The third question, however, needs more clarification. Some Third World churchmen are visiting the United States and setting up qualifications for the kind of missionaries they would like, and they are getting the ear of sending churches. One man in particular from Latin America, whose name is not important here, has said that the church he represents wants only those missionaries willing to participate in the changing of Latin American social structures and in the liberation of the Latin American man. He wants social revolutionaries, not evangelists.

By reacting to this attitude, I do not want to give the impression that I oppose the Latin American social revolution. In other writings I have declared myself a supporter of it. Nor do I want to give the impression that it is in any way wrong for this man and other Latin churchmen to participate in the revolution to the degree their consciences direct them. I do contend, however, that neither he, nor his church, nor the pope himself has any right to say that a Spirit-filled missionary, called of God to preach the gospel of Christ to the fourth world, to turn men from darkness to light and baptize them into the church, should not fulfill his calling.

If he is talking about the kind of missionary who has felt led to "help the church," whose objective is the Third World church rather than the non-Christians of the fourth world, who has fallen into the syndrome of church development—in that case he and his colleagues have a perfect right to tell any missionary to go home or stay home. Let the members of any church or denomination decide what is right for the internal functioning of their church. Let them set up personnel requirements and accept only workers they desire and approve. But if the Third World churchman has lost his vision for a world without Christ and without hope, if he no longer is concerned that people who die without repentance and faith go to an eternal punishment in hell, if he is more burdened for the salvation of society than the salvation of souls, he of all people is least qualified to decide whether *evangelistic* missionaries should fulfill Christ's command to make disciples in the fourth world, even when that part of the fourth world is in his own country. The source of the missionary mandate is the triune God, not the church. The final accounting will be given before the judgment seat of Christ, not before some ministerial council or ecclesiastical assembly.

This is why asking whether the Upper Zaxonians want any more missionaries is not the right question. The right question is: Are there any men and women in the fourth world in Upper Zax who need Christ, who are receptive to the gospel, and to whom missionaries from Lower Bovima (the hypothetical sending country in this case) can effectively communicate? If the answer is yes, they must go, unless, of course, there is a high degree of assurance that the Upper Zax church will indeed take care of that fourth world in terms of reaping all the harvest there before it is too late.

WHERE HAVE WE GOOFED?

This doesn't mean that anyone should thumb his nose at the church. Harmonious relationships, I repeat, are the best of all possibilities. But we do learn from history and from men like Martin Luther, John Wesley, William Carey and A. B. Simpson that the establishment should not be allowed to stand in the way of fulfilling God's will. Remember the Jesus People?

It is a sad but true fact that many Third World churches do not have a vital burden for the fourth world. How could this have happened? There are three major causes:

1. *A lack of missionary teaching.* For some strange reason, missionaries have not made it a point to teach missions to the emerging churches. Chua Wee Hian once said, "Most of my missionary friends confess that they have never preached a single sermon on missions to the young churches."[8] Exceptions to this are described elsewhere in this book, especially with the Sudan Interior Mission in Nigeria and the Christian and Missionary Alliance in Asia. But the general rule holds, and missionaries should correct this serious omission as soon as possible.

2. *A lack of missionary example.* If missionaries have decided to "leave evangelism to the natives," no wonder the natives have little evangelistic burden. Missionaries should set the example for the church if they expect the church to develop the proper vision for the fourth world.

3. *Nominality in the church.* While two of the three causes of the lack of missionary vision in some newer churches can be traced to the missionaries themselves, a third relates directly to the church. Especially when the second generation comes

into leadership, nominality is likely to set in, just as it has done in so many churches in the sending countries. The only cure for this is a renewed vision under the supervision and power of the Holy Spirit.

CONCLUDING RECOMMENDATIONS

In conclusion, I would mention five recommendations to missions which desire to maintain the best relationships with the churches they are involved with, and at the same time not betray their own true nature. This is a fine and difficult line to walk. Mistakes are inevitably made; tensions inevitably arise. But hopefully they are *creative* tensions, and when they are resolved, both mission and church have benefited.

1. Maintain as the guiding principle for mission policy effective discipling of the fourth world. Jesus came to seek and to save the lost, and missions must not deviate from that. Although constantly tempted to stay behind with the ninety-nine, they may not do this as long as there is one more lost sheep to find and fold.

2. Do all possible to transmit the vision for the lost to the emerging church. From the very beginning teach the newborn babes in Christ that part of their commitment to the Lord is to use their gifts in the effective fulfillment of the Great Commission.

3. Avoid the syndrome of church development. Do not become unduly involved in the internal development of the church. Trust the new believers to the Holy Spirit, give them responsibility early in their Christian experience, allow them to develop their own relevant patterns of church organization, liturgy, leadership, finances and training.

4. When structures need to be developed, choose the structure of mission-church relationship on pragmatic grounds. Make whatever arrangement will best make disciples in the fourth world.

The ideal structure combines resources from mission and church in a concerted effort to win the fourth world for Christ;

together they are discipling peoples and multiplying churches for God's glory.

The second-best situation occurs when the church has no resources to offer but gives the mission her moral support as the mission continues to move into the fourth world with the gospel.

The last resort is necessary only when the church is obstinate and opposes the mission's ministry to the fourth world. In this case "we must obey God rather than man" as long as people in the fourth world are waiting for Christ.

5. Help each emerging church or denomination develop a missionary sending program of its own. This, when successful, completes the cycle of world evangelism. The new church spawns a new mission. The full sequence, as Ralph Winter has already pointed out, is not mission-church, nor even church-mission-church, but rather, church-mission-church-mission. No mission should feel that its task is accomplished, even as far as the emerging church is concerned, until that church has become an active missionary church.

NOTES

1. Joseph S. McCullough, "Our First Priority," *The Andean Outlook* (Plainfield, N.J.), Fall, 1971, p. 7.
2. Lloyd E. Kwast, *The Discipling of West Cameroon, A Study of Baptist Growth* (Grand Rapids: Eerdmans, 1971), p. 148.
3. Louis L. King, "Mission/Church Relations Overseas," in *Missions in Creative Tension* ed. Vergil Gerber (South Pasadena, Calif.: William Carey Library, 1971), p. 181.
4. Ibid., p. 175.
5. George W. Peters, "Mission/Church Relations Overseas," in *Missions in Creative Tension*, p. 230.
6. Ibid., p. 208.
7. Donald McGavran, "Will Green Lake Betray the Two Billion?" *Church Growth Bulletin* (Palo Alto), July 1971, p. 152.
8. Chua Wee Hian, "Encouraging Missionary Movement in Asian Churches," *Christianity Today,* June 20, 1969, p. 11.

*This chapter is a strong, biblical oriented argument
for the perennial need of foreign missionaries.
But the kind of missionary and the auspices under which he works are carefully defined. Robertson McQuilkin warns against uncritical acceptance of either the old comity system or the new
"organizational fundamentalism" of amalgamation.
Here is some fresh, pragmatic input for the current dialogue.*

17

THE FOREIGN MISSIONARY–
A VANISHING BREED?

by J. Robertson McQuilkin

Is there still a valid role for foreign missionaries? Raised by
honest people, this question has been accused of deflecting
many young people from the mission field, of sending tremors
through the ranks of missionaries, and of causing many to
leave the foreign field.

Whether or not this question alone can bear such heavy responsibility, it obviously is the type of question that, just by
being raised, has enormous practical impact. Therefore, it must
be answered. At root it is a theological question, not merely a
pragmatic problem. Consequently, it must be answered theologically: Is there still a valid role for foreign missionaries?

J. Robertson McQuilkin has been President of Columbia Bible
College since 1968. Previously he served for twelve years as a pioneer
missionary to Japan under The Evangelical Alliance Mission. Dr. Mc-
Quilkin is a graduate of Columbia Bible College and Fuller Theological
Seminary. His articles on mission theory and practice have appeared
in leading evangelical periodicals.

To answer this, four other previous questions must be handled. They are:

1. What is the primary mission of the church?
2. What is the evangelistic mission of the church?
3. When may the mission be judged complete?
4. Who is responsible to accomplish this mission?

I will simply outline a brief answer to the first three questions, laying the groundwork upon which I build an answer to the last question, really the central issue.

What Is the Primary Mission of the Church?

According to the Bible, the church has many functions or purposes. The congregation of God's people is a *temple* for worship and observing the ordinances, a *family* for the fellowship and discipline of its members, a *school* to teach and learn the Word of God, and a *fold* for pastoral care, counseling and healing. All of these are functions of the ministry of the church for its own members. Incidentally, all of these functions will be fulfilled far more effectively when God's people are with Him in His presence, the "church triumphant." But is there no ministry of the church toward the world, a function that only the "church militant" here on earth can fulfill? What is its obligation toward those outside the family of God?

The apostle tells us that we are to do good unto all men, speaking of financial assistance (Gal 6:10). Though he qualifies it by saying, "especially to those of the household of faith," a reader of the New Testament would be dull indeed not to sense that God's people should be concerned for the welfare of those outside the family—their physical and social welfare as well as spiritual. The church is concerned for the whole man.

But the underlying assumption of this paper is that such a mission is not the *primary* mission of the church. The primary mission of the church we call *the* mission, the *Great* Commission, repeated with a different emphasis by our Lord on at least four different occasions following His resurrection.

This is the same mission that brought Christ to earth. "Jesus Christ came into the world to save sinners" (1 Ti 1:15). "The Son of man is come to seek and to save that which was lost" (Lk 19:10). This great mission of our Saviour in providing eternal redemption for lost and aliented men is the same mission which He gave His disciples to complete. The "Wheaton Declaration" puts it this way:

> We regard as crucial the "evangelistic mandate." The gospel must be preached in our generation to the peoples of every tribe, tongue and nation. This is the supreme task of the Church.[1]

The church thus has many functions and even more than one responsibility to those outside the church. However, the primary mission of the church to those outside is to bring them inside the evangelistic mandate of our Lord. What is that mandate?

WHAT IS THE EVANGELISTIC MISSION OF THE CHURCH?

The evangelistic mission of the church includes three elements: proclamation, persuasion, and establishing congregations of God's people.

Our mission is to go into all the world and proclaim the good news to every person (Mk 16:15), to be a witness to the very ends of the earth (Ac 1:8), to proclaim repentance and remission of sins to all nations (Lk 24:47). Of course, a proclamation of the gospel, even when "proclamation" is taken to mean effective communication, does not exhaust the responsibility of the church in its evangelistic mission.

The church is responsible not only to inform people but to win them. Only when men are won will God be satisfied. The great Commissioner defined the mission as discipling the peoples (Mt 28:19).

Finally, not only are the people of God responsible to win men to faith in Christ, but they are responsible to bring them into the visible congregation or family of God's children. If there is no such congregation it must be established. "I will build my church" (Mt 16:18) states in advance what Christ intended to do, and the book of Acts shows how the Great Commission was understood by those who heard it. They set about establishing churches. Birth is an individual matter, but in God's plan it is birth into the family.

Once a congregation has been formed, there is the immediate need for all the functions of the church. If the evangelist has the capability or gift of providing for these other functions, his role may begin to change. Normally, however, the congregation itself as it begins to mature, should provide for these various ministries. Certainly if the evangelist continues to "evangelize" the Christians, there will be little maturing. And if he alone provides for all the pastoral and teaching ministry, the church may be stunted in its growth. The ideal would be for the church to mature rapidly, assume its responsibility for ministry to its own, and join the evangelist in winning those yet outside.

These three, then, are the components of the church's evangelistic responsibility: proclamation, persuasion, and establishing congregations of believers.

The official stand of the United Presbyterian Church emphasizes these three elements:

> The supreme and controlling aim of the Christian mission to the world is to make the Lord Jesus Christ known to all men as their divine and only Savior and to persuade them to become his disciples and responsible members of his church in which Christians of all lands share in evangelizing the world and permeating all of life with the Spirit and Truth of Christ.[2]

The International Missionary Council meeting in Madras in 1938 put it this way:

> Evangelism . . . must so present Christ Jesus in the power of the Holy Spirit, that men shall come to put their trust in God through Him as their Savior and serve Him as their Lord in the fellowship of His church.[3]

This is the evangelistic responsibility of the church. When it has been fully discharged, what will the world look like?

WHEN MAY THE EVANGELISTIC MISSION OF THE CHURCH BE JUDGED COMPLETE?

Since this question is eschatological, it may not be possible to answer it with dogmatic precision. But we can judge to some extent. The church's responsibility can hardly be assumed discharged until every person has had opportunity to hear with understanding the good news of the way to life in Christ.

Of course, saturation proclamation alone does not fully discharge the church's responsibility. That will not be until all whom God is calling have responded to the call, accepting Christ as Lord and Saviour, and have been brought into the fellowship of His people. God alone may judge when this has been accomplished. And yet, so long as the Lord Himself does not proclaim a consummation by His own appearance, the church must assume that it is her responsibility to do what He said to do.

Without trying to probe the part of God's purpose He has not seen fit to reveal, what does the present state of obedience to His command seem to be? Has the evangelistic mission been accomplished? Actually the need is greater today than it ever has been. There are more people outside of Christ in the one land of Indonesia than there were in the entire Roman Empire when the Great Commission was given. According to the conclusions of some demographers, if our Lord should return today there would be more people in hell from this generation than from all preceding generations combined.

The evangelistic task is great and growing greater. But who, specifically, among all Christians, is responsible for seeing that it is done? Are local Christians alone responsible? What of lost people who are out of reach of any "local Christians"? What of people who live within reach but are not being reached? Are such people the responsibility of Christians from afar, that is, of foreigners? If so, of which foreigners? American foreigners? Only foreigners invited by local Christians to do the job? Or also foreigners sent by their own people to do the job?

WHO IS RESPONSIBLE TO ACCOMPLISH THIS MISSION?

The apostolic church did not take this great evangelistic mission as the responsibility of a select group of full-time professionals. The early church accepted the mandate as the responsibility of every disciple of Christ. Not all would be equally effective in bringing unbelievers to a commitment of faith. Not all would be equally effective in landing "fish," but all were equally responsible to be good bait in (1) demonstrating a supernatural quality of life, and (2) giving testimony (witness) to genuine, personal experience. The evangelistic responsibility is for all Christians, particularly all Christians in concert. Together they win men, each contributing his share. The body as a whole reproduces. We might call this "evangelism through the total church-in-witness."

But God also gave evangelists to the church, those who were particularly gifted in "landing fish," bringing men to commitment. Thus some Christians were given ability to be more *persuasive* than others, though all were to be faithful *proclaimers*. These evangelists were never intended to function independently of the church, but were designed as representatives of the church. Patricularly for people at a distance, whom the "total church-in-witness" could not reach, God provided the means whereby the church could delegate this evangelistic responsibility to certain of its members, gifted and sent to accomplish that mission.

Paul was such a representative of the church at Antioch, reporting back to the church what had been accomplished. This same function continued on after the apostolic era.

Eusebius, writing of the time from A.D. 100-150, speaks of "numberless apostles" or "preaching evangelists" who were living then. He describes them:

They performed the office of Evangelists to those who had not yet heard the faith, whilst, with a noble ambition to proclaim Christ, they also delivered to them the books of the Holy Gospels. After laying the foundation of the faith in foreign parts as the particular object of their mission, and after appointing others as shepherds of the flocks, and committing to these the care of those that had been recently introduced, they went again to other regions and nations, with the grace and cooperation of God.[4]

The contemporary word *missionary* does not precisely describe this function, however. As we now use it, the term has to do with location rather than vocation. No matter what the vocation, one seems to be a missionary if he is employed by a church in one place to serve in some way elsewhere. Especially, we use the term when a person serves in a culture other than his own, while being supported or paid by a church or mission in his own culture. Normally this means an overseas ministry and thus the term *missionary* normally means an overseas servant of the church.

This definition contributes to some of the confusion concerning the "missionary call." Actually the "call" may have little or nothing in common with what has traditonally been considered a "call to the ministry." What it really boils down to is geographical guidance—the conviction that God wants one to work in some place other than his native land. Each person who has such a conviction may be considered to have a "missionary call." He may be an airplane mechanic or a farmer; but if he is convinced that he should do this in a foreign land and is to be paid by the church of his own land, he has a "missionary call."

This particular definition of *missionary* means that we only confuse the issue by asking a general question such as that proposed as the theme of this chapter, "Is there still a valid role for foreign missionaries?" Of what role do we speak? We must discern the exact role or it will be impossible to judge whether or not the need for that role still exists.

For example, does the role of the outsider or foreigner include supplying funds for the relief of human need or to provide financial aid to a weaker sister church? Then foreign *funds* are what is necessary and the foreign *person* may actually prove an embarrassment. This administrative role of distributing money sent by more affluent Christians of other lands, if necessary at all, could hardly call for a large foreign staff. Is the foreigner a technical expert with skills needed more in another land than his own? Then, so long as some area of the world needs him, and wants him, the doctor, educator and agriculturalist will have such a role.

Is the foreigner's role that of ministering to Christians as teacher, pastor or administrator? If so, his role is normally a diminishing one in a maturing church. Furthermore, once the church has come into being, such ministers should be invited or called by those who desire the service or ministry, not sent by others who feel the ministry is needed. Of course, in the life of an emerging church there may be a legitimate period of weaning when maternalism or paternalistic oversight may be needed or at least tolerated. But in the nature of the case the need for roles of ministry to Christians imposed by "sending churches" from outside will decrease in direct proportion to the success or spiritual growth of the church.

THE EVANGELISTIC ROLE

But what if the role is evangelistic, particularly pioneer evangelism? This original missionary role will never cease to exist until the evangelistic mandate of the church is finished.

It may be argued that the responsibility for a given area passes from the foreign sending church to the local church once it has been established. This may be a legitimate delegation of responsibility, just as the original sending congregation may have delegated its evangelistic responsibility for those at a distance to the specially called evangelistic missionary at an earlier stage of evangelistic outreach.

But if there is a church that either cannot or will not reach the lost nearby, those churches outside that range of direct responsibility cannot delegate their evangelistic responsibility to it any more than they could to a nonfunctioning evangelist. The church universal has an obligation to all people outside of Christ, and it may not attempt to discharge this responsibility by delegating it to representatives who are not fulfilling it. God alone may judge whether they cannot or simply will not, but the church at large must judge whether a local congregation or group of congregations is in fact fulfilling the responsibility.

Adaptation to local circumstances can make the evangelistic task more successful: sometimes in cooperation with others, sometimes independently of others, sometimes under the direction of others. Perhaps certain people should be sent to one area and not to another. But the evangelistic representative is sent to a lost world by a sending, responsible church, not called or invited to a receiving church. He may be invited by one church to join it in evangelism so that his home or original sending church may be joined by a second forwarding church, nearer the evangelistic objective. Paul asked the church in Rome to share in sending him to Spain, for example.

Recognizing these things, evangelical missions generally bypass the old denominational comity system which allocated evangelistic responsibility for an area to one mission. The system served some good purposes, no doubt, but when it became a hindrance to completing the task, God raised up dynamic groups that bypassed the system. So with emerging nationalistic comity. If it aids in completing the evangelistic mandate, good. But if it blocks it, God will raise up fresh, dynamic movements and will bypass the new system just as he did the old.

We tend to accept the new way as inevitable. For example, in commenting on the "nationalization" of the Africa Inland Mission in Kenya, the news writer for *Christianity Today* assumed this. He said, ". . . mission societies similar to the AIM were watching and looking for guidelines . . . many of them doubtless will follow the AIM's lead . . . the 1970's will be the decade for 'passing the baton.' "[5]

Often the sole criterion in judging whether or not organizational changes should be made seems to be the question of unity and harmony, what will make for smoother running of the organizational machinery and more pleasant interpersonal relations. This undoubtedly has entered our missiological bloodstream through massive transfusions of ecumenical thinking. To be sure, the unity of the body of Christ is of great importance indeed. But it is not the only criterion.

Donald McGavran puts the primary criterion into clear focus:

> Is the over-riding goal cordial church-mission relationships? . . . If principles governing cordial relationships are stated regardless as to whether they guarantee an ever more effective evangelization, the two billion will be betrayed. . . . *Church-Mission relationships have little importance in themselves. They are important chiefly if they enable effective discipling of men and ethne to take place.*⁶

If evangelical missions dissolve staff, facilities and organization into a national church because they have no choice (the government demands it, for example) or because the evangelistic mandate in that area is being fully cared for by the national church, or because, through amalgamation, both foreigner and national can become more effective in the evangelistic responsibility, the amalgamation may indeed be the step of wisdom. However, if action is taken because of an uneasy feeling that this type of union is the only truly right way and as a consequence the evangelistic initiative is lost, the error is fatal.

The danger inherent in this indiscriminate move to amalgamation of church and mission was seen more than ten years ago by the director of the Missionary Research Library. Herbert C. Jackson says:

> A second "old pattern" I would propose is the restoration of an aggressive independence of foreign mission activity, breaking the current pattern which holds that missions must

be completely subservient to the younger churches and to the cooperative relationship in the rather narrow and technical sense in which we in the ecumenical groups have come to use that expression. This is not to be understood in any sense as a rejection of ecumenicity, which I believe profoundly to be the work of the Holy Spirit in our age; but it is to recognize that quite unintentionally a tyranny has arisen which stifles apostolate and militates very greatly against any real fulfillment of the great commission and against the freedom of the Holy Spirit to move where he will. . . .

The current view of both younger churchmen and older churchmen is that "mission" and missionary agencies must be subject to the younger churches, and work only where and when and how the younger churches should dictate. This has produced a retraction in the missionary witness that is worse than tragic and at the same time when there are still vast areas that have not heard the gospel. . . . We must have a breakdown of the contemporary view that if a church is established in a given country, or even in a region of a country, it has "homestead rights" (if not squatter's rights) and no one may enter except with the approval of the existing church, to work under the direction of that church. . . .

We must replace the present pattern in the cooperative groups, to once again swing wide open the doors so that the largest possible number of missionaries may enter to proclaim the gospel to as many people as possible.[7]

Jackson has given us fair warning of what we may expect if we blindly follow the evolutionary interpretation of missions, accepting as inevitable and good whatever the "new pattern" may be. In area after area, the evangelistic mandate is going unfulfilled because a miniscule group of Christians has assumed or has been delegated full evangelistic responsibility for a population it cannot reach alone.

Of course there are areas in which the local church is discharging effectively the responsibility for evangelization and little, if any, outside help is needed. A mission that has served

in such an area will need to refocus its aims and perhaps reallo-
cate its resources, keeping in mind the primary mission.

But instead of concentrating on our primary reason for existence as missions and missionaries, namely, to develop new
relationships and innovative programs to forward this evangelistic task, we tend to resist change—or seek change—for ex-
traneous reasons.

On the one hand we tend to conform to the old structures,
sending unneeded or uninvited servants to churches that feel
increasingly responsible for their own ministry. We may do so
because "the old is good"; God has seen fit to bless the ways of
godly men who laid the foundations. Change is difficult and
dangerous. Besides, jobs and income may be threatened by the
new way.

On the other hand, we become fascinated by the new organizational orthodoxy: amalgamated mission and church. And
we rush to the altar of union as the only really valid option.
Then we sit and wait for an invitation from the "receiving
church," while neither they nor we evangelize the unreached
world.

Does the answer lie in such either/or solutions? Why do we
lump all "missionary" activity into a single rigid structural relationship? Why do we not distinguish the roles of those we
send overseas? Certainly when *ministry* to the *church* is the
task, a move toward the servant role is long overdue in many
places. But when our *mission* to the *world* is the task, we must
maintain enough structural flexibility to assure its completion.

If the historic missions can cut free from inhibiting traditions
concerning the role of the "missionary," refuse indiscriminate
adoption of emerging organizational fundamentalism, and act
creatively, the role of world evangelization through them may
well be accomplished. However, if they become bound by
either the old or the new, God may well pass them by and accomplish His purpose of world redemption through new, free,
dynamic movements.

CONCLUSION

"Is there still a valid role for the foreign missionary?" We may answer categorically: so long as the evangelistic mandate has not been completed, the church of Jesus Christ has need for representatives with evangelistic ability to which it may delegate this responsibility. The role of the missionary evangelist is more needed today than ever before.

Therefore, we can face young men who are seeking the will of God for life investment and say: If God has given you a gift and calling of service to the church—teaching, pastoring, healing, literature—you may serve in needy America or needy Africa, long-term or short-term, full-time or part-time. But you must go as a servant of the church to which you minister. If you do go to a foreign land, you would be wise to ride light in the saddle—you may be phased out instead of fused in.

But if God has called and gifted you to bring sinners to repentance and plant the church of Christ, here is a band of pioneer evangelists we call a "mission." It works in partnership with other groups—other missions, churches at home, churches overseas—in some cases by fusion in a single organization, in some cases by consultation with other autonomous organizations. But, my young friend, they're in business till Jesus comes. They are obeying His great command. They have His promises. They will succeed, for the gates of hell shall not prevail against them.

NOTES

1. Harold Lindsell, ed., *The Church's Worldwide Mission* (Waco, Tex.: Word, 1966), p. 221.
2. *Missionary Research Bulletin*, 11, no. 8.
3. *Christianity Today* 11, no. 3 (Nov. 11, 1966): 4-5.
4. Philip Schaff, *The Oldest Church Manual Called the "Teaching of the Twelve Apostles"* (New York: Funk & Wagnalls, 1886), p. 68.
5. *Christianity Today* 16, no. 5 (Dec. 3, 1971): 41.
6. Donald McGavran, ed., *Church Growth Bulletin* 7, no. 6 (July 1971): 151-52.
7. Herbert C. Jackson, ed., *Occasional Bulletin* 12, no. 10 (Dec. 1961).

Part VI

Third World Missions

The Planting of Younger Missions first appeared in
Church/Mission Tensions Today edited by C. Peter
Wagner and published by Moody Press.

The Two Structures of the Christian Mission first
appeared in Volume II, No. 1, January, 1974 of
Missiology: An International Review.

"Missions from the Third World" is composed of selections from
a book of the same title by James Wong, Peter Larson and Edward
Pentecost. In the course of their studies for their master's degrees at
the School of World Mission at Fuller Theological Seminary, they
gathered the very pertinent but almost unknown data here presented. James Wong, an Anglican priest, is the director of the Chruch
Growth Study Center in Singapore. Peter Larson is a missionary of
the Baptist General Conference in Argentina. Edward Pentecost is
currently on the faculty of Dallas Theological Seminary in their
missions department. He formerly taught at the Philadelphia School
of the Bible and served as a missionary to Mexico.

*Missionaries and mission strategists commonly talk
about planting younger churches in the mission
fields they are sent to. This is all to the good. But
in this chapter, which may turn out to be a mile-
stone in contemporary missionary thought, Ralph
Winter raises a question that is not commonly
talked about in missionary circles: How about
planting younger* missions? *The matter of moving*
beyond *the national church is something which
was not stressed at Green Lake, but which is
brought out strongly by Winter and other contributors to this symposium. Here, not only the
goals, but the accompanying structures are analyzed with unusual perception.*

18

THE PLANTING OF YOUNGER
MISSIONS

by RALPH D. WINTER

I was in the Philippines recently, staying in the Conservative
Baptist Mission guest home while being involved in a seminar
on theological education by extension. To my delight, different missionaries and nationals were invited to be present at
mealtime from day to day, and through these contacts I re-

RALPH D. WINTER is Associate Professor of the Historical Development of the Christian Mission in the School of World Mission at Fuller
Theological Seminary, a position he accepted after ten years of experience as a United Presbyterian missionary in Guatemala. He holds the
B.S. degree from California Institute of Technology, the B.D. from
Princeton Theological Seminary, the M.A. in Education from Columbia University and the Ph.D. in Anthropology from Cornell. Dr. Winter
is widely respected as a missionary opinion-former through his writ-

ceived a good impression of how determinedly the Conservative Baptist missionaries and national church leaders were involved in church-planting.[1]

I observed, however, that the American missionaries, while
they participate in local church life, are themselves preeminently members of a nonchurch organization (based in the USA)
called the Conservative Baptist Foreign Mission Society. The
national leaders in the Philippines neither have joined this
United States organization, nor have they formed a parallel
mission structure of their own. I do not know that anyone has
tried to stop them from doing so. I suppose the idea simply
has not come up.

I would like to bring it up here and now. I have selected
the people in the CBFMS because they are so up-to-date; if I
can make a point in regard to their operation, it will have to
apply to practically every other mission!

CLEAR GOALS, CONFUSED MEANS

In Manila there is no question about clarity of purpose in
church-planting. The goal is an autonomous, nationally run
Conservative Baptist Association in the Philippines, or perhaps an even larger association including other Baptists. "Some
day" this Philippine association may sprout its own home mission society or foreign mission society. But when? How will it
go about it? Why not now? Why is not a nationally run mission as clearly and definitely a goal as is church-planting? That
is, why do the various goals prominent in everyone's mind not
include both *church*-planting and *mission*-planting? And why
do we talk so little about such things? Or, to take another tack,
why is it that only the foreign missionary (no doubt not by

ings such as *The Twenty-Five Unbelievable Year*s (cited by several
authors in this symposium), and for his role as one of the architects
of the extension seminary movement. The book he edited, *Theological
Education by Extension,* has become a cornerstone for that movement,
worldwide.

plan, but by default) has the right, the duty or the opportunity to "go here or to go there and plant a church"?

In the present circumstances, for example, if the Conservative Baptist Mission in the Philippines for any reason decides that its particular family of churches ought to be extended to some other country (or even to some other part of the Philippines), everyone would be likely to assume that it will take foreign money, foreign personnel, and even a decision by foreigners. There may be exceptions, but at least this is the usual approach. Without any foreign help, the local churches may be doing an excellent job reaching out evangelistically in their own localities. But if a new church is going to be established at a distance, especially in another dialect area, that will very likely be the work of the foreigner. Why? Because for some strange reason the only *mission* in the situation is a foreigner's mission, and because the vaunted goal of producing a nationally run *church,* as valuable and praiseworthy as such a goal is, has not automatically included the establishment of nationally run *missions* as part of the package.

This is not to say the idea has never been thought of. The American Presbyterian missionaries in Korea, for example, long ago saw fulfillment of their dream of a national church that would send foreign missionaries. The United Church of Christ in the Philippines sends foreign missionaries. The members of the Latin America Mission are in the throes of mutating into an association of autonomous missions in which Latin as well as Anglo Westerners are involved, but they do not include nor at the moment plan to deal with the far more drastic cross-cultural task of reaching the aboriginal, non-Western inhabitants of Latin America. There are many other examples. And as to the future, just wait: the recently established Conservative Baptist Association in the Philippines will before long be sending foreign missionaries.

Nevertheless, what I would like to know is why the sending of missionaries by the younger church is so relatively rare a phenomenon, and, if discussed, is so widely conceived to be a "later on" type of thing. Just as a new convert ought to be able immediately to witness to his new faith (and a great deal is lost if he does not), so a newly founded church ought not only to love Jesus Christ but to be able immediately to show and share its love in obedience to the Great Commission. How long did it take for the congregation at Antioch to be able to commission its first missionaries? Were they premature?

Space does not allow us to describe the outstanding mission work done by Pacific Islanders (over 1,000 in a list recently compiled), by Vietnamese nationals in the seventeenth and eighteenth centuries, or by the famous Celtic Peregrini and their Anglo-Saxon imitators, for example. Perhaps what we must at least point out is that the churches emerging from the Reformation must not be taken as an example. They took more than 250 years to get around to any kind of serious mission effort, but even then it was not more than on a relatively small scale for an entire century.

The most curious thing of all is the fact that precisely those people most interested in church growth often are not effectively concerned about what makes congregations multiply. Those who concede that church-planting is the primary instrument whereby mankind can be redeemed do not always seem to be effectively employing those key structures that specialize in church-planting. We hear cries on every side to the effect that an indigenous national church is our goal, but the unnoticed assumptions are (1) that only a Western mission can start a new work across cultural boundaries, and (2) that once such a church is established, the church itself will somehow just grow and plant itself in every direction. What illogically follows is this: United States churches need explicit mission organizations to reach out effectively for them, but overseas churches can get along without such structures. The goals are clear; the means to reach them are still largely obscured.

WHAT GREEN LAKE DID NOT SAY

Admittedly this chapter covers a subject the Green Lake

Conference did not plan to take up. As GL '71 unfolded, we all began to realize that what has carelessly been termed "church/mission relations" really refers, it turns out, to mission/church relations: the relations between an American *mission* and an overseas national *church* (which is probably the product of the U.S. mission's work over the years). To these mission/church relations, GL '71 added church/mission relations, namely, the relation of the *churches* back home to the *mission* they support. So now we have what George Peters characterized as the official docket of the conference, namely, church/mission/church relations. This included three focuses: (1) the church at home, (2) the missions which are their overseas arm, and (3) the churches overseas resulting from these missionary efforts. We can call this "second-generation church-planting" and diagram it as in Figure 1.

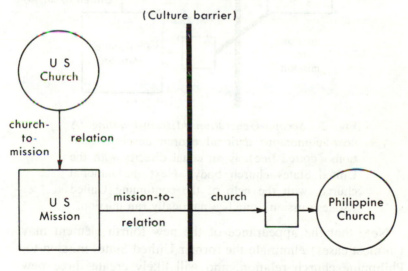

Fig. 1. *Second-Generation Church-Planting.* A new church is "planted" by a United States-based mission across a cultural barrier (mottled line).

It is greatly to be appreciated that this post-GL '71 symposium has allowed for an additional element to enter the picture, namely, the *mission* outreach of the *younger churches*. Thus, while Green Lake tended to confine itself to church/mission/ church relations, this symposium covers greater ground, namely, church/mission/church/mission relations. This may be termed "second-generation *mission*-planting," and diagramed as in Figure 2.

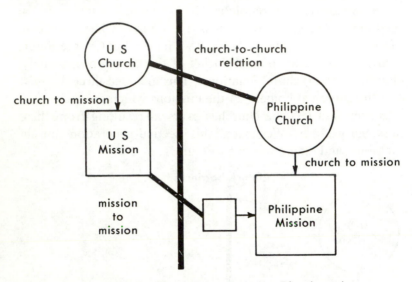

Fig. 2. *Second-Generation Mission-Planting.* A now-autonomous national church develops relations (dotted line) as an equal directly with the United States church body. Next the national church, with the help of the continuing United States mission, founds a nationally run mission.

Note that the appearance of the new fourth element may (in most cases) eliminate the former United States mission-to-Philippine church relation, and will likely create three new ones: (1) United States *church*-to-Philippine *church*, (2) United States *mission*-to-Philippine *mission*, and (3) a new kind of Philippine *church*-to-Philippine *mission* relation that is parallel to the existing United States *church*-to-United States *mission* relation.

In Figure 3 we are anticipating not only the existence of an autonomous Philippine mission, but also its success in establishing a third-generation church across some new cultural barrier. (The existence of such barriers is the primary reason for needing a specialized mission organization, in contrast to ordinary church evangelism, to accomplish such a task.) We call this step "third-generation church-planting." By this time it is possible that the United States mission has reduced its staff sufficiently to be able to move into a new field in a similar way to plant another second-generation church.

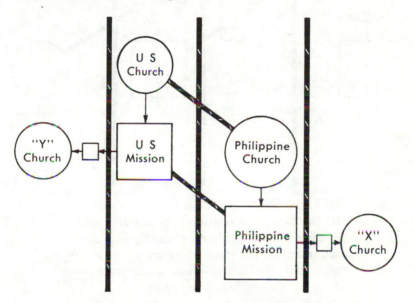

Fig. 3. *Third-Generation Church-Planting.* Both national church and national mission are now autonomous. The national mission establishes relations as an equal with the United States mission, and both it and the United States mission (elsewhere) plant churches across new cultural barriers. This is "third-generation church-planting" for the United States mission and "second-generation church-planting" for the Philippine mission.

Figure 4 assumes that the new third-generation church has now been encouraged to plant its own mission agency before the second-generation mission considers its task finished.

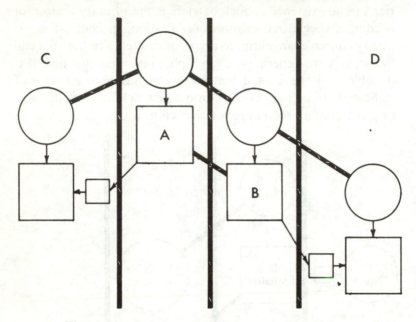

Fig. 4. Both (A) the United States mission and (B) the Philippine mission help establish nationally run *missions* in cultures C and D, respectively, each repeating the stage of Figure 2. In healthy church and mission multiplication this process will continue indefinitely.

FIRST REACTIONS

At this point some may recoil in horror at the thought of all this new machinery to be set up. Some readers may even have compared this to Rube Goldberg. It isn't that we object to the nationals getting in and doing things for themselves. We just somehow can't see the desirability of the nationals, with their limited resources and perhaps in some cases limited knowledge of the rest of the world, having to get involved in all the administrative paper work needed to set up and operate a competent mission agency. It is parallel to our feeling that every nation doesn't have to be a member of the nuclear club. Why should every small nation have to figure out how to make an atomic bomb? Some people may even feel that nationals can't be trusted that far! Can they not be trusted to send missionaries on their own? Western missions made a lot of mistakes in the beginning, and by now they have learned much about government red tape, anthropology, etc. Why should national leaders who have huge problems at home be bothered at this early stage with the problems of other nations?

Furthermore, it is rather mind-boggling to imagine how many new mission organizations will jump into existence around the world if this new kind of mission theory is pursued. The number of new churches (and whole demoninations) springing up in the non-Western world is already astronomical, especially in Africa. You can image the statisticians at the World Council of Churches or the World Evangelical Fellowship going out of their minds trying to keep track of all the new denominations being born (currently at the rate of at least one a day). Isn't that bad enough? So the question naturally arises: Are we serious about every church communion in the world getting into the mission business?

Let's think about it some more. For one thing, we're not necessarily suggesting that the Dani tribespeople of West Irian send a missionary to the Eskimos. Let's reemphasize right here that a specialized mission structure is required not just for work in foreign countries, but also for work in foreign *cultures,* which may or may not be found merely in foreign countries. One of our common weaknesses is that we often take cultural differences more seriously when a political boundary is crossed than when we reflect upon groups of different culture within our own country, especially when those groups are minorities and may appear to be unpatriotic in their adherence to their traditional customs. Certainly, wherever it is feasible, full-fledged work in a foreign country is desirable for several rea-

sons. It not only puts the new national mission on a par with
the United States mission which caused its own birth; it also
creates a parallelism of circumstances and experience as national workers discover what it feels like to present the gospel
while working as aliens in a foreign country. This kind of experience may for the first time introduce key leaders and their
families to the psychological dimension of sacrifice involved
in being a missionary. Nationals with such experience behind
them will be the first to see the foreign missionary in a new
light.

However, no matter what the miscellaneous factors pro and
con may be, there are two overarching mandates that throw
the whole subject of younger missions into the very highest
priority.

THE DEMOGRAPHIC IMPERATIVE

In a recent article I found myself presenting a chart which
indicated the existence of 2,150,000,000 non-Christian Asians.
While Christians constitute a higher percentage of the Asian
population than ever before, a far larger number of Asians do
not know Christ than when William Carey first headed for
India. We must be deeply grateful to God and to earlier pioneers that there are over ten million Christians in India, for
example, but the perplexing fact is that there are at least 500
subcultures in India alone, as distinct from each other socially
as the blacks and whites in Birmingham, Alabama, and that in
at least 480 of these entire subcultures there are no Christians
at all. Very bluntly, normal evangelistic outreach from existing Christian churches in India is utterly inadequate to face
this challenge.

Note that I am not making a case here for the need of United
States missionaries, although in many of these subcultures
Western missionaries might be just as acceptable, or more so,
than any Indian or Asian. What I am saying is that not even
the Indian Christians can do this job unless (1) they understand it to be a task of full-blown *missionary* complexity, and

(2) they set up the proper *mission* machinery to do the job.

What is most needed in India today is the development of liberating fellowships of Christian faith among the hundreds of millions of Indian people who live in the hundreds of unreached subcultures. But the point is that these essential, crucial new fellowships in the unreached subcultures will not be planted by existing *churches* as much as by *mission* structures that can effectively express the true Christian obedience of the existing churches.

We hear that there are already one hundred such mission agencies in India, either for evangelism within the pockets of population where there are already Christians, or for real cross-cultural mission into pockets that are as yet unreached. But who cares? No one even has a list of these organizations. No one thinks it is important enough to make such a list. The new, immeasurably improved, *World Christian Handbook* for 1973 is projected for publications without such a list. There have long been directories of missions originating in the Western world; no one has yet begun a directory of the missions originating in the non-Western world.

This is not a bizarre, offbeat curiosity. It is impressively clear that the two thousand million non-Christian Asians will not be reached unless it can become fashionable for the *younger churches* to establish *younger missions*.

THE THEOLOGICAL IMPERATIVE

One reason why some apathy about missions has been growing in the United States recently has been all the talk (shall we say the "crowing"?) that has gone on during the past twenty-five years about the "great new fact of our time," that is, the emergence of a worldwide family of believers representing every country (but not every subculture) on the face of the globe. As we have seen, this quite distorts the picture demographically. Theologically it is very nearly totally misleading.

When pushed excessively, this "great new fact" ignores the

theological reality of the diverse subcultures of mankind. Let's take a hypothetical example. If the United States were an unreached country and Christians from Japan planted a church in Seattle, another in San Francisco, and a third in Los Angeles and then headed home feeling satisfied that the United States had now been reached for Christ, this would be the kind of demographic nonsense we pointed out above. But if the three churches that were planted by the Japanese mission were all among the Navajo Indians, it would become a *theological* absurdity as well. And it would be an even greater absurdity if all the rest of the United States were (like Africa and Asia) cut up into hundreds of radically different subcultures rather than being relatively unified in language and culture. This is only a parable of the whole non-Western world today.

The theological imperative, however, does not merely arise from such practical considerations of tough cross-cultural mission. It goes much deeper. Do we dare say that whether or not there is anyone to "win" in foreign countries, that God does not intend for national churches to be isolated from Christians of radically diverse culture? Do we dare say that the Great Commission will not be fulfilled merely by the planting of an indigenous church in every culture so long as those churches remain isolated? Surely the Bible teaches us that the worldwide multitude of Christians constitutes a body, and that the various members and organs of that body need each other. Isn't it possible, therefore, to assume on theological grounds that even if everyone in the world were converted to Christ, Christians in one culture would still need to know Christians in other places? And their growth in faith and love would have to consist in part of some kind of nonassimilative integration which would neither arbitrarily break down all the cultural differences nor allow the diverse elements of the body to wither and die, or be stunted due to the lack of proper circulation of witness and testimony through the whole body.

This is the ultimate reason for missions. God has allowed a gorgeous diversity among the butterflies, the leaves, the flowers, and the human families of mankind. If He does not intend to reduce the number of butterflies and flowers to a single model, He may not intend to eliminate all the ethnic, racial and linguistic differences in the world today. If He doesn't, then there is (and always will be) a powerful case for special mission organizations to facilitate the intercultural contact and to provide the lifeblood that will enable the whole body to flourish through interdependence, rather than to languish in fragmented isolation or to be stultified in a monotonous uniformity.

The theological imperative means that we condemn national churches to stultification if we frustrate their right and their duty to enter into serious mission. This ominous stagnation can occur to missionless churches in the Celebes as easily as it can develop among complacent nonmissionary minded Christians in a Detroit or London suburb. This is a theological dimension that has nothing to do with arithmetic or demography.

THE BACKGROUND OF THE IMPASSE

At least two assumptions may contribute to the widespread blindness about the need for younger missions as well as younger churches. One of these arose years ago in what is now called the ecumenical camp. The other, which leads almost precisely to the same conclusion, is a pattern of thought common among the most fervent Evangelicals.

Ironically, the first assumption began to develop at that time in history when the older historic denominations' mission efforts were staffed and run primarily by people who would be considered clearly evangelical today. It was D. L. Moody who launched John R. Mott into the explosively powerful Student Volunteer Movement, for example, and it was these early evangelical student leaders and their followers who, in country after country around the world, organized the missionary councils. By 1928 there were twenty-three. By 1948 there were thirty, and virtually every "mission field" country of the non-Western world and even of the sending countries had its missionary council or Christian council. Note that in only three of these was there any reference to "churches" in the title. They were missionary councils or "Christian" councils, but *not* councils of churches. This means that in India, for example, both national churches and *foreign* mission societies were originally represented in the national Christian council. Also, as a minor element, there already were indigenous mission societies of certain special types, such as quasi-nationalized offices of the American Bible Society or of the YMCA. The development of younger *churches* was the focus of attention, and apparently it was almost automatically supposed that *missionary societies* could only come from abroad. This fact later became a booby trap. Western mission societies themselves usually took the initiative to withdraw from these councils (in order to let national churches "run their own show") and, as a well-intentioned but tragic parting shot, they often even recommended either directly or indirectly that only *churches* should be allowed as members in the councils they left behind.

This fateful step assured the free sway of authority by national leaders, but it also swept the American Bible Society and the YMCA *and all future indigenous mission societies!* The National Christian Council of India in 1956 determined that "only organized church bodies are entitled to direct representation in the Council."[2] As a result, many Christian councils actually changed their names to "councils of churches." Still other councils, as that of India, for example, changed their nature (as above) without changing their names.

However, it is not as though everyone simply forgot about the need for mission work to be carried forward by personnel and funds from within the new nations and the younger churches. By this time in history it was felt that all missions should properly result from the direct initiative of *church* organizations as such. The move to exclude all but churches from these new councils did not, it was thought, do any more than eliminate *foreign* missions. Missions sponsored by national Christians, it was assumed, would quite naturally and normally be represented in the meetings of those new church councils by the appropriate respresentatives of the churches themselves. Thus the unquestionable principle stressing the autonomy of the national church was implemented in such a way as to exclude without a hearing the cause of the voluntary society. The reason the records do not show any great tussle at the time is partly because of the confusion of the two issues and of the predominant urgency after 1945 of getting the foreigners out of the picture. It also resulted from the fact that by this time most of the larger and older voluntary societies had already severed ties with these councils, and were thus not present to voice any opinion as to the structural implications of the new development. This leads us to the second basic assumption which has caused blindness among present-day Evangelicals about the need for younger missions.

There is no disguising the fact that a great deal (perhaps by now it would be fair to say the bulk) of mission efforts has been and is the work of people who normally call themselves Evangelicals. Evangelicals have expressed their missionary interest both inside and outside the older denominations. Every move by the older denominations to decrease foreign mission efforts has resulted in proportionate transferral of personnel and funds to newer "more mission-minded" denominations (and their mission boards) or to interdenominational missions, old and new. Thus, the average missionary overseas has tended to be either a strong Evangelical working within an older denomination (and thus believing that churches as such can and should send missions) or increasingly he is likely to be a missionary working for an interdenominational society, in which case he commonly believes that while older, perhaps liberalized, denominations back home can't be expected to send many missionaries, certainly the new churches overseas (started from scratch by evangelical fervor and developing with close dependence upon the Word of God) will surely be as missionary-minded as the missionary himself.

Thus, by 1972 we see that on every side, whether liberal or

conservative, there is a nearly unanimous assumption that the autonomous mission society in the mission land is either wrong and shouldn't exist or that it will be necessary only as an emergency measure someday in the future when younger churches follow the path of older United States denominations and "go liberal."

CONCLUSION

It is painful to add one more reason for blindness about the need for younger missions. True passion for the lost today is relatively scarce, even among missionaries. You don't have to be very daring to be a missionary today. As one missionary put it, "Circumstances have changed so much that it takes more courage to go home to the States than it does to go overseas." In the case of the United Presbyterians, for example, a young seminary graduate can very likely get a higher salary by going overseas as a missionary (if there is any budget for him at all) than he can by starting at the bottom rung of the ladder in church life back home. In general, American missions are a very elaborate end product of a massive century and a half of institutional development. The early missionaries were generally poor people who went from a poor country. But it did not take them long to build up institutions and vast land holdings—in some cases little empires—and in all cases a vast array of paraphernalia unimaginably beyond the ability of the national churches to duplicate.

Thus, even in an economic sense, the missionary from a well-heeled country is his own worst enemy should he ever want to promote a bleeding, sacrificial outpouring in foreign missions on the part of Christians in the national churches of the Third World. They literally cannot "go and do likewise."

Let us envision for a moment the young United States mission candidate. He may have to scrounge around for the wherewithal to buy his family a car, a camera, and a washing machine (just the "bare necessities" of the US life-style). Once on the field he will make expensive plane flights to the capital city for necessary medical help from real medical doctors. Even the most pitiable, poverty-stricken new missionary appears quite wealthy to the national Christian of most mission lands. For example, he may purchase just a few native trinkets to dress up his home for the benefit of the occasional tourist from America. What he buys for this purpose may appear in the national's eyes to be a shockingly trivial use of items which are to him culturally functional and essential, and may even cost him a year's savings!

Quite obviously missions, United States style, are out of reach to the Third World churches. National churches are as unlikely to be capable of following the life-style of United States missions as they are able to own as many cars per family. The economic gap is so great that the only possible solution is for autonomous younger missions to enter the picture on their own and be able to do things their own way. This may or may not mean they will set up their own promotional office in Wheaton, Illinois. In any case, it will be a whole new ball game.

We may end the century somewhat in the way foreign missions first began (in Protestant hands), with German candidates going under Danish auspices supported by British funds. Entirely new patterns may develop once the ingenuity and creativity of the younger churches reign free. One thing is clear: We cannot promote second-generation churches without promoting second-generation missions. The great new fact of *our* time must be the emergence of Third World *missions*. This is the next phase of missions today.

NOTES

1. The word *plant* is not ill-chosen. To say *establish* would be presumptuous by contrast. *Plant* means precisely that you take into your hands life which is beyond your power and help it to take root and grow by a process which is beyond your power. *Planting* is a delicate but very much needed task in which man assists God.
2. Harold E. Fey, ed., *The Ecumenical Advance: A History of the Ecumenical Movement*, vol. 2, 1948–1968 (Philadelphia: Westminster, 1970), p. 98.

The Two Structures of God's Redemptive Mission[1]

RALPH D. WINTER

19

IT is the thesis of this article that whether Christianity takes on Western or Asian form, there will still be two basic kinds of structures that will make up the movement. Most of the emphasis will be placed on pointing out the existence of these two structures as they have continuously appeared across the centuries. This will serve to define, illustrate and compare their nature and importance. The writer will also endeavor to explain why he believes our efforts today in any part of the world will be most effective only if both of these two structures are fully and properly involved. Finally, it is hoped that this material will highlight the degree of urgency at this conference to foster every effort to promote better understanding and harmony between these two structures.

Redemptive Structures in New Testament Times

First of all let us recognize the structure so fondly called "the New Testament Church" as basically a Christian synagogue.[2] Paul's missionary work consisted primarily of going to synagogues scattered across the Roman Empire, beginning in Asia Minor, and making clear to the Jewish and Gentile believers in those synagogues that the Messiah had come in Jesus Christ, the Son of God; that in Christ a final authority even greater than Moses existed; and that this made possible the winning of the Gentiles without forcing upon them any literal cultural adaptation to the ritual provisions of the Mosaic Law. An outward novelty of Paul's work was the development eventually of wholly new synagogues that were not only Christian, but Greek.

Very few Christians, casually reading the New Testament, and with only the New Testament available to them, would surmise the degree to which there had been Jewish evangelists who went before Paul all over the Empire, people whom Jesus himself described as "traversing land and sea to make a single proselyte." Paul followed their path; he built on their efforts and went beyond them with the new gospel he preached, which allowed the Greeks to remain Greeks and not be circumcised and culturally assimilated into the Jewish way of life.[3]

Yet, not only did Paul apparently go to every existing synagogue of Asia,[4] after which he declared, ". . . all Asia has heard the gospel," but, when occasion demanded, he established brand new synagogue-type fellowships of believers as the basic unit of his missionary activity. The first structure in the New Testament scene is thus what is often called the *New Testament church*. It was essentially built along Jewish synagogue lines,[5] embracing the community of the faithful in any given place. The defining characteristic of this structure is that it included old and young, male and female. Note, too, that Paul was willing to build such fellowships out of former Jews as well as non-Jewish Greeks.

There is a second, quite different structure in the New Testament context. While we know very little about the structure of the evangelistic outreach within which pre-Pauline Jewish proselytizers worked, we do know, as already mentioned, that they operated all over the Roman Empire. It would be surprising if Paul didn't follow somewhat the same procedures. And we know a great deal more about the way Paul operated. He was, true enough, sent out by the church in Antioch. But once away from Antioch he seemed very much on his own. The little team he formed was economically self-sufficient when occasion demanded. It was also dependent, from time to time, not alone upon the Antioch church, but upon other churches that had risen as a result of evangelistic labors. Paul's team may certainly be considered a structure. While its design and form is not made concrete for us on the basis of remaining documents, neither, of course, is the New Testament church so defined concretely for us in the pages of the New Testament. In both cases, the absence of any such definition implies the pre-existence of a commonly understood pattern of relationship, whether in the case of the church or the missionary band which Paul formed.

Thus, on the one hand, the structure we call the *New Testament church* is a prototype of all subsequent Christian fellowships where old and young, male and female are gathered together as normal biological families in aggregate. On the other hand,

Paul's *missionary band* can be considered a prototype of all
subsequent missionary endeavors organized out of committed,
experienced workers who affiliated themselves as a second
decision beyond membership in the first structure.

Note well the *additional* commitment. Note also that the
structure that resulted was something definitely more than the
extended outreach of the Antioch church. No matter what we
think the structure was, we know that it was not simply the
Antioch church operating at a distance from its home base. It
was something else, something different. We will consider the
missionary band the second of the two redemptive structures in
New Testament times.

In conclusion, it is very important to note that neither of these
two structures was, as it were, "let down from heaven" in a special
way. It may be shocking at first to think that God made use of
either a *Jewish* synagogue pattern or a *Jewish* evangelistic pattern.
But this must not be more surprising than the fact that God
employed the use of the pagan Greek language, the Holy Spirit
guiding the biblical writers to lay hold of such terms as *kurios*
(originally a pagan term), and pound them into shape to carry
the Christian revelation. The New Testament refers to a
synagogue dedicated to Satan, but this did not mean that
Christians, to avoid such a pattern, could not fellowship together
in the synagogue pattern. These considerations prepare us for
what comes next in the history of the expansion of the gospel,
because we see other patterns chosen by Christians at a later date
whose origins are just as clearly "borrowed patterns" as were
those in the New Testament period.

In fact, the profound missiological implication of all this is that
the New Testament is trying to show us *how to borrow effective
patterns;* it is trying to free all future missionaries from the need
to follow the precise *forms* of the Jewish synagogue and Jewish
missionary band, and yet to allow them to choose comparable
indigenous structures in the countless new situations across
history and around the world — structures which will corres-
pond faithfully to the *function* of the patterns Paul employed, if
not their *form!* It is no wonder that a considerable body of
literature in the field of missiology today underlies the fact that
world Christianity has generally employed the various existing
languages and cultures of the world-human community — more
so than any other religion — and in so doing, has cast into a

shadow all efforts to canonize as universal any kind of mechanically formal extension of the New Testament church. As Kraft has said earlier, we seek *dynamic equivalence* (1973:39 ff.) not formal replication.

The Early Development of Christian Structures Within Roman Culture

We have seen how the Christian movement built itself upon two different kinds of structures that had pre-existed in the Jewish cultural tradition. It is now our task to see if the *functional* equivalents of these same two structures were to appear in the Roman cultural tradition as the gospel invaded that larger world.

Of course, the original synagogue pattern persisted as a Christian structure for some time. Rivalry between Christians and Jews, however, tended to defeat this as a Christian pattern, and in some cases to force it out of existence, especially where it was possible for Jewish congregations of the dispersion to arouse public persecution of the apparently deviant Christian synagogues. Unlike the Jews, Christians had no official license for their alternative to the Roman Imperial cult.[6] Thus, whereas each synagogue was considerably independent of the others, the Christian pattern was soon assimilated to the Roman context, and bishops became invested with authority over more than one congregation with a territorial jurisdiction not altogether different from the pattern of Roman civil government. This tendency is well confirmed by the time the official recognition of Christianity had its full impact: the very Latin word for Roman magisterial territories was appropriated — the *diocese* — within which parishes are to be found on the local level.

In any case, while the more "congregational" pattern of the independent synagogue became pervasively replaced by a "connectional" Roman pattern, the new Christian *parish church* still preserved the basic constituency of the synagogue, namely, the combination of old and young, male and female — that is, a biologically perpetuating organism.

Meanwhile, the monastic tradition in various early forms, developed as a second structure. This new, widely proliferating structure undoubtedly had no connection at all with the missionary band in which Paul was involved. Indeed, it more substantially drew from Roman military structure than from any other single source. Pachomius, a former military man, gained three thousand followers and attracted the attention of people like Basil of Caesarea, and then through Basil, John Cassian, who laboured in southern Gaul at a later date (Latourette, 1953:181, 221-234). These men thus carried forward a disciplined structure, borrowed primarily from the military, which allowed nominal Christians to make a second-level choice — an additional specific commitment.

Perhaps it would be well to pause here for a moment. Any reference to the monasteries gives Protestants culture shock. The Protestant Reformation fought desperately against certain degraded conditions at the very end of the 1000-year medieval period. We have no desire to deny the fact that conditions in monasteries were not always ideal; what the average Protestant knows about monasteries may be correct for certain situations; but the popular Protestant stereotype surely cannot describe correctly all that happened during the 1000 years! During those centuries there were many different eras and epochs and a wide variety of monastic movements, radically different from each other, as we shall see in a minute; and any generalization about so vast a phenomenon is bound to be simply an unreliable and no doubt prejudiced caricature.

Let me give just one example of how far wrong our Protestant stereotypes can be. We often hear that the monks "fled the world." Compare that idea with this description by a Baptist missionary scholar:

The Benedictine rule and the many derived from it probably helped to give dignity to labour, including manual labour in the fields. This was in striking contrast with the aristocratic conviction of the servile status of manual work which prevailed in much of ancient society and which was also the attitude of the warriors and non-monastic ecclesiastics who constituted the upper middle classes of the Middle Ages . . . To the monasteries . . . was obviously due much clearing of land and improvement in methods of agriculture. In the midst of barbarism, the monasteries were centres of orderly and settled life and examples of the skillful management of the soil. Under the Carolingians monks were assigned the duty of road-building and road repair. Until the rise of the towns in the eleventh century, they were pioneers in industry and commerce. The shops of the monasteries preserved the industries of Roman times . . . The earliest use of marl in improving the soil is attributed to them. The great French monastic orders led in the agricultural colonization of Western Europe. Especially did the Cistercians make their houses centres of agriculture and contribute to improvements in that occupation. With their lay brothers and their hired labourers, they became great landed proprietors. In

Hungary and on the German frontier the Cistercians were particularly important in reducing the soil to cultivation and in furthering colonization. In Poland, too, the German monasteries set advanced standards in agriculture and introduced artisans and craftsmen (Latourette, 1938:379-380).

For mission leaders the shattering of the "monks fled the world" stereotype is even more dramatically and decisively reinforced by the magnificent record of the Irish *peregrini,* who were Celtic monks who did more to reach out to convert Anglo-Saxons than did Augustine's mission, and who contributed more to the evangelization of Western Europe, even Central Europe, than any other force.[7]

From its very inception this second kind of structure was highly significant to the growth and development of the Christian movement. Even though Protestants have an inbuilt prejudice against it for various reasons, as we have seen, there is no denying the fact that apart from this structure it would be hard even to imagine the vital continuity of the Christian tradition across the centuries. Protestants are equally dismayed by the other structure — the parish and diocesan structure. It is, in fact, the relative weakness and nominality of the diocesan structure that makes the monastic structure so significant. Men like Jerome and Augustine, for example, are thought of by Protestants not as monks but as great scholars; and people like John Calvin lean very heavily upon writings that derive from such monks. But Protestants do not usually give any credit to the specific structure within which Jerome and Augustine and many other monastic scholars worked, a structure without which Protestant labors would have had very little to build on, not even a Bible.

We must now follow these threads into the next period, where we will see the formal emergence of the major monastic structures. It is sufficient at this point merely to note that there are already by the fourth century two very different kinds of structures — the diocese and the monastery — both of them significant in the transmission and expansion of Christianity. They are each patterns borrowed from the cultural context of their time, just as were the earlier Christian synagogue and missionary band.

It is even more important for our purpose here to note that while these two structures are *formally* different from — and historically unrelated to — the two in New Testament times, they are nevertheless *functionally* the same. In order to speak conveniently about the continuing similarities in function, let us now call the synagogue and diocese *modalities,* and the missionary band and monastery, *sodalities.* Elsewhere I have developed these terms in detail, but briefly, a modality is a structured fellowship in which there is no distinction of sex or age, while a sodality is a structured fellowship in which membership involves an adult second decision beyond modality membership, and is limited by either age or sex or marital status. In this use of these terms, both the *denomination* and the *local congregation* are modalities, while a mission agency or a local men's club are sodalities (Winter, 1970:52-62).

In this early post-Biblical period there was little relation between modality and sodality, while in Paul's time his missionary band specifically nourished the churches — a most significant symbiosis. We shall now see how the medieval period essentially recovered the healthy New Testament relationship between modality and sodality.

The Medieval Synthesis of Modality and Sodality

We can say that the Medieval period began when the Roman Empire in the West started to break down. To some extent the diocesan pattern, following as it did the Roman civil-governmental pattern, tended to break down at the same time. The monastic (or sodality) pattern turned out to be much more durable, and as a result gained greater importance in the early medieval period than it might have otherwise. The survival of the modality (diocesan Christianity) was further compromised by the fact that the invaders of this early medieval period generally belonged to a different brand of Christian belief — they were Arians. As a result, in many places there were both "Arian" and "Catholic" Christian churches on opposite corners of a main street — something like today, where we have Methodist and Presbyterian churches across the street from each other.

Again, however, it is not our purpose to downplay the significance of the parish or diocesan form of Christianity, but simply to point out that during this early period of the Medieval epoch the specialized house called the *monastery,* or its equivalent, became ever so much more important in the perpetuation of the Christian movement than was the organized system of parishes, which we often call the church *as if there were no other structure making up the church.*

Perhaps the most outstanding illustration in the early medieval period of the importance of the relationship between modality and sodality is the collaboration between Gregory the Great and the man later called Augustine of Canterbury. While Gregory, as the bishop of the diocese of Rome, was the head of a modality, both he and Augustine were the products of monastic houses — a fact which reflects the dominance even then of the sodality pattern of Christian structure. In any case, Gregory called upon his friend Augustine to undertake a major mission to England in order to try to plant diocesan structure there, where Celtic Christianity had been deeply wounded by the invasion of Saxon warriors from the continent.

As strong as Gregory was in his own diocese, he simply had no structure to call upon to reach out in this intended mission other than the sodality, which at this point was a Benedictine monastery. This is why he ended up asking Augustine and a group of other members of the same monastery to undertake this rather dangerous journey and important mission on his behalf. The purpose of the mission, curiously, was not to extend the Benedictine form of monasticism. The remnant of the Celtic "church" in England was itself a network of sodalities since there was no parish system in the Celtic area. No, Augustine went to England to establish diocesan Christianity, though he himself was not a diocesan priest.

This is quite characteristic. During a lengthy period of time, perhaps a thousand years, the building and rebuilding of the modalities was mainly the work of the sodalities. That is to say, the monasteries were uniformly the source and the real focus point of new energy and vitality which flowed into the diocesan side of the Christian movement. We think of the momentous Cluny reform, then the Cistercians, then the Friars, and finally the Jesuits — all of them strictly sodalities, but sodalities which contributed massively to the building and the rebuilding of the *Corpus Cristianum,* the network of dioceses, which Protestants often identify as "the" Christian movement.

At many points there was rivalry between these two structures, between bishop and abbot, diocese and monastery, modality and sodality, but the great achievement of the medieval period is the ultimate synthesis, delicately achieved, whereby Catholic orders were able to function along with Catholic parishes and dioceses without the two structures conflicting with each other to the point of a setback to the movement. The harmony between the modality and the sodality achieved by the Roman Church is perhaps the most significant characteristic of this phase of the world Christian movement and continues to be Rome's greatest organizational advantage to this day.

Note, however, that it is not our intention to claim that any one organization of either the modality or sodality variety was continuously the champion of vitality and vigor throughout the thousands of years of the medieval epoch. As a matter of actual fact, there really is no very impressive organizational continuity in the Christian movement, either in the form of modality or sodality. (The list of bishops at Rome is at many points a most shaky construct and unfortunately does not even provide a focus for the entire Christian movement.) On the other hand, it is clear that the sodality, as it was recreated again and again by different leaders, was almost always the prime mover, the source of inspiration and renewal which overflowed into the papacy and created the reform movements which blessed diocesan Christianity from time to time. The most significant instance of this is the accession to the papal throne of Hildebrand (Gregory VII), who brought the ideals, commitment and discipline of the monastic movement right into the Vatican itself. In this sense are not then the papacy, the College of Cardinals, the diocese, and the parish structure of the Roman Church in some respects a secondary element, a derivation from the monastic tradition rather than vice versa? In any case, it seems appropriate that the priests of the monastic tradition are called *regular priests,* while the priests of the diocese and parish are called *secular priests.* The former are voluntarily bound by a *regula,* while the latter as a group were other than, outside of ("cut off") or somehow less than the second-decision communities bound by regula. Whenever a house or project or parish run by the regular clergy is brought under the domination of the secular clergy, this is a form of the "secularization" of that entity. In the lengthy "Investiture Controversy," the regular clergy finally gained clear authority for at least semi-autonomous operation, and the secularization of the orders was averted.

We may note that the same structural danger of *secularization* exists today whenever the special concerns of an elite mission sodality fall under the complete domination of an ecclesiastical government, since the Christian modalities (churches) inevitably represent the much broader and, no doubt, mainly inward concerns of a large body of all kinds of Christians, who, as "first-decision" members, are generally less select.

We cannot leave the medieval period without referring to the many unofficial and often persecuted movements which also mark the era. In all of this, the Bible itself is perhaps the ultimate prime mover, as we see in the case of Peter Waldo. His work stands as a powerful demonstration of the simple power of a vernacular translation of the Bible where the people were unable to appreciate either Jerome's classical translation or the celebration of the Mass in Latin. A large number of groups referred to as "Anabaptists" are to be found in many parts of Europe. One of the chief characteristics of these renewal movements is that they did not attempt to elicit merely celibate participation, although this was one of their traits on occasion, but often simply developed whole "new communities" of believers and their families, attempting by biological and cultural transmission to preserve a high and enlightened form of Christianity. These groups usually faced such strong opposition and grave limitations that it would be very unfair to judge their virility by their progress. It is important to note, however, that the average Mennonite or Salvation Army community, where whole families are members, typified the desire for a "pure" church, or what is often called a "believers" church, and constitutes a most significant experiment in Christian structure. Such a structure stands, in a certain sense, midway between a modality and a sodality, since it has the constituency of the modality (involving full families) and yet, in its earlier years, may have the vitality and selectivity of a sodality. We will return to this phenomenon in the next section.

We have space here only to point out that in terms of the durability and quality of the Christian faith, the 1000-year medieval period is virtually impossible to account for apart from the role of the sodalities. What happened in Rome is merely the tip of the iceberg at best, and represents a rather superficial and political level. It is quite a contrast to the foundational well-springs of Biblical study and radical obedience represented by the various sodalities of this momentous millennium.

The Protestant Recovery of the Sodality[8]

The Protestant movement started out by attempting to do without any kind of sodality structure. Martin Luther had been discontent with the apparent polarization between the vitality he eventually discovered in his own order and the very nominal parish life of his time. Being dissatisfied with this cleavage, he abandoned the sodality in which he finally found faith and took advantage of the political forces of his time to launch a full-scale renewal movement on the general level of church life. At first, he even tried to do without the characteristically Roman diocesan structure, but eventually the Lutheran movement produced a Lutheran diocesan structure which to a considerable extent represented the readoption of the Roman diocesan tradition. The Lutheran movement did not in a comparable sense readopt the sodalities, the Catholic orders, that had been so prominent in the Roman tradition.

This omission, in my evaluation, represents the greatest error of the Reformation and the greatest weakness of the resulting Protestant tradition. Had it not been for the so-called Pietist movement, the Protestants would have been totally devoid of any organized renewing structures within their tradition. The Pietist tradition, in every new emergence of its force, was very definitely a sodality, inasmuch as it was a case of adults meeting together and committing themselves to new beginnings and higher goals as Christians without conflicting with the stated meetings of the existing church. This phenomenon of sodality nourishing modality is prominent in the case of the early work of John Wesley. He absolutely prohibited any abandonment of the Parish churches. A contemporary example is the widely influential so-called *East African Revival,* which has now involved a million people but has very carefully avoided any clash with the functioning of local churches. The churches that have not fought against this movement have been greatly blessed by it.

However, the Pietist movement, along with the Anabaptist new communities, eventually dropped back to the level of the nominal commitment of a second and third generation of biological growth; it reverted to the ordinary pattern of congregational life. It reverted from the level of the sodality to the level of the modality, and in most cases, rather soon became ineffective either as a mission structure or as a renewing force.

What interests us most is the fact that in failing to exploit the power of the sodality, the Protestants had no mechanism for missions for almost three hundred years, until William Carey proposed "the use of means for the conversion of the heathen." His key word *means* refers specifically to the need for a sodality, for the organized but non-ecclesiastical initiative of the warm-hearted. Thus, the resulting Baptist Missionary Society is one of the most significant organizational developments in the Protestant tradition. It set off a rush to the use of this kind of "means" for the conversion of the heathen, and we find in the next few years a number of societies forming along similar lines: the LMS and NMS in 1795, the CMS in 1799, the CFBS in 1804, the BCFM in 1810, the ABMB in 1814, the GMS in 1815, the DMS in 1821, the FEM in 1822, and the BM in 1824 — twelve societies in thirty-two years. Once this method of operation was clearly understood by the Protestants, three hundred years of latent energies burst forth in what became, in Latourette's phrase, "The Great Century."

The Nineteenth Century is thus the first century in which Protestants were actively engaged in missions. For reasons which we have not space here to explain, it was also the century of the lowest ebb of Catholic mission energy. Amazingly, in this one century Protestants, building on the unprecedented world expansion of the West, caught up with eighteen centuries of earlier mission efforts. There is simply no question that what was done in this century moved the Protestant stream from a self-contained, impotent European backwater into a world force in Christianity. Looking back from where we stand today, of course, it is hard to believe how recently the Protestant movement has become prominent.

Organizationally speaking, however, the vehicle that allowed the Protestant movement to become vital was the structural development of the sodality, which harvested the vital "voluntarism" latent in Protestantism, and surfaced in new mission agencies of all kinds, both at home and overseas. Wave after wave of evangelical initiatives transformed the entire map of Christianity, especially in the United States, but also in England, and to a lesser degree in Scandinavia and on the continent. By 1840, the phenomenon of mission sodalities was so prominent in the United States that the phrase "the Evangelical Empire" and other equivalent phrases were used to refer to it, and now began a trickle of ecclesiastical opposition to this bright new emergence of the second structure. This brings us to our next point.

The Contemporary Misunderstanding of the Mission Sodality

Almost all mission efforts in the Nineteenth Century, whether sponsored by interdenominational boards or denominational boards, were substantially the work of initiatives that were mainly independent of the ecclesiastical structures to which they were related. Toward the latter half of the Nineteenth Century, there seemed increasingly to be two separate structural traditions (Winter, 1970:57, 58; 1971:94, 95).

On the one hand, there were men like Henry Venn and Rufus Anderson, who were the strategic thinkers at the helm of older societies — the Church Missionary Society (CMS) in England, and the American Board of Commissioners for Foreign Missions (ABCFM), respectively. These men championed the semi-autonomous mission sodality, and they voiced an attitude which was not at first contradicted by any significant part of the leaders of the ecclesiastical structures. On the other hand, there was the centralizing perspective of denominational leaders, principally the Presbyterians, which gained ground almost without any reversal throughout the latter two-thirds of the Nineteenth Century, so that by the early part of the Twentieth Century the once-independent structures which had been merely *related* to the denominations gradually became *dominated* by the churches. Partially as a result, toward the end of the Nineteenth Century, there was a new burst of totally separate mission sodalities called the *Faith Missions,* with Hudson Taylor's CIM taking the lead. It is not widely recognized that this pattern was mainly a recrudescence of the pattern that had been established earlier in the century, prior to the trend toward denominational boards.

All of these changes took place very gradually. Attitudes at any point are hard to pin down, but it does seem clear that Protestants were always a bit unsure about the legitimacy of the second structure, the sodality. The Anabaptist tradition consistently emphasized the concept of a pure community of believers and thus was uninterested in a voluntarism that would involve only part of the believing community. U.S. denominations for their part, lacking tax support as on the

Continent, were generally a more selective and vital fellowship than the European state churches, and at least in their youthful exuberance, felt quite capable as denominations of providing all of the necessary initiative for overseas mission. It is for this latter reason that the many new denominations of the U.S. have tended to act as though centralized church control of mission efforts is the only proper pattern.

As a result, by the Second World War, a very nearly complete transmutation had taken place in the case of almost all mission efforts related to denominational structures. That is, almost all older denominational boards, though once semi-autonomous or very nearly independent, had by this time become very dependent — very much involved, perhaps even integrated into the financial machinery of a denomination, becoming part of unified budget provisions and so forth. At the same time, and partially as a result, a whole new host of independent mission structures burst forth again, especially after the Second World War. As in the case of the earlier emergence of the Faith Missions, these tended to pay little attention to denominational leaders and their aspirations for church-centered mission. The Anglican church with its CMS, USPG, etc., displays the medieval synthesis, and so, almost unconsciously, does the American CBA with its associated CBFMS, CBHMS structures. Thus, to this day, among Protestants, there continues to be deep confusion about the legitimacy and proper relationship of the two structures that have manifested themselves throughout the history of the Christian movement.

To make matters worse, Protestant blindness about the need for mission sodalities has had a very tragic influence on mission fields. Protestants, being modality-minded, their missions have tended to assume that merely modalities, e.g., churches, need to be established. Even in the case where mission work is being pursued by what are essentially semi-autonomous mission sodalities, it is modalities, not sodalities, that are the only goal. That is to say, the mission agencies (even those that have most independent from themselves been denominations back home) have tended in their mission work very simply to set up churches and not to plant, in addition, mission sodalities in the so-called mission lands (Winter, 1972:129-136).

As we look back on it today, it is surprising that most Protestant missionaries, working with (mission) structures that did not exist in the Protestant tradition for hundreds of years and without whose existence there would have been no mission initiative, have nevertheless been blind to the significance of the very structure within which they have worked. In this blindness they have merely planted churches and have not effectively concerned themselves to make sure that the kind of mission structure within which they operate also be set up on the field. As a matter of fact, many of the mission agencies founded after World War II, out of extreme deference to existing church movements already established in foreign lands, have not even tried to set up *churches,* and have worked for many years merely as auxiliary agencies in various service capacities trying to help the churches that were already there.

Without being critical of the vast plethora of existing mission "service agencies," I believe to be highly significant two closely related emphases of the church growth movement. First of all there needs to be deliberate, intentional effort to establish (church) fellowships of believers no matter what else is being done in a given situation, and we must believe sincerely that this kind of organization implantation is one of the most important things that can be accomplished. Thus, even if an agency specializes in medical work, or orphan work, or radio work, or whatever, it must be aware of, and concerned about, the interface between that activity and the church-planting function. So far, so good. But, secondly, in addition to this older, well-known concern for the establishment of churches, there have appeared in church growth circles a number of chapters and articles which indicate very clearly the need for the intentional and deliberate implantation of mission sodalities (Winter, 1965, 1970, 1971, 1972, 1973, 1974; Winter and Beaver, 1970). It is at this point, I believe, that classical mission efforts, especially in the Protestant sphere, have most grieviously suffered from poor strategy.

The question we must ask is how long it will be before the younger churches of the so-called mission territories of the non-Western world come to that epochal conclusion (to which the Protestant movement in Europe only tardily came), namely, that there needs to be sodality structures, such as William Carey's "use of means," in order for church people to reach out in vital initiatives in mission, especially cross-cultural mission. There are already some hopeful signs that this tragic delay will not continue. We see, for example, the outstanding work of the Melanesian Brotherhood in the Solomon Islands (Tippett, 1967:50-53). Some of the research going on right now is uncovering the details of that and other sodality initiatives that were built out of believers in the national churches in the non-Western world (Larson, 1973). As far as I am concerned, the most important single reason for this All-Asia Mission Consultation is the possibility that it shall highlight the legitimacy and the significance of the *intentional development of mission sodalities,* both denominational and interdenominational.

Conclusion

This article has been in no sense an attempt to decry or to criticize the organized church. It has assumed both the necessity and the importance of the parish structure, the diocesan structure, the denominational structure, the ecclesiastical structure. The modality structure in the view of this article is a significant and absolutely essential structure. All that is attempted here is to explore some of the historical patterns which make clear that God, through His Holy Spirit, has clearly and consistently used another structure other than (and sometimes instead of) the modality structure. It is our attempt here to help church leaders and others to understand the legitimacy of *both* structures, and the necessity for both structures not only to exist but to work together harmoniously for the fulfillment of the Great Commission, and for the fulfillment of all that God desires for our time.[9]

It may well be that these words will be futile and that in the non-Western world, just as it has been in the Western world, a misunderstanding of the relationship of these two structures will continue to be one of the most serious stumbling blocks to effective steps forward in mission. But I would hope that it would not be so; I would hope that the churches planted in Korea and in other parts of Asia, and in the non-Western world in general, would awake to the significance of the sodality structure and not misunderstand its importance. This means, for one thing, that they should not work from ecclesiastical centers of power to frustrate the formation of those necessary sodalities, which by the dozens, hundreds, yea thousands, will nourish and bless the modality structures today as they have in the past, wherever that relationship has been harmonious and well-understood.

There is not time here to elaborate, but it might, in conclusion, be pointed out that a meeting of strictly church leaders will characteristically overlook the emphasis of this article. This is why the All-Asia Mission Consultation, drawing, as it has, delegates from sodalities in mission rather than churchmen, as such, is in this sense a much more significant gathering than one sponsored by a council of churches, in which case the delegates are chosen by the initiative of church leaders and their conciliar representatives. This is not to say that churches should never get together as churches, but it is to point out that that is only one kind of a gathering and that something else is also necessary. May I then once more underline and thus applaud the strategic significance of this kind of a meeting in the development of the work of God in Asia?

Notes

1. Address to the All-Asia Mission Consultation, Seoul '73, Korea, August 27-September 1, 1973.

2. One can hardly conceive of more providentially supplied means for the Christian mission to reach the gentile community. Wherever the community of Christ went, it found at hand the tools needed to reach the nations: a people living under covenant promise and a responsible election, and the scriptures, God's revelation to all men. The open synagogue was the place where all these things converged. In the synagogue, the Christians were offered an inviting door of access to every Jewish community. It was in the synagogue that the first Gentile converts declared their faith in Jesus (De Ridder, 1971:87).

3. Representative of those scholars who have noted Paul's Jewish moorings, Schoeps says:

> According to Gal. 1:16, Paul recognized already at the time of his Damascus experience that the mission to the Gentiles was his special charge in the service of Christ. Hence, he was at once confronted by the problem as to what mode of procedure should be adopted for the admission of Gentile converts. Already in the matter of Jewish mission to the Gentile world the question had arisen as to the extent to which the law of Moses should be obligatory for proselytes. It had proved difficult of solution and had led to semi-solutions and compromises, after the pattern of which the Jewish-Christian first church proposed to proceed, by insisting on the *Berith Mila, Kashruth,* as also the *Tahara* ritual through the custom of baptism. This was a normal solution such as we should have expected Jewish Christians to adopt; and had it not been for the intervention of Paul, it would never have become a subject of lengthy discussion. As is well-known, Paul's abrupt repudiation of all claims of the law on the Gentiles in his missionary practice was based on a deliberate position with regard to the Mosaic law (1961:64-65).

4. In Paul's day *Asia* meant what we today call Asia Minor, or present-day Turkey. In those days no one dreamed how far the term would later be extended.

5. That Christians in Jerusalem organized themselves for worship on the synagogue pattern is evident from the appointment of elders and the adoption of the service of prayer. The provision of a daily dole for widows and the needy reflects the current synagogue practice (Acts 2:42, 6:1). It is possible that the epistle of James reflects the prevailing Jerusalem situation: in James 2:2 reference is made to a wealthy man coming *'into your assembly.'* The term translated 'assembly' is literally

'synagogue', not the more usual word 'church' (Barker, Lane and Michaels, 1969:126-127).

6. Christians, it is said, resorted to the formation of "burial clubs," which were legal, as one vehicle of fellowship and worship.

7. It is Latourette who judges the mission from Rome less effective than the initiatives of the Celtic sodalities.

Had the Roman mission never come, the conversion of the English would probably have been accomplished by Celts from Scotland and Ireland and by a scattered few from the domains of the Franks. Moreover, it might have been completed almost as early as it was even without Roman aid (1938:60, 72; cf. McNeill, 1974:192).

8. This section is further expanded in Winter, 1970:19-22.

9. In a chapter, "Organization of Missions Today" in Dayton, 1973, I worked out a classification of the relation between mission sodalities and churches. More recent discussion and improved diagrammatic presentation of this classification is found in Winter, 1974:21-22. Not all types of relationships between modalities and sodalities are equally good. This is another very large subject.

References Cited

Barker, Glenn W., William L. Lane and J. Ramsey Michaels
  1969   *The New Testament Speaks* New York, Harper & Row

Dayton, Edward R. (ed.)
  1973   *Mission Handbook: North American Protestant Ministries Overseas* Monrovia: MARC, 10th ed.

DeRidder, Richard R.
  1971   *The Dispersion of the People of God* Netherlands: J.H. Kok, N.V. Kampen

Kraft, Charles
  1973   "Dynamic Equivalence Churches" in *Missiology, An International Review* Vol. I, No. 1

Larson, Peter A.
  1973   "Third World Missionary Agencies: Research in Progress" in *Missiology: An International Review* Vol. I, No. 2

Latourette, Kenneth Scott
  1938   *A History of Christianity, Vol. II, The Thousand Years of Uncertainty* New York: Harper & Brothers
  1953   *A History of Christianity* New York: Harper & Brothers

McNeill, John T.
  1974   *The Celtic Churches, A History, A.D. 200 to 1200* Chicago: The University of Chicago Press

Schoeps, Hans Joachim
  1961   *Paul* Philadelphia: The Westminster Press

Tippett, Alan R.
  1967   *Solomon Islands Christianity* London: Lutterworth Press

Wagner, Peter C. (ed.)
  1972   *Church/Mission Tensions Today* Chicago: Moody Press

Winter, Ralph D.
  1969   "The Anatomy of the Christian Mission" in *Evangelical Missions Quarterly* Vol. V, No. 2
  1970   "The Warp and the Woof of the Christian Movement" chapter in Winter and Beaver, 1970

1971   "The New Missions and the Mission of the Church" in *International Review of Mission* Vol. LX, No. 237, pp. 89-100

1972   "The Planting of Younger Missions" chapter 7 in Wagner, 1972

1973   "Organization of Missions Today" chapter in Dayton, 1973, pp. 10-15

1974   "Seeing the Task Graphically" *Evangelical Missions Quarterly,* Vol X, No. 1

Winter, Ralph D. and R. Pierce Beaver

1970   *The Warp and the Woof: Organizing for Mission* South Pasadena: William Carey Library

20

MISSIONS FROM
THE THIRD WORLD

James Wong, Edward Pentecost and Peter Larson

Creative, dynamic power was unleashed through the Person of
Jesus Christ. The cross — resurrection — pentecost event has been
the focal point of the divine — human encounter for millions of
people who have lived in the shadow of these tremendous acts of
God's grace. The clarion call of Jesus, given first to the Jewish
disciples, has continued to find echo in the corridors of men's
thoughts, and to fire the flame of love within his heart. Through
the energizing work of His Spirit, Christ's followers have sensed
a holy compunction to "Go and Tell'. The simple sharing of the
Good News concerning the Saviour has been the foundational
backbone of an amazing and important chapter in human history
— that of the expansion of the Christian faith through her missionary activity and zeal. Under His Lordship and direction, vast
amounts of creative energy have been expended by both individuals
and groups of committed personnel in the communication of this
message.

Set-backs, obstacles, and various kinds of persecution have
occurred. The perception of a bright and glorious missionary
vision has been dimmed, at times, through disobedience and
neglect upon the part of those who have claimed relationship to
Jesus. And yet, even in the face of what has seemed overwhelming odds, the triumph of the Resurrection has been heralded
around the world, and has found receptivity on every continent.

With the ascendency of Western European political and economic expansion during the Sixteenth to Nineteeth Centuries, Protestant Christians belatedly began to follow an earlier pattern of missionary effort that had been given by the missionary orders (Jesuits, Dominicans, Franciscans, Etc.) of the Roman Catholic Church. Having their roots in Reformation theology, Protestants needed the impulse provided by Pietism, the Evangelical Awakening and the organizational structures of Mission Societies, to spur them into united missionary action. With the spirtual backing of these great movements, the Nineteenth Century became a "Great Century" for the advance of Protestant Christianity.

The greatest number of Christians were to be found in Europe and the Americas. From this Eurican base (in this term meaning Europe and North America) a great army of missionaries were sent out to the great non Western areas of the world. In many cases the missionaries followed their governments in colonization efforts. Having as they did a European origin and being closely identified with Western imperialism of the colonization period, it is not difficult to understand the reason why Christianity came to be viewed as something "Western" and as the "White man's religion." Undoubtedly in limited areas and for a short period of time this identification of Christianity with the West worked favorably towards the extension of the Faith. But, with the recent surge of new nationhood after the Second World War, and the new political alignments which have drastically changed the political picture of our world, Dr. Winter's thesis regarding the "Retreat of the West" is substantiated. (Winter 1970: 11-20) With this marked decline of Western prestige and the continued close identification of Christianity with the White man, a stone of stumbling arose to hinder many people from committing their lives to Jesus Christ.

With regards to Protestant Christianity, two Twentieth Century phenomena have had profound implications. The first stems from Edinburgh 1910, from whence issued conversations and interest concerning Latin America. The outgrowth of this was the new ideological position that became widely held which enabled Latin

America to be viewed as a "mission" area and to which an increasing flow of missionary personnel was channeled. Coupled with this was the amazing growth of Pentecostalism which is called by some the "Third Force."

The second very significant development has been the rise of the "Younger Churches." Having had the numerical growth and experience of the Nineteenth Century upon which to build, these churches located in Africa and Asia have come of age during this century. Mainly through People's Movements, large numbers of multi-individual decisions have taken place without an accompanying social dislocation. Strong Churches have emerged such as the Korean Presbyterians, the Karen Baptists of Burma or the

Lutheran Bataks of Indonesia. These Younger Churches have manifested missionary passion and enthusiasm. The same missionary impulses that were seen in the book of Acts and throughout the history of the Christian Faith are also seen in the activity of these Younger Churches. Fantastic sacrifices, deep devotion, and a yieldedness to the purposes of God characterizes many of these non-European, non-American Christians.

The same tendency to identify Christianity with the West has had its parallel regarding missionary activity. Far too often Christians of the West have been totally ignorant regarding the missionary passion of the Younger Churches, and have tended to be interested only in what happens to the Christian missionaries that are sent out of Eurics. This is unfortunate and short sighted. The large number of Western missionaries has suggested that the phenomenon of missionary activity also is purely a Western monopoly. This is not true to the facts. Kenneth Scott Latourette has admirably demonstrated in his monumental series, *A History of the Expansion of Christianity,* that a solid, definite characteristic of this Faith has been its missionary outreach and extension, whether it be from the West or the East or from the North or the South. This missionary Characteristic is inherent within its constitution. Christianity entails a missionary purpose and activity.

The Great Commission of Jesus Christ is given to all of His followers, whether white or black, rich or poor, literate or illiterate.

PURPOSE OF THIS STUDY

The present day Protestant missionary enterprise is a vast and multi-faceted undertaking. Extending to numerous units of many societies, and employing almost a bewildering variation of methods and philosophy in its undertaking, it presents a many-pronged thrust in seeking to communicate Christ to the *Two Billion* plus who largely remain outside an effective hearing of the Gospel. Part of this many pronged missionary approach has been the development of non-Western, and Third World groups of organized Christians who keenly sense their personal responsibility to the Great Commission of Jesus Christ. These men and women have banded together in order to support, sustain and encourage a missionary endeavour that will make Christ a live option not only for people speaking the same language, but for others of different cultures and countries. With this in mind, this study seeks to gather basic data relating to the Protestant Missionary sending agencies in the Third World. (We mean by this those areas of Asia, Africa, Oceania and Latin America.)

Special attention has been given to mission work which concerns itself primarily with cross-cultural and cross-geographical evangelism and church planting, in contrast to social service and itinerant ministries. The basic data gathered are analyzed and compiled into this book. In a covering letter that was sent to those individuals who may have had information the purposes were stated as follows:

1. Help the national churches in Asia, Oceania, Africa and Latin America to know the present extent of indigenous missionary activities, within their regions, and to encourage one another in obedience to our Lord's Comission.

2. Provide names and addresses through which these national churches and missionary agencies can communicate with each other.

3. Stimulate a greater faithfulness in discerning where the ripened harvest fields really are and where more laborers need to be thrust forth.

4. Assist in the mutual learning process through shared experiences of problems in missionary work from an indigenous perspective.

5. Place current mission facts in clearer focus so that worldwide recognition will be given to such non-Western missionary agencies, and correct the common viewpoint that all missionary organizations in the world originate from the Western countries.

6. Encourage the development of a new and creative relationship with the older missionary societies from the West so that together we may arrive at a better understanding of the Church's missionary responsibility to the Two Billion who do not know Christ. (See Appendix A for copy of covering letter.)

METHODOLOGY

I. RESEARCH TEAM CONSTITUTED

A small research team was formed from the School of World Missions, Fuller Theological Seminary, Pasadena, California at the instigation of Professor C. Peter Wagner. Inspired by his characteristic enthusiasm and capable direction the team of Edward Pentecost, James Wong, and Peter Larson began their task. Initially, Dr. Ralph Winter, another faculty member of the School of World Missions, contributed a questionnaire that had been developed by a former student and twenty-five names of possible contacts.

II. RESEARCH TOOLS

A. Questionnaire, Contact, And Covering Letters

Through a contact made with World Vision's Missions Advanced Research and Communication Center (MARC), the formal development of an adequate questionnaire was begun. Both William Needham and Edward Dayton gave invaluable assistance in the formulation of this questionnaire. (See Appendix B and C.) This questionnaire, together with its Spanish translation sought to enlist the following information:

1. The names and locations of the national missionary agencies.
2. Their histories.
3. Growth statistics.
4. Types of ministry.
5. The countries and cultures to which they send missionaries.
6. Financial policy.
7. Church affiliations.
8. Their major emphases and future plans.

The questionnaires, covering letters and a contact letter were sent to 697 potential respondents asking for this information. By April 30, 1972 233 had responded which means a percentage response of 33.4%.

Resume

Members of the team working on this project had found the study a source of challenge and inspiration. From the findings of this very preliminary survey we sensed the power of God in the widening scope and extent of missionary activity going on among the Third World Churches. All indications point to the increasing part that these non-Western missionaries will take in the world-wide missionary advance of the Gospel. Western Christians will be challenged as increasing knowledge of Third World missionary activity becomes known. To this end, there is satisfaction upon the part of the team and grateful for the guidance of the Lord in enabling this study to take place.

In resumé form the following findings are again stated:

1. The percentage response of 697 to whom a request for information went out was 33.4% or 233 replies. (Since the dateline of April 30, 1972, we have received 11 additional replies which gives us a total of 244 or 35%).

2. Identified are 46 sending countries in the report plus New Guinea as now we have information in our Appendix E. Total — 47.

3. The agencies reported in the study were 203. Since the finalization of the statistical study, it has been found that Japan was credited with one too many agencies. The number of Japanese agencies is 31 instead of 32, and the total adjusted to 200. But since April 30, 9 additional agencies have been reported and their data included in Appendix E. The total thus stands at 211.

4. Of these agencies 100 are New Agencies, not listed in the *Encyclopedia of Modern Christian Missions,* which have been detailed in the study, plus the nine listed in Appendix E. Total for New Agencies is 109.

5. Area wise, as to the number of agencies with the additional information that is contained in Appendix E, it would be as follows:

Area	Sending Countries	Number of Agencies
Asia	19	110
Latin America	14	62
Africa	12	33
Western (3rd World)	2	7

6. The reported number of missionaries — 2971, with the recent addition of 23 from those listed in Appendix E brings the total up to 2994.

7.   Estimated number of missionaries including those agencies for whom we have no statistics — 3411.

8.   The average number of missionaries per statistic reporting agency — 26.2. (Based on 113 reporting agencies.) When calculated on the total of agencies listed the staff would average 14.7 missionaries per agency.

9.   Nineteen agencies are listing 20 or more missionaries.

10. Latin America was the area where we found the most new agencies in our study (the 49 listed in the study plus one additional agency — 50.)

11. There are 86 receiving countries (including 6 Islands which are possession of another country) to which are being sent Third World missionaries.

12. Asia as an area, in terms of the number of countries involved, lead both in the sending and the receiving of missionaries. This points to the area with the greatest amount of Third World activity.

13. Sixty-five ethnic groups are listed among whom are working the Third World missionaries. This does not include major groups such as English, Chinese, Japanese, etc., except where they would be an overseas minority.

14. Evangelism and church planting occupies the great majority, 89%, of missionary activity for whom we have data.

15. The types of societies in which missionary activities are taking place is very evenly distributed, with the large cities holding a slight edge.

Third World missionary effort in its historical perspective may have been overlooked in the West as the focus usually was upon the Western missionary. However, this does not mean that there was no Third World missionary activities. Quite to the contrary, when one thinks of the Karens of Burma who as early as 1833 were involved with American missionaries in seeking to present the Gospel to other tribal groups. By 1850 the truly indigenous Bassien Home Mission Society was established. This type of activity also was being reproduced in Oceania on a larger scale. Mission sending agencies, while not in great numbers, existed in India, Burma, Malaysia and Japan by the very early years of the twentieth century.

The extent to which Western missionaries encouraged Third World missionary outreach is somewhat debated. One opinion says that their encouragement has been rather slight. Men such as Chua Wee Hian have indicted the Western missionaries in their failure to encourage those of the Far East. It is his contention that the Western missionary, in desiring to take the center of the stage too often, has desired to create and maintain the policies and administration. (1969:11) This certainly has been part of the picture, for which those of the West must confess they are guilty. But, there is another side. Perhaps the proportion has been small, and their numbers few, but there have been Western missionaries such as John Williams, Rufus Anderson, or present day missionaries like Denis Lane of the Overseas Missionary Fellowship who have and are encouraging Third World Christians to put their shoulders to the task of missionary advance.

PROPOSALS

Just the surface of a vast amount of research material has been scratched regarding Third World Missionary agencies. Needed will be a continuation study group dedicated to the task of gathering new data regarding Third World missions. We consider this project and the publication of this book as only the first step forward. It is here that the School of World Mission and Institute of Church Growth can give continuing impetus in the broadening of this initial research project. Not only will constant verification be needed to update the information, but in-depth studies should be undertaken concerning organizational structures, financial policy, types of affiliations, ethnic units, and other related topics. Very important would be a study in the types of organizational structures that are being followed, their relationship to patterns developed in the West as well as indigenous patterns.

A network of concerned missionary strategists in each country should be formed who will engage in uncovering primary data regarding Third World missionary activity. A starting place for this is among both national leaders and the Western missionaries who attend the School of World Mission and Institute of Church Growth. Guidelines and types of material to be looked for could be given. This network should not confine itself to those of the faculty or student body of the School of World Mission, but should seek to incorporate the interest and enthusiasm of other individuals and groups.

Encouragement, as Dr. Ralph Winter has suggested, to plant missions as well as churches, should be done. The Christian and Missionary Alliance has set an example which should be studied with great care, and put into practice by many other Western missionary agencies. Perhaps, more important, however, is what happens among the Younger Churches which might be of encouragement in their increased missionary activity. The suggestion shared by many regarding the value of regional missionary conferences where Third World missionaries could meet and discuss common concerns is one proposal that could have far reaching significance in the future development and strengthening of the Third World missionary enterprise.

We believe that there are greater resources and personnel of the Third World whom the Lord is desiring to be thrust forth to the missionary task.

As we prayerfully ponder the actual situation, the words of Dr. Forman come to us in which he relates that at a recent meeting of the South Pacific Association of Theological Schools, a resolution was drawn up by that group and sent as a plea to the World Council of Churches urging that places might be found around the world where Islanders could be continued to be used as missionaries. Forman goes on to ask, "How can they be used?" (Forman 1970:216). From the lessons of history we would answer that they have demonstrated ability, courage and missionary heroism at its finest. This should be repeated today in missionary advance. It must be a missionary advance that has been prompted because of the outpouring of the Holy Spirit and through His leading in adequate organizational structures.

NINETEENTH AND EARLY TWENTIETH CENTURY THIRD WORLD MISSIONARY ACTIVITY

The Great Century of the Protestant missions is studded with the names of outstanding missionaries, such as Livingstone, Morrison, and Judson. While it would be a grave mistake to down play their victories of faith, at the same time it is unfortunate that more is not known concerning those non-western missionary heroes of the faith upon whom the mantle of dynamic faith fell. These men, like Joseph Merrick, Ini Kopuria and Joeli Bulu were also gifted men and filled with the love of Christ that impelled them across formidable frontiers in order that Jesus Christ might be made known. They were men who felt that the Great Commission of Christ was unchanging in its demands, and thus invalidates the argument that it was given for just a select company of people for a given time. It was their keen feeling that its command and implications could not be monopolized by just part of the Church or for just the Western Christians but was applicable for each individual regardless of his own particular cultural heritage.

The same staggering barriers had to be surmounted that were faced by their Western counterparts. Extremes of climate, diseases, difficult languages, persecutions, and even misunderstandings dogged their steps. Often extremes of personal sacrifice were made because of lack of economic support. At times they were told to stay in their place by the white missionary who thought they would be of more value to the Lord's work in their home area. Some were outwardly discouraged because the Westerner desired to take the center of the stage. And yet, our impression is that the same missionary passion was filling the lives of Christians from the Third World during these years.

The purpose of this study is to explore examples of this missionary activity. Our danger is that these examples might be used to make generalizations regarding the scope of the Third World missionary activity which might not be characteristic for the entire period or the entire area. This limitation is recognized, but it is my feeling that given the sources and the time, countless other examples would also substantiate the basic premise that Third World missionary activity was taking place on a scale that has not been given its due recognition.

AN AFRICAN-AMERICAN EXAMPLE

An interesting example of Third World missionary activity is that which began in the Jamaica Baptist Churches during the 1830's and which found its outlet in the West Cameroons. The story of this development has been written by Lloyd Kwast who begins the historical treatment of the growth of Baptist work by saying, "The story of the evangelization of West Cameroon does not begin in Europe or North America, as one would suppose, but on the small Caribbean island of Jamaica." (Kwast 1968: 60)

Emancipation of the slaves in Jamaica came in 1838, and with this freedom, there arose a concern among those who had accepted the Gospel, to return to West Africa in order to carry the message of salvation to their ancestral lands. Letters were written as early as 1839 to the Baptist Missionary Society of Great Britain, reporting the concerns of the Negro Christians for West Africa, and some of them had volunteered to make the return trip. It was because of this apparent concern that the Society made plans for the opening of a new field in West Africa. After the initial exploratory trips had been taken, in 1843 Joseph Merrick and Alexander Fuller, two Jamaicans of West African ancestry, together with Dr. G. K. Prince, set sail for Fernando Po. This latter place was an island just off the Cameroon coast where a large number of liberated slaves had gathered and was to be the site for the first missionary effort.

Additional personnel came five months later made up of thirty-nine Jamaicans and two additional English missionaries. Kwast comments here as to these Jamaicans.

> The harsh terrain and climate, disease and sickness, loneliness and discouragement, and incessant harassment by Spanish Roman Catholics led to an early return of many of Jamaicans to the West Indies in 1847. (Kwast 1968:63)

However, one Negro Jamaican made his way from Fernando Po to the Cameroon River estuary on the African coast where, with his wife he settled at Bimbia among the Isubu people. Very able, really a gifted man, he quickly set out to learn their language. By 1846, one year after he had initiated his labours, he had not only learned their language and reduced it to writing, but had produced a translation of Matthew's Gospel. He conducted the first regular church services, erected a printing press and pushed on into the interior to preach to the Bakweri tribe. During the next three years he continued to print and translate the Scriptures. Genesis was completed in 1847 and part of John's Gospel in 1848. Kwast describes this man as a noble man of God, who gave himself to his task in an unselfish way. Unfortunately, "Worn out by his many labors for Christ, and disease stricken by his deadly environment, Joseph Merrick died a most untimely death in 1849." (Kwast 1968: 64)

Other Jamaicans continued to contribute to the initial missionary advance. Especially significant was their contribution as teachers in the first schools that were set up under the Mission auspices in which the plan was to evangelize the resistant tribal peoples through the children who would be sent to the schools.

This example of Jamaican interest and support illustrates the axiom that the missionary call and vision has not been relegated to "Western" Christians alone, but pervades those of the Younger Churches as well. The pattern suggested here, wherein the initial vision belonged to the Negro Jamaican Christians, but who were helped to fulfill this vision through the activity of a "Western" sending agency, may have been a rather normal type of structural pattern, through which these missionaries of the Third World were able to fulfill their God-given task.

THE KARENS OF BURMA

The story of Adoniram Judson and the beginning of Baptist church growth in Burma is a thrilling account. Great growth has occurred since those very discouraging years of pain and anguish that were experienced by Judson and other early missionaries among the Burmese people. To a large measure, this growth was the result of receptivity found among the Karen people who were predominantly animistic in their religion. It was under the ministry of George Boardman that Ko Tha Bya, the first Karen was won to Christ. He became a flaming evangelist to his own people, and along with Boardman saw the beginning of peoples movements to Christ among the Karens. (Latourette 1944: 231) While the account of the Karen movement to Christ is fascinating, our purpose is to discern and point to the cross-cultural missionary activity that very soon was to occur.

A very fine paper has been written by Herman Tegenfeldt regarding this missionary movement among the Karens. From his material we will take the following gleanings which illustrate for us the early missionary vision for the reaching of other ethnic groups which was part of the history of the expansion of Christianity in Burma.

As early as 1833 Mission Societies were formed by the Karens in both the Moulmein and the Tavoy areas which had in themselves seen good church growth. These efforts were made with considerable American missionary involvement. (This point shows that American missionaries were interested that the Karen's begin their own cross-cultural missionary efforts to other ethnic groups, as well as across the neighboring boundaries.) Later in 1850 a more truly indigenous Bassein Home Mission Society was established among the Karens primarily for the support of evangelists to their own people. This entailed, however, crossing political boundaries such as the boundary with Thailand in order to evangelize those Karens living in the neighboring country. Numerous difficulties were encountered because of the unfriendly relationships between the two governments. This meant that the Karen evangelists often merely slipped across the Thai-Burma border to preach in the hill country where Thai officials seldom visited.

Another outreach of the Bassein Home Mission Society was to appoint three men to go to a hill people several hundred miles north of Mandalay. These hill people (the Kachins) were considered by the Karens as their cose relatives. The journey was made in 1859 and after spending some months among the Kachin people, the three missionaries returned to the Bassein Mission with the news that the Kachins were different from the Karens as to their language and other aspects of their culture. They seem to have been impressed with more war-like nature of the Kachins. At that time little additional effort was made by the Karens to evangelize the Kachins.

The American missionaries, too, became concerned for the Kachin area, seeing not only the area within Burma, but coming to feel that it would be a place from which they might reach into Yunnan. It was not until 17 years after the journey of the three Karens into Kachin territory, however, that J. N. Cushing went with a Karen evangelist, Bogalay, to Bhamo. Bogalay was designated and supported by the Bassein Home Mission Society for the Kachin work. (Tegenfeldt: 15) Bogalay went on into the hills to live, while Cushing remained in Bhamo. After only a few months the Karen evangelist returned to his home area. He was replaced by two others who sought to give continuity to the work.

Reflected in Tegenfeldt's account is seen the anguish and sacrifice that was made by these early Karen missionaries. He quotes S'Peh who had taken Bogalay's place in the hills as he writes, "I was attacked with fever three times ... I am not very strong." He went on to say " ... If my wife comes, and our support is continued, I am ready to cast in my lot with these poor Ka-Khyens, to suffer with them, and to lead them with my whole heart to Christ, as Moses cast in his lot with the children of Israel." (Baptist Missionary Magazine 1879: 165 as quoted by Tegenfeldt: 16).

The American missionaries were encouraging and pleading with the Karens to send more Karen missionary help. A Karen pastor gave a powerful challenge to which other Karen young men responded. By 1878 there were two Karen couples and two other young men serving and co-operating with the American missionary in the Kachin outreach. After five years of this labour, the first 7 Kachins were baptized. With the growth of the Kachin work, the Karens contributed not only in the initial evangelism but also became an important source for the teachers and the head masters in the schools that were developed in the Kachin area. Karen women performed in an outstanding way, not only as teachers in the Kachin area, but also as nurses, and as Bible women.

A brief mention must be made of other ethnic groups to which the Karen's shared in taking the Gospel, which is also outlined in Tegenfeldt's paper in greater detail. Missionary activity was begun as early as 1859 to the Asho Chins in the Prome area. Five years later part of the Karen missionary efforts for this group was in reducing the Asho Chin language to writing. At the turn of the twentieth century the Karen missionary effort was also extended to the Zomi Chins. Five years after their initial efforts among these hill Chins, the first two were won to Christ. As a tribute to their efforts among the Chins, Rev. Cope wrote the following description:

> We owe everything to the Karens. We do not know what we would do without them. When Mr. Carson first came up he brought three or four Karens with him and from that time on, with a few exceptions, they have proven splendid men on whom one could place no end of responsibility. For a long time they were the only evangelists here. They went out to strange villages where no preparations had been made for them and where they were threatened direly. The first Chin Christians came seven days' journey from Haka where a Henzada Karen, Thra Shwe Zan, worked alone, seeing the missionaries only once a year. The Chin preachers were put under these Karens and some of our finest workers were trained by them. They learned the language, learned the ways of the people, and won their confidence. In the first literary work I did, it was the Karens who helped me. In the school work as well we have Karen Headmasters, and they proved as valuable there as in the evangelistic work. (Shwe Wa and Sowards, quoted by Tegenfeldt: 20).

Additional effort was made among the Lahus, Was, Akhas, Shans and the Nagas. Some of this is very recent times. It should also be mentioned that the Karens of Lower Burma have taken into their homes promising young people from the tribals, endeavoring to give them a good education and Christian training. These young people were then expected to return to their own peoples.

Interesting are Tegenfeldt's conclusions which may be summarized:

1. A missionary vision and passion has been part of the Karen church growth story.
2. Early concern was primarily for groups with whom they sensed common bonds of relationship such as the Kachins and Chins, and with whom they shared a common tradition of the Lost Book.
3. Karen missionaries were supported by their fellows, through the Bassein Home Missionary Society. They also received support from the American mission, from institutions in which they served, and from the people to whom they ministered.
4. The Karen missionaries endeavoured to learn the local languages and were instrumental in Bible translation among the Asho Chin and the Lisu.
5. Their outstanding musical ability was a great contribution to the congregational singing and choirs among the people to whom they had gone.
6. The missionary example of the very early Karen converts seemed to have set the tone for Karen outreach.
7. Missionary outreach to the Burmese Buddhist was not to same degree of scale nor intensity as to the other tribal groups.

KOREAN PRESBYTERIANS

The growth of the Korean Presbyterian Church has been widely acclaimed. A great part of this was due to its growth numerically as it is carefully documented in Shearer's book, *Wildfire: Church Growth in Korea*. Part of its fame has come because of its example through the persecutions and wars through which it has been called to come. Closely associated with the Korean

Presbyterian Church were the revival movements of the Holy Spirit and a philosophy of missionary thinking which was adopted by the Northern Presbyterian Mission in Korea, called the Nevius Method. This policy had been developed by John Nevius in the 1880's while he was a missionary in China. His original book, *Planting and Development of Missionary Churches,* was first published in 1888 in which he enunciated six very important cardinal points which sought to permit great growth of indigenous churches. In reading the thrust of his material, the impression is made that he was struggling for local church growth rather than missionary growth across frontiers and boundaries. This is evident from his main concern that the local church be self supporting and self governing. The stress was that each convert abide in his calling, earning a living as he did before he became a Christian. This is reminiscent of Luther's same contention that each one remain in the calling wherein he had been called (I Cor. 7: 20), and which became a deterrent regarding missionary expansion. Nevius does provide for paid evangelists or helpers for the foreign missionary, but here again, the emphasis seems to be upon the planting of the Church in one's own geographical and cultural area. Nevius emphasized that new churches should be planted by existing churches with the local Christians earning their own living while visiting their friends and kinsmen in their web relationships. Dr. McGavran's evaluation of the principles is that they were pragmatically sound, a workable system and in line with psychology. He continues in saying, "It kept missions from seeming foreign. It was capable of infinite expansion, and it presented the Gospel in a true light. It multiplied sound, self-propagating congregations." (McGavran 1970: 339)

But, whether or not the Nevius plan encouraged the Korean churches to view their responsibility for the evangelization and church planting effort in other parts of Asia and the world is a moot question. From this distance in time, it would appear that the implications for a worldwide missionary effort were more implicit than explicitly stated. Shearer is relatively quiet as to Korean missionary activity outside the Korean borders. This does not necessarily mean that it was not taking place, at least in a limited fashion, but it does seem to indicate that the emphasis was upon church growth within the Korean milieu itself.

Won Yong Koh, from the School of World Missions, Fuller Theological Seminary, wrote a paper regarding the missionary movement of the Korean Presbyterian Church. A resume of his findings follows. They reflect his own personal participation in this missionary expansion. They exemplify something of the wonderful dynamic of the Korean Christian movement, even though Nevius in his plan had not placed great stress in the sending of missionaries cross-culturally.

Koh feels that the missionary movement was the direct result of the great revival in 1907. Six years later in 1913 the Korean Presbyterians seem to have had a Mission Board of the General Assembly of the Church, and through this Board the first three candidates were selected and sent to China. These were the first missionaries to foreign peoples. (Koh 1971: 2) While these three were considered the first missionaries to a people of different culture, there had been Koreans who had crossed political boundaries since 1907 to work among Koreans living in Japan, China, Manchuria, and Russia. The first of these was Rev. Kee Pung Lee who had gone to Cheju Island.

Five years after the men were sent to China, the three missionaries came back to Korea, having successfully served in China. They had seen twenty baptized and six congregations formed. From the data, it appears that the financial support for the re-emplacements who were sent to China came from the funds of the Korean Presbyterian Church. Koh mentions the economic factor as the Church members were very poor to the extent that they did not have enough to eat and it was not without considerable sacrifice that this support was raised. Even in the midst of the intense trials through which the Koreans had to pass, they desired to continue their missionary efforts. Though the Japanese made life difficult, in 1919 the Church also sent three missionaries again to China. These men served long terms of service, one coming back to Korea after the Second World War and one of the others remaining until 1957 when he was deported by the

Red Chinese government. During those years of the Chinese effort, the evangelistic missionaries were aided by able, dedicated Christian medical doctors. Koh says that these Korean doctors co-operated with the missionaries in evangelism, many Chinese came to Christ, churches were established, and the organization of a district of churches in San-Pong Province was also effected. (1970: 6)

From this glimpse of the Korean Presbyterians that Koh has given to us, and from Shearer's material, we can make the following deductions concerning the initial phase of Korean Presbyterian activity prior to World War II.

1. The Korean Presbyterian Church from the time of the Great Revival in 1907, began expressing its dynamic vigour not only in local church growth but by sending out missionaries to Northeastern Asia.

2. This early missionary effort followed very soon after a decade, 1895-1905, that Shearer entitled, "Explosion in the Church." It was not too long after the initiation of Presbyterian work in Korea which began about 1885.

3. The earliest Koreans who went forth did so in order to minister to the large numbers of Koreans who had emigrated North into Manchuria. The search for a better life seems to have been the main reason for this migration as Japan began to take over the economy. Shearer says that the oppressed Koreans "began to look for greener pastures in Manchuria." (1966: 60) From the suggestions regarding the widespread economic pinch, it is noteworthy that the Presbyterians were able to send out a few missionaries.

4. The great task of planting the church in many parts of Korea so consumed the energies and thinking of the Western missionaries that outreach into Manchuria was seen as not advisable, in that their forces would be spread too thin. One wonders if this might have hampered the missionary zeal of Koreans who had a vision for reaching out. A logical type of American missionary response in the

midst of such great opportunity would have been to encourage the Koreans to remain in their calling and to remain in their own geographical area in order that church growth might continue.

5. The Nevius method did not primarily address itself to missionary expansion that would be cross-cultural from the indigenous church's point of view, but created guide lines for the Western missionaries in their guidance and activity among the Koreans. It would be interesting to know if the early Korean missionaries also followed the Nevius method in their mission activity beyond the boundaries of Korea.

6. Of very special concern to the Korean Christians was the area of Northeastern Asia, including Manchuria, Russia and Japan. Political events such as the power struggle between those nations caused very serious obstacles for the Korean missionary advance.

7. From Koh's further comments, the Korean missionary advance into other areas, such as Southeast Asia did not take place until after the Korean war and after the end of Korean missionary work in Red China. This would bring us into the modern period.

BATAK MISSIONARIES

Another one of the great Younger Churches is the Lutheran Batak Church of Indonesia. The missionary zeal of the Batak Christians has been well substantiated. In 1899 the Kongsi Batak (Home Missionary Society) was founded, but the primary emphasis appears to be in its evangelistic responsibility to its own people and to carry on some of the philanthropic work previously carried on by the Rhenish Mission. This missionary work met with many difficulties as the Bataks sought to communicate to other Batak groups. The principal reason for this was the attraction to local autonomy and a decentralized organization structure that was the prevailing attitude among the various groups. While this was the case, nevertheless, the enthusiasm, and dedication of the Toba Batak members was an important factor in the spread of the faith through Batakland. (Beyerhaus and Lefever 1964: 82).

The Kongsi Batak did not flourish until after 1921 when it was reorganized and integrated into the Church by Johannes Warneck and re-named, Zending Batak, Batak Mission. After the change it proved extremely successful.

Particular attention was given to the many Bataks migrating throughout the East Indies, whether it be to isolated islands, rural areas or to the great cities. A second front was opened about 1930 when three Batak evangelists began among the Senoi aboriginal people of West Malaysia. From what Pederson says, this work was continued into the early 1960's although it had always been a controversial and sensitive issue. (Pederson 1970: 76).

An interesting feature is the way that money for sending evangelists was gathered. This was done at an annual mission festival that followed the harvest. This harvest festival was popular in pre-Christian Batak society as one of the ceremonies of the traditional religion and was taken over by the Church as an opportunity for the Bataks to show their gratitude to God and to share with others the blessings that He had given in the harvest.

An additional feature of great significance in the missionary movement of the Bataks was the migration of large numbers of Batak Christians to other areas of Indonesia. As they moved, they took their faith with them, and it was not uncommon for them to secure positions of authority such as teachers. These migrants remained faithful as well as evangelistic. Pederson says of the migration, "Travelling individually, in families, or in colonies, this migration has had virtually no outside financial help, encouragement or organized guidance." (Pederson 1970:77). In seeking to summarize, the following might be learned.

1. Missionary vision was part of the built-in mechanism of Batak faith. It expressed primarily itself through efforts to reach other Bataks, although in more recent times they have pursued cross-cultural missionary work.

2. Quite early (1899) a mission society was founded, and which has functioned much better after 1921 when it was closely integrated into the organizational structure. One wonders if the conflict might not have developed because of its sodality image in a church organization that was very strong as a modal group. Perhaps, Warneck's ideas regarding church polity were having some influence in causing the friction and the lack of support with this missionary society.

3. Migration was a chief instrument in missionary expansion and the role of the Batak as a teacher should not be underestimated.

4. A traditional form, such as the harvest festival, was harnessed by the Church for missionary purposes.

OCEANIA

The area of Oceania presents many challenges and lessons from the powerful movement of the Holy Spirit through which great church growth and numerous peoples movements have taken place. Latourette calls the nineteenth century record of the spread of Christianity among the Pacific Islanders as "one of the most spectacular in the history of that or of any other faith." (Latourette 1943:263). Missionary annals are replete with stories of famous missionary heroes such as John Williams, John G. Patton, the Selwyns, James Chalmers and many others whose lives of faith and courage have been a source of inspiration to the Western Church. However, those who bore the brunt of insecurity and hardship were not the Western missionaries but the Pacific Islands missionaries who from the very early beginnings were in the thick of the fray. Charles Forman concludes that the "Islanders suffered far more than their European colleagues even though the latter had much to endure." (Forman 1970:216).

The qualities of bravery, devotion, and enthusiasm for the missionary enterprise were noteworthy among these very fine Third World missionaries. Untold suffering was the lot of many of them as they suffered from hostility, endured without food and water, and at times fled under the cover of darkness because of the persecutions. Some were not allowed to flee in those moments of intense opposition as they were tied to rafts and cut adrift, or eaten. Martyrdom was a price that was paid by Pacific Islanders as well as Western missionaries as they sought to extend the Gospel of Christ across the Pacific.

Dr. Ralph Winter points to the crucial importance of the missionaries in relationship to church growth as he notes that the highest percentage of church membership in any non-Western region of the world is found in Oceania, and it is also this region which has seen such an outstanding record of islanders going as missionaries to the other islands. (Winter 1971:200.) While too little is generally known about these outstanding national missionaries, Dr. Alan Tippett, Dr. Charles Forman and others in their writings have been pointing to their importance. The College Chapel of the Pacific Theological College in Fiji has been dedicated to those who have gone out as missionaries. Charles Forman says that a list which stands at over 1,000 national missionaries, not including their wives, has been made with the principal sending Churches being Fiji (Methodists) with 269, Samoa (Congregational) 209, the Cook Islands — 197, and the Solomon Islands — 139. (1970:215)

While the purpose of this chapter is not to detail all the missionary effort by national Christians, as this is far beyond the capacity of the writer, the following examples are given to show something of the scope of this development, in pointing to this interesting and challenging aspect of missionary work — the crucial involvement of Third World missionaries.

As one follows Latourette in his description of the Expansion of Christianity regarding the islands of the Pacific, the magnitude of this Third World missionary movement is striking. With the initial thrusts of evangelism made toward Tahiti at the turn of the nineteenth century, it is interesting that as soon as 1830 the first national missionaries were being sent forth. This was the period of John Williams who soon saw the dynamic possibilities of the missionary passion of the islanders, and who encouraged them in their vision for other islands and peoples. Retracing our steps we find in 1820, Christianity entering the Austral Islands through the people of Rurutu who, because of contrary winds, had been forced to go to Raiatea. There they saw what Christainity was doing on the island, felt that this was good, and when they went back to their homes, they took as missionaries some of the Raiatea Christians. This met with immediate success. (Latourette 1943:208)

John Williams, at many points was aided by national missionaries. Even prior to 1830, missionaries from the Society Islands were helping him on Rarotonga. There he built a college for the training of these men and Latourette goes on to say that "from it teachers went out to the New Hebrides, Samoa, the Loyalty Islands and New Guinea. They had a remarkable part in spreading Christianity in the Pacific." (1943: 209) In opening the work in the New Hebrides, Williams expected to use Samoans as the missionaries. The initial missionary expansion met with opposition and John Williams was slain on Nov. 20, 1839. This probably happened in retaliation for the cruel treatment meted out to the nationals by white men who a short time before had been searching for sandal wood. The Samoan teachers and Christians persisted, however, even though in 1841 a group of them were also killed on the island of Futuna. By 1845 they had made some progress and were reinforced with the arrival of other white missionaries. Again, Latourette summarizes the national missionary effort by saying, "In the southern portions of the New Hebrides . . . Christians from the Pacific had a larger share." (1943: 228) The Samoans' and Rarotongans were important not only in the New Hebrides, but also effective in introducing Christ in the islands of Ninu, Tokelau, Ellice and Gilbert Islands. (Orr 1962:8)

Another of the early Western missionaries who encouraged this development was George Augustus Selwyn, the first Anglican Bishop of New Zealand and Melanesia. His plan was to take boys from the islands to New Zealand for their training, and then to send them back to their homes as missionaries. With an able colleague in John C. Patterson, this plan was put into effect with the transfer of the training center to Norfolk Island.

In many areas the national missionaries preceeded the Westerner. Examples of this is the entrance to New Guinea, as the Congregationalists sent men from Samoa, the Cook Islands and the Loyalty Islands to that area, or the Fijians who sent to the Bismark Achipelago. (Forman 1970:215) As we shall see in a moment, Tongans went first to Fiji with the white missionary following later. Sometimes they were under direct supervision of the white missionary and given a stipend by him. In many other cases they were months and even years without the personal supervision of western missionaries. Not unusual was an accompanying achievement of church growth as they preached, taught and led groups of people to Christ. One of these examples has been ably recounted by Dr. Alan Tippett regarding the island of Fiji. It is from his writings that the following account comes.

In the great outpouring of the Holy Spirit in Tonga in 1834, prayers of concern for Fiji were expressed with calls for missionary service. As a result, Josua Mateinaniu, a "good and zealous" exhorter was sent from Tonga to Fiji. 1835 really marked the official beginning of Christianity in Fiji for it was in that year that the most important message was sent by King George of Tonga to the paramount chief, Tui Nayau, King of Lau, presenting a case for Christianity in the chiefly way. In this message, George of Tonga related all the benefits that he and Tonga had received through the Gospel. The first Tongan preachers who were sent were all selected men, high chiefs in their own right so that the Gospel was presented with status. One of the greatest of these was Joeli Bulu, who became one of the great island missionaries. They went communicating the Gospel in Tongan. Nineteen days after their arrival in Naufaha, about fifty people had decided to become Christians. The year 1835 also saw the arrival of David Cargill and William Cross, who had come by way of Tonga with the Tongans and Fijians that they had prepared for the work.

This suggests prior effort and preparation which was exactly what had been done. Six years before in 1829 a Tongan teacher had been sent to "spy out the land." There was, also, a group of Tongans living on Fiji who had been given to adventure and plunder. The movement of God in the Tonga Islands began to affect these Tongans living in Fiji as well, and a marked transformation began to appear. Dr. Tippett says of these Tongans that they travelled on board the long distance canoes and organized devotionals rather than continue their acts of plunder. Quoting Thomas Williams Tippett says, "No better pioneers could be found," (Tippett: 1962:16) Also prior to 1835 nationals had been appointed in 1832 to serve an apprenticeship to be served in Tonga but with the long range plan that they be used in Fiji. The advantages of these men for pioneer missionary activity were: 1. They knew the Pacific and the Island people, 2. Understood the Tongan language, 3. They knew how other island people had become Christians, 4. Through this apprenticeship system, the able men were selected, 5. Inspiration and dedication was felt as a team and 6. Confirmation of God's call in being sent was also experienced as a team. (Tippett 1962:34)

Extreme care was exercised regarding the custom of the people as they presented the Gospel in a chiefly way. The case in point here was the way that King George of Tonga aided the entire missionary advance by making his approach in the chiefly way. The indigenous trainees spear headed the attack as men who faced death daily and for whom life meant the propagation of the faith.

The initial missionary movement from Tonga to Fiji was repeated hundreds of times as a separate missionary thrust had to be sparked off for every island, and in every valley. God used a particular type of Christian. The Fijians, upon receiving the Gospel from the Tongans began to reproduce this same kind of missionary expansion. The Holy Spirit moved in a powerful way through the active preaching. Often there were emotional accompaniments, which the Western missionaries described in a terminology much like that of Wesley. The outpourings usually began in meetings when there was some focus upon the sacrificial and saving work of Christ. These outpourings resulted in missionary expansion as the Western missionaries such as Calvert

would take those who had been touched, to other parts of Fiji.
There was no thought of educating in order to evangelize, rather
the idea that education should follow a deep experience with
Christ.

All types of obstacles needed to be overcome. Not among the
least was the inter-tribal wars. In one area of Kadavu, the
spread of the Gospel grew out of a request of the chief, Tui
Yale, who sent to Varani of Viwa for help in war. Varani had
become a Christian and he sent back a message that he had no
army to give but would send another type of soldier. This was
to be a soldier of the faith — Paula Vea, who had come as a
missionary from Tonga to Fiji. After initial church growth had
taken place, Vea sent a plea for additional help to the Western
missionary, Moore. The latter recruited nineteen exhorters, without training but full of the Holy Ghost who had recently been
touched in an awakening on two Lau islands — Matuku, and
Totoya. These men came to work with Vea and a circuit of
preaching points was developed with their help.

In summary, from this area we learn:
1. The wide scale of the national missionary movement in
    Oceania.
2. The close co-operation between national and western
    missionaries.
3. The numerical importance of the national missionary
    force and its possible correlation with the high percentage
    of Christians who now make up the population.
4. The keen interest of Western missionaries such as John
    Williams and George Selwyn, in the missionary vision of
    the islanders, setting up missionary training colleges.
5. The close relationship that awakenings had with the ability
    and enthusiasm to send out missionaries.
6. The anthropological insight with which some of the ad-
    vances were made.
7. The advantages inherent in a well prepared spiritual island
    missionary.

A SODALITY — THE MELANESIAN BROTHERHOOD

A very important place in indigenous mission structures in the Pacific Islands must be given to a "thoroughly indigenous mechanism" called the Melanesian Brotherhood. This was a structured missionary agency that was something quite unique in the history of Pacific missions. (Tippett 1967:45). Tippett attributes its importance to the fact that it was a Melanesian concept for Melanesian action, in which the national island people were able to take the movement into their hearts and give to it the support it needed. This support was primarily through the establishment of a Company of Companions who would pray daily for the missionary brothers and their work. (1967:51)

The Melanesian Brotherhood, called the *Retatasiu*, which means "Company of Brothers", began during the 1920's through the dynamic of a Guadalcanal native, Ini Kopuria. He had been a pupil of Bishop Steward who had taught him as a small boy at Maravovo. A well known story of his class room experience occurred when Ini proposed a fast during Lent by not speaking until Easter, and he asked not to be questioned in class as well. (Fox 1958:193). Evidently he did not like the humdrum of school life, as a teacher, so he returned to the Solomon Islands from Norfolk Island to serve in the armed constabulary in which service he served two years. An accident occurred and he was hospitalized. During the time of his convalescence, through reflection upon his life and upon the Lord's will, he heard the voice of God saying,

> "All this I gave to you:
> What have you given to Me?" (Tippett 1967: 50)

It seemed to Ini as if the Lord had given him a specific challenge. He returned to talk with Bishop Steward who in turn guided his ideas into the structural forms that became the Melanesian Brotherhood. Fox suggests that he was also helped by Arthur Hopkins with whom he also stayed at the time. He further intimates that the form of the Brotherhood could have stemmed from an earlier attempt that Fox himself had made in using young Melanesian lads to go into the hill villages, two by

two, for evangelism. He had called this the St. Aidan's Brotherhood. (1962:67). Whatever the model that might have influenced
him, Ini Kopuria furnished the inspiration and spark that ignited
others to engage in the task of evangelism. Their purpose was,
"to proclaim the teaching of Jesus Christ among the heathen,
not to work among the Christians." (Tippett, 1967:51)

Under the guidance and encouragement of Bishop Steward,
together with six others, the Brotherhood was initiated. They
were resolved to go in obedience wherever Bishop Steward would
send them. The rules were simple with missionary evangelism
taking precedence. The idea was to go first to Guadalcanar,
then to the rest of Melanesia, on to New Guinea, Indonesia and
beyond. Going two by two, each Brother was to take a vow not
to marry, nor to take pay and to obey those who were over him.
This vow was for the duration of a year at which time it could
be renewed. Ini took the vow for life, as well as one other.
They went, barefoot and bareheaded with the distinctive dress
of a black loin cloth and white sash. On Sundays and other
special religious days they would wear a white loin cloth and
a black sah. (Fox 1962:69)

The Brotherhood was organized in Households of twelve, each
under an Elder Brother wherein a disciplinary check was made
on each other. Criticism of another Brother was not allowed
to outsiders. A time for voicing of this type of criticism was
given at the annual meeting when all the groups met together
at the headquarters. This was held on Saint Simon's and St.
Jude's Day which celebrated as well Ini Kopuria's vow taking.
Each household reported to the whole group regarding what had
been done during the year, with both praise and concern being
voiced for the missionary activity. The commissioning of the
novices each year was done by the Bishop who would see Jesus'
words, "Let your light so shine before men that they may see
your good works and glorify your Father which is in heaven."
These novices had two years of prior preparation before the
taking of their vows.

After this service of renewed consecration, these would scatter out across the islands and work out from their Households. Great changes came to some of the areas where they worked, such as Santa Cruz or Lord Howe Island where a wonderful work of God was accomplished and many were baptized.

The Brotherhood ascertained by trial whether or not there was a vocation to religious life among the Melanesians. (Tippett 1967:51) At one point in its history its numbers grew to about a hundred and fifty. A good deal of time was spent practicing singing, during the time that they would be together as a group as well as in Bible study.

Problems were encountered with the passage of time. Fox felt that one of the weaknesses was that they were allowed to spend such a short time, only three months, in a village where they had been able to found a Christian school. Then it was to be handed over to a Christian teacher who often was of another denomination. The difficulty of finding good men who would be able to train the novices was another problem. This, perhaps, was due in part to the number of Brothers who became Anglican priests after serving in the Brotherhood. Too often the white missionaries were critical of the young men, feeling that they were there more for the adventure and the glamour than anything else. They were also misused by the established churches so as to furnish cheap labor for all sorts of menial tasks in building a church, helping to move a school, etc. (Fox 1962:76)

Parallel to the Brotherhood was the Order of the Companions who prayed for the Brotherhood and for the local church. They were also to do something for the village such as cleaning the church, visiting the sick or gathering firewood for old people. Their numbers grew to 1500 who not only prayed for the missionary effort of the Brotherhood, but also supported them through offerings.

With the coming of the Second World War and the Japanese invasion and the leadership gap after the departure and death of Ini, the ranks of the Brotherhood have been reduced. Yet, their ministry is important especially if they might be freed for the continued thrust into more and more pagan areas.

Lessons of interest for us include:

1. The validity and usefulness of a sodality to the Younger Church.
2. The ability of an organizational structure that would function on indigenous resources.
3. The close co-operation between the western missionaries and the national founder who innovated at this point.
4. The principle of group dynamics in the team approach to evangelism, as well as comradship among its members.
5. The means whereby grievances and criticisms were given an opportunity within the structure, but which at the same time, minimized the tension.
6. The discipline, commitment, and success in helping the Church to grow.
7. The preparation given to the novices as well as the trial period that it provided to young men who were considering the Anglican priesthood.

Regional Analysis and Interpretation

AFRICA

Africa presents a most interesting pattern related to its missionary picture. Almost all activities are either to or from Africa itself. As a sending continent, whereas Africa reports 24 sending societies, only one is sending missionaries out of Africa itself. That is the **Church of the Lord Throughout the World** (Aladura) which sends to England and to New York, with one person each. Likewise as a receiving continent its chief activity in Third-World missions is from within. Of the 52 reported groups from Third-World, only 10 are from outside of Africa.

Examination shows that the different missionary activities largely fall into groupings according to four relationships.

First, the traditional well-recognized denominational churches, which are today related to the World Council of Churches and the Ecumenical movement. To the questionnaire sent, replies were received from the Christian Council of Nigeria, the All-African Conference of Churches, and the Christian Council of Malawi. All of these responded in the negative, stating that they had no missionary sending activity.

The one group that has missionary activity which would fit into the grouping was **The Church of the Province of South Africa,** with headquarters in Johannesburg, which is the Anglican Church of South Africa. The response was that it is engaged in missionary work to various groups of peoples of South Africa, and adjoining territory.

Second, is the group of the newer denominations, and the independent missionary boards working in Africa, such as those which have relationship with the U.S. based boards, and thus affiliated with the Evangelical Foreign Missions Association and the Interdenominational Foreign Missions Association.

In this group were several responses, such as the following:

> **Africa Gospel Church**
> **Africa Inland Church Missionary Board**
> **Christian and Missionary Alliance**
> **Evangelical Church of West Africa**
> **Nigerian Baptist Convention**

These groups are patterned after and related to the mother organization. In many cases the mission board, now operating with national personnel, is set up with a joint committee of missionaries from the U. S. and national pastors. Much of the work is possible because of U. S. funds which are available to sustain the groundwork, and to give support to the outreach. The personnel are national believers from the different congregations, who to a greater or lesser degree are responsible for the financial support of their own representatives. Report comes from the

Evangelical Church of West Africa of the development of a new missionary-sending society of some 100 missionaries with an annual unsubsidized budget of over $20,000 (U.S.).

Many problems which were long ago faced by the foreign missionaries are now avoided, as the supervision and oversight in close cooperation has brought confidence and mutual sharing in the new enterprise undertaken by the African Church.

The missionaries operating this pattern are ministering in many different geographical, tribal, lingual and cultural situations. Many are not expecting to be permanent "missionaries" who will necessarily give their whole life to "missionary" work, but will go for as long as is necessary until the church is established in the new location. Often they will be replaced by another later, and return as a much more mature pastor who has vision to send others out as he himself went out. It is a method that is productive of vision and practical ministry that enriches in personal growth, and produces new churches where the Word is proclaimed.

Third, is the group of separated national churches which have formed their own mission board. This group is small, but is represented by the **African Brotherhood Church** and the **Gospel Furthering Church.** These had their origin in the nationalistic reaction against a foreign mission board, which had planted the parent church. When the separation came, a new church was established on equal lines to the parent pattern. As far as can be determined, there is little missionary outreach from these groups. The burden of sustenance of the individual churches and in the formation of national relationships is not allowing much in the way of financial support of an outreach ministry. However growth and extension are reported. Lack of finances is hindering the undertaking of any large-scale program.

Fourth, is the independent and indigenous church movements. These are the "Prophet movements" of which there are over 50 and they have gained considerable recognition. Among them are the following which have gained considerable missionary impetus:

Eglise de Jesus-Christ sur la Terre par la Prophete Simon Kimbangu, of Zaire.
Christ Apostolic Church, of Nigeria.
Church of the Lodr Throughout the World, (Aladura,) of Nigeria.

The pattern of missionary outreach seems to be distinctive in character, being representative of many indigenous and independent movements throughout history. Individuals are not sent by the church or local body, but feel a sense of responsibility and concern. Therefore as individuals they use migration to extend the message. Often the entire family, goes to another region, sets up house and farms within the new area, and simply continues its life style in another location. In the course of establishing a new home in the new region there is testimony to the new religion and so the message is proclaimed. The religion is not the religion of an outsider, but rather of a "new insider" which means the individual is an advocate, gathers a following, becoming an innovator within the new society. Such is the case of the **Church of the Lord Throughout the World,** where its representatives have migrated to England and the U. S. to reach certain groups, seeking them out, and settling among them in the new chosen homeland. Their message is a report of one, a new "Prophet" who has appeared in the land from which the people migrated, and those people are led to feel an affinity for the new religion of the land from which they migrated.

At this point it would be hard to tell whether the second or the fourth group is growing fastest, but certainly the first and the third groups as mentioned above are almost completely out of the picture as far as missionary outreach is concerned.

Prediction would lead one to say that as long as the second group recognizes the "gifts of the Spirit" and invites men to minister with the national brethren because it recognizes gifted men of the Lord, a stronger international character of missionary endeavour will be developed in the future. Group four will most probably come to tension over the validity of one or another prophet, but will develop within a completely African frame of reference, and so may have an abiding appeal. Where Scripture is the basis, there will be growing harmony between the followers of different prophets. Where the Scripture is not the basis, surely more heresy will follow and the movement will become more and more individualistic, and rejected by the other groups as being non-Christian.

ASIA'S INVOLVEMENT IN MISSIONS

The Protestant missionary movement has been going on in Asia for more than 170 years. Wherever the missionaries went, new churches were established. Thus, in every country today there is a witnessing and worshiping community of Christians. Nevertheless, only a tiny minority of the population in Asia as a whole has been evangelized. The work of mission is far from finished. If the gospel is to be spread widely and speedily, the churches in Asia, as well as those from the West, must renew their efforts to be actively involved in missions.

In the past, the evangelization of Asia has been retarded because of the failure of Western missions to encourage Asian Christians to organize their own missions and thereby extend the faith. They planted churches, but kept these churches from attaining any real measure of maturity. Consequently, most of these younger churches remained on the receiving end of the gospel. This failure of the older missions to stimulate the organization of new missions has been a significant factor in accounting for the relatively slow progress in spreading the gospel throughout a greater part of Asia during the past 150 years.

THE EARLY BEGINNINGS OF ASIAN MISSIONS

It is significant that India was not only the first country to receive a Protestant missionary,[1] but also had the honor of being one of the first missionary-sending countries in Asia. In 1884,

1. William Carey arrived in Calcutta on November 11, 1793 to begin his work.

the **Methodist Conference of South India** decided to start a mission to Malaysia. The following year William F. Oldham, who was born in India, was sent to Singapore as their first missionary. Some twenty years later, the late Bishop V. S. Azariah was instrumental in founding the **Indian Missionary Society** in 1903.

About the same time, in another part of Asia, the first Korean missionary was sent by the recently-formed **Korean Presbyterian Church** to Cheju Island in 1907. The Rev. Kee Pung Lee was among the first seven national pastors to be ordained by this Korean Church. Although many more nationals were needed for their growing church, they felt it their responsibility and privilege to send this brother to proclaim the gospel to the inhabitants of this island, south of Korea, whose culture and language were different.

Five years later, after the General Assembly of the Korean Presbyterian Church was inaugurated, three more missionaries were sent to China. Since 1913, this Korean Church has sent missionaries not only to China, but also to Russia, Tokyo and Manchuria. Thus it has been estimated by Won Yong Koh that by the second world war "around 100 Korean missionaries had served in different parts of the North East Asia mission fields."[2]

Even prior to these missionary-sending involvements by the Church in India and Korea, the Protestant Churches in Hawaii, Fiji and Samoa were already active in sending their own local missionaries to different islands in the Pacific. For example, in 1875 a group of Fijian Christians crossed to the island of New Britain as missionaries. Throughout the period, missionary activities were spontaneously carried out by the churches in the Oceania. Thus, in his response to our survey questionnaire, the President of the Methodist Conference in Fiji gave this account:

> While records are known to be incomplete, a total of 533 men and women have been documented as having served as missionaries of the Methodist Church in Fiji to other countries.

THE GROWTH OF THE MISSIONARY MOVEMENT IN ASIA

Japan, Korea, Hong Kong and the Philippines have sent a fairly significant number of missionaries overseas, while Taiwan, Vietnam, Singapore-Malaysia, and Indonesia have also started. Both Burma and India, with vast populations of different tribal, caste and linguistic backgrounds, have cross-cultural missions within the sub-continent as well as foreign missions.

However, from the questionnaire survey, out of 30 distinct foreign missionary societies in these Asian countries which responded, 22 of them (73%) were formed only after 1960. In this sense, a majority of the organizations are very young and, as expected, still small in size.

Japan leads the list in the number of mission agencies. Together with Korea, these two countries present a good example of growing missionary involvement. In July 1971, eleven of the indigenous missionary-sending agencies organized themselves into the **Japan Overseas Missionary Association.** The purpose of this association is "to seek cooperatively more efficient ways of promoting foreign missions among evangelical churches in Japan."[3] Besides coordinating the efforts of its constituent members, this Missionary Association will seek to find out needs and opportunities of foreign mission fields, as well as to sponsor a training program for Japanese missionaries.

The example of Korea is equally encouraging. In March, 1968, the **Korean Evangelistic Inter-Mission Alliance,** KEIMA (now known as **Korean International Mission, Inc.**) was founded by Pastor David J. Cho. It seeks to promote inter-missionary activities at home and abroad with the primary purpose of "training

---

2. In an article "The Missionary Vision of the Korean Church" written for the "Strategy in Missions" course at the School of World Mission, Pasadena, 1972.

3. "Japan Overseas Missionary Association Formed" in *Japan Harvest,* Fall 1971 issue.

and sending forth missionaries from Korea into the harvest fields of the world." Since its founding, it has sent four couples and two single men to serve in Hong Kong, Iran, Thailand and Brunei, with five more couples being prepared to go overseas. The support of these missionaries has largely come from churches and Christians in Korea. However, besides K.I.M., the Presbyterian and Methodist Churches in Korea have also sent a number of missionaries to various parts of Asia, as well as to distant Ethiopia, Mexico and Brazil.

India, a nation with the second largest population in the world, is both a mission field and a mission-sending country. With only two percent of the population claiming nominal allegiance to Christianity, there is an obvious need for more extensive missionary witness within the country. In spite of this fact. the Church in India had not use this as an excuse for not being prepared to engage in foreign missionary activities. The great commission, which the Lord gave to His Church in all places, at all times, is to bear witness for Him **both** in Jerusalem (home mission) **and** to the ends of the earth (foreign mission).

Altogether, eleven societies replied to the questionaire, giving a description of their missionary activities. Six of these work within the country — their missionaries serving in different parts and often engaging in cross-cultural and linguistic communication. However, the data supplied was not sufficient to conclude whether they were strictly "home missions" or to be regarded as "foreign missions." Five others reported that they have sent missionaries to East Africa, the Adaman Island, Nepal, Afghanistan, Sikkim, Bhutan, Nagaland, the Burma border, Thailand and Sarawak. These foreign mission societies are the **Board of Missions of the Methodist Church in Southern Asia** (reconstituted in 1920), the **United Church of North India Missions Board** (1955), **All India Prayer Fellowship** (1957), **Christian and Missionary Alliance Church of India** (1961) and the **Indian Evangelical Mission** (1965).

OLDER MISSIONS ESTABLISHING YOUNGER MISSIONS

During the past decade, two well-known western missions have led the way in the founding of younger missions in Asia. The

Christian and Missionary Alliance has the honour of being the pioneer in mission planting in Asia. Beginning in 1961, six of the C&MA churches began to send missionaries abroad. The data below summarizes the number of Asian missionaries sent out by the various churches in 1970:

CHURCH

The Japan Alliance	2	to Brazil
The C&MA Church of India	2	to Adaman Island
Gospel Church of Thailand	2	to Laos
The Alliance Church of Hong Kong	10	to Vietnam, Taiwan Malaysia, Indonesia
The Evangelical Church of Vietnam	2	to Laos
	16	to Tribal Groups within Vietnam
The C&MA Church of the Philippines	4	to Indonesia

As a result of this growing missionary involvement, these Churches met together for an Asian Missionary Consultation in March, 1970. As a result the **C&MA Missions Fellowship of Asia** was formed. The constitution of this Fellowship states that it purposes "to fulfill the command of Jesus Christ by promoting the program of foreign missions in Christian and Missionary Alliance churches throughout Asia."

The second western missionary society which opened its membership to include nationals is the older and larger **Overseas Missionary Fellowship.** Beginning in 1965, the O.M.F. encouraged the formation of home Councils in the Asian countries, enabling Asian Christians to have a specific missionary interest, and through joining this large international missionary fellowship, be represented widely overseas. Presently, fifteen Asian missionaries, supported by their respective home countries, work in Singapore-Malaysia, Korea, Philippines, Thailand and Hong Kong.

SOME CHARACTERISTICS AND CONTRIBUTIONS
OF ASIAN MISSIONS

The emergence of these younger missions are a sign of growing maturity in the Asian churches. All over Asia the people are becoming increasingly receptive to the gospel message. So it is timely that Asian Christians express their obedience to the Lord's great commission by being more missionary minded. A study of the expansion of Christianity shows that as the number of missionary societies increase, greater progress is made in the advancement of the gospel. It is obvious that this did not take place in all parts of the world at the same time. Indeed, there were different periods when God was seen to be active through the Church in winning the populations to Himself. Hence, many of us in Asia today are conscious that now is God's time (*kairos*) for discipling the nations in Asia. So, His people must be ready to allow God to use them for the evangelization not only of Asia, but through them, of the whole world.

P. Octavianus, the founding director of the **Indonesian Missionary Fellowship,** writing in an article, "Asia Future and Our Response," contends that as God worked through the missionary movement, beginning from the Mediterranean, then from Europe, England and across the Atlantic from North America, the time has now come for Him to work through the churches in Asia. He believes that God is specially pouring His Holy Spirit upon many Asian Christians to prepare them for world-wide missionary expansion:

> In the middle of the twentieth century the "rain" of the Holy Spirit has begun to fall. Although there are as yet only scattered drops, it is a sign of the beginning of the "latter rain" in the world at large, and in Southeast Asia and East Asia in particular. All the things that we are experiencing in Asia at the present time indicate to me the fulfillment of the promise of God in Joel 2:23-28....[4]

It can be expected, therefore, as the Asian churches grow in their missionary commitment, they will contribute new ideas and new ways to help towards the fulfillment of the missionary mandate.

---

4. *Asian Outreach*, No. 10, p. 14.

Compared with western missionaries, Asians have the advantage of experiencing less culture shock. Therefore, due to common cultural values and traditions, they would find greater ease in adjusting to new situations. As Asians, they will also be able to adapt themselves to a social level more similar to the population of the receiving country and so again help to establish common points of socio-economic contact with the people. From the economic point of view, the fact that Asian missions are not financially as well endowed can also have advantage. Their missionaries will not be looked upon as sources for raising "inter-church aid" and are less likely to be engaged in expensive programs of institutional work. Their limited supply of funds can stimulate their missionaries to concentrate on the essential of missions — evangelism and church planting.

Asian missionaries can have advantage over their western counterparts in establishing an indigenous image of the Church. To find Asians preaching the gospel to fellow Asians and commending Christ to them will help to correct the mistaken notion that Christianity is a western religion. Asian mission societies can also play an effective role in helping the local churches to develop greater missionary commitment. With better promotion, more nationals can be challenged and recruited to missionary service.

PROBLEMS ENCOUNTERED BY ASIAN MISSIONS

Although Asian missionaries find many encouraging factors on their side, when they begin to serve as cross-cultural missionaries within the Asian context, they will also encounter a number of problems. Some of these are listed below. They are not meant to discourage the Churches in Asia from continuing to expand their missionary movement, but rather, to enable them to face up to these real problems and find solutions to overcome them.

1. GOVERNMENT RESTRICTIONS

All sovereign nations in the world feel they have the unquestionable right to accept only those nationalities they prefer. It is unfortunate that in Asia today Asians of one nationality find serious difficulty in obtaining visas to work in another Asian country. For example, a Korean finds difficulty in entering Japan, a Taiwanese does not have a passport to visit any country he chooses, a Chinese is not particularly welcomed by a number of Southeast Asian nations, and so on. This problem of visa restrictions is often particularly serious for Asian nationals moving from one country to another. This is due to political bias towards the different nationalities by the governments concerned.

2. LACK OF EXPERIENCE

As most Asian missions were formed only recently, they lack experience in both management and mission relationships with one another. Since their formation, many of them have not been able to get together, either on a national basis (an exception is Japan) or a Pan-Asian basis whereby they can discuss mutual problems, share ideas and insights and plan together for a common thrust to advance their cause.

New missionaries recruited by these small societies are often inadequately prepared for overseas assignments. Once out in the field, their missionaries are practically on their own; they seek to establish their work without the guidance and counsel of more experienced missionaries. Consequently, those who are confronted with cross-cultural adjustments are left without assistance from older colleagues.

3. CHURCH-MISSION RELATIONSHIPS

The problem of church-mission relationships is faced by Asian missions just as much as by the older western missions. It operates at both ends — at the home base as well as in the receiving country. Is the Mission society recognized and supported by the home churches? This is important because they must count on a number of churches in the sending country so they can be assured of a wide base of continual financial support for their programs. If the home churches recognize the value of their function and encourage them in their work, this also means that some of their members may offer to join their society as missionaries. Support and recognition from the home Church will thus help in their recruitment program. It is therefore important that understanding and cooperation must be cultivated with a large number of home churches in the sending country. Most of the present Asian missions, because of their "independence" attitude and their poor relationship with the older mainline Churches, often function with this handicap.

Missionaries on the field also face the same problem of relating themselves and their work to the Churches in the receiving country. Uncertainty as to whether they should start new churches or feed converts to existing local churches can generate tensions. Just as these missions function "incognito" in sending countries, their missionaries are similarly regarded as such in the receiving countries. Sometimes Asian missionaries face unusual barriers in receiving countries and to their surprise find themselves less welcome than western missionaries.

4. INADEQUATE FINANCIAL SUPPORT

This could be an important factor; seriously hindering the growth and expansion of many established missions. In the home country, many of the older and larger Churches, being more affluent, are not missionary minded. Currently, most of the support for Asian missions come either from individuals or the smaller independent congregations. So, various missionary societies, as for example the **Alliance Mission** in Hong Kong and the **Asian Evangelistic Fellowship** in Singapore, have more volunteers than funds to send them overseas for missionary service. It would appear that as they stir up missionary enthusiasm and interest in the home churches, they should also find ways to challenge Christians to give generously and sacrificially to send more missionary recruits to the field.

5. LACK OF TRAINING

Very few of the Bible colleges or seminaries offer in their curricula "Missions" as a subject. Very few missionary training schools exist in the countries of Asia. Consequently, those who are sent overseas either do not have the benefit of training or are ill-prepared for cross-cultural missionary service. The danger is that as these Asian missionaries find themselves unable to relate cross-culturally, they can become discouraged and unable to make a strong contribution to their work. Many of these Asian missionaries need training so they can become effective church planters.

THE FUTURE OF ASIAN MISSIONS

As more national missions emerge in Asian countries, there is an urgent need for some form of meaningful relationship to link them with the older western missions. Two kinds of missionary conferences for the purpose of mutual learning, fellowship and sharing of past experiences will help in the world-wide missionary enterprise. First, the younger Missions in Asia need to meet together to get to know each other. This can be followed by a larger meeting of all Missions, on a world-wide basis, at which the task of fulfilling the great commission in each generation can be reviewed and strategies to accomplish the goal can be planned together. If positive partnership can be formed between the older and younger Missions, much benefit will be mutually derived from such consultations.

Missions today, young and old, cannot afford to operate without exact knowledge of the changing world. Research, planning for church growth and understanding of where receptive peoples are found across the Continents are indispensable to the task of effective missions. The mistakes and failures of the past must be noted and new styles of cross-cultural communication which will lead to church growth must be explored. In view of all these, as the Asian missions face the future (which have tremendous opportunities to disciple responsive populations to Christ) they must regard the establishment of an Asian Church Growth and Missionary Research Center as important. They should, therefore, unite to support such a Center when it is formed.

LATIN AMERICAN ANALYSIS

In reflecting upon the responses from Latin America regarding Third World Missions, a sense of excitement dawns. There is a realization of the greatness of the power of God as one sees not only the increasing numerical growth in Latin America of those who love Jesus Christ, but also a dynamic national leadership in the indigenous churches. One indication of this increasing dynamism is the expanded missionary vision and practice in the sending of Latin American missionaries.

To be remembered is the fact that Protestant missionary activity has really come into its own during this century, and the church growth that has been experienced has largely come within the last twenty-five years. It would be remiss to suggest that no Third World missionary effort by Latin American Churches existed prior to World War II. The contrary seems to be the case, even though the principle thrust was missionary work within the Continent. J. B. A. Kessler, Jr. recounts the story of Baltazar and Andreas Rubio who in 1936 were working as pastors in the Nazarene congregations along the coast in Perú. They felt the call of God upon them to go to a tribal group, the Aguarunas, where the Roger Winans, a Nazarene North American missionary couple, had been pioneering the evangelistic effort to reach this tribe With the help of the Winans they were able to use the language fairly soon. Kessler says, "Baltazar and Rubio worked for many years among the Aguarunas, and in this way the evangelization of this tribe became a project that affected the whole Nazarene Church in Peru." (1967: 273).

The early pattern suggests that national missionaries began working cross-culturally in conjunction with North American mission agencies. The Methodists of Argentina sent a doctor to Bolivia, the Presbyterians of Brazil sent to Portugal, the Baptists of Brazil to Bolivia, and the Christian and Missionary Alliance to Uruguay and Paraguay. Santo Barbieri by 1960 was saying, "Happily, there is a promising beginning toward the discharge of the missionary imperative on the part of some groups." (1961: 155) Another Methodist writing at the same time says that "the churches themselves are reaching out in home and foreign mission projects and in the establishment of humanitarian institutes, schools, hospitals and orphanages." (Derby 1961: 11, 12).

However, most of the missionary activity, as it was called, was done within the borders of their own countries, or to another Latin American neighbor. Very few were sent to other continents, with the exception of North America. The proximity to its Northern neighbor has meant that for one reason or another Latin American Evangelicals have found varying degrees of ministry among the Spanish speakers who reside within the boundaries of the United States. As far as we are able to determine this type of missionary activity was based on informal structural patterns and there were no Latin American missionary agencies formed during the pre-1950's expressly for the evangelization of the Spanish peoples of the United States. Perhaps additional research may reveal their existence.

Another early pattern which was followed was through migration. Victor Monterroso told the writer of his experiences in Southern Argentina among the Chilean Pentecostals who had formed churches in this way. The pastor of a Pentecostal Church in Santiago del Estero also told the writer of the missionary impact of Chilenos who had come to Santiago del Estero, Argentina, during the 1940's and who had provided a spark for the development of their work. This type of missionary work by migration has continued, and while not formally structured, is a factor in Latin American missionary outreach. From a questionnaire returned from the National Presbyterian Church of Guatemala, the same picture was given for the beginning of their missionary work in Honduras. Twelve years ago, some Presbyterian elders from Guatemala had gone to Honduras and established there a lumber mill. They saw the need, and began to witness as there were no other Evangelical churches in the area. Help was sent to the area during the subsequent years by the church in Guatemala.

PRESENT RESPONSES

DENOMINATIONS

With the development of autonomous national denominational Churches, such as the **Argentine Baptist Convention,** or the **Brazilian Presbyterian Church,** mission boards of these Churches have also been formed under national leadership for the purpose of sending missionaries. According to Dr. Ralph Winter's categories they would be modal societies, closely tied to the denomination for both personnel and funds. The **Brazilian Baptist Convention,** the **Assemblies of God** in Brazil, as well as some smaller denominational groups have strong programs and are contemplating missionary expansion within their own groups. The Christian and Missionary Alliance, while not as numerically as strong in Latin America as they are in other areas of the world, has nevertheless presented the same example of seeking to foster and promote national missionary agencies. David Volstad, Area Secretary for the C. and M.A. for South America, in a letter of reply, commented upon the Argentine church that is supporting three couples, as well as a new effort of their churches in Puerto Rico, Colombia, Ecuador and Perú in supporting a Puerto Rican worker in Venezuela. The notable thing about this is that there are four national Churches that are supporting, in Volstad's opinion, "may point to a future Missions Fellowship of Latin America, such as was founded in Asia some years ago." (Letter 72-194, see Basic Data File, Puerto Rico, Christian and Missionary Alliance.) Suffice it to say that, denominational programs should be increasing their missionary sending.

PENTECOSTAL CHURCHES

These Churches are part of the denominational picture, but special note must be made with relationship to their missionary passion and great potential due in part to their numerical strength. There is the feeling of confidence that God is going to use them in the missionary enterprise across the world. I remember Hugo Contreras, who since has gone from Argentina to Spain with his family as an evangelistic missionary, relating how that in a number of prayer groups associated with the **Renovación Cristiana in Argentina,** God had been impressing upon numerous individuals as to the importance of Latin American missionaries in the task of world evangelism. Reflected in the lives of these brethren was not only confidence that God was to mightily use them in the missionary endeavour, but also courage and joy in the midst of hardships. This type of an attitude is repeated in other parts of Latin America.

Everett Carver, a fellow missionary associate at the School of World Mission, and who has served in Puerto Rico and Cuba, tells of the missionary vision of the Iglesia de Dios Pentecostal of Puerto Rico, who since 1950 have sent missionaries to twelve mission fields. He lists the following countries to which they are sending missionaries — U.S.A., Dominican Republic, Virgin Islands, Haiti, Panamá, Venezuela, Honduras, Mexico, Portugal, Spain, Colombia, Costa Rica and formerly Cuba. This gives an idea of their dynamic outreach.

Dr. Herbert Kane recently sent to us three pages from a Master's Thesis of Trinity Seminary written this year in which the author[1] tells of the missionary outreach of the United Pentecostal Church. The Church is called a very missionary minded Church, sending their workers to more *departamentos* and other points within the Country of Colombia than any other Protestant Church, as well as sending nine Colombian missionaries to three other Countries — Ecuador, Bolivia and Spain. (1972: 130). The author goes on to say that these missionaries receive the equivalent of two hundred dollars (U.S.) per month in support. He says that a big factor in this outreach program is because these Pentecostals give sc liberally. Missionary emphasis is made in the local churches with a special service once a month. Also through publications, the news and needs of the missionaries are kept before the local people. One of the great moments during the year is the last day of the annual convention which is also dedicated to their missionary program.

INTERDENOMINATIONAL GROUPS

This is another missionary structure which is being reproduced in Latin America somewhat from the molds that are seen in the independent missionary agencies from Eurica. Agencies such as **New Tribes Mission, Unevangelized Fields Mission, World-Wide Evangelization Crusade** in Brazil are examples of this development. In this movement auxiliary and sometimes fully autonomous societies have been encouraged to form under national leadership and with the full support coming from indigenous sources. The Brazilian branch of the **Christian Literature Crusade** has announced their first training course for Brazilians that have been recruited for foreign missions. The first course began March 20, 1972, which prepared the eight who had enrolled. Two of these are preparing specifically for missionary work in Spain and Africa.

---

1. We do not know at this time the author's name, nor the title of the Thesis.

Another such group is the **International Missionary Fellowship of Jamaica.** This is an indigenous faith organization created to help qualified missionary candidates to fulfill their calling. It was begun in 1962 through three men — a Chinese-Jamaican, a British IVF worker and an American independent missionary who consulted with Dr. G. Christian Weiss of Back to the Bible Broadcast. From that time they have sent 15 West Indian missionaries to Haiti, Bolivia and the Dominican Republic. This Mission has a missionary internship program in which the candidates receive practical training and which allows the mission to establish contact with an IFMA mission in which the missionaries are accepted as Associate Missionaries. Thomas Northen, in the reply to us noted, "We plan to see the IMF concept of missions developed in other countries, particularly where nationalism runs high. We have done it successfully in Guyana... where there is a Guyana Missionary Fellowship serving in Guyana, closely coordinated with our IMF." (See Appendix E for International Missionary Fellowship Data File.)

Another Eurica based group, the Salvation Army, has been sending Argentine missionaries through its organization to other countries for some time.

A Mission that has been admired and closely watched not only because of Evangelism in Depth, but also because of its attempt to incorporate into its structure Latin American leadership, has been the **Latin American Mission.** Significant strides were made from the time of Kenneth Strachen to the present to provide for more Latin American initiative and responsibility in an extension of the partnership idea. Horace Fenton said, "I believe that L.A.M. cannot be really effective in its evangelistic objective until fully rooted in Latin America." He went on to say that, "I feel that the gradual partnership program cannot produce what we are after. There are only a limited number of Latins who will continue to honor us with their membership in our mission unless there are basic and deep changes in our whole structure." (Latin American Evangelist 1971: 2)

Perhaps part of the reasoning behind this thinking is that which was expressed by Dennis Clark when he said, "It seems almost too late for Western societies to recruit the national because, with very few exceptions the stigma of being labeled a 'stooge' or 'puppet' reduces usefulness." (1971: 45)

The restructuring of the L.A.M. is well underway, placing emphasis upon the major responsibility and leadership in Latin American hands. The structure consists of a federation of autonomous ministries in which the various departments of ministry will have freedom to work with and through the Evangelical Churches in Latin America. At present they are in a seventeen month transition period. The Latin American Mission as a North American sending agency is one among the eight or ten different member entities.

Dayton Roberts, of the community of Latin American Evangelical Ministries, as the new community is called, pin pointed a very specific concern in stating that they are attempting to explore how to develop more successfully and realistically the local resources for the support of the Lord's work in Latin America.

IMMIGRANT CHURCHES

Part of the picture in Latin America is the receiving of Third World missionaries for ministry among immigrant populations such as the Japanese who have immigrated especially to Brazil in large numbers. Agencies from Japan, as would be expected, are sending these missionaries not only to Brazil, but to other Countries as well. Both Argentina and Bolivia have received Japanese missionaries. Katsumi Yamahata describes his life to the "Lost Sheep of Bolivia." He points out that those among whom he ministered tried to be Japanese even in that remote corner of the earth. He sensed his duty not only to be a bearer of the Gospel but also to furnish a spiritual bridge between Japan and Okinawa and the Bolivian Japanese.

396 THIRD WORLD MISSIONS

IN RETROSPECT

Exciting events are taking place in Latin America among Evangelical Christians. One of the most significant is the indigenous missionary vision. New Agencies are coming into being such as the **Asociación Misionera Evangélica Nacional of Peru** or the **Asociación de Iglesias Evangelicas Libres of Venezuela,** with whom Professor C. Peter Wagner had a recent interview. The strength of Brazil is beginning to show. As noted in the statistical summaries, Latin America in the number of agencies and missionaries, is behind Asia. But with the acquired data for newer agencies, the growth of missionary activity in Latin America seems to be increasing. We would trust that it would continue to flourish and prosper.

It is our hope that the increased missionary passion of our Latin American brethren might be consumated in the establishment of many missionary agencies.

Part VII

Introducing Theological Education by Extension

C. Peter Wagner

and Ralph R. Covell

Part VII, which introduces the Theological Education by Extension concept is taken in its entirety from *An Extension Seminary Primer* by Ralph R. Covell and C. Peter Wagner.

Ralph R. Covell is the head of the department of Missions at the Denver Conservative Baptist Theological Seminary. He was a missionary for one term in China and for three terms in Taiwan. His work in Taiwan, in addition to the translation of the New Testament, included the founding and development of a Bible institute into a seminary for training Christian leaders in that country.

21
CHANGING PATTERNS OF
MINISTERIAL TRAINING

A modest experiment with a new form of ministerial training in Guatemala in 1962 has, within a decade, not only drawn
the attention of theological educators world-wide, but also
caused many to rethink their patterns and presuppositions for
theological education. As Ralph Winter, one of the architects
of the extension seminary, says, "We do at least now have a
movement on our hands."[1]

The movement, quite naturally, spread first of all from
Guatemala to other Latin American countries, notably Colombia,
Bolivia and Brazil. Soon CAMEO (the joint committee of Interdenominational Foreign Mission Association and Evangelical
Foreign Missions Association to Assist Missionary Education
Overseas), under the leadership of Raymond Buker, Sr., became
interested in the concept and sponsored a workshop in Wheaton
in 1968, well attended by missionaries from most parts of the
world. This in turn produced invitations for similar workshops
in Asia and Africa, the first round of them being held in the
Summer of 1970. England and Spain have workshops scheduled for
early 1971.

From its present application in younger churches, interest
in extension theological education is now increasing in U.S.A.
seminaries. An excellent study by F. Ross Kinsler of the Presbyterian Seminary in Guatemala has outlined ways in which
extension principles could help overcome certain deficiencies
in U.S. theological education.[2] Taking a broader view which
includes developments in secular education, Ted Ward of Michigan
State University has observed that "theological education by
extension is rapidly moving to a leadership position among the
educational movements of the day."[3]

In the secular world, where educators have realized that their institutions will not be able to sustain growth rates equal to those of the population explosion, methods which have been found helpful in the extension seminary are being applied. In January of 1971 "The Open University" in England will begin courses leading to a B.A. degree. As *The Expository Times* reports, "This will prove a real godsend to older men and women who feel equipped to proceed to degree work, but cannot absent themselves from the duties which provide their livelihood, or to women who cannot discard the responsibilities of home and family."[4]

The Israeli government for a number of years has attempted to teach Hebrew to new immigrants by "taking the school to adults." The pilot projects consisted of residential schools, but when it became obvious that these would not keep pace with the needs, an extension program was inaugurated. By 1965 half of the immigrant students (10,500 of 21,350) were studying in extension centers called *"ulpaniyot."*[5]

CHANGING PATTERNS OF THE CHURCH

One of the phenomena of today's rapidly-changing world has been a noticeable change in patterns of the church. The New Testament does not purport to give us a master blueprint for church form. Although some still do consider a particular church structure "more biblical" than others, a new openness toward differing forms of the church seems to be characteristic of Christians today.

The church, in its simplest form, is where the believers are. When the IVCF group meets on campus, for example, this is a type of functional church meeting. Christian businessmen, nurses, military officers, scientists, and others who have common secular interests form associations which (in spite of predictable denials) become kinds of churches outside the church. Some interdenominational missions in foreign cities become functional churches when they hold their own Sunday worship in English. Organizations such as the Gideons or Young Life or Christian Endeavor have functioned as churches for some people.

Home Bible studies are becoming popular in some areas, and are considered their "church" by many who attend them. Groups of Christians in the charismatic movement sometimes meet outside their own church buildings and programs. If a conflict occurs, some will feel so loyal to their ad hoc meetings than they prefer to split from their traditional church rather than give up the new form they have discovered. The term "under-ground church" is now commonplace.

In Red China faithful Christians can meet secretly in groups which must not exceed two or three--a form of the church reminiscent of the catacombs. In Indonesia groups of evangelical Christians from the Reformed Protestant Churches have begun what they call "by-pass" groups. They think they are by-passing the church, but in reality they have developed a new form of church. The Philippine Congress on Evangelism recommended the formation of 10,000 "cell groups" as the basis of future church growth there. These cell groups will not look much like our traditional churches.

Rapidly-growing cities with limited real estate such as Hong Kong and Singapore have brought about the development of still another form--"churches in the flats." Mac Bradshaw anticipates that "land area for church buildings will be scarce and prohibitively priced. Life patterns for high-rise flat dwellers will not likely be conducive to crossing town for the 11 a.m. Sunday service."[6] The newly-emerging forms of house churches which own no real estate of their own may even be closer to New Testament patterns than the "cathedral on the corner," according to Bradshaw.

Many missiologists believe that we are now on the threshold of the greatest ingathering into the Christian Church that the world has yet experienced. McGavran, with his characteristic optimism, has recently said that we are today witnessing "the sunrise of missions." President Doan-van-Mieng of the Vietnamese National Church is entirely serious when he claims that the Lord has spoken to him and to the church he leads to set their long-range goal at winning ten million Vietnamese for Christ. If these men prove to be right, this degree of accelerated church growth will undoubtedly produce new sets of changing patterns of the church. Leaders will do well to be alert for them.

CHANGING PATTERNS OF THE MINISTRY

As Christians recognize and encourage changing patterns of the church, they realize that an immediate corollary of this will be new forms of the ministry. Bradshaw says that in the exploding cities of Asia, "full-time ministers will no doubt continue to be needed. Yet the brunt of the responsibility for shepherding the small house congregations will of necessity fall upon the shoulders of a new task force of semi-professional ministers . . . Self-supporting status will be essential because most flat churches will be too small in numbers to support a full-time pastor."[7]

From the other side of the world, Mario Rivas, President of
the Bolivian Baptist Union, makes a plea for a new dynamic
nationalism in his church. It may be necessary "to give up the
idea of a paid ministry," he suggests. "Let's forget the
idealistic position of a full-time pastorate if the situation
so demands. Let's get out into the community and work like
other men, earning our daily bread through radio broadcasting,
teaching, public offices, and above that offer our talents for
the glory of God. Many pastors are doing it already."[8]

In a recent book on Indonesia, Ebbie Smith urges his Baptist colleagues there to set as a goal the planting of 50 new
churches a year. But he recognizes that "Baptists cannot provide places of worship and trained pastors for fifty new congregations a year for the next ten years."[9] Thus, he recommends
house churches and unpaid pastors. "Unpaid or slightly paid
non-seminary trained pastors should be recognized and allowed
to function fully as pastors, leading their congregations with
full freedom, drawing their authority from the Lord and the
congregation they lead."[10] This type of creative thinking is
by no means confined to Bradshaw, Rivas, and Smith. On all six
continents Christian leaders have become convinced that a total
rethinking of the form and function of the ministry is long
overdue.

Basic to the newer ideas of the ministry is the concept of
ordination. Some younger churches have found themselves with a
two-level hierarchy they had neither planned nor desired--
ordained and unordained ministers. Functionally they are doing
the same job in many cases, but for one reason or other ordination is denied to some, relegating them to a second-class
status. Some churches insist that ordained ministers be full-
time, thus excluding the biblical pattern of a tent-making
ministry. Educational levels form another rather artificial
barrier in certain circumstances. Institutions have been
created with academic levels which exclude many functional
pastors on principle. In some cases, more emphasis seems to be
placed on academic attainment than on spiritual gifts.

The widespread concern in many younger churches to "raise
the standards of the ministry" seems to be somewhat misguided,
since again it is usually linked directly to certain academic
levels. An uncritical application of this principle could well
serve to cripple the ministry rather than upgrade it. The use
of the term "lay pastors" is well-intentioned, but tends to
accentuate their second-class rating. In one church I know
this was carried to such an extreme that, whereas both ordained
and unordained pastors could pronounce the benediction, only

the ordained pastors were allowed to raise their hands while
doing it!

Raising the standards of the ministry usually has a corollary: the desire to "upgrade the seminary." This, unwisely,
has become one of the major goals of theological educators in
many parts of the world. It is commonly interpreted as meaning
raising the admission requirements another notch, and if possible eliminating a lower notch. The net result is that the
gap between first and second class pastors is widened even more,
and the institution runs the risk of educating pastors right
out of the system. This is one reason why so many of the best
educated ministers in the younger churches buy one-way tickets
to the U.S.A. They no longer fit in their own system.

More important than higher and higher academic requirements should be spiritual and cultural standards. A man of God
who is fully accepted by his peers as a leader, who has spiritual gifts which equip him for his task, and who leads his church
forward in winning people to Christ and planting new churches,
is the man who should be studying in our institutions regardless
of his previous academic opportunities. Unhappily, many who
fit this description have not been eligible for our seminaries,
and therefore have been excluded from the possibility of
ordination.

The vested interests of the ordained clergy have at times
prevented broader concepts of the ministry. In some cases,
consciously or unconsciously, ordained men have created something of a "preachers' union" and decreed a closed shop. Since
both the mission subsidy fund and the number of well-paying
churches are limited, new competition is discouraged in one way
or another. The danger of this mentality is evident, especially
when applied to planting new churches. Some denominations discourage the organization of a church until a pastor is available, thus making the rate of church multiplication dependent
upon the ability of a seminary to produce graduates. This
thinking needs to be changed. It can become an unwholesome
deterrent to healthy church growth.

CHANGING PATTERNS OF LEADERSHIP TRAINING

Once changing patterns of the church and the ministry are
recognized, the problem of ministerial training must be faced.
Here again we find changing patterns in today's world. Both
Bradshaw and Smith recommend for their specific areas of Asia
what is now known as the extension seminary. This has been
used by some institutions in Latin America since 1962, and
estimates indicate that some fifty institutions there are using

these methods to train something over 2,000 students. As to
Africa, Gerald Bates of Burundi writes, "The extension seminary
and its use of programmed learning offer a viable alternative
to some present forms of education which are falling far short
in the matter of leadership training, particularly for the pastorate, in Africa."[11]

    Recent studies have shown that, in spite of vast cultural
differences between them, churches in Asia, Africa and Latin
America share with remarkable correlation a set of deficiencies
in their traditional theological education programs. To one
degree or another these might be corrected by adapting extension seminary principles to their particular situation.

    What are these principles?

PHILOSOPHY OF EXTENSION

    The extension seminary involves first of all a change in
mental attitude for those who have been involved in traditional
institutions. If we were to seek a slogan for this change, I
would call it "the humanization of theological education."

    This intentionally implies that our past efforts at train-
ing the ministry have not quite been human enough. I think
that most of us who honestly examine ourselves on this matter
will admit that this has often been true. At least the recent
workshops in Asia have reflected a new openness on the part of
both missionaries and nationals to recognize past shortcomings
and face the future more realistically. This process is part
of what Ted Ward calls "a profound alteration of institutions
of long standing and rich tradition."[12]

    For one thing we have tended to be institution-centered
rather than person-centered. We have wrongly asked "how?"
before asking "whom?" We have started with an institutional
structure which we may have adapted to a degree to the culture
of our particular field, but which was, nevertheless, heavily
laden with inevitable cultural baggage. Then we have set up
certain requirements for admission and opened the doors. Those
who could fit our requirements could come in, but the others
stayed out. In other words, the person to be trained had to
conform to our institution.

    The extension philosophy involves starting with the <u>person</u>
rather than the <u>institution</u>. If a given person should be
receiving ministerial training, the institution should see that
he gets it, according to this new mentality. No possible alteration of the structure of the institution should be discounted

which will enable more of God's chosen men to take theological studies. As the seminary or Bible school conforms to the student to be trained rather than vice-versa, it is to that degree "humanizing theological education."

Theological educators are now coming to recognize that the task of the seminary is not to <u>make</u> leaders. As John Meadowcroft of West Pakistan puts it, "By some kind of metamorphosis, a young fellow who has no qualities of leadership is expected to emerge from the chrysalis of the seminary as a 'leader of the community.' And he also considers himself to be. The fact, however, is that nothing will make a man a leader if he does not possess the attributes already."[13] The calling of the seminary is to <u>train</u> the leaders that God has already made. If this is admitted, the question prior to all others becomes: Whom do we teach?

That God, and not man, sovereignly distributes gifts of the ministry to the members of the body of Christ "as it hath pleased Him" is clear from I Corinthians 12. The task of the church is not to endow these gifts, but rather to recognize them, help develop them, admonish Christians to use them, and publically authorize their use through the laying on of hands. Our seminaries and Bible schools should set their sights on this objective--training men and women who are the gifted ones of God for the ministry: pastors, teachers, evangelists, and others.

Especially in the younger, rapidly-growing churches of the world, these gifts are most evident in men and women somewhat older than the students we have usually been training. Cultures which respect age more than we do in contemporary U.S.A. ordinarily will not allow a younger person to assume a position of true leadership (although at times a leadership title may be granted). Qualifications for leadership usually include maturity, marriage, a family, the ability to earn a living through a contribution to the community, and church responsibilities properly executed. Some of these leaders have been recognized by their people but cannot be ordained by their churches because they are unable to conform to any known institution. Others have had some theological training earlier in life and have been ordained; but with the rising standards of education, they feel the need of more studies. A leader of the Indian church says: "The average pastor in India does not know how to lead a soul to Christ or to preach expository messages." Those of us in theological education need to be concerned about this kind of situation.

This points up the need for in-service training, perhaps
to an even greater degree than for pre-service training.
Nevertheless our concentration to the present has largely been
on the pre-service variety of training. The recognition of
this basic principle was one of the factors that sparked the
Presbyterian Seminary in Guatemala to launch the first extension program eight years ago. In one of the pioneer documents
of the extension seminary movement, James Emery of Guatemala
said, "The people who most need the training are not those who
traditionally attend the seminary, but those of the larger
group who are more mature, and with experience."[14]

HOW THE SEMINARY EXTENDS

As the extension seminary principles have developed over
the past few years, the sense in which seminaries have "extended" has become clearer.

From the beginning it should be kept in mind that we are
suggesting an *extension*, not an *extermination* of the present
structures. Years of sharing extension principles with others
have taught us that most of the initial opposition to the new
ideas comes from those who interpret the extension program as
a threat to their existing institutions. They have made an
"either-or" case of extension versus residence. This is unfair
and hasty. The two programs are complementary, not contradic-
tory. Most (although not all) residential institutions are
serving a very useful function and should be continued. But
few (or perhaps none) are doing as much as they *should* or *could*
do. In order better to accomplish their goal of training the
ministry for the church, they should think in terms of extending their present ministry.

Theological educators who are willing to become student-
centered rather than institution-centered in their outlook will
want to consider extending their present structures in six
ways:

1. Geographical extension. This refers to the place or
places where students are taught. Due to any number of circumstances, many gifted church leaders cannot leave their own
homes and move into a residential institution. If they are to
be trained, then, the institution must somehow move to them.
This may mean that a professor in Bolivia travels six hours on
the train to meet a group of students every week, or that his
counterpart in West Kalimantan contracts the Missionary Avia-
tion Fellowship plane for two days a week to visit three centers, or that the students from one area meet their teacher

under a bridge as they did in Guatemala. By whatever means are necessary, the professor moves out to his students.

Some professors, accustomed to the more sedentary and contemplative life of the ivory tower will say, "this is not for me!" But scores of others are saying, "this is what I have been looking for."

2. Extension in time. Schedules in the extension seminary are drawn up *after* asking the student: When can you study? I know of one weekly meeting at 6:00 a.m., another at 10:00 p.m., and others in between. Urban centers usually meet at night since students are tied to strict daily schedules. Rural centers often meet during the day since farmers' schedules are more flexible. After the sun sets, farmers usually think more of bed than of books.

The time factor is not only important as to the hour, but also as to the seasons. One center operating among potato farmers inadvisedly scheduled its courses to run through the potato harvest. It soon had to close down and rearrange the program. Whereas ordinarily all extension centers adhere to the academic year of the base institution, ample room for adjustment must be allowed.

Some students have more leisure time for study than others. Thus the speed at which students complete their studies will have to vary. This variation is usually not made according to the rate at which a student completes a given subject, but rather according to the number of subjects the student handles in any given semester. If he can afford six hours a week, he can take just one subject, but if he can afford eighteen hours a week, he may take three.

3. Cultural extension. As the insights of cultural anthropology filter down to grass roots, missionary educators have become more aware of patterns of culture and sub-culture all over the world. Even people living within the same city, group themselves into distinct sub-cultures, as a short drive from Beverly Hills, through Watts and to East Los Angeles would prove. Molds of thinking in each sub-culture are different, and proper theological education will be tailor-made for each one. Institutions that are not extended will often require that a student from one culture take his training within another one. Experience has shown that this cultural extraction is not ideal.

In the July, 1970, Asia Evangelical Theological Consultation held in Singapore, Dr. Ogill Kim of Korea said, "The

training of national theological faculty members can best be
done in their own countries. We must get rid of the mentality
of being students of Western theology. Asians are leaders of
the theology of Asia."[15] Professor Bong Rin Ro of the Discipleship Training Center in Singapore laments the fact that
"many Asian Christians uphold the West as their theological
model. Thousands of young people have made an exodus, particularly to the U.S. for their education."[16]

Observations like these do not relate only to those vast
cultural differences between the Eastern and Western Hemi-
spheres. They exist also within the same country. Leaders of
rural churches in South Viet Nam, for example, were recently
discussing the problems that sending their ministerial candidates to study in the city raised. They said, "When our men
return to the country they are not the same. They want their
salary in cash, not in rice and chickens; they won't walk
through the rice paddies because they will get their trousers
wet; they are not even able to sit and talk with us because
they have brought their city schedules back with them and no
longer have any time."

The extension seminary attempts to adapt to people who
need training by making sure that the teaching is relevant to
the culture in which they have been called to minister in the
future. This is one reason why the leaders of the Latin American Intertext program have rather firmly insisted that their
materials all be prepared originally in either Spanish or Portuguese in spite of a great deal of pressure from other parts
of the world to do them in English. Not only will this provide
material in the most useful languages there, but it will also
tend to force authors to develop their materials in thought
patterns characteristic of the culture of their students.

The extension seminary enables students to take full
theological training while continuing to live within their own
culture. This reduces the danger of deculturization, known in
one of its international aspects as the "brain drain." While
it is true that many examples of dedicated people who have
studied in a second culture and have returned successfully to
the first can be found, most theological educators and church
leaders will agree that the trend is in the opposite direction.

4. <u>Academic extension</u>. It has already been mentioned
that many of us have fallen into the mentality that certain
minimum academic requirements are necessary for the Christian
ministry, and that these requirements should be universally
applied. Further analysis, however, will probably indicate
that academic standards for the ministry are better determined

by the academic levels of the people in the pews than by the
seminary board. It may be true that college and seminary are
basic for a U.S.A. suburban pastor, and that seminaries now
need to replace the B.D. with a professional doctorate to keep
their graduates on an academic par with the increasing number
of Ph.D.'s in their congregations. This standard is not necessary among the mountain peoples of Taiwan, however, nor perhaps
even for effective ministry in the black ghettos of the inner
cities of the U.S.A.

Thousands of leaders of third world churches have been
able to attain only minimal levels of general education, and
they find themselves in no position to return to school.
Should these men be excluded from theological training on those
grounds, when God himself has placed them in the ministry? The
seminary must extend itself to such men. Some extension programs have geared theological education to as low as second
grade levels, especially when the church in question will grant
ordination (or whatever form of ministerial recognition is
employed) to these leaders. Others, such as the Presbyterians
in Guatemala, have developed subsidiary programs to raise the
general educational level to sixth grade before they begin
theological training. Either way extends the seminary
academically.

5. _Economic extension_. The expense involved in training
men for ordination (whether this term is understood formally or
functionally is irrelevant here) in the younger churches is
higher than many of us may think. A competent observer has
recently stated that on a world scale the cost of this educational system may be second only to that of training physicians
in the U.S.A. When the cost of providing missionary professors,
buildings and grounds, the low student-teacher ratios, and the
high drop-out quotient are considered, this might well be the
case.

On most mission fields where indigenous church principles
are applied, missions have found that one of the last aspects
of the church-related work which can be turned over to the
churches is the ministerial training program. This is due
largely to the economic structure which is often entirely out
of keeping with what the churches can afford. If a less expensive way to train ministers could be found, some of the national
churches could exercise greater responsibility in this crucially important aspect of their development toward full
maturity.

The extension seminary may prove to be a step in that
direction. Studies that have been made indicate a reduction in

costs, although more research is still needed. The George
Allan Theological Seminary in Bolivia, for example, has found
that their urban residence program costs about $90.00 annually
per student-subject, the rural residence program about $30.00
per student-subject, and the extension program about $15.00 per
student-subject. Other than the modest initial cost of setting
up the extension centers, most of this sum represents travel
for professors. The students pay their own way--travel ex-
penses, room and board, and textbooks. They also help reduce
general costs by paying a monthly tuition. This sounds like
something that any church can afford.

     6. Ecclesiastical extension. The widespread divorce of
the seminary from the local church has been recognized by leaders of many denominations in recent years. As Sam Rowen says,
"The development or training of Christians should take place in
a genuine church-life situation. Only as the church becomes
aware of the need for the systematic study of the Word of God
will there be developed the proper attitude towards theological
training . . . . Theological training should be church-
centered."[17]

     Until recently, few had been able to suggest ways and
means to reverse the trend of separation. But placing theological training back in the local church has been a welcome by-
product of some extension seminaries. In many cases classes
are actually held on church premises. Seminary professors
visit the churches and interact with church members as well as
with students, keeping themselves in direct touch with their
thinking and attitudes. This makes them ever so much more
effective as teachers. Students, for their part, are not ex-
tracted from their local church for an extended period of time,
but they continually relate their studies to the realistic conditions of the grass-roots level.

NOTES FOR CHAPTER 1

1. Ralph D. Winter, ed., Theological Education by Extension,
    South Pasadena, William Carey Library, 1969, p. xvii.

2. F. Ross Kinsler, "Extend the Seminaries," chapter in Theo-
    logical Education by Extension, Ralph D. Winter, ed.,
    pp. 245-255.

3. Ted and Margaret Ward, Programmed Instruction for Theolog-
    ical Education by Extension, CAMEO, East Lansing, 1970,
    p. 115.

4. "The Open University," *The Expository Times*, April, 1970, p. 224.

5. Ministry of Education and Culture, Israel, <u>School Comes To Adults</u>, Jerusalem, 1965, p. 57.

6. Malcolm Bradshaw, *Theological Education by Extension*, leaflet.

7. <u>Ibid</u>.

8. Mario Rivas, "Nueva Vision de la Iglesia Nacional," article in *Chasqui*, Los Angeles, September, 1970.

9. Ebbie Smith, <u>God's Miracles: Indonesian Church Growth</u>, South Pasadena, William Carey Library, 1970, p. 195.

10. <u>Ibid</u>., pp. 195-196.

11. Gerald Bates, *The Extension Seminary, Its Potential for African Young Churches*, mimeographed paper, Lansing, Michigan State University, 1970, 13 pp.

12. Ward, <u>Programmed Instruction for Theological Education by Extension</u>, p. 115.

13. John G. Meadowcroft, *Theological Education by Extension*, mimeographed paper, Gujranwala, West Pakistan, 1970, p. 6.

14. James H. Emery, "The Preparation of Leaders in a Ladino-Indian Church," *Practical Anthropology*, Vol. 10, No. 3, 1963, pp. 127-134.

15. Okgill Kim, quoted in privately-circulated minutes of the Asia Evangelical Theological Consultation, Singapore, July 5-7, 1970.

16. Bong Rin Ro, "Some Thoughts on the Future of Theological Education in Asia," *The Asian Challenge*, Vol. 2, September, 1970, p. 49.

17. Samuel F. Rowen, "Let's Train the Right People," *Whitened Harvest*, Fall, 1968, supplement.

22
HOW GOD MAKES MINISTERS

It has already been mentioned that the question which should be asked prior to establishing any institution designed to train the ministry is: *whom* do we teach?

It has also been mentioned that our seminaries and Bible institutes do not *make* leaders, but rather they *train* leaders whom God has already made. To understand how God makes the leaders whom we should be training, we need to analyze the biblical teaching on the matter. It revolves basically around the concept of spiritual gifts.

I Corinthians 12:1 says, "Now concerning spiritual gifts, brethren, I would not have you ignorant." Ignorance of spiritual gifts is a dangerous sin of omission for anyone involved in theological education. It is surprising, however, to learn how many Christians who have given their lives to training the ministry hold very superficial views on spiritual gifts.

The opposite of ignorance is knowledge. God wants us to have a thorough knowledge of spiritual gifts, particularly if we are engaged in developing these gifts. First of all, we need a knowledge of the theory, or better yet the theology, of spiritual gifts. Secondly, we need a personal knowledge of what spiritual gifts we ourselves have. Relatively few Christians, including some seminary professors, have taken the time and effort necessary to discover their own gifts. Some don't even realize they have a gift at all! They are surprised when they are told that I Corinthians 12:7, "the manifestation of the Spirit is given to every man," applies to them personally.

Part of our trouble begins in the pulpit. Few churches in the U.S.A. emphasize the spiritual gifts as does, for example, the Peninsula Bible Church of Palo Alto, California. They have

even developed a new slogan: "body-life evangelism." This is
undoubtedly one reason why this is one of the most active and
fast-growing churches in the country. A deep hunger for
more teaching concerning spiritual gifts may be part of the
reason why the charismatic movement is enjoying so much success
on a pandenominational level.

Before we identify the spiritual gifts specifically, we
need to make two contrasts. First, spiritual gifts are not the
same as natural talents. While there might be a close relationship between the two in some cases, they are widely separated in others. Natural talents are abilities which to one
degree or another every member of the human race possesses.
Spiritual gifts are supernatural endowments which God himself
gives to a person when he becomes a Christian and thus enters
as a functioning member of the body of Christ. In some instances, such as the gift of teaching for example, the natural
talent which a person has before becoming a Christian may well
be the spiritual gift he receives in the body of Christ. On
the other hand, when it comes to such gifts as prophecy or
tongues, the chances that these would carry over from some
natural talent that a person might have had are very slim
indeed.

The second important contrast is between spiritual gifts
and spiritual fruit. The fruit of the Spirit is listed in
Galatians 5:22: love, joy, peace, and the rest. Some err by
speaking of "the gift of love," when love really is the fruit
of the Spirit. The basic difference is that whereas only certain members of the body of Christ are expected to have a particular gift, such as the gift of pastor for example, all members of the body are expected to have the fruit. This is one
reason why, right in the middle of the key scriptural passage
on gifts (I Corinthians 12-14), the chapter on love, the fruit,
is included as "the more excellent way." The first three
verses of I Corinthians 13 contrast many different gifts
(tongues, prophecy, wisdom, knowledge, faith, etc.) with the
fruit. Spiritual fruit is a *sine qua non* for an effective use
of spiritual gifts, but the two are distinct works of the Holy
Spirit. Whereas there is a close relationship between a person's sanctification and the spiritual fruit characteristic of
his life, there is no such relationship between sanctification
and the spiritual gifts he possesses. The Corinthians are the
best example of the latter. They had all the gifts (I Corinthians 1:7), but were among the most carnal brethren described
in the New Testament.

Three key passages list the spiritual gifts in the body of
Christ: I Corinthians 12, Romans 12, and Ephesians 4.

Granting one or two possible discrepancies in exegesis, if you
correlate all the gifts in those passages, and add I Corinthians 7:7 and I Corinthians 13:3, you come out with a list
something like this: apostleship, prophecy, teaching, evangelism, pastor, ministry, administration, wisdom, knowledge, faith,
exhortation, miracles, healing, tongues, interpretation of
tongues, discerning of spirits, giving, mercy, celibacy, and
martyrdom.

No other specific gifts are mentioned in the New Testament,
but the very fact that none of the individual lists is exhaus-
tive would lead us to think that there may be others. What
they might be, I do not know, but the possibility is open.
Most Christians I know who have given adequate attention to
spiritual gifts can locate theirs somewhere in the list we have
made. Some may have one gift, some may have more than one.

Paul's choice of the human body as an illustration was a
very happy one. Understanding what he means does not depend on
coming from a particular culture or having a certain level of
education. Everyone has at least an elementary understanding
of the body. The body as an illustration is given in all three
of the major passages on gifts mentioned above. What are some
of the lessons learned here?

As the human body is made up of a large number of diverse
members, so is the body of Christ. The reason for the diversity is unknown. What we do know is that the Spirit places the
gifts in the members "as He will" (I Corinthians 12:11). The
mystery of the diversity of gifts is parallel to the mystery of
cell differentiation in the human body. Cell *division* in
biology is well known and understood. Cell *differentiation*, or
the process by which from one cell others divide off to form a
kidney and others to form an eyeball, remains unknown to modern
science. In the body of Christ, God entrusts his children with
cell *division*--bringing new members into the body through evangelism (Romans 10:13-15). But he does not entrust them with
differentiation, the awarding of spiritual gifts to his children; he reserves this for himself alone (I Corinthians 12:18).

No church in the world is without gifts if it is a truly
Christian church. Christ promised: "I will build my church"
(Matthew 16:18), and as I Corinthians 12 tells us, one of the
ways he accomplishes this is to distribute the spiritual gifts.
Not even a theological seminary has the power or authority to
award a spiritual gift.

In spite of the great diversity of gifts, they are all coordinated under one head, both in the human body and in the

body of Christ. No Christian can use his gift or gifts independently of the other Christians around him. No member of our human body could function properly if it were not connected organically to the head. Every member is to some degree dependent upon every other member. This is why "the eye cannot say to the hand, I have no need of you" (I Corinthians 12:21). Granted, some members of the body may be more beautiful than others. Lovers look at each other's eyes--not at their feet! But if the whole body were an eye, it would then be grotesque and ugly, no longer beautiful. To have three or four eyes would also detract from, not add to, their beauty. We can trust God, who fashioned the human body so perfectly, to fashion the body of Christ in the same way.

What does this mean for us?

Romans 12 tells us to present our bodies a living sacrifice to God. In order to do this, we must be "transformed" and "prove what is that good, and acceptable, and perfect will of God" (Romans 12:1-2). We must not make the mistake of isolating these verses from the total context of spiritual gifts in Romans 12, because one will only know the will of God for his life in a full way if he understands what spiritual gifts he has and what he is expected to do with them.

One of the features of this understanding is to be content with the gifts God gives to each one of us. Each Christian is to evaluate himself "soberly, according as God hath dealt to every man the measure of faith" (Romans 12:3). At the same time we should be content with what God has *not* given us, for a Christian should "not think of himself more highly than he ought to think" (Romans 12:3). The only way accurately to evaluate one's own responsibility before God is to recognize his spiritual gifts (Romans 12:6).

Perhaps all do not have as prolonged an experience as I had in this process. During my entire first term as a missionary, for example, I was disturbed and frustrated because I did not see substantial results from my evangelistic efforts, public or personal. I wanted to be another Billy Graham. I did not discount the possibility of a spiritual obstacle, but after much prayer and heart searching I could not discover one. Finally God brought me to the realization that I did not have the gift of an evangelist, and it was like a great burden being lifted off my back. I now know that God is not going to hold me responsible for the gift of evangelist at the judgment day because he didn't give it to me in the first place. I would still love to have the evangelistic power of Billy Graham, but I am no longer frustrated because I do not have it. I have come to a similar conclusion concerning the gift of pastor and other gifts.

At the same time, I now am quite aware that God has given me the gifts of teaching and administration. I feel I must dedicate my time and effort to developing and using these gifts, because I will have to give account for my stewardship over them some day.

This personal process of realistically evaluating one's exact place in the body of Christ yields three spiritual advantages. It reduces the possibility of false pride, since one realizes he has nothing to do with the fact that certain gifts have been bestowed upon him by God. It eliminates the type of false humility that says, "I can't do anything in my church--I don't have what it takes." And it prevents the envy that can so easily creep into the human heart because someone else might have a more beautiful or spectacular gift than I have.

Now, what does all this have to do with the extension seminary?

Possessing a spiritual gift and recognizing it is only the first step. From there on, a Christian is responsible for developing it. Paul wrote to Timothy to "stir up the gift of God which is in thee" (II Timothy 1:6).

In a very broad sense, this applies to every member of the body of Christ and the gifts he possesses. In a special sense, however, this refers to gifts of leadership in the church, or what we often call gifts of "ministry." Basically (although no absolute line can be drawn), the gifts of ministry are grouped in Ephesians 4:11. They would include apostleship, prophecy, evangelism, pastor, and teacher--maybe more from the other lists, although the details are not important at this juncture. What is important is that these special gifts are recognized publicly by the church by the laying on of hands. Paul speaks of Timothy's gift as "by the putting on of my hands," (II Timothy 1:6), and "with the laying on of the hands of the presbytery" (I Timothy 4:14). Paul even refers to himself in this specialized sense by saying that "God put me into the ministry" (I Timothy 1:12).

At this point a helpful distinction can be made between what we might call "theological education" and "Christian education." Whereas Christian education involves the edification of the entire body of Christ, the training of every Christian; theological education is more specialized, referring primarily to the training of the leadership of the Church.

It is the task of theological education to locate the persons to whom God has given these specialized gifts of the ministry, and assist them to develop their gifts to the highest degree possible. The specific objective is to provide them the training that will allow them to meet whatever requirement their church or denomination has established for public recognition as a minister. This is usually called ordination, but not always. Some churches with a lower view of the ordained ministry, such as the Plymouth Brethren, will ordain a large quantity of elders and not distinguish a professional pastor from the other elders. Other churches, such as the Anglican, place much higher formal requirements on the candidate for ordination. Sometimes ordination is symbolized by the use of the title "Reverend," sometimes "pastor" indicates functional ordination, and a wide variation of these definitions can be found in different ecclesiastical groups.

Theological education is not concerned with the way a given denomination publicly recognizes its ministry. It is concerned with preparing those whom God has called to this ministry, helping them meet whatever their church's standards might be. Theological education fails to the degree that it excludes gifted men and women who should be preparing themselves for their church's ministry.

The starting point for any program of theological education should be the *person* whom God has gifted for the ministry. This person-centeredness unfortunately has not been generally characteristic of many of our seminaries and Bible institutes in the past. The very structure of our institutions has excluded many of the men who have proven that they are gifted, while they include large quantities of young people who may wish they were gifted or who hope they might be gifted some day, but who have not yet been accepted by their churches as legitimate leaders. Melvin Hodges puts it very well when he says: "It is important that the missionary shall not limit his leadership training to the bright young men who at first glance would appear to be the best material. This is one of the fundamental errors of modern missions. The missionary has failed to see the importance of making place for mature men--the "elders" of the New Testament. Instead, he has gathered around him a group of the brightest minds, usually boys from the Mission School or children of converts, to give them special instruction."[1]

If we base our leadership training on spiritual gifts which have been tried and proven, we will find that the majority of our students are mature men with homes, families, jobs, and community responsibilities. This is a description which does not too well fit the typical student whom most of us have been training through the years. It *does* fit I Timothy 3:1-7.

One of the most difficult problems for those who are being initiated into the principles of the extension seminary is to conjure up the proper mental image when the word "student" is mentioned. "We must train our young people for the ministry," is uppermost in our minds, when in many cases the grandfather, not the young person, is the one who has been gifted, and therefore called, and who needs the training. An excellent analysis of this situation by Ross Kinsler bears repeating here: "This is not simply a matter of mobilizing the layman. It is also a question of leadership. Technical studies (and common sense) indicate that the present system of theological training and ordination is ineffectual in the selection and development of leaders. On the one hand, the seminaries are set up for men and women who are young, just out of college, and who have had almost no chance to prove themselves in the world or even to develop their gifts in the church . . . On the other hand those men and women who do prove themselves in the world and gain experience and earn positions of leadership in the organizations of the church find it almost impossible to go to seminary, and must always sit under the tutelage of the former group.[2]

Confusion as to the "call to the ministry" is one of the roots of the problem. The self-assertion that a person has received a mystical call to the ministry should not be sufficient for seminary admission. The confirmation of the church, such as took place in the case of Barnabas and Saul in Acts 13:1-3, is equally necessary. But responsible churches will only confirm a call when sufficient evidence of possessing the spiritual gift has been accumulated. This, almost invariably, implies a spiritual, social, psychological, and physical maturity which we have not insisted on to any great extent in the past. Receiving the spiritual gift of pastor, for example, must not be distinguished from the call to the pastorate. When the church recognizes that a person has the gift of pastor they *ipso facto* confirm his call to the pastorate.

Many theological educators, especially those who are now involved in extension seminary programs, admit that much time and money has been invested in training good people, but people who after all had not been gifted by God for the ministry. Of course, there are many outstanding exceptions to this. Thousands of today's effective church leaders have been trained in traditional institutions. But this is not the point we are making here. While we are pleased with those who *have* been trained, we are pointing out that we have not been sufficiently concerned with those who *have not* or *are not* being trained. As has been mentioned before, the good that our traditional system is doing should be preserved and continued, but the challenge of doing even better should be accepted and acted upon.

The theological basis for this challenge, therefore, is the New Testament teaching on spiritual gifts. Basing ministerial training on gifted men will force our training schools to become more person-centered and thus help us in the process of humanizing theological education.

"Concerning spiritual gifts, brethren, I would not have you ignorant" (I Corinthians 12:1).

NOTES FOR CHAPTER 3

1. Melvin L. Hodges, "The Selection of Ministerial Candidates," *Church Growth Bulletin Volumes I-V*, Donald A. McGavran, ed., South Pasadena, William Carey Library, 1969, p. 232.

2. F. Ross Kinsler, "Extend the Seminaries," Theological Education by Extension, Ralph D. Winter, ed., South Pasadena, William Carey Library, 1969, pp. 246-247.

23
FORMS OF
THEOLOGICAL EDUCATION
THROUGH HISTORY

The past has a great future. Much can be learned by
briefly examining the history of theological education. Not
only are we helped to avoid the mistakes of the past, but we
will derive comfort in learning that current problems were
faced by other generations. They, too, struggled with the dichotomy of the clergy and laity, saw the need for a ministry on
various academic levels, sought to resolve the tension between
theory and practice, and emphasized the need for tutorial as
well as formal training.

Our present pattern of theological education is a relative
newcomer on the scene of ministerial training. It cannot be
absolutized as the "Biblical" way of training people--the only
way that God has given to his church. Little value, then, will
come by uncritically exporting it as a pattern for overseas
churches. Rather, we should encourage them to see how the Holy
Spirit can help in developing an education more functional to
their own environment and their needs.

Form in theological education must be separated from the
function or purpose of the church in any given age or environment. The church has always developed a variety of forms to
fulfill its God-given function of training leaders to meet specific needs. This function is clearly rooted in the Scripture.
But there is no one Biblical form by which this function must
be carried out. A particular form is useful and worthy to be
perpetuated only as it is a vehicle for meeting the ministerial
needs that the church has. When it is dysfunctional, it can
only be discarded.

Many missionaries, unfortunately, have frequently confused
form and function. Their experience in the lands from which
they come has introduced them to one or more forms of

theological education. These forms have been relatively efficient in meeting the needs of an affluent, but rather static
church with well established norms for ministry. The problem
has come when these forms used in North America, Great Britain
and the Continent have been transplanted into an overseas environment where the ministerial function has been far different.

NEW TESTAMENT PERIOD TO THE REFORMATION

The church has always had some form of training for its
leaders. In the New Testament period there were no formal
theological schools. The disciples of Jesus learned by being
with him (Mark 3:13-19). They apparently had general knowledge
equal to that of their peers, but, lacking formal education,
they were accused of being "uneducated, common men"
(Acts 4:13). Paul received a classical training at the University of Tarsus and a rabbinic education in Jerusalem.

Paul followed the apprentice method of Jesus in training a
company of men who travelled with him. Carefully selected by
him during his missionary journeys, these men were trained "on
the job" in the truths of Scripture, and perhaps in the knowledge common to the men among whom they worked. And Paul, in
turn, expected Timothy and others to train faithful men of
proven teaching ability who would be continuing links in this
educational chain.

Vast geographical areas needed to be conquered for Christ
during this era. Consequently, great stress was placed upon a
lay leadership which quickly took the church into every corner
of the Roman Empire. Sole dependence on a formally trained
ministry would not, as Kenneth Latourette points out,[1] have
enabled the early church to expand so rapidly.

In Alexandria, about 230 A.D., Origen upgraded into an advanced theological school what Clement had started as an informal adult Bible study. The subjects included Bible training,
natural sciences, geometry, astronomy, philosophy, and ethics.
The church was faced with devastating attacks from philosophic
critics and consequently needed a ministry to defend the faith.
Theological education in this part of the Roman Empire assumed
the form of a school of religious apologetics. Its curriculum
was not shaped by an arbitrary standard, but by a practical
need.

This formal pattern of theological education in schools
was not followed in the fourth and fifth centuries. Rather,
the clergy received ministerial training, often from an early

age, through personal tutorial sessions with a bishop and older
priests.

By the beginning of the sixth century the structure of the
Roman Empire was collapsing. Invasions by Goths, Vandals,
Franks, Visigoths, and Lombards rent the fabric of classical
civilization and brought culture to such a low ebb that the ensuing period is sometimes referred to as the "Dark Ages." If
the light of the orthodox Christian faith and culture was to
shine in Southern and Western Europe, outposts for evangelism
and civilization must be established. The form adequate to
perform this function, as well as to train a portion of the
church's leadership, was the monastery.

Many of these monasteries were staffed by missionaries
from England and Ireland. As their work of conversion and
civilization progressed, they took young boys into the monastery and trained them to be monks. The curriculum was a simple
one of reading, writing and memorizing much of the Bible. Included also was basic doctrine and some knowledge of the
liturgy.

Today we talk about penetrating the world. At this period
of church history the task was to escape from the pollution of
the world and to reestablish a Christian culture into which the
non-Christians could be invited. The monastery form does not
fulfill the function of today's church, but without it Christianity would not have survived in Western Europe.

The episcopal school was another form of ministerial
training in the medieval period. Here again was the tutorial
method with a group of students gathered around a bishop to receive training in church dogma, liturgy and canon law. At an
earlier time their secular education came through the ordinary
Roman schools of the day. When the Roman system of classical
education was destroyed by the barbarian invasions, the episcopal schools, as well as the monasteries, assumed the responsibility of giving the secular training upon which the theological education was based. These episcopal schools formed one
strand of the movement which ultimately led, in the twelfth and
thirteenth centuries, to the founding of Europe's first univer-
sities--institutions whose *raison d'etre* was the teaching of
theology.

INFLUENCE OF THE REFORMATION

As a result of the Protestant Reformation, the Bible was
rediscovered. Believers in the evangelical churches desperately wanted to understand God's Word. Consequently, a great

emphasis was placed upon catechetical preaching that would explain Biblical truth. Every church had at least one daily service with a sermon, and some churches had several such services. One great need, then, was a leadership that would meet the need of the churches for Biblical instruction. Little wonder that in the academy established by Calvin in Geneva preaching was central in the curriculum. Anything else would have been dysfunctional. Form and function in ministerial training were closely linked.

In seventeenth century England there was both a highly trained ministry and an untrained one. A reformation in learning had stimulated the founding of hundreds of neighborhood grammar schools throughout England. These schools trained boys for the church of England, and religion was the core of the curriculum. The grammar schools fed into English universities in which theology, again, was the central academic interest. Subjects normally associated now with the university such as science, medicine and law were pursued in other schools.

The thorough training required by the Anglicans for the ordained ministry was also a concern shared by the Puritans. In 1644 a Parliamentary ordinance was passed that required all ministerial candidates to read Hebrew and Greek.

Why did both the Anglicans and Puritans feel that at least a portion of their clergy needed this type of training? Was it an arbitrary standard? Not at all! Both groups were confronted by intellectual attacks from Roman Catholic scholars well-versed in Hebrew and Greek.

Nevertheless, a widespread ignorance existed among most of the clergy in England during the seventeenth century. Perhaps no more than one out of six had sufficient training to be ordained or licensed as preachers. "Many knew little or no Latin and less Scripture--some could barely read the English services of the new Prayer Book."[2]

Despite this lack of formal educational background, provision was made for these men to receive instruction fitting them for ministry in the smaller, more isolated parishes. They studied the Bible and Bullinger's Decades, a book of sermons. Licensed preachers in their vicinity supervised their studies and made quarterly reports on their academic and practical progress. Arch deacons examined them regularly and reported the results.

An important task for the ministry during this period was to catechize the parish by families and give pastoral

counseling. For this purpose manuals on counseling were prepared for private study. In addition, older ministers with experience in counseling established informal training classes in
their homes to give instruction in this art. The function
which the church and its ministry must perform was implemented
by the form of theological education.

During this period of English history, some questioned the
need for a partly or fully trained ministry. The role of the
laity was emphasized, and schooling was thought unnecessary.
The need for a converted ministry caused piety to be given priority over formal education. Some claimed that since the ministry is a Divine calling God alone can do the equipping. Others
asked why Hebrew and Greek were necessary if the original manu-
scripts were not extant. And obviously God did use men without
the proper education--John Bunyan being the most notable
example.[3]

THEOLOGICAL EDUCATION IN AMERICA

When the Puritans settled in New England they brought
their concept of the ministry with them. They expected their
clergymen, who would form the intellectual elite of New England,
to be well-trained men. This stress upon educational qualifications led to the founding of Harvard College in 1636, and in
the ensuing colonial period nine colleges were founded which
had similar purposes.

College training was intended to give the minister his
basic general education. Specific theological instruction was
acquired through study under the supervision of established
clergymen. These clergymen, in some instances, were ministerial
professors who used the college as a base from which to go out
and train ministerial candidates in various areas.

In other cases, the clergymen who did the training were
parish ministers who opened up their homes to students, provided them with room and board, guided their study and afforded
them practical experience in ministerial duties.

During the first half of the eighteenth century, in the
middle colonies, it was the custom for Presbyterian churches to
have pastors trained in the universities or colleges in Ireland,
Scotland or New England. Several difficulties made this pattern unacceptable to some. If the pastors originally came to
the middle colonies from these other areas, it was not easy to
learn much about their background. It was expensive to go
abroad or to New England for study. Furthermore, there was no
certainty that the students would return, and, if they did, it

was only with difficulty that they could fit into the local situation.

Meanwhile, another form of ministerial training had developed. William Tennant had come to Pennsylvania as a boy of thirteen. He received most of his education from his father and concluded that if he could learn in this fashion, it would be possible for others as well. He made this vision a reality by establishing the "log cabin" school in Bucks County, Pennsylvania, where he taught and prepared local men for the ministry. The facility was not ideal--a roughly formed structure only twenty feet by twenty feet. The studies, however, included what normally was received in a university plus a training in divinity.

The Synod objected to this type of theological education. One man, they claimed, could not give a thorough education. Moreover, piety seemed to be exalted over knowledge.

Particular needs on the American frontier led to another very functional form of theological education. Here the cry was for evangelists--those experienced and gifted in leading men to personal decision for Christ. The intellectual church leaders or parish ministers of the Atlantic seaboard were not what the situation demanded.

Evangelists were produced by a type of extension training. Personal study, a circuit of preaching points, periodic tutoring, and quarterly examinations were utilized to prepare men who conquered the frontier for Christ. These Methodist and Baptist circuit riders on the frontier used stumps, blocks, old logs and wagon beds for their pulpit. Wherever they were is where the school was! One of these men, Peter Cartwright, made fun of the intellectual Easterners, but he himself had studied literary theological books under an elder and had been examined quarterly. His education was not an inferior one, but a different one. More important, his training was functional to his calling.

This pattern on the American frontier was indebted greatly to the Wesleyan movement in England. Although Wesley's circuit riders were extremely busy in their itinerant ministry their formal education was not neglected. Some of these preachers claimed that to study the Bible was enough. To this Wesley retorted, "If you need no books but the Bible, you are above St. Paul. If you have no taste for reading, then get a taste for it or return to your trade." When they objected that they had no books to study, Wesley answered, "I will give each of you as fast as you can read them books to the value of five pounds."

True to his word he published a Christian library of forty volumes for his preachers and demanded that they study five hours
a day while they preached the Word of God. As a result of this
procedure Wesley claimed that, "There was not one of them who
could not pass an examination in substantial, practical, experimental divinity, as few of our candidates for holy orders even
in the University."[4]

The Dutch Reformed Church founded the first separate theological seminary in America at Flatbush, Long Island, New York,
in 1774. However, this form of theological education did not
become popular until the early nineteenth century when seventeen permanent institutions were established.[5]

The decisive turning point in American theological education was the independence of the colonies. At this juncture
professional schools arose in law and medicine, and it seemed
natural that theological training should follow suit. With beginning disestablishment of religion in the thirteen states a
new spirit of competition developed among the denominations.
Each group wanted its own school to perpetuate its own distinctives. The conviction also increased among many that one man
was unable to effectively train in the many, varied aspects of
the ministry.

The separate seminary did not replace other forms of theological education. Methodist preachers continued to be educated on horseback. One man reports how he reviewed grammar as
he rode to his engagements. He parsed sentences while he
visited with friends. During one year his reading diet was
twenty-five books of history and theology. His teacher was a
local preacher. Another lamented that his "facilities" for
study were not equal to those in fine libraries, but that "he
had some acquaintance with the Hebrew and Greek languages."[6]

The separate theological training school has been the most
commonly perpetuated form for the training of the ministry in
younger churches around the world. Unfortunately, the impression is often given that this is the only form that God has
provided for his church. Where this conviction has taken hold
of mission and church leaders, great resistance has developed
to different patterns that may be more functional.

NEW EXPERIMENTS

As theories of progressive education have gained currency
in the West, the environment has been created for innovative
approaches in both general and theological education. Moreover,

new approaches to the form of the church and of the ministry have created a demand for new forms of theological education.

McCormick Theological Seminary in Chicago has adopted a program of Individualized Guided Education, the first step of which is to complete a basic level of studies. Each student will follow this level at a speed commensurate with his own background, ability, and maturity. Resources available to him are personal counseling by his faculty advisor, a syllabus of courses, projects, seminars, specimens of the qualifying examinations and a clear statement of the faculty expectations for student achievement. No student will follow exactly the same route in reaching this initial goal.

After completing his qualifying examinations, the student is aided in structuring an individualized program of studies at a more advanced level. Here again his work is personalized in terms of his achievement, his interests and his needs in present and future ministry. The content of the curriculum and the form of his study program are highly functional.[7]

Many seminaries are developing their programs in close relationship with action training centers. Two insights have guided these efforts: Theology can only by understood in life situations as a "doing theology." Students have too frequently been "recruited from the religious ghetto, trained in an insulated seminary and returned to the sheltering religiosity of the status quo church."[8]

Saint Paul School of Theology in Kansas City has been an innovator in this emphasis of "action and reflection." In the student's first year he is required to be involved each of three quarters in a minimum of six hours weekly in a specific mission in the world. During the summer of 1970, seven conservative evangelical seminaries cooperated in the Urban Ministry Program for Seminarians (UMPS) in Chicago's inner city. At least four hours of academic credit were given to each student participant by his respective institution.

Episcopalians have been involved in a unique experiment in theological education in Los Angeles. Students are men with successful careers in law, medicine, business and education who are seriously considering the possibility of the ministry. They need not leave their vocations or their families to go away to school. Classes are held on Friday evenings and Saturday. The curriculum is the same as that of the regular five-day seminary program. At the end of four years a basic decision must be made. If the student opts for a ministry in the church, he leaves his job, studies in a resident institution for one year, and then actively enters a church vocation. If, after these four years of study and evaluation, he feels that he is not gifted for a full-time church ministry, he continues in his secular vocation and serves Christ as a committed and knowledgeable layman.

Fuller Theological Seminary has established an extension center to offer credit in degree work in Fresno, California. In this center, operated in cooperation with the Mennonite Brethren Biblical Seminary, the professor is in contact with his students a maximum of three or four times in a ten-week quarter. Guided study, research papers, periodic seminars, and a final examination are being utilized in these non-resident courses.[9]

Innovations of this type in theological training are paralleled in the field of general education. One of the most interesting of these is the open university in Great Britain. This school, which commenced offering courses in January, 1971, will provide educational opportunity leading to a university degree for older men and women who can neither forsake jobs or families in order to be internal students for several years on the campus. In describing this innovative educational program, one writer observes that it will "tap the great unused reservoir of human talent and potential."[10] This is the goal of the extension theological seminary--to tap God-equipped men with ability to pastor existing churches and to plant new ones. Missionaries and national church leaders will be more open to this possibility as they see the variety of forms that God has given his church throughout history for ministerial training.

NOTES FOR CHAPTER 6

1. Kenneth Latourette, <u>A History of the Expansion of Chris-</u><u>tianity</u>, Vol. 1, <u>The First Five Centuries</u>, New York, Harper, 1937, p. 116.

2. Richard Niebuhr and Daniel Williams (ed.), <u>The Ministry in</u> <u>Historical Perspective</u>, New York, Harper, 1956, p. 186.

3. <u>Ibid</u>., p. 206.

4. C. W. Ransom, <u>The Christian Minister in India</u>, London, Lutterworth Press, p. 267.

5. Niebuhr and Williams, <u>The Ministry</u>, Ch. 8.

   Also see Robert Kelly, <u>Theological Education in America</u>, New York, George H. Doran Company, 1924, p. 25.

6. Frederick Norwood, "Americanization of the Wesleyan Itin-erant," in Gerald McCullah (ed.), <u>The Ministry in the</u> <u>Methodist Heritage,</u> Nashville, Board of Education of the Methodist Church, 1960, p. 55.

7. Arthur McKay, "McCormick Theological Seminary," *Nexus*, Vol. 12, Spring, 1969, pp. 27-30.

8. W. Paul James, "Action Training and the Seminaries: Four Possibilities," *Theological Education*, Winter, 1970, pp. 152-159.

9. *Theology News and Notes*, Fuller Theological Seminary, November, 1970, p. 14.

10. "The Open University," *Expository Times*, April, 1970, 81:7, p. 224.

24

"TRAINING IN THE STREETS" IN CHILE

We have seen that throughout the history of the Christian church many different forms of theological training have been used to advantage for the development of the ministry. Even today some churches outside of the main stream so well known in the traditionally Protestant countries have developed forms of ministerial training quite unlike anything we have been used to. One of the most unusual, and at the same time successful, forms has been developed through the years in the indigenous Pentecostal churches of Chile. In order to understand it, let's take an imaginary visit to that long, thin country on South America's west coast.

We plan our visit so that we are in the capital city of Santiago on a Sunday. Around five o'clock we take a bus and get off anywhere around the railroad station, then begin walking down one of the larger streets. If we look both ways at every intersection, it will not be long before we spot a crowd on a street corner or in a small plaza. Immediately we hear either singing or a voice coming over the portable amplifier, and we know we have found one of the several open air meetings held by groups from the Methodist Pentecostal Church, one of the larger indigenous groups in Chile.

As we approach the crowd, which might number between fifty and 300, we make sure we have our Bibles in our hands in plain sight. With these we will be accepted as *hermanos*, and no one will try to convert us on the spot. Our group might include 75 other people with Bibles under their arms. Maybe fifteen or twenty will have guitars and accordions, long red sashes flowing from the guitars. Between songs, three or four will step up to the microphone and give their personal testimony of how God saved them from drink, adultery, wife-beating, stealing, and cheating, and gave them a new life. They will recommend

the same to the group of curious onlookers gathered around.
"Glorias" and "amens" will ring out from the other Christians
from time to time.

When the meeting is finished, the listeners are not asked
to come to church "sometime" and given a tract. They are invited to "come along" with the crowd to church that very night.
Many decide to go, the group begins to march through the street
singing and reciting Bible verses in unison, and then stops for
a similar meeting on another street corner.

The leader keeps check on his watch, and at the proper
time the final parade begins toward what is known as the
Jotabeche Church, bringing the newly-found visitors along with
them. The same thing had been happening in virtually every
neighborhood within parading distance of the church. At about
seven o'clock the several groups converge on the church from
all sides. No motor traffic moves on Jotabeche Street at this
time. The church officers come out in front of the church and
form two lines of welcome, while the open-air campaigners file
between them and enter the church building, singing the praises
of Zion.

The several Chilean Pentecostal denominations (most of
which are splits from one another and have a common ancestry)
trace their beginnings to a Pentecostal revival in the Methodist Church in 1909, and a break from Methodism by Rev. Willis
Hoover. Other than Hoover, these churches, which comprise over
80 percent of Chilean Protestantism now, have had no missionary
influence of any consequence. Unlike many other churches in
Latin America they have been free to develop along cultural
lines which are indigenous to the Chileans, and therefore many
things they do seem strange to other Protestants, both Latin
Americans and Anglo-Saxons. But they do not seem strange to
Chileans, and a result has been one of the fastest-growing
churches in Latin America.

The half hour between seven and seven thirty, for example
is a bedlam of noise and confusion. Singing stops, but a
social time begins. Everyone greets everyone else, asks about
their family's health, tells what the Lord has done for them
during the past week, and shares in a time of fellowship. Anyone who wants a good seat has to get there early. The Jotabeche Church (at least the last time I went) seats only 5,000,
and the overflow has to listen through loudspeakers in the
street. The orchestra, composed mostly of guitars and accordions, gathers in the balcony--500 strong--and tunes the instruments, forming a background of musical cacophony to the chatter-
ing below.

A few minutes after seven thirty, pastor Javier Vasquez steps on the platform with the ten or so others who will take part in the service. The noise stops, and the service begins. Faces radiate joy--the people would rather be in church than anywhere else in the world. During the special numbers or hymns a dozen or two will stand and begin to dance through the aisles in rhythm to the music with upraised hands. Some prayer times will sound like a free-for-all, but they will all stop at a signal, keeping everything decent and in order. Instead of passing offering plates, the pastor invites all 5,000 to come up front and leave their offerings at the altar, causing a seeming mass confusion, but a pattern well accepted by the congregation. After the service a long line forms in front of the pulpit to shake hands with the pastor, give him a present, or have him pray briefly for their health or some spiritual problem.

Although I haven't been able to double check this, I was told in Santiago that when Javier Vasquez was elected pastor of the church, he received 40,000 secret ballot votes! These came not only from the Jotabeche Church itself, since that is only the "mother church." Some 35 daughter churches also participated in the election. Little wonder that most Chilean politicians are interested in keeping on the good side of the evangelicals there!

Vasquez has his church organized like an army. Not only do the open air teams go out on Sunday afternoon, but an elite corps of around eighty bicycle riders in red and white uniforms go out with guitars and Bibles to many parts of the city outside of walking distance. One Tuesday night Pastor Vasquez invited me to speak to his men's group. A fierce wind and rainstorm drenched the city about an hour before the meeting, and lasted through the night. I thought the meeting might be called off, but went along with wet shoes and all. Vasquez apologized to me that only 400 men had come that night! I learned that they form what is called the "volunteer army," several hundred men who put themselves at the orders of the pastor to move out in any type of ministry--hospital or jail visitation, praying for the sick, open air meetings, planting of new churches--or what have you. They are all working men who support their families well with their jobs, but give their spare time to the work of the Lord.

One of the phenomena of the Chilean Pentecostals is what has been called "growth by splits." A man like Pastor Vasquez obviously has outstanding gifts of leadership. He knows how to manage his huge church with the skill of an army general. He has many characteristics of the type of man called a *caudillo*

in the political world in Latin America. Most of the growing
Pentecostal churches in Chile are led by pastors of the
caudillo type, which is a familiar and well-accepted pattern
among the Chileans. But the disadvantage is that there is seldom room for two *caudillos* in the same church. As Catholic
sociologist Emilio Willems says: "Two opposing principles are
operative in the Pentecostal sects, one 'democratic' and the
other 'authoritarian.' They clash as soon as rival leaders
with similar divine endowments arise and accuse the ones in
power of misusing their authority or, as they sometimes put it,
of 'antidemocratic behavior.' If the rival is able to sway
enough followers, the split occurs and a new sect is born.
There is much bitterness during the conflict, and such words as
'caudillo' and 'cacique' are freely used, but little of it
seems to remain once the secession has taken place."[1] Back in
1942, for example, Bishop Enrique Chavez had come up through
the ranks in the Jotabeche Church, but he found no room at the
top. In *caudillo* style he split off from the Methodist Pentecostals in 1946, took some people with him, and started his own
denomination called The Pentecostal Church of Chile. According
to Jesuit Ignacio Vergara, in only ten years Chavez' work was
"enormous." Not only did he have a central church which was a
"virtual basilica," but that mother church had given birth to
26 other congregations, and a total of 136 preaching points.[2]
Statistics in Chile are hard to come by, but estimates of current membership of Bishop Chavez' church run from 13,500 (Read,
Monterroso and Johnson) to over 60,000 (Chavez). According to
Kessler, Chavez "does not share the horror for church division
which is usually felt in ecumenical circles." He believes
"that division has helped the astonishing growth of the Pentecostal churches in Chile more than it has hindered it."[3] Read,
Monterroso and Johnson say, "The influence of strong personali-
ties vying for leadership has produced a proliferation of Pentecostal groups and denominations. The dynamic force behind a
newborn church creates a certain spiritual momentum that results
in growth."[4]

Not only did Chavez' split-off grow, but so did the church
he split from. Just this year the Jotabeche Church left the
building that could hold only 5,000 and moved into a gigantic
new edifice that seats 16,000, has rooms for 200 overnight
guests, and boasts its own independent water and electrical
supply. It was all built with Chilean money--not a cent of
foreign subsidy!

HOW THE LEADERS ARE TRAINED

The question we have been leading up to is this: how are
leaders like Vasquez and Chavez trained? It is hard to believe

at first, but none of the great leaders of the Chilean Pentecostal churches have been for one day to a seminary or Bible
institute. The training system of these churches is so different from what other churches have developed in the twentieth
century, that it remained a complete mystery to most outsiders.
In fact it was commonly said that the pastors were "untrained,"
and scores of others felt very sorry for the Chilean Pentecostal ministers.

Now the picture is clearer. A brilliant study published
by sociologist Christian Lalive D'Epinay in 1967 has given the
rest of the world light on the matter. Now we can understand
the inner operation of this strange, but highly successful,
method of "training in the streets."[5]

Using a slightly different analogy and classification,
Lalive's findings can be described as seven rungs on the ladder
up to the pastorate. Anyone can start, in fact all are expected to try the first rung. Any of the six rungs may break,
sending the candidate back to the ranks. The rungs may be described as follows:

1. Street preaching. When a person is converted, he or
she is expected to give his testimony in public in a street
meeting the very next Sunday. Experience will show that some
are gifted and successful in this ministry and if so they can
go up to the next rung.

2. Sunday School class. Sunday School meets on Sunday
morning. If the teacher can communicate simple Bible truths to
his students, and hold the interest of the class, he may be advanced to a more important class, and he passes this test.

3. "Preacher." As a "preacher" the candidate is permitted to lead worship and is asked to bring messages on occasion.
If his pastor is pleased with his performance, he will promote
him to the following rung.

4. New preaching point. When he is sent out to a new
preaching point (*avanzada*), his success is measured in an objective way--he must produce converts to demonstrate to others
that God has given him the gifts necessary for the ministry.
If he does, his position can become official on the next rung.

5. Christian worker. Upon application to the Annual Conference of pastors, he is proposed and accepted as a Christian
worker (*obrero del Senor*). This gives him an official title
for the first time, and he is under the orders of the denominational leadership.

6. <u>Pastor-deacon</u>. He is assigned an area (*vina nueva*) in which he is expected to plant a church. As this takes place he may be named pastor-deacon. If he does not gain converts and form the nucleus of a new church, he goes no higher, nor does he receive the title.

7. <u>Pastor</u>. The probationer (*probando*) then comes up against his last test. In order to be promoted to pastor, he must present sufficient evidence to the Annual Conference that he can leave the secular world, dedicate his full time to the ministry, and be financially supported in it by the congregation he has gathered together.

As we have seen in the preceding chapter, this is not the first time in history that the Christian church has used the apprenticeship system to train the ministry. But it is one of the least known cases today, and an example of a system that seems to work. The result is one of the fastest growing complexes of churches in Latin America.

This is no three-year Bible institute program. It may take the candidate twenty years to reach the top rung. But by the time he reaches it, both he and the church are quite certain that he has the gifts, the spirituality, and the dedication needed for the Christian ministry. One of the results of such a long process is that 57 percent of the pastors are over fifty years of age. Also 56 percent have less than six grades of primary school. But they are God's men for the job, and as such officially recognized by their churches.

Few seminary-trained pastors receive the affection and allegiance of their people that the Chilean Pentecostal pastors do. David Brackenridge describes the pastor's position in these words: "It is astonishing to note the care and reverence the people show towards their pastor. Everything is done for him. Besides monetary support, members bring gifts of meat, vegetables and fruit. His table is usually full. He entertains lavishly and no member is turned away who is in need. But it must be said that the pastor controls everything--finances and all the activities. Nothing is done without his consent."[6]

Curiously, through the years many of the relatively static, non-growing denominations have tried to help the Pentecostals improve their ministerial training. This was partly the reason why the conciliar groups set up the Theological Community in Santiago some years ago. The U.S.A. Assemblies of God also expected that the indigenous Pentecostal churches would use their Bible institute in Santiago. Others have tried; all have been notably unsuccessful. The Pentecostals prefer "training in the streets." As a matter of fact, the top leaders consistently turn down lavish scholarship offers, knowing that if they enter some institution they will lose their status in most of the churches. Lalive makes this astute commentary: "Without claiming that there may be a *causal* relationship between the theological level of the pastors and the evangelical dynamism of their denominations, the existence of correlation between these two facts makes us less confident of the benefits of theological education, and even of the method of training in the developed countries which we impose on Protestants in the developing nations."[7]

One disadvantage of training in the streets becomes evident to the observer who listens to the sermons preached by the pastors from the pulpits of these churches. This is the appalling lack of theological and even biblical content. The susceptibility of such a large mass of Christians to the entrance of some heresy is terrifying to one who holds in high esteem the "faith once delivered to the saints." God has seemed to protect the Chileans against this to now, although similar groups in Brazil and Mexico have developed a very low (not to say erroneous) doctrine of the Trinity, for example.

It seems to us who are working in extension theological education that this system could be used to great advantage to the Chilean Pentecostals. They may need it, they may not. Lalive says, "Who should be teaching whom? What right have the Presbyterians and Methodists to teach the Pentecostals, who are a living illustration of the fact that quality of faith has nothing to do with lucidity of dogmas or with perfection of discipline?"[8] This has been presented to them, but predictably the response has been much less than enthusiastic.

When I recently told a group of pastors in Viet Nam about the frustration that the indifference of the Chilean Pentecostals to extension produced, one of them raised his hand and said he had a suggestion. "This might take a longer time than you have," he said, "but I know how you could convince them. Just go there, climb up the ladder to the seventh rung, and then tell them about extension."

He was right!

NOTES FOR CHAPTER 7

1. Emilio Willems, Followers of the New Faith, Vanderbilt University Press, 1967, pp. 113-114.

2. Ignacio Vergara, El Protestantismo en Chile, Santiago, Editorial del Pacifico, 1962, p. 163.

3. J. B. A. Kessler, Jr., A Study of the Old Protestant Missions and Churches in Peru and Chile, Goes, Oostervaan & le Cointre N.V., 1967, p. 318.

4. William R. Read, Victor M. Monterroso, and Harmon A. Johnson, Latin American Church Growth, Grand Rapids, Eerdmans, 1969, p. 104.

5. Christian Lalive d'Epinay, "The Training of Pastors and Theological Education, the Case of Chile," *International Review of Missions*, Geneva, W.C.C., Vol. LVI, N . 222, April, 1967, pp. 185-192.

6. Brackenridge quoted by J. B. A. Kessler, A Study of the Older Protestant Missions . . ., p. 318.

7. Christian Lalive, "The Training of Pastors . . ." p. 185.

8. Ibid., pp. 185-186.

25

THE BIRTH OF
THE EXTENSION SEMINARY

The extension seminary was born in Latin America. Part of
the web of circumstances which brought this about can now be
reduced to some clear statistical data. Rough as this data
might be, it still sketches the broad outlines of one of the
world's most serious "ordination gaps."

The influential book, Latin American Church Growth, estimates the number of evangelical (Protestant) churches in Latin
America at 75,000.[1] Whereas each one of these churches has
leaders, it is estimated that only 15,000 of them have enjoyed
what might be considered adequate theological training. This
leaves 60,000 who still need training. As has been mentioned
previously, these are almost invariably mature men whose leadership ability and spiritual gifts have been tried and found true.

Many think that 60,000 is a highly conservative estimate.
They talk of recent statistics of Brazil alone where of some
16,000 who hold the title of "pastor" (they are functionally
ordained), 11,500 of them have not had formal theological
training. This would be par for the course, if it were not for
some 40,000 others in Brazil who are actually leading congregations, but who do not even have the title of pastor. Many of
them are termed "lay pastors." As a matter of fact, 100,000
untrained church leaders in Latin America might be the best
figure, admitting that it is largely a symbolic number.

The present efforts to train these leaders are dramatically described by Read, Monterroso and Johnson: "At the
present rate of growth, approximately 5,000 new congregations
are formed in Latin America each year. If all the students in
the 360 existing theological training institutions were to become pastors after graduation, there still would be an

insufficient supply of pastors for the new congregations alone,
to say nothing of those already existing."[2]

The 100,000 are doing their best. God has gifted them and
they are faithfully using their gifts. But understandably,
many of them feel personal frustration when they come to the
self-realization that they are considered second class pastors
because they have not had formal training, and that under the
traditional system of theological education they find it virtually impossible to make up for their deficiency. It is not
surprising that their congregations often suffer from spiritual
malnutrition, and that some missionaries from well-fed congregations under skillful pastoral care in the homelands hastily
judge their Latin American brethren as being terribly "unspir-
itual." The 100,000 would dearly like to remedy the situation,
and this is one of the reasons why the new extension system has
been so well received in these circles.

Perhaps the most insidious danger lurking within the complex of the Latin American ordination gap is the possibility
that large segments of the Latin American church will fall away
into heresy. As Ralph Winter has said: "The greatest *encouragement* in missions today is that the Christian movement is
outrunning the traditional methods of ministerial training, but
the greatest *tragedy*, both in the U.S. and abroad, is that we
are ecclesiastically and institutionally arthritic at the point
of *bending* to give appropriate, solid, theological education to
the real leaders that emerge in the normal outworking of our
internal church life. Without this critical retooling of our
theological education, church growth may in many areas wander
into Mormon-type heresies instead of producing a Biblically-
based evangelicalism. In some places this is already happening
before our eyes.[3]

THE GUATEMALA EXPERIMENT

Some years before these general statistical studies were
made for Latin America as a whole, the Presbyterian Church in
Guatemala did some mathematical work of its own. They had an
excellent seminary of the traditional cut in the capital,
Guatemala City, and it had been serving the denomination for
twenty-five years. But in 1962 the leaders took an inventory,
and discovered that in twenty-five years the seminary had prepared only ten pastors who were actively serving the denomination. This in itself was quite a startling realization, but
more so was a glance into the future. At that time only five
or six students were enrolled in the seminary, hardly sufficient to take care of the 200 growing churches which belonged
to the Presbyterian denomination.

Such a dramatic ordination gap indicated that something was wrong somewhere. It was not atypical of other churches in Latin America, but in his providence, God had raised up a special trio of missionaries and placed them together in Guatemala at that time. The three were thoroughly evangelical in their convictions, burdened for the training of the ministry, concerned about the future growth of the Presbyterian Church in Guatemala, and unusually creative in their thinking. Ralph Winter, for example, had gone through a hodge-podge of academic disciplines that dovetailed perfectly for the situation God put him in. His university training (and family background) was engineering (Cal Tech), his masters degree in education (Columbia), his doctorate in anthropology (Cornell), and his B.D. from Princeton. James Emery was a General Electric engineer-cum-theologian and a Hartford graduate in anthropology, who had become an expert in the Indian cultures of Guatemala. Ross Kinsler, a theologian-pastor, with his doctorate from Edinburgh, joined these two innovators to complete the team of God's educational pioneers. Together the three cross-fertilized each other's ideas and set themselves to come up with some answer to their church's ordination gap.

The Guatemala trio was thoroughly familiar with the several solutions that others had previously attempted to train those who could not enter traditional seminaries. They studied the possibilities of offering more scholarship help, of changing their academic year around, of correspondence courses, of night schools, of regional laymen's training institutes, and of other methods. None of these fitted their particular set of problems.

Finally they realized that one of the major difficulties was that their seminary was located in Guatemala City, while the majority of their churches were located out in the rural areas in the western part of the country. It became evident that the leaders they wanted to train were not going to come to Guatemala City for training, so they concluded that part of the solution lay in moving the seminary out to the region where their churches were located. Because of the multiplicity of sub-cultures and different academic levels they first experimented with separate training programs for each ethnic group, but "it only produced a caste system, dividing rather than uniting the church."[4]

After much predictable debate among the Guatemalan leaders, the Church came to the radical decision of selling their seminary in the city, and using the funds to build a new campus out in the town of San Felipe, located in the midst of their most dense cluster of churches. Once the new seminary campus was

built, another major problem raised its head. The church
leaders still did not matriculate in the seminary! The trouble
was that the seminary in San Felipe had simply moved geographically, but it had kept its same structure.

A radical change in structure was the solution proposed.
The seminary obviously was too centralized--everything was located in one place, and the church leaders could not adjust
their lives to fit into a program that required extended periods of residence away from their homes. It made little difference if the residence center was in far off Guatemala City
or in nearby San Felipe. Such an adjustment was simply not
possible for the majority.

From this sprang the idea of the decentralized seminary.
If the leaders couldn't come to the seminary, the seminary
could be broken up into pieces with a piece placed within easy
reach of each interested church leader. Residence in a central
institution then would not be required, but the important principle was that no matter where a piece of the seminary might be
located the students would be receiving the same theological
training they would have received if they had gone to San
Felipe to live. This was no short term laymen's institute that
gave good teaching but that could not prepare men for Presbyterian ordination. It was to be first class ministerial
training.

Several regional centers were thus set up, where the student would meet once a week with a professor from the seminary,
receive help on his studies of the previous week, and take home
assignments for the coming week. The same textbooks used in
the residence program were the basis of the study program.

The new structure seemed to work. Enrollment increased at
once from seven to fifty students. Finally the real church
leaders were studying in the seminary. But the next major
problem in the experiment soon became evident: the students
were not learning much! Somehow the educational process had
broken down.

The minds of the engineers went to work, using that envi-
able ability to erase the past and focus on the present problem
and its solution. Here a graduate degree in education also
helped. By 1963 the value of programmed, self-instructional
study materials had been widely accepted by educational psy-
chologists. The trio decided that if the traditional textbooks
were inadequate for the new structure, they would set out to
write new textbooks that were. Thus began the most physically
and emotionally trying phase of the project. Gallons of

midnight oil as well as grueling self-discipline were needed as this first generation of extension materials was produced, tested, and revised. Although the materials were primitive as compared to what is being done today, they seemed to work. They were written in such a way that the student took active participation in the learning process as he worked through them. Eventually tests showed that many of the extension students were pulling better grades in the same subjects as the residence students! The shape of the future was beginning to take form in Guatemala.

But even the self-instructional materials had to be prepared to teach a student who had reached a predetermined academic level. Those who were more advanced or too far behind academically did not learn as much as they should from the books. The design of the materials was varied somewhat to make them multi-level so that each student could study at his own level. In the same seminary, then, students ranging from sixth-grade graduates to university men were studying, each at his appropriate level.

Two-thirds of the church leaders who should have been studying, however, did not have the six grades of primary necessary to study at the lowest level. How to solve this problem? These men could not be by-passed. Two alternatives were possible: lower the seminary requirements or raise the level of the leaders. Both these alternatives have subsequently been used to advantage. In the George Allan Seminary in Bolivia, for example, mature men who have had only a second-grade level of studies are taking approved theological training. In the Guatemalan Presbyterian Church, however, a higher academic level of the ministry is insisted upon for ordination. The level of the church leaders had to be raised there.

In order to accomplish this, a set of materials was prepared which would allow the leaders to bring themselves up to sixth grade levels. This was not a part of the seminary program, but it was encouraged by the seminary. Books on natural sciences, geography, mathematics, hygiene, Spanish, and Bible were prepared by Guatemalan educators. Then the government was approached to see if it would grant a sixth-grade diploma to men who had studied these materials and passed the government examinations. The government was extremely receptive to the idea, not only for church leaders, but for the population across the board. This encouraged the Lincoln Schools for adult education to be established under the leadership of Raul Echeverria, a Presbyterian layman. His materials became some of Guatemala's best-selling books, and recently he was decorated by the President with the "Order of the Quetzal,"

Guatemala's highest honor! Furthermore, scores of church leaders finally earned their primary school diplomas and enrolled in the seminary.

Looking back at this pioneer experiment in the rural area of Guatemala, the critical observer now can pick out many flaws. Since then much has been learned and much has been changed. To be true to the creative genius of the trio of architects of the extension seminary, the program must never stagnate or crystalize--it must remain pliable, constantly adapting to new situations and correcting past shortcomings.

The advantages at that time, however, far outweighed the shortcomings. Ralph Winter has listed five of the advantages which were evident to the Guatemalan educators from the beginning:

1. The door was opened for leaders who desired to reach a higher level of training.

2. The leaders could receive their theological training within the context of their own sub-culture.

3. The system permitted those students who had low motivation to leave without losing face.

4. Instead of lowering academic levels, it was observed that the extension student learns better and develops better study habits in his home.

5. The project is more economical than the conventional seminary, and it saves much time for the professor.[5]

Thus a radical departure from the traditional structure of theological education was born in the tiny Central American republic of Guatemala. It spread next to other Latin American countries.

NOTES FOR CHAPTER 8

1. William R. Read, Victor M. Monterroso, and Harmon Johnson, Latin American Church Growth, Grand Rapids, Eerdmans, 1969, p. 326.

2. Ibid.

3. Ralph D. Winter, "New Winds Blowing," Church Growth Bulletin, Vols. I - V, Donald A. McGavran, ed., South Pasadena, William Carey Library, 1969, p. 242.

4. Ralph D. Winter, "This Seminary Goes to the Student," *World Vision Magazine*, July-August, 1966, p. 11.

5. Raul Winter, *El Seminario de Extension de Guatemala*, El Seminario de Extension, informe del cursillo en Cochabamba, Bolivia, del 3 al 7 de agosto, 1968, p. 10.

26

HOW THE EXTENSION CENTER WORKS

We can no longer postpone describing some of the more practical aspects of the extension seminary. What actually happens in an extension program in full operation?

In order to understand this, we first must agree on some definitions, especially those of the different academic levels. It has already been mentioned that in many of the institutions using the extension method, students are taking their work on several different academic levels. This multi-level situation was one of the problems which seminaries and Bible institutes faced for many years in Latin America and in other places where the ministry for the younger churches was being trained. Most teachers had experienced time and time again the impossible situation of having right in the same classroom some students with a high school diploma and others with barely five or six years of primary school. To attempt to gear subject matter to reach a happy medium in such circumstances is a formidable challenge even to the most expert pedagogue.

The built-in flexibility of the extension seminary allows students on many different levels to study for the ministry, but it takes them out of the same classroom and gives them material especially designed for their particular level. Chapter 13 will describe how this material is produced, but at this point we only need to know that to operate an extension seminary properly, programmed material for each course on each level is essential.

The delegates to the Armenia workshop brought with them a large amount of cumulative experience in training pastors for the Latin American churches. As they pondered together the necessity of defining the levels at which men and women were studying in the seminaries and Bible institutes of the

continent, they established a scheme of academic levels which
has been accepted by nearly every institution developing extension programs. The broad outlines of the academic divisions
are as follows:

Name of level	Academic prerequisites for beginning the course
Licentiate (B.D.)	Two or three years of university
Bachelor	High School diploma
Diploma	Primary School diploma (six years)
Certificate A	Two or three years of primary school
Certificate B	Little or no formal training, but functional literacy in vernacular

When students enroll in the seminary they are placed in
their proper level. Many institutions have found that since
they are dealing largely with mature men in the student body,
their formal attainments often do not reflect their ability to
handle the theological studies on a given level. Placement
tests have been devised which fit each student into his proper
level. This leaves room for the self-educated man to take more
advanced studies, and also weeds out the person who may have
slid through to a diploma on the basis of a fast tongue and
winsome personality instead of actual academic attainment.

In order to describe the operation of the extension seminary, let us set up a hypothetical example, and call it Bible
Theological Seminary (B.T.S.). The B.T.S. has a base institution, two extension departments, and six extension centers.
One hundred twenty students are in training, forty in residence
and eighty in extension.

The base institution seems to be a necessary beginning for
an extension program. Whether one can operate without it remains to be seen—I have not heard of one. The base institution is usually located in a city, and is the seminary or Bible
institute that is being "extended." It is the stable and
visible center of activities, the institution that grants the
diplomas or degrees. But it must not gain the image that it is
the location of the seminary—wherever an extension center
exists, the seminary is there also. This is an important feature of the extension mystique.

The main offices of the seminary are located in the base
institution. The rector or director lives here, as does the
other administrative personnel. A residence program operates
here, and so perhaps a good number of the full-time faculty

members are also in residence. The main library is housed on
the premises. Especially for those institutions teaching on
the higher levels, a first class library is obviously essential,
and cannot be duplicated in every extension center. It is well
to develop a general catalog of all books of the whole institution, whether the main library or the functional libraries in
the centers, in the base institution.

If some of the professors of the B.T.S. are programming
materials for their students, a publications department for the
institution might also be located in the base institution.
This may not be much more than a typewriter, a mimeograph machine, and a mailing desk, but it can be a most important element not only for the B.T.S., but also for sister institutions
offering instruction in the same languages.

The forty residence students in our hypothetical seminary
are all studying on the diploma and bachelor levels. But there
is an extension center located here as well. This is set up
for students from the city who for one reason or another cannot
enroll in the residence program, but who are taking one or two
extension courses. A wider variety of courses can be offered
here because of the larger number of available professors. It
has been found that potential faculty increases greatly when
the professor only has to meet his students once a week. Some
administrators, for example, who could not allow themselves to
be tied down to an ordinary teaching schedule, accept an extension course because of the flexibility of the time table.
First of all, the professor can arrange any time at all during
the week that is mutually convenient for himself and his students. I once had a small extension class on Protestant Christianity meet in my own office, where I installed a blackboard,
on Tuesdays at 1:00 - 2:00 p.m., around a pot of coffee and
dessert which my wife prepared. It was a delightful learning
situation!

The second advantage, time-wise, for a part-time teacher
is that the preparation can be handled at more leisure. The
professor does not have to prepare lectures as such. He needs
to be familiar with his subject matter, of course, but does not
need to develop the tightly-knit pedagogical structure of a
lecture. This has already been done for him by the author of
the programmed text the students are using, as will be explained
in more detail in Chapter 12. His work is more in the areas of
testing, counseling, and trouble-shooting. He might need as
many hours per week as he would if he were lecturing, but the
number of weekly deadlines is greatly reduced.

Let's say that B.T.S. extension center in the base institution holds its weekly meetings on Thursday night and at different times during Saturday. There are fifteen bachelor students and ten diploma students. On Thursday night one of the
full-time professors holds an extension class in his regular
seminary classroom with five of the bachelor students. Two
other part-time professors, who do not teach in residence,
teach extension on Saturdays, right in the seminary building.
Saturday may not be the best time to teach, but for many students it is the only time they could meet with their professors,
and those who have developed an extension mentality combined
with their love for theological training realize that they must
adjust to it.

We have said that B.T.S. has two extension departments.
If we call them the Northern Department and the Southern Department we can easily distinguish them. The Northern Department is a distance from the seminary, and is self-contained.
That is, no faculty members travel out from the base institution to teach there. Their faculty members are all residents
in the region of the department. The dean of the department
lives in Center No. 2, and he travels out to Center No. 3. The
pastor of the church in Center No. 2 is also a professor, and
he travels with the dean. Center No. 2 is an urban center, and
the classes are held in the dean's house, some on Wednesday
night and some on Saturday morning. Three are studying on the
bachelor level and eight on the diploma level.

In order to identify this as an extension center, a sign
painted with the same kind of lettering and the same colors as
the sign over the base institution is placed over the door.
This is simply a reminder that when the students enter the
building usually thought of as the dean's house, they are
entering the Bible Theological Seminary just as literally as
they would be if they had traveled to the base institution. On
Wednesday nights and Saturday mornings, that *is* the seminary.
This must be stressed because it has been one of the most difficult mental adjustments for those not thoroughly familiar
with extension theological education.

Center No. 3, also under the Northern Department, is
located in a rural area 35 miles away. For the extension classes there, the dean and the professor get on a bus Monday afternoon, have supper with the pastor of the church there, and hold
classes that night in the local church building, using the
Sunday School rooms. A sign "Bible Theological Seminary" has
been nailed over the side entrance to the church, making this
another part of the general institution. This is the only time
classes are held, so the two diploma students and twenty

certificate A students all gather there. Some have to travel
most of the day from their own churches to make the weekly
meeting. The local pastor has built a shed-like room on the
side of his house where many of these pastors from out of town
sleep before traveling back the following day. The dean and
the professor from Center No. 2 also stay overnight at the pastor's house.

Now is the time to pause and describe a hypothetical
schedule for Center No. 3. The meeting begins at 6:30 p.m.
with all 22 students present. The first half hour is a devo-
tional time. At 7:00 the dean takes the two diploma students
in the study of Romans and Galatians while the professor takes
the twenty certificate students in Life of Christ. At 8:00 ten
of the certificate students leave, because they have chosen to
take only one course this semester. The other ten stay, and
they are divided into two separate classes, the dean taking the
five who have elected homiletics, and the pastor of the local
church taking the five who have elected Genesis-Exodus. The
professor in the meantime teaches theology to the two diploma-
level students.

Each class session has several objectives. First the professor uses about ten minutes to give an examination on the
materials the students had been studying the previous week.
Twenty minutes is used for a discussion of the answers to the
test, providing the students immediate feedback, 25 minutes for
a general discussion and application of the previous week's
work with the students raising any problems they might have run
into, and the final five minutes going over the assignment for
the following week.

At 9:00 the pastor's wife invites students and faculty
alike to a cup of tea. Some have to leave early, but others
sleep right there. At times lively discussions of the matters
brought to the surface in the classes go on until midnight or
more--an unparalleled opportunity for professors to get to know
their students. The next day the dean and the professor take
the bus home.

The Southern Department also has a resident dean, but no
resident professors. It is near enough to the base institution
so that a professor from there can assist him in two of his
three centers. On Tuesday morning the professor from the base
institution drives his car to Center No. 4, where the dean has
traveled on the bus. The center there is a rented room in a
block of stores in the business section of town. On one side
is a small grocery store, on the other a barber shop. But over
the room is the ubiquitous sign, "Bible Theological Seminary."

Classes are held in late morning and early afternoon for the
five diploma students. Then the dean gets into the professor's
car and they drive to Center No. 5.

Here, as in Center No. 3, the church becomes the seminary
building on Tuesday nights, and an appropriate sign indicates
it. A full night's program includes two bachelor students,
three diploma students, and two certificate students. After
staying at the center overnight, the professor drops off the
dean at his house, and continues back to the base institution.

On Thursday the dean travels alone to Center No. 6 where
he has ten certificate students in a rural community. The sign
here is found nailed over the door of a thatched-roof hut which
is the home of one of the students. The dean stays here also.
He meets with his students for several hours during Friday,
stays a second night, and travels home on Saturday.

This dean is relatively busy. He is involved every day,
Tuesday through Saturday, in extension work. He does not work
only eight hours a day, for in a sense he is on the job from
the time he leaves his home until he arrives back. His teaching does not start and stop with the classroom. He is with his
students for long periods of time. He eats meals with them,
stays in their homes, meets their families, travels with them,
and often stays a longer time for an evangelistic campaign or
Bible teaching in their churches.

But he is only a hypothetical dean. As an example from
real life, I could choose Peter Savage, Rector of the George
Allan Seminary in Bolivia, where I also teach. Since most of
my work is administrative, my involvement in extension is mini-
mal--one course on the bachelor level. But Savage has involved
himself more than the average.

On Thursday he boards the mission plane at 7:00 a.m., for
the hour's flight to the Choro center on the bleak Altiplano.
There he meets with 35 certificate students (one of whom has
traveled two hours on his bicycle including crossing a shallow
lake with the bicycle on his back and breaking ice with his
bare feet!) until noon. He flies back to Cochabamba, takes his
wife out for a game of tennis, catches up on administrative
work Thursday night, begins his Friday schedule with a Greek
class at 6:00 a.m. (to accommodate university students who have
to be at their other classes at 8:00), meets with several classes in the Cochabamba urban extension department on Saturday,
and then flies on Sunday morning to the tropical area of
Bolivia where he takes the San Antonio center on Sunday, the
Desengano center on Monday, the Santa Ana center on Tuesday,

and flies back to Cochabamba early Wednesday morning. Charitably, the circuit which takes him to the tropical area repeats every two weeks instead of every week.

THE TEN REQUIREMENTS FOR AN EXTENSION CENTER

In order to inaugurate an extension center, ten prerequisites are necessary. I will attempt to list them here in order of priority:

1. <u>Students</u>. It is worth repeating that the extension seminary begins with the students. Here is the starting point. Never attempt to set up an extension center, and then hope that students might come. The center is where the students already are. In a year or two it might be in a different place, if the student demand shifts. For this reason, the roots of a center never should be in too deep.

2. <u>Faculty</u>. Obviously teachers are needed. Since extension makes demands upon professors that are quite different from the conventional teaching job, all teachers are not prepared to participate in extension, but the search for those who are is worth the effort.

3. <u>Self-teaching materials</u>. Either these materials must be previously available or the professors must prepare their own as they go along. More about this in Chapter 13.

4. <u>Transportation for professors</u>. Geographical problems present themselves in every extension project. Some arrangement must be made to get the professors to their centers every week. This is often the most expensive aspect of extension theological education. In some cases, such as Kalimantan in Indonesia, extension would be unthinkable without the use of aircraft.

5. <u>Classrooms</u>. A place is needed to hang the "sign," and give tangible expression to the presence of a seminary. Already several possibilities of how such a room or rooms can be provided have been mentioned. At times a rental item will have to be built into the budget.

6. <u>Furniture</u>. One of the initial capital expenditures for setting up an extension center is the purchase of a blackboard, tables, chairs, bookcases, etc. Including the cost of the functional library, a sum of $300.00 has been calculated as an average budget for establishing a center.

7. <u>Schedule</u>. The students and the professor have to agree mutually upon a schedule. A great deal of flexibility is available at this point, of course.

8. <u>Placement examination</u>. Each culture or ethnic group will need its own placement exam to see that the students are using the self-instructional material which will best be able to teach them.

9. <u>Functional library</u>. Students at the diploma level or above need a library of a limited number of books such as commentaries, Bible dictionaries, concordances, and other research material. These books are on loan from the base institution's library, and are recalled if they are not used. This is why it is called a "functional" library.

10. <u>Secretary</u>. Some person needs to be in charge of taking attendance, collecting fees, keeping the other records, and whatever else might be involved in the administration of a center. Sometimes the local pastor can do this, sometimes one of the advanced students, sometimes the dean's wife or a professor's wife. Ideally, the secretary is a person who lives at the center, not one who comes and goes.

27

THE EXTENSION SEMINARY
AND CHURCH GROWTH

The primary thrust of the extension seminary is to extend the church of Jesus Christ. To extend the seminary geographically, culturally, economically, and academically to fit the needs and capabilities of the student without the church being multiplied will be to fail.

The goal of mission activity is not to develop a new and more effective system of theological education but to fulfill the Great Commission--the quantitative and qualitative growth of the church. The value of extension training awaits the verdict of history--at least a ten or fifteen-year period during which time a careful analysis must be made of the actual church growth that has occurred.

In the provision of God such a "breakthrough" in leadership development could not have come at a more opportune time. The church of Jesus Christ in Africasia is at the threshold of unprecedented advance. All previous mission history pales in significance before the dimension of today's potential. The church in Latin America is growing at the rate of 10 percent annually, well beyond the 3 percent rate of natural population increase.[1] David Barrett predicts, on the basis of a careful statistical analysis, that the church in Black Africa will constitute 57 percent of the total population below the Sahara by A.D. 2000.[2] The cyclic pattern of the advance and recession of the church of Christ noted by Dr. Latourette will no longer be determined solely by the state of the church in Europe and North America.[3] These areas will slip into the limbo of relative insignificance, while the center of the Christian movement will move to "the younger churches," particularly the church in Africa.

God has laid the burden of evangelism upon his people worldwide. Sparked by the Berlin Congress on Evangelism in 1966, regional and national conferences on evangelism have been held in the United States, Africa, Latin America and Asia. During 1970 alone conferences on evangelism have met in India, Thailand, the Philippines, Taiwan and in the United States for the Latin American population. A saturation evangelism campaign was held in Shikoku, Japan, a spirit of revival and evangelism has continued in Indonesia, and an intensive Evangelism-Deep-and-Wide program is gaining momentum in Vietnam.[4]

How can the extension seminary contribute to this growth? Three possibilities are most apparent. Extension programs will train the leaders who have come to the surface in these rapidly multiplying congregations. New churches will die or turn toward heresy without adequately trained leaders. The extension seminary will train leaders from static churches to be the evangelists in programs of new outreach. Finally, this method of decentralized training will afford new opportunities for pastors to "upgrade" their education and to feel more confident in facing the challenges of the present day which demand new forms for the church and its ministry.

It would be easy for today's strategists to be messianic in their emphasis and gratuitously assume that theological education has never produced church growth. Mission history reveals repeated examples of innovative and functional forms that Christ has used to build his Church. The apprentice method characterizing the primitive church and the Methodist movement in both England and the United States stands out. The Ruanda scheme used by the Church Mission Society integrates periods of study and church involvement, rewarding those who showed academic ability, spiritual growth, and gifts of ministry with opportunity for further study and work advancement.[5] The Chilean Pentecostal Church has trained its pastors "on the street." Promotion depended upon measurable spiritual productivity.

The Assemblies of God Bible School in San Salvador, El Salvador, has maximized practical work, often demanding that students evidence their ability to plant churches before they can complete their academic training program. Many mission groups and national churches periodically hold short-term Bible schools, evening classes, or a variety of special training programs, all of which are semi-extension and aim to upgrade every level of present church leadership for a diversity of ministries. Some traditional programs of theological education emphasize proven principles of church growth. We would be blind either not to note these noteworthy efforts or to assume that they are the rule rather than the exception.

Static traditionalism is the normal pattern in overseas theological education and has tended to inhibit the extension of the church. The widespread interest in extension education is a measure of the dissatisfaction felt. Dr. McGavran has observed that one of the basic points of "church growth" philosophy is that "theological education should be revamped so that seminaries graduate many men successful in church planting."[6] Why this need for revamping? Where are the problems? In what specific ways may the extension seminary, if properly implemented, serve as a corrective?

Traditional seminary programs *extract* men from their natural environment in the world and insulate them from real life situations. The "ghetto mentality" produced by this artificial learning situation reinforces the concept of the church as a place to which the world is to come rather than as a staging base from which it penetrates the world. Inflexible attitudes are developed in training with little possibility of adjustment to the changing forms of ministry and church planting demanded, for example, by burgeoning urban regions like Hong Kong, Saigon, and Calcutta. If the seminary does "business as usual" its graduates will only engage in church housekeeping. A less institutionalized seminary training may help future pastors see the viability of flexible forms of ecclesiastical life--the house church, for example.

Furthermore, the "leader-to-be" is separated from his own people and may find it difficult to return to them, particularly if they are in a rural area or from a cultural minority group. The graduate from such a program has the status of a semi-professional. He has gone away to school and now qualifies to move into the elite leadership of the church. He must have a role equal to his attainment. The Hakka populace of Taiwan has been deprived of all potential for the planting of new churches, since the young Hakka men sent to Taipei or Tainan for training in two major Presbyterian seminaries have settled down in more convenient pastorates among the Taiwanese. Would this have happened if they had been trained in the Hakka areas?

Even where graduates do return to their original homes for service it may be with attitudes that make it difficult for them to serve effectively. Dr. George Vicedom recommended that the Yuli Theological Institute on the East Coast of Taiwan be decentralized to better meet the needs of students studying there from the ten tribal groups.[7] Sheer idealism and totally impractical for a traditional seminary program was the verdict, and his advice was rejected with the consequent loss in growth potential. His suggestion could easily have been implemented by the concept of extension.

Training by extraction is expensive. Heavy subsidy is the name of the game. The student--usually a young man with no job and with no secular vocational experience--develops a spirit of dependence. As the seminary has supported him with mission funds, perhaps creating a token campus job for him, so will the mission continue to support him after graduation. Thus a system of subsidized church pastors is created which limits church extension to the availability of outside resources. Furthermore, the only viable pattern within this system will be the "full-time" pastor. The extension seminary creates the possibility of another pattern--a temporary or permanent "part-time" ministry. If a man has been trained while making his living in the world, he will not need to be weaned from mission funds nor will he find it demeaning to his status to continue along the same path.

Training by *extraction* is never certain whether or not it has a product. The students may or may not become leaders; they may or may not have Spirit-given gifts for leadership. The attrition rate before graduation is 30-40 percent, but, even more tragic, the only thing we know for sure about those who remain is that they can get passing grades! Can they produce in the work of Christ? The extension seminary trains more mature men already working in churches. They will produce because they are producing. They are leading men and exercising the gifts given to them for ministry by God the Holy Spirit.

Some extension programs radically emphasize leadership development. The Honduras Extension Bible Institute, run by C.B.H.M.S., is calling those who study "worker" rather than "student." Courses are highly functional. The one which introduces the New Testament is called "Communication of the New Testament." The goal of the institute is "to equip and mobilize dedicated workers to carry on by themselves immediately the spiritual production both of individual Christians and of churches."[8]

Culture in most areas of the world is a mosaic with a number of homogeneous groups. Church growth will best be promoted by training leaders from each group where there are churches or where church planting is projected. Training by extraction is a "melting pot" approach. Differences are minimized with little allowance for the variety of backgrounds represented in the student body. Under pressures to develop a unified curriculum and methodology, no creative thought can be devoted to

preparing the student to meet the specific needs of his particular cultural group. Potentialities and possibilities of various church growth patterns are overlooked by the cultural
levelling process of the educational approach. The extension
seminary is better able to develop multi-cultural curriculums
and to utilize "on-the-spot" training to stimulate creative
student response to their own cultures.

The traditional seminary program can inhibit church growth
by preparing leadership on only one or two levels. Concentration is usually on the middle-class student who may be ill-
prepared either to reach the lower classes (the so-called
"masses" of church growth theory) below him or the intellectual
classes above him. Efficiency of operation, centralized location, common classes and other factors dictate concentration on
one or two levels with the result that the needs of the entire
church are not fully met. The extension seminary can do a good
job of education for ministry on several academic levels. It
trains the men whom God has equipped, irrespective of their
educational backgrounds. Ralph Winter observes that an "unexpected discovery" of the extension program of the Evangelical
Seminary in Guatemala was that "extension centers allowed us to
reach up to higher as well as down to lower academic levels
than we had operated on before."[9]

A warning is necessary at this point. Extension training
is the "in" thing. Everyone wants to get on the bandwagon.
Any kind of an effort, as long as it tips its hat to the name
"extension," is seen as a panacea for every ill of the church.
Many half-hearted programs, with ill-conceived materials, and
giving no academic credit to a potpourri of students, lumped
together in "catch-all" lay-training courses, are being dignified as extension training. Little wonder that some church
leaders are adverse to granting ordained status in their
churches to such ill-prepared leaders. Dr. Winter cautions
that extension can go wrong if it loses sight of the "primary
goal of the early proponents of theological education by extension which is to reach out to the real pastoral leadership of
the church with first rate theological education that will
allow these men of high potential to become more than second-
class leaders."[10] First-rate extension training will gradually
diminish status consciousness among church leaders and increasingly make it possible for churches to ordain men trained by
extension as well as those who have graduated from the more
traditional schools.

No observation came more frequently in Asia from workshop
delegates than this critical one, "Our churches are not growing
and we have enough leaders at present. Are extension methods

as necessary then for us as in Latin America?" This very
statement misses the point that the extension seminary can
train men gifted in evangelism for massive new outreach with
the Gospel. Vast, untapped resources are to be found in "God's
frozen people." Here is the army that can penetrate a world
for Christ. Many of them will never be reached in our traditional seminaries. And as long as we put all our eggs in the
extraction basket we will limp along with only a very small
portion of the resources God has given his church.

The church must grow qualitatively in biblical knowledge,
in Christian piety, and in many forms of dedicated service.
Pastors long for renewed learning opportunities. If they must
leave their sphere of ministry and go away to school, both
quantitative and qualitative growth will suffer. How far superior to train them where they are as they continue to serve
Christ.

The extension seminary and church growth? In a nutshell,
decentralized theological education enables us to prepare more
and better leaders on a variety of levels and from a variety of
homogeneous cultural units. These men will take places of innovative leadership within rapidly multiplying new churches and
spearhead evangelistic outreach into whitened harvest fields.

Index